Developmentalism

CRITICAL FRONTIERS OF THEORY, RESEARCH, AND POLICY IN INTERNATIONAL DEVELOPMENT STUDIES

Series Editors

Andrew Fischer, Giles Mohan, Tanja Müller, and Alfredo Saad Filho

Critical Frontiers of Theory, Research, and Policy in International Development Studies is the official book series of the Development Studies Association of the UK and Ireland (DSA).

The series profiles research monographs that will shape the theory, practice, and teaching of international development for a new generation of scholars, students, and practitioners. The objective is to set high quality standards within the field of development studies to nurture and advance the field, as is the central mandate of the DSA. Critical scholarship is especially encouraged, within the spirit of development studies as an interdisciplinary and applied field, dealing centrally with local, national, and global processes of structural transformation, and associated political, social, and cultural change, as well as critical reflections on achieving social justice. In particular, the series seeks to highlight analyses of historical development experiences as an important methodological and epistemological strength of the field of development studies.

Developmentalism

The Normative and Transformative within Capitalism

GRAHAM HARRISON

OXFORD
UNIVERSITY PRESS

OXFORD
UNIVERSITY PRESS

Great Clarendon Street, Oxford, OX2 6DP,
United Kingdom

Oxford University Press is a department of the University of Oxford.
It furthers the University's objective of excellence in research, scholarship,
and education by publishing worldwide. Oxford is a registered trade mark of
Oxford University Press in the UK and in certain other countries

First Edition published in 2020

Impression: 3

Published in the United States of America by Oxford University Press
198 Madison Avenue, New York, NY 10016, United States of America

British Library Cataloguing in Publication Data
Data available

Library of Congress Control Number: 2019955332

ISBN 978-0-19-878579-8

Printed and bound by
CPI Group (UK) Ltd, Croydon, CR0 4YY

Contents

Acknowledgements vii

SECTION 1: DEVELOPMENTALISM AS A POLITICAL THEORY OF TRANSFORMATION

1. Introduction 3
2. Capitalist Development 21
3. Capabilities and the Limits of Liberal Development 48
4. Realism, Values, and Development 65

SECTION 2: CASE STUDIES

5. Britain 91
6. America 132
7. The Post-Imperial Era and Japan 168
8. Taiwan and Israel 194
9. Rwanda and China 219
10. Conclusion 248

Bibliography 261
Index 281

Acknowledgements

This book is dedicated to Jane, Jack, and Lydia.

Conversations with Duncan Higgins and Matt Sleat helped the book along the way and gave some encouragement. The School of Government and International Affairs at Durham made much-appreciated efforts to give me the time to complete the writing. Many thanks to those at Oxford University Press who helped with the production of this book: Adam Swallow for supporting the original proposal, the referees whose comments were extremely helpful, Katie Bishop who was really supportive in the final stage of writing, and Julie Musk whose copyediting meticulously got the text into shape.

In memoriam, George.

SECTION 1

DEVELOPMENTALISM AS A POLITICAL THEORY OF TRANSFORMATION

1
Introduction

Tanzania 2090

Let us start this book with a scenario. It is 2090. In 2090, Tanzania is a middle-income country in which the per capita income (adjusted by imaginary future economists to 2018 prices) is $12,000. Tanzania has a network of cities throughout its provinces, all connected by well-maintained highways and railways; it has a working national energy grid, having escaped from the regular power failures of the early 2000s. Tanzania's economy has diversified significantly into a range of services and industries that connect with the East African region and global markets. The agriculturally rich zones in the south and around the northern highlands are highly capitalized commercial farming zones, served by various local goods and services, market towns, and infrastructure. They produce large amounts of food for national consumption and export. Reliable wage employment—albeit still at modest real income levels—has expanded secularly, a process that has generated increasing tax and savings rates. Savings have increased capital for investment and tax revenues have enabled the Tanzanian government to sustain a system of social support with little dependence on the caprice and agenda-setting of aid donors and lenders.

Currently, Tanzania has a per capita income of about $3,000. Its road system is constrained to a small number of national highways, a set of tarmacked but poorly maintained secondary roads, and a large number of roads constructed out of compacted soil which are often destroyed or eroded by rainfall. The energy supply to Dar es Salaam, the commercial centre of the country, is sporadic and often worse in other towns and cities. Rural electrification is absent, the vast majority of rural dwellers relying on kerosene lamps, wood or charcoal fires, and the occasional generator or solar panel. Tanzania's economy remains fundamentally based in low-productivity smallholder agriculture and a welter of small-scale informal goods and services activities which are in some combination low-technology, precarious, and defined by small-scale investment; 47.5 per cent of its export value is derived from just three commodity groups: gold, nuts, and raw tobacco. Financial markets are extremely thin and spatially constrained. The state's ability to raise tax

Developmentalism: The Normative and Transformative within Capitalism. Graham G.M. Harrison, Oxford University Press (2020). © Graham G.M. Harrison.
DOI: 10.1093/oso/9780198785798.001.0001

revenues is poor, and successive governments find themselves struggling to deal with dependency on external aid and credit.[1]

This opening might seem like a flight of fancy, describing a future Tanzania radically different from the actually existing Tanzania of today. But this future Tanzania is not fanciful. In fact, it is based on a property of the global capitalist system in which, from the mid-nineteenth century, countries with socio-economic conditions not dissimilar to real and present Tanzania have transformed over historically short periods of time into countries in which the majority of people's incomes have increased multiple times to provide what one might call the basic modern comforts of life. These countries have also developed weighty socio-economic infrastructures: transport, education, health, regimes of taxation, security, various regulatory and legalistic authorities, and so on. They have also shifted from relatively undiversified and low-productivity labour to higher and more diversified labour, broadly away from agriculture and into industry and services.

The G25+

The G25+ countries have one thing in common: a fully realized capitalist transformation. Countries with sustained economic growth and increases in income per capita have generated the vast majority of the world's poverty reduction and they very clearly fit within a group we shall call 'capitalist dominant'. Coates[2] offers a list of as many as twenty-five countries that have grown and sustained high levels of income per capita: Britain, America, New Zealand, Australia, Sweden, Switzerland, Denmark, Norway, Finland, Austria, Portugal, Ireland, Italy, Germany, Belgium, the Netherlands, Spain, France, Canada, Portugal, Singapore, Greece, Japan, Taiwan, and South Korea. One may wish to add or subtract at the margins, but this list stands as a strong representation of the world's wealthiest and most dynamic political economies.

There is also a group of countries that one might characterize as catching up, and these are countries in which (in our terminology) capitalism is ascendant. Kroeber[3] identifies fourteen countries that have, between 1970

[1] On the contemporary political economy of Tanzania's development, see Andrew Coulson, *Tanzania: A Political Economy* (2013), Michael Lofchie, *The Political Economy of Tanzania: Decline and Recovery* (2014), and Hazel Gray, *Turbulence and Order in Economic Development* (2018).

[2] David Coates, *Models of Capitalism. Growth and Stagnation in the Modern Era* (2000): 3.

[3] Arthur Kroeber, *China's Economy. What Everyone Needs to Know* (2016): 10.

and 2010, increased GDP per capita relative to America by ten percentage points or more and these include those countries from southern Europe and East Asia that have achieved the greatest levels of industrialization. Again, one might add or subtract around the edges: the BRIC economies, or the MINTs (Mexico, Indonesia, Nigeria, and Turkey) for example. But a list like this one certainly exists for anyone interested in the political economy of development. Within this latter 'ascendant' group, some have done considerably better than others. And, for many, it is far from obvious that one would want unconditionally to celebrate their transformations. Nor is there any guarantee that a country that reaches a certain level of economic growth will not encounter regressions of one kind or another.[4] But between these two lists of 'dominant' and 'ascendant' capitalisms you have the world's major capitalist economies and the sites within which the world's major poverty reduction over 300 years has taken place.

None of Coates' 'G25' countries in the present-day is anything like Tanzania, and it is far from clear how Tanzania becomes like one or some of these countries. Nor is it clear what one might make of the process through which Tanzania's potential transition might be realized. So, schematically to present Tanzania Today with Future Tanzania and make reference to G20 Past and G20 Present seems like a crude historical framework that lacks any workable analytical co-ordinates through which to say anything realistic and empirically focused about how life might improve for Tanzania's large population of poor people.

Nevertheless, the intellectual condition of globalized modernity is strongly coloured by both comparison[5] and the sensibility that history is driven by material progress. Indeed, there has been an acceleration and intensification in the metrics and data of comparison, most obviously expressed in just the issue we have started the book with: global poverty. The master episteme of international development is derived from the comparison of relative progress in measures of socio-economic achievement between countries across time. It follows that any discussion of global development necessarily has to make some sense of how Tanzania looks in comparison with other states and also to ask questions about how countries have changed and are changing,

[4] A significant aspect of this concern is the discussion among economists about a middle-income trap. See, for example, Andy Sumner 'Global Poverty and the New Bottom Billion: What if Three-quarters of the World's Poor Live in Middle-Income Countries?' (2014).

[5] For a specific and deep study of modernity and the politics of comparison, see Benedict Anderson, *The Spectre of Comparisons* (2008). The episteme of comparative measurement is as old as capitalism and its 'improvement' aesthetic—see Paul Slack, *The Invention of Improvement* (2015).

and how they might look in the future. At its core, the historiography of development is about what worked in some countries in the past and what that means for the future in other countries. If one does not like this kind of historiography—and there are some strong arguments that protest this approach to the global[6]—that is fine, but it does require one to find a different meta-narrative to the one we call development. Indeed, the term 'development' intrinsically summons up this sensibility of political time: prospective, progressive, subject to manipulation, but hardly absent of risk.[7]

Tanzania 2020

Tanzania has approximately 28 per cent of its people in extreme poverty—that is, a daily income of less than $1.90 per day. Life expectancy is 64 years. For most Tanzanians, work is extremely hard and minimally rewarding. It is also precarious. Low-productivity labour is set within social infrastructures that are weak and unreliable, whether in relation to transport, banking, energy supply, education and training, or law. Getting from T2020 to T2090 necessarily would require radical change over a fairly compressed period: one hundred years or so.

This way of understanding development—rapid, structural, modernizing—has been subjected to a considerable amount of criticism within political studies of development. Development in the sense we are suggesting here is seen as authoritarian, eurocentric, racist, and imperialist.[8] Approaches to development that identify with rights, capabilities, indigeneity, and 'grass-roots' have enjoyed considerably greater normative appeal since the early 1980s. This is not our approach. Development in the sense that we shall consider throughout this book is fit for the purpose of discussing the possibility of T2090. It does not set it limits at the point where small-scale farmers live out their existing livelihoods in moderate relative comfort.[9] As I shall argue in

[6] Post-colonial and post-development approaches eschew the concept of 'development'.

[7] On the intellectual lineages of this characterization see Michael Cowen and Robert Shenton, *Doctrines of Development* (1996). Marshall Berman insightfully encapsulates the cultural history of modernity as the 'desire for development' in *All that Is Solid Melts into Air. The Experience of Modernity* (2010): 39.

[8] Arturo Escobar, *Encountering Development: The Making and Unmaking of the Third World* (1995); Majid Rahnema and Victoria Bawtree, *The Post-Development Reader* (1997).

[9] This characterization relates to what de la Rocha calls the myth of survival. Mercedes Gonzales de la Rocha, 'The Construction of the Myth of Survival' (2007): 43. A full genealogy of this approach to development might start in the mid-1970s when the International Labour Organization and other United Nation organizations promoted the Basic Needs Approach.

Chapter 3, the current orthodoxies of development define the possibilities for change in precisely this latter fashion through concepts like capabilities, resilience, and livelihoods. The notion of development as we shall define it at least has the scope of ambition to maintain the possibility of a radical transformation in people's lives towards a material condition in which work, income, and the social infrastructures of daily activities are proximate to those that most people would consider 'ordinary lives' in the G25+ countries—a kind of life that large numbers of people live or that they can realistically and reasonably expect and demand through political processes.

We can do this simply because this is a core historical insight that one can glean from concrete histories of capitalist development. Although there is no desire in this book to generate romanticized historiographies of capitalist development, we need also to be able to recognize the remarkable progress that developed capitalist societies have achieved. The generalized conditions of material progress within developed capitalist societies are perhaps so pervasive and obvious that it is intellectually banal to recognize them and consider them as evidence of remarkable material and productive progress. But they are very easily recognizable if one does not live in these conditions. It is a personal point, but during those periods when I undertook fieldwork in rural East Africa, a commonly expressed desire was to move to America or Europe, not to be subjected to the moderate ameliorative adjustments of an NGO (non-governmental organization) project. It is a speculative point, but intuitively convincing to imagine that a smallholder farmer or artisanal fisher might be offered a small loan, improved tools, or free literacy classes. They might accept these sorts of things and the project within which they are situated might consider its grassroots values realized through improved catches or yields. But what if that person was offered an alternative option: to live in Britain or Norway with access to a flat with water and electricity, a welfare state, and far greater access to wage labour that pays better (even for casualized low-wage work) than one might find in nearby commercial farms and industries? One might argue that this fictional individual would rather be at home in their community. But surely, then, the forging of material conditions roughly akin to those in Britain or Norway in more parts of the world is what development should be about?

Without this scope of ambition, we will argue, development is defined through relativistic lenses in which poverty is moderately and incrementally reduced through the uplift of market forces and well-appointed aid. Indeed, the term 'poverty' might be questioned or critiqued as a narrowly material categorization. Economic growth might be allocated an auxiliary status in the definition of development rather than a principal one. There might be cautionary tales of growth not generating happiness. And comparisons between one place and another might be questioned on the basis of ethnocentrism. This book will see development differently. It will—with fairly detailed empirical historical material—identify capitalist development as a kind of structural transformation, a transformation that is inescapably the precursor through which the possibility of mass material well-being becomes possible.

Thus, it is a strong premise of this book's line of inquiry that what Tanzania and other countries with mass extreme poverty need is capitalist development: a radical and broad-ranging social transformation that has at its core mass poverty alleviation and a broader set of improvements in work and social infrastructure. This is neither wishful thinking nor a plainly eurocentric imposition of one model onto other places. It is the means through which one might think about what is most plainly the major-order issue in large parts of the world.

Two Cheers for Development

Pain and Gain

This is not a book that aims simply to reassert a kind of modernizing development canon that is already well established; rather, it is a critical political economy which is aimed at not rejecting development or defining it outside of its core historic promise, but at foregrounding in a dialectical fashion its internal tensions. One of the main tensions is normative. The more grandiose one's development vision, the less easy it is properly to encapsulate within it a sense of human agency or make value judgements about processes of social change[10] which might 'discount those social costs—including "peasant elimination"—as the necessary price of progress'.[11] Keynes famously declared that in the long run we are all dead, and in the *longue durée* of development one might suppose the same thing. The implication here is that longer-term and broader framings of development proportionately reduce the value of individual lives. To borrow an aphorism from another rather different politician, one death is a tragedy, a million deaths is a statistic.

Although we are claiming that development is a 'grand' capitalist transformation, we shall develop an analytical framework that does not avoid the

[10] A strong version of this argument is found in Gavin Williams, 'Taking the Part of Peasants: Rural Development in Nigeria and Tanzania' (1976).

[11] Henry Bernstein, *Class Dynamics of Agrarian Change* (2010): 304.

normative challenges through crude prospective utilitarianism in which certain kinds of pain are justified by certain kinds of future gain. We coin the normative tension between progress and agency as a tension between the normative and the transformative, although we will also argue that ultimately one cannot entirely resolve this tension.

A second tension derives from the fact that when we use the term 'development' we mean *capitalist* development. To suppose that development occurs without a political economy of capitalism is to lose sight of its key properties and in many instances to absolve capitalism of the deprivations in its own historical processes by supposing that extreme poverty is a product of the persistence of extra-capitalist ways of life, or externalities in the economist's parlance. Most fundamentally, capitalist development is based on processes of sustained and transformative accumulation. By this we mean not simply economic growth. Expanded accumulation involves increasing proletarianization, investment in new forms of production, the movement of capital into more complex and diverse activities, and increases in productivity. This is what we shall conceptualize in Chapter 2 as its 'real' developmental property. This is far from the whole story, as we shall go on to see; but it is the beginning of all stories of development. Capitalist accumulation is based on the changing dynamics and intensities of exploitation, much of which is both harsh and disruptive. It also generates all manner of struggle and contention. It moves to reorganize the social relations of gender, race, and place. Furthermore, in contemporary accounts of lived experience, capitalist development does not look like it. It tends to be experienced as disruptive, messy, and contested—not as well-planned progress. It might offer opportunities for improvements in the life of a people, or all manner of fears about a lapse into chaos or decline; or most likely both.

Thus, is it impossible to be unconditionally positive about capitalist development even when it generates mass poverty reduction and development 'miracles'. There is a balance in evaluation to be made in regards to the ways in which capitalist development creates the conditions of possibility for mass material well-being and generalized social disruption, exploitation, and inequality within concrete and complex social processes of expanding accumulation. This evaluative balance is intrinsically contested.

A Commonwealth

Furthermore, capitalist development is not teleological. Neither does it have a clear and stable endpoint in terms of the dynamics of its processes, nor does it have a coherent and stable image of the 'good life' to which we should cleave. Developed countries remain characterized by all manner of inequality, exploitation, struggle, and privation. The fact that these phenomena are less extensive and severe in degree or that the political processes in developed countries make their reduction more possible should not distract from the fact that capitalism is tendentially exploitative and largely indifferent to human suffering unless the suffering humans rebel. It requires robust political mobilizations to compel capital to take on the accoutrements of a more humane way of life. And, even then, it will not relinquish its control over the full flourishing of human endeavours.

As a result, this book is an argument about the unprecedented ability of a specific set of capitalist processes—here coined as development—to generate mass poverty reduction. But this is 'two cheers' for capitalism, not three. The second cheer is the conditions of possibility it creates for a politics of commonwealth in which growing and productive capitalist economies provide for a shared material well-being. The third cheer—not dealt with in this book—would be for the supersession of capitalism's exploitative core property into a more fundamentally socialized way of life in which industry, science, work, and creativity are not subjected to the logics of property rights, competition, and profit. That would be, then, three cheers for socialism.

Nevertheless, the 'first cheer' is some achievement. Consider our G25+ list. Twenty-five countries sit within it, and different country specialists might want to make a case for the addition of a few more or less—this out of no more than 250 years in a state system that now has 195 members. In a very crude ratio, it is one country every 10 years or so: 250 years of global capitalism have generated twenty-something developed countries. This basic statistic is misleading in many ways, but it does say something about the likelihood of achieving development and it implies—rightly—that achieving capitalist development is extremely hard. Addressing the twentieth century as the century of development, North et al. rightly state that

> Twenty-five or so countries...achieved high incomes by the late twentieth century. Viewed in the context of long-run history, the developed world was decidedly abnormal while the slow or nondeveloping world appeared normal.[12]

[12] Douglass North et al., *In the Shadow of Violence. Politics, Economics, and the Problems of Development* (2013): 9.

One might think that this is a rather dour way of framing development: a social condition that is hardly unconditionally worthy of celebration, that requires all manner of problematic processes to be realized, and which in any case is extremely hard to achieve. The history of capitalist development is more about failure than success; it is more about austere global conditions than enabling ones. This framing certainly contrasts with the aspirational optimism of liberal approaches to development. But this approach is simply a realistic addressing of the conditions of global capitalism. And, in another sense, it is *more* aspirational than liberal approaches to development because it both insists on a considerable degree of ambition and seeks to identify through a roughly dialectic historical method the ways in which development is not simply achieved but also contested and won. Indeed, the conceptualization of agency through struggle will serve as a key point in our analytical framework.

Understanding Tanzania's Failure

Tanzania is, then, normal. It has failed to develop, although it has certainly demonstrated some political will to do so. Historically, Tanzania has not been short of ambition. Indeed, it was selected by James Scott[13] as one of his country case studies of 'high modernism' in his influential *Seeing Like a State*. High modernism is Scott's term for systemic programmes of social engineering that rapidly transform societies into conditions of capitalist modernity. His critique is based on a normative and empirical incredulity regarding the success of this kind of programme. Tanzania's *ujamaa vijijini* (roughly village socialism) programme is treated by Scott in this vein. From 1967 and especially from 1973, the Tanzanian government aimed to reorganize Tanzania's rural population of smallholders into communal villages with a view to providing social infrastructure, imposing state authority, and disseminating more 'advanced' agricultural production techniques through co-operative fields, government fields, and extension services.[14]

Articulated through ideas of national self-determination, socialism, and equality, the Tanzanian villagization programme was connected to other areas of strong state action to generate industrial growth through the creation of a

[13] James Scott, *Seeing Like a State: How Certain Schemes to Improve the Human Condition Have Failed* (1999).
[14] Kjell Havnevik, *Tanzania: The Limits of Development from Above* (1993); Leander Schneider, *Government of Development. Peasants and Politicians in Tanzania* (2014).

large state-owned enterprise sector, one of the largest in Africa. It also came with a strong emphasis on education and modern citizenship. And it failed in pretty much every aspect.

The extent and nature of its failure has, naturally, been the focus of considerable research and discussion. Some have identified how the institutions of government were not effective in carrying out the tasks of development.[15] Some have argued that the programme was so authoritarian that it was resisted by ordinary people, and indeed, the last thing one would want is for it to be successful.[16] Some have identified specific policy errors.[17] Some have highlighted how the entire programme was based on an unprogressive class project which was not focused on the mass well-being of Tanzanians.[18] Some have highlighted the adverse global circumstances within which Tanzania was situated, while others have identified how in some respect Tanzania worked with relatively high levels of international support.[19]

The fact of the failure of *ujamaa* is commonly recognized; the causes and explanations of failure are more contested. Most prominently, debate has focused around the failure of 'socialism' in post-colonial countries to generate sustained growth and accumulation.[20] Furthermore, the Tanzanian development programme might have been undesirable, poorly designed, unachievable, or some combination of these. The political drivers of the programme might have been dominated by different social forces. There might have been an overestimation of state capacity to re-engineer societies and/or an underestimation of the social forces to resist the state. It is precisely within these issues that the exacting challenges of capitalist development take place, not simply for Tanzania but for all countries. In this light, Tanzania's development failure under *ujamaa vijijini* is a failure of the state to generate a capitalist transformation. Seen through this historical point-of-reference, the various interpretations of Tanzania's misfortunes can be collated into a single frame of reference in which questions of too much or too little state action become adjusted into questions about the ways in which state action generated increases in productivity or supported processes of accumulation (or not). Questions of 'high modernism' become refocused around the class struggles

[15] Goran Hyden, *Beyond* Ujamaa *in Tanzania: Underdevelopment and an Uncaptured Peasantry* (1980).

[16] Scott, *Seeing Like a State.*

[17] Frank Ellis 'Agricultural Price Policy in Tanzania' (1982); Joel Barkan, *Beyond Capitalism Versus Socialism in Kenya and Tanzania* (1994).

[18] Issa Shivji, *The State and the Working People in Tanzania* (1986).

[19] Michael Jennings, 'Almost an Oxfam in itself: Oxfam, *Ujamaa* and Development in Tanzania' (2002).

[20] A sensibility crudely encapsulated in the title of Arne Bigsten and Anders Danielson, *Tanzania: Is the Ugly Duckling Finally Growing up?* (2001).

generated by development strategy: in terms of both the social base of state power and the mobilizations provoked by grandiose social engineering.

Introducing Developmentalism

The Politics of Development

If Tanzania's troubled history of *ujamaa vijijini* is fundamentally one of failed capitalist development, it is important not to account for this solely in an economistic or technical fashion. The foundations of political economy from Adam Smith[21] onwards have been oriented towards the identification of the social, political, and economic conditions for capitalist growth and transformation. The success or (more likely) failure to develop is, from a political economy perspective, an outcome of the dynamics of the political (re)ordering of accumulation.

However, the importance of politics does not only relate to the generation and sustaining of expanded accumulation—this is a necessary but not sufficient condition for capitalist development. Development requires the deployment of effective political power to regulate the processes of accumulation towards a broader socio-economic transformation and to realize a politics of commonwealth in which the surpluses generated by accumulation are subjected to strong claims and capacity to provide for a broad material well-being. This goes way beyond 'good governance', the most explicit political formulation offered by liberal theories of development. In this book, we will set out a model of developmentalism which aims to provide a framework through which to understand how some countries—a few countries—endured the major order challenges of development sufficiently robustly to generate sustained growth, expanding social provision, and achieve mass poverty reduction, even as so much social disruption, new inequality, hardship, and uncertainty swirled around them.

Developmentalism is, then, fundamentally about the way in which political power is exercised to promote sustained accumulation. It has a set of cardinal

[21] It is noteworthy that Smith is often seen as the progenitor of classical economics and is sometimes bundled into a genealogy of neoliberalism. A complete reading of *Theory of Moral Sentiments* or *Wealth of Nations* clearly shows a far more inclusive consideration of political economy, something Marx recognized even in his proceedings to critique Smith's understanding of capital, labour, and civil society.

features: the dynamics of interaction between the state and major concentrations of property; the coherence and social determination of ruling elites; the ideologies of statehood and their ability to generate stable projects of social engineering; the extent to which the state and capital endure crisis; and the socio-political dynamics of popular mobilization and contestation in pursuit of the commonwealth. Each of these themes can be understood as components of an encompassing process of capitalist development that takes place over a period of decades, leading to a systemic transformation in the political economy of a country. They might be seen as mutually dependent aspects of a complex and exacting project of transformation. Of course, each component needs considerable elaboration and consideration in light of actually existing development projects. Before we do this we should note here some conceptual co-ordinates that give developmentalism its moorings.

Developmentalism is offered as a contribution to a Marxist tradition of understanding development. It acknowledges a dialectic in Marx's more historical writing on capitalist development in which capitalism can possibly generate remarkable transformations in societies that produce considerable wealth, increased productivity, technological change, and new possibilities for collective agency. Nevertheless, these possibilities are accompanied by systemic impoverishment, intensification of labour, dispossession, and new or renewed forms of inequality. It is within this 'agonistic' historical tendency that politics is enacted, both as a form of governance and as a set of political contentions that generate mass mobilizations around class, gender, race, and region, commonly in intersectional modes and expressing varied normative framings.

At the heart of this dialectic in capitalist development is a core feature which identifies the major-order challenge of developmentalism: capitalist development inevitably involves the allocation of pain, disruption, and suffering and it does so in ways that are not simply 'necessary' but rather more contested and uncertain. There is no consequentialist wisdom in forcible state action, not least because coercion destabilizes the temporal framing of cause and effect. The allocation of pain is done for more ideological and interest-based reasons that might be transcribed into a ledger book of utility and disutility. We will unpack the meaning of this approach later.

Developmentalism is not a concept offered in order to construct a single framework to understand and predict development success. Far less is it a way to develop models of development to be emulated. Although we shall try to be as detailed as possible in our conceptualizations, the underlying purpose is to think heuristically about development as a concrete and broad social project. There is no single road to development. There are no hard and fast causes and consequences. But there are some historically adduced and inescapable issues and questions that all development transformations have to face in ways that are contextually specific. In this context, we can sketch the main co-ordinates of developmentalism.

Developmentalism as the Existential Politics of the State

Developmentalism commonly involves a conflation of existential threat to the state with the success of capitalist transformation. Put plainly, the politics of developmentalism is fuelled by its articulation to the principle of political imperatives of states: to secure national security and sovereignty in the context of threat. In a nutshell, developmentalism is possible where development is not normatively attractive but existentially necessary.

The harnessing of developmental ambition as a national threat response is far from automatic; there are many examples of besieged states acting in non-developmental ways. But it is within this conflation that developmentalism as a political project's necessary tenacity resides. Recall that we have characterized the project to transform a society into a fully capitalist one as extremely demanding. This means that it necessarily has to be based on a remarkably determined state. The determinedness of developmentalism is expressed through ideology, institutions, and patterns of political practice over a period of decades and therefore enduring through all manner of contingencies. It involves imposing the state on a territory and securing that territory against external threats. That development might be desirable or preferable is not enough. The rigours of capitalist development—its instabilities, privations, and contestations—are categorically far stronger than can be met by an elite that declares development as an aspiration or vision to nurture the gradual improvement in its citizens' lives. The major-order challenge of capitalist development requires a similarly major-order political foundation.

The Basic Legitimacy of Development

The 'security imperative' is the principal component of developmentalism's political foundation. The second is the coupling of legitimacy with development. Legitimacy and security both might be understood as mutually dependent first-order political demands imposed on states that are attempting to undergo capitalist development. Legitimacy here is not a political property attained through a social contract, democratic representation, or conformity to human rights. Developmental legitimacy is defined by the extent to which a government can use its authority to generate growth and regulate that growth into something like shared social progress. Legitimacy is understood here not as popularity or as having a 'social base' for a particular ruling elite but rather as something more fundamental. It is about the acceptance of state power by its population expressed through practices and habits of obedience, conformity, and participation in the actions of the state. It is about the establishment of the state as a largely unquestioned principal authoritative agency. This is a bare but fundamental legitimacy that is not straightforwardly won or sustained. Developmentalism is a profoundly ideological project. Indeed, the ideology of developmentalism is constitutively defined by its combination of nationalism and commonwealth in the name of sovereignty. We identify security and legitimacy as fundamental or primary political imperatives in the sense that Bernard Williams defines the unique nature of politics in the basic legitimacy demand, a concept we will return to in Chapter 4.

The legitimacy in developmentalism is best understood as recombinations of a set of claims and appeals propounded by states as they pursue major social transition. I will sketch these here with no claim to their order of importance which is historically contextual. First, let us look at legitimacy through the imposition of order. Bearing in mind how disruptive, risky, volatile, and unpredictable capitalist development is, a state can claim a legitimacy that derives from its unique ability to authoritatively and coercively regulate social change. Making significant social change orderly is no small feat and the extent to which this is achieved makes a considerable difference to the authority and legitimacy of the state. When states lose control and cannot account for the nature of change within their territory, legitimacy is undermined. Predictable and orderly social life throughout capitalist transformation necessarily requires sustained, stable, and authoritative state action. Of course, this kind of political dispensation is never perfectly achieved, but within the generalized anxieties about change and the efforts of states to ensure a sense of direction there is a considerable claim to legitimacy.

As we have seen, our historicizing of developmentalism is not sequential but dialectic. This is how we might understand the interplay of 'progress' and 'order': the political management of both within a situation where these two properties cannot be perfectly harmonized. This dialecticism is also present in the interplay between expanded accumulation and expanded and generalized material well-being. And, in this respect too, we can readily see a vital component of developmentalism's legitimacy: the construction of a commonwealth. When one discusses generalized material well-being, one commonly finds considerations of equity (often measured through the Gini coefficient), the extent of basic social provision (things like primary healthcare and education, access to clean water), and generalized income levels. We use the term commonwealth here to articulate these specific and measurable forms of social progress into something more richly political. We draw on a particular tradition of discourse about the commonwealth which is defined by moral economy.[22] The term moral economy focuses our attention on the ways in which broad populations (a 'crowd'; not political thinkers and politicians) construct normativities about economic change and their impact on the masses. Commonwealth, then, is a normatively infused, generally shared, and politically significant ideal which advocates in various ways for a 'just' transformation. The extent to which capitalist development is considered just is situational, but it is underpinned by a specific political-normative consideration: to what degree is the wealth generated by accumulation shared by all?

Although it is difficult to imagine a commonwealth without a consideration of things like average income, Gini coefficients, and expenditure in social infrastructures, we should allow that it might contain other broader aspects. Levels of wage employment, land reform, the regulation of staple food price and availability, and support for the provision of an expansive range of goods such as housing, public transport, and leisure can also be included. The politics of commonwealth is expansive, not simply 'basic needs'. Indeed, it is a major component of our analysis that capitalist transformation is developmental precisely because it opens up political possibilities for stronger and more ambitious political demands for a shared well-being. In sum, we understand the commonwealth as a moral economy of shared improvements in life both provoked and enabled by expanded accumulation. This is, of course, entirely manifested in concrete political economies, not through ideal thinking about a difference principle.[23]

The basic legitimacy demand for developmentalism is, then, a property of states that ensures orderly life and some form of 'development performance' in which mass poverty is addressed through state action. This does not involve a social contract or a specific form of governance derived from idealized

[22] The *locus classicus* here is Edward Thompson, *The Making of the English Working Class* (1980). James Scott uses the term in *The Moral Economy of the Peasant: Rebellion and Subsistence in Southeast Asia* (1977). See also James Carrier, 'Moral Economy: What's in a Name?' (2018).

[23] See here, of course, John Rawls, *A Theory of Justice* (1971), esp. pp. 75–81.

justice principles. Indeed, empirical studies of legitimacy tend to identify performance-related concerns rather than a respect for human rights.[24]

To summarize so far, developmentalism is a strategy that effectively combines the existence of the state with capitalist transformation articulated through ideologies that fix this strategy within a claim to legitimacy. We shall see throughout our case studies in Section 2 that broader social well-being is slowly won through hard battles.

In accordance with our realist approach, we recognize this tension between accumulation and broader social well-being as constitutive of developmental politics. It cannot be resolved and it is not simply a stagism in which a 'difficult' period generates a 'reward' when a 'take-off' is achieved.[25] The allocation of pain and gain are dialectically active and contain the aspiration or possibility of commonwealth, no more. In this sense—and again contra correspondence theories of social change—legitimacy is not won through a fairly simple positive cycle between state performance, economic growth, social policy, and popular fealty. Legitimacy might also involve the construction of myths[26] and propaganda: attempts to deceive, dissemble, and quash rebellious narratives. In this sense, the developmentalist 'state is first and foremost an exercise in legitimation... [and] in every sense of the term a triumph of concealment'.[27] Rich political narratives about development contain something metaphysical: an imagined national destiny and grandeur; the righting of an epochal wrong; the fulfilling of a religious providence. There are ceremonies as well as statistics. New investments might improve national accounts but they are also physical realizations of prestige. When the mythologies and prestige become the heart of the government's legitimacy claim, they are not developmental; when they embellish the tensions of transition in order to shore up the legitimacy of a transition, they are. The conditions within which one distinguishes one from the other are situational and ultimately subject to interpretation.

Class, Power, and Accumulation

Developmentalism tends to emerge within elites that seize power after periods of extreme disruption, perhaps even 'immigrating' into the country and

[24] Bruce Gilley, *The Right to Rule: How States Win and Lose Legitimacy* (2009).

[25] Something of this can be seen in the influential model of Walt Rostow, *The Stages of Economic Growth* (1971).

[26] An early recognition of this is given in Albert Hirschman, *Development Projects Observed* (2002).

[27] Philip Abrams, 'Notes on the Difficulty of Studying the State' (1988).

therefore having social identities that are partially 'expatriate' or 'missionary'. These elites tend to treat societies as in need of massive and radical transformation, tend to give little value to the existing and diverse cultures and habits of societies, and tend to perceive their own security and right to rule as derived from effective social engineering in the name of economic strengthening. These elites are not commonly a capitalist class, but they identify within a dynamic capitalism the essential vector for them to realize their goals.

Developmentalism requires a robust and coherent project of state-building. This is not necessarily in the sense of a liberal expansion of rule of law and citizenship, but rather something altogether deeper and likely more forceful: resettlement, the rezoning of space, the assertion of new systems of property, the disciplining of social resistance or radical labour movements, the restraining or closing down of political opposition.

The political economy of developmentalism has to produce (fairly quickly) certain kinds of relations between state and capital. These relations are varied, but all can be characterized as producing a situation in which states facilitate the 'upgrading' and expansion of a capitalist class, and capitalists 'lock in'[28] states to a mode of governance that responds effectively to changes in relations and strategies of production. The comparative political economy literature tends to frame the state–capital relation in terms of embedded autonomy[29] and crony capitalism, the former being functional and the latter dysfunctional. The perspective here is that both dynamics exist and are manifestations of developmentalism. Their combination is a political and strategic matter, set within the context of a shared desire to expand processes of accumulation.

Developmentalism has to be a flexible political practice. Capitalist transformation does not follow a single pathway or plan; it is simply too disruptive and unstable. Politically, there is art and chance in managing capitalist , as the circumstances within which policy is made change. What might seem like a successful governing regime for growth for a period will create conditions for its own partial obsolescence. Furthermore, social protest, conflict, changes in global trade and investment, spikes in inflation, burst asset bubbles, or drops in growth require from governments extremely challenging combinations of muscularity and flexibility. All developmentalisms are proven in their ability to survive crises. Crisis events are not unexpected external events that fall upon otherwise successful development; they are intrinsic to capitalist

[28] Vivek Chibber, *Locked in Place* (2003).
[29] Peter Evans, *Embedded Autonomy: States and Industrial Transformation* (1995).

transformation. Developmentalism is a politics that endures, responds, and eventually reinvents itself.

The co-ordinates of developmentalism set out above locate the challenges of capitalist development within an exacting political strategy and political economy in which the processes of transformation, growth, and improvements in the material well-being of the population are both hard-won and contested. This generates very pertinent questions about the normative content of development. Both as an ideology and as a bundle of concrete processes of change, development centrally evokes value judgements. This is what distinguishes social change—which might involve all manner of content—from development which has a connotation of improvement, progress, or betterment.

The co-ordinates of developmentalism set out in the section 'The Politics of Development' imply that development is immanently disruptive, requires authoritarian state action, generates social harm to some and maybe many, and is based on a process of accumulation that is intrinsically exploitative. There is, then, a fundamental tension between capitalist development and the normative political theories of rights and justice. At a high level of abstraction, one is a normative framework that affirms the value of individual freedom, the other is a framework that affirms the value of material improvement.

The most common response to this difference is to make a series of theoretical and analytical manoeuvres which do not so much engage with the antagonism between incommensurate normative frameworks as much as define them away. This is a key feature of liberal historiography, and we shall see in Chapter 3 how the capabilities approach makes a similar manoeuvre. Perhaps the best-known example of the conflation of development values and rights values can be found in Amartya Sen's work.[30]

Taking on board the limitations of liberal historiography, we will accept that there is no logical or complete correspondence between rights and development. Analytically, there is always a point at which one has to concede that these two meta-values—the desire for the realization of individual rights and the desire to see speedy and radical social transformations towards productive economies with a material commonwealth—are antagonistic. This is not a fatalistic or pessimistic approach; it is a realistic one.

[30] Amartya Sen, *Development as Freedom* (1999).

2

Capitalist Development

Introduction

Phenomenal Progress and Structure

Capitalist development is not simply growth, poverty reduction, reduced levels of inequality, or improvements in social indicators. Indeed, these changes—and the indices that measure and compare them—are manifestations of deeper social processes which are difficult to assess without establishing some connection to a theory of capitalism based on the systemic reorganization of property, labour, accumulation, and political power. Without this connection, 2 year's high GDP growth in Costa Rica compared with Mexico might lead one to suppose that the former is 'catching up' with the latter. It might lead one to identify and celebrate reductions in poverty in one country which are the result of high inflows of aid or a sudden increase in the price of a major export. In either case, the phenomenal progress of one country against another or within certain measures of development offers up limited insight unless we endeavour to understand the deeper social processes that generate this. When reduced inequality and improved social provision are taking place, they require careful investigation in order to analyse their causes, sustainability, and the likelihood of further improvement. Without some articulation of apparent indicators of progress to deeper and systemic social transformations, we might find ourselves lost for an explanation if progress halts or reverses. We might also neglect the ways in which progress is contextual and therefore supported or enabled by a range of processes and relations which may or may not persist.

The history of development policymaking and aid is strewn with moments of optimism, celebration, and advocacy which prove to be short-lived as the particular improvements in economic growth, poverty reduction, and so on fall away. Indeed, these are more common than robust examples of development success. Nevertheless, these narratives of progress are essential to intergovernmental discourses of development; without them, the entire project would come to appear as unlikely and demanding as it actually is.

Developmentalism: The Normative and Transformative within Capitalism. Graham G.M. Harrison, Oxford University Press (2020). © Graham G.M. Harrison.
DOI: 10.1093/oso/9780198785798.001.0001

Narratives of progress—especially when framed within prospective optimism—enable even the most ungrounded heroic projects to enjoy widespread support and legitimacy, such as the current Sustainable Development Goals. Mainstream accounts of development identify proximate and readily seeable causative factors: a specific policy, institution, aid mechanism, or programme. It is within this remit that the majority of development research resides. And, although there are clearly important questions concerning aid performance, good governance, institutional form, the selection of one policy in preference to another, and so on, these are not considerations that fundamentally address how the conditions of possibility for capitalist development occur. As such, they are themselves contingent—dependent rather than independent variables.

Rather than setting an agenda based on the identification of the right aid or policy regime, the best-designed project, or the institutional innovation, we accept that development is a process of structural transformation. McMillan and Rodrik argue that 'one of the earliest and most central insights of the literature on economic development is that development entails structural change. The countries that manage to pull themselves out of poverty and get richer are those that are able to diversify away from agriculture and other traditional products'.[1] The premise that development involves a structural transformation in which political economies undergo holistic and integrated changes from low-productivity agrarian to higher-productivity industrial production has been the foundation for almost all development economics until the rise of neoclassical economics.[2]

The corollary of a structuralist approach to development is not an abandonment of agency or an apolitical determinism—although it might mean these things. The defining of development as structural transformation means that one assumes that there are deep underdetermining relations that condition, enable, and constrain the possibilities and politics of specific and concrete change. It requires an ontology in which there is a social realm not easily identified in manifest and specific social phenomena. If we seek the causes of development, we might characterize structure as the causes of causes. Less easily identified, these are the structures and relations of labour, property, and

[1] Margaret McMillan and Dani Rodrik, 'Globalization, Structural Change and Productivity Growth' (2011): 1.

[2] Among a large and diverse literature, see Dani Rodrik, *In Search of Prosperity. Analytical Narratives on Economic Growth* (2003), James Cypher and James Dietz, *The Process of Economic Development* (2004), Ha-Joon Chang and Irene Grabel, *Reclaiming Development. An Alternative Economic Policy Manual* (2004), Michael Tribe et al., *Economics and Development Studies* (2010), Emery Hunt and Mark Lautzenheiser, *History of Economic Thought* (2011), Justin Lin, *The Quest for Prosperity* (2012).

accumulation which create the predispositions, possibilities, and adversities within which the more easily seen and discrete facets of macroeconomic policy, aid, and project execution are realized.

Critical Realism

A set of interconnected and 'deep' features in the social relations of capitalism drive a developmental social transition, the manifestations of which allow economists and policymakers to survey and audit societies and to identify empirical evidence of progress. We argue that positive changes in indices are only sustainable and meaningful if they interconnect with other phenomenal changes and with deeper processes of social change: in a phrase, capitalist development is 'more than just events'.[3] There is something systemic and totalizing about capitalist development that cannot be captured by discrete empirical observations over 2 or 3 years.

Critical realism offers a useful and epistemologically detailed means to make distinctions between different 'depths' of development.[4] Roy Bhaskar sets out an understanding of societies through three interconnected and mutually interactive levels: the empirical, the actual, and the real.[5] To put it schematically, the empirical is what is observed; the actual are the myriad social phenomena that are readily apparent whether observed or not; and the real are the mechanisms that underpin and generate the layers 'above'.[6] So, in terms of poverty reduction, we might say that the empirical is a sampled survey of people's income and assets to quantify whether a population has become richer or poorer. The actual is that population's entire material product, something that exists but that is extremely difficult to quantify. And the real is the social relations of production that underdetermine the dynamism and limitations to production and which can only be recognized through theoretically informed concepts.

Critical realism guides us to start from the assumption that there are core realities to a political economy and that it requires theoretical effort to perceive them. As such, Critical realism is not a positivist correspondence theory

[3] Joe O'Mahoney and Steve Vincent, 'Critical Realism as an Empirical Project' (2014): 3.

[4] It should be noted that critical realism seems fairly open and at times unclear in its constitutive features. We shall take it as a loose tradition and seek ways in which it helps us with our matters at hand rather than as a formally specified paradigm. On this, see Geoffrey Hodgson, 'Some Claims Made for Critical Realism in Economics: Two Case Studies' (2004).

[5] Roy Bhaskar, 'Philosophy and Scientific Realism' (1998): 41 *et seq.*

[6] Bhaskar, 'Philosophy': 34.

which aspires to a perfect match of empirical evidence and a theoretical model. It is, rather, a *procedural* orientation in which one assumes that the reality of a political economy underdetermines the manifest actualities and empirics: it gives us ways to assess them, their relations to each other, and their deeper import.

It is important to clarify at this point that this layering of social phenomena is not an Althusserian base-superstructure ontology. We will use terms such as 'causal mechanism', or 'underdetermination'[7] to maintain an analysis in which a deep reality of capitalism is not determinative in the sense that one might read-off a logic demanded by capital, but rather it fundamentally produces the nature of development in all of its complexity.[8] The real of capitalism has 'causal power'.[9] The underlying social relations of capitalism are both too important to ignore and too important simply to assume as structural determinants. Indeed, in the discussion of these Critical Realist categorizations, there is always the possibility that the real changes precisely because it must be theoretically adumbrated and is therefore subject to further empirical and analytical reflection.[10] It is simply that this possibility of change is based on the premise that there is a reality to capitalist development, that it is difficult to change, and that we cannot fully see it in the world of empirical instances.

A great deal of the methodological procedure signalled by this insistence on 'the real' within the social relations of capitalism is, of course, derived from Marx. One of the most-discussed aspects of Marx's writing is his methodological and analytical procedures, mainly in *Capital I*[11] in which he aims to identify what might be called actual phenomena such as commodities or money and seek out the occluded social relations that generate their forms, content, and movement: 'forms of appearance of essential relations'.[12]

Marx understands capitalism's historically distinctive features as both occluded and fundamental. He sustains this general analytical orientation through a conceptual language of 'unlocking' the realities of capitalist social

[7] Bob Jessop, 'The Regulation Approach and Critical Realism' (2002): 103.

[8] Douglas Porpora, 'Four Concepts of Social Structure' (1998).

[9] Andrew Sayer, *Realism and Social Science* (2000): 14.

[10] Stephen Ackroyd and Jan Karlsson set out the core procedures through which 'generative mechanisms' can be partially identified through the empirical identification of processes in their 'Critical Realism, Research Techniques and Research Designs' (2014).

[11] The majority of my discussion of Marx bases itself on *Capital I* (1995) as the only fully realized and detailed political economy that Marx wrote.

[12] Marx, in David Harvey, *A Companion to Marx's Capital* (2010): 241.

relations from their fetishized appearances. One might, again, charge Marx or Marxist traditions within the political economy of relying on crude determinations such as 'false consciousness', teleological stagist historiographies, or 'logics' of capitalism. But this is not how Marx wrote[13] and nor is it necessary to resort to structuralism and determinative thinking in which an unchanging feature of capitalism generates immutable socio-political effects that can only change when the structure does. In fact, taken as a whole, Marx's writings clearly do not signal this analytical procedure at all. It would be a closer representation of Marx's political economy to say that the mystified social relations of capitalism are unstably unified in visible social phenomena and agencies in ways that create dialectical change. There is, as a result, a common epistemology within and between the Marxist and Critical Realist traditions.[14] The distinction between the actual and the real might be characterized as 'forms of appearance of essential relations'.

We can start, then, from a theorization of capitalism which seeks to identify the 'real' or deep conditioning features of its political economy and maintain broad scope for agency, contingency, and dynamic or unstable social change. Recall that the empirical level is one constructed through epistemic action. The way evidence is generated, composed, and communicated constitutes the empirical matters. It is of course true that the 'actual' features of a society provide the remit within which actual evidence is created, but it hardly determines it. Selections and prioritizations are made, norms infused, and rhetorical and discursive strategies deployed. Furthermore, the relation between the actual and the real—the totality of an economy's production, and the productive relations that realize that production for example—are neither fixed nor stable. Because real causes are imperfectly visible, they are subjected to analytical contestation rather than empirical verification. The Marxist critical realism deployed in this book aims to understand how the real/deep conditioning factors of capitalism are generated in order to consider the 'empirics' of concrete development processes.[15]

[13] Mischaracterization of Marx is rife. For a consideration of this with relevance to our arguments, see Norman Geras, 'Seven Types of Obloquy: Travesties of Marxism' (1990).

[14] Andrew Brown et al., Critical Realism and Marxism (2002); Richard Westra, 'Roy Bhaskar's Critical Realism and the Social Science of Marxian Economics' (2019).

[15] A far richer theoretical treatment of the direction of flow suggested here can be found in Jonathan Joseph, 'Five Ways in which Critical Realism Can Help Marxism' (2002).

Historiographies of Development

Origins and Transformations

There is a requirement within this framework to understand development not through empirical renditions of the present in comparison with other cases or with other 'snapshots' in nearby years, but through a theory of historical change. It is only through a theory of history that deep causes can be discerned, discussed, and assessed; and it is for this reason that this book takes its point of departure as the late eighteenth century. This is when a totalizing industrial capitalism started to emerge, forging those deep social relations that subsequently pose both possibility and difficulty for countries. It is within the jaws of possibility and adversity posed by the British capitalist industrialization that development has been constructed in myriad forms in other countries. To speak of development outside this frame of reference is to deplete the term of any distinct historical meaning. To discuss development within more constrained timeframes is to remove from the scope of analysis the establishment of those deep causes that profoundly underdetermine the nature of and prospects for development. We aim for a historical account that has as its concern not only the causes of development—the policies, resource transfers, strategies, institutions—but also the causes of causes—the social relations of capitalism and the dynamics therein which enable sustained accumulation and growth.

Setting out a theory of history is vital for those wishing to adopt a 'deep causes' approach to social change. Without it, the realities that underpin a political economy can start to resemble something like a metaphysics. That is to say, if the profound conditioning forces of a political economy are not subjected to a historical account as to their creation at particular periods and their change over time, they come to resemble a mystical/religious phenomenon as a result of their purported timelessness or immanence in the nature of being: the invisible hand, the human *geist*, natural providence, or god.

Associating the deep causes of social change with a specific historical periodization ensures the analytical connections one might make between the real, actual, and empirical are bound together in a 'disenchanted' fashion, one that accepts that 'things have not always been like this', and questions 'why are things like this?'; and more ambitiously, 'how might things be different?'. The insights offered in the connections between deep causes, the actual world, and the ways in which we understand the world are only as good as they sustain a sense of historical pertinence. It is most palpably the case that capitalism has only expanded, encroached, and intensified throughout human societies since the late 1700s. If a theory of development is not also a theory of capitalism, it is difficult to see how it can operate as a historical theory at all.

We can illustrate the theoretical position with a couple of brief examples. Development research on agriculture has largely focused on small-scale family farming. Throughout the 1970s, this field of research conceptualized these farmers as a class: the peasantry.[16] Indeed, the strongest intellectual drivers of this research were concerned with how one conceptualized the historical origins of the peasantry and how one understood the nature of the peasantry within global capitalism. Peasantries were not only a 'modern' part of capitalism, but also either being undermined or sustained by capitalist social relations. Furthermore, peasantries were not timeless traditional forms of life, but created recently by forces such as colonialism, mercantilism, and capitalism itself. These research agendas were often shorthanded as the agrarian question.[17]

In the 1980s, research on agriculture and development came to be focused not so much on questions of the peasantry's place in capitalist social relations but more on the ways in which farming systems might be understood in more detail and how this understanding might open up possibilities for interventions to improve those systems. These interventions were described in terms such as appropriate or intermediate technologies. They tended to define their objects of interest simply as 'farmers' or smallholders. The conceptual frameworks within which smallholders were located were livelihoods within communities. The temporal frame of reference was the present and immediate future.[18]

There is a considerable difference in talking about peasantries or talking about smallholders/farmers. The analytical language of smallholders and livelihoods is very amenable to empirical research. There is now a strong literature on research methods to generate empirical material on smallholder livelihoods, much of which is extremely revealing. The use of assets, labour, management of environment, credit, collective work, and so on provide rich representations of life in agricultural regions. They might open up discussions about how support for these farmers might be prioritized, not least because

[16] The following books capture a sense of peasant studies and development in the 1970s: Judith Heyer et al., *Rural Development in Tropical Africa* (1981); John Harriss, *Rural Development: Theories of Peasant Economy and Agrarian Change* (1982).

[17] Again, from a large literature, two overviews: Henry Bernstein, *Class Dynamics of Agrarian Change* (2010); Philip McMichael, *Food Regimes and Agrarian Questions* (2013).

[18] For example, Martin Whiteside, *Living Farms* (1998); Frank Ellis, *Rural Livelihoods and Diversity in Developing Countries* (2000).

these research traditions often build on the expressed preferences of the farmers themselves as part of a norm of 'putting the last first'.[19] The primary orientation of smallholder research is to glean a weighty body of empirical material to understand the contemporary conditions of small-scale agriculture with a view to improving practices of policymaking, resource transfer, and institutional support. This research is important, often revealing, and focuses on making concrete improvements to people's lives.

But the smallholder/livelihoods approach does not necessarily or often concern itself with the deeper historical underdeterminations of capitalist social relations. It might recognize how markets are dysfunctional, poorer households labour scarce, or credit usurious. It is less likely to see smallholder production as interlaced within broader social relations of production and exchange that exert limitations and possibilities on the prospects of smallholder farming. It takes detailed snapshots of the contemporary and considers its possibilities of change in the near-future.[20]

Thus, the smallholder definition and approach does not endeavour to conceptualize smallholders as a class with a specified set of processes and relations that connect to patterns of accumulation, (self) exploitation, and property. The latter kind of framing requires a conceptualization of the peasantry not as the actual aggregation of smallholders in a region or country but rather as a historically informed proposition about how agriculture is transformed under capitalism and what class relations this generates. This is not a deterministic argument; it is a conceptual one that inescapably calibrates the scope and meaning of the observed changes taking place within agriculture. It also opens up a different set of questions to those set by the smallholder/livelihoods framing which relate to the forms of differentiation, reallocation of property, articulation between classes, and deeper logics of political power that strongly condition the effects and prospects of not only discrete interventions into farming livelihoods but also their limitations.

One would not wish to draw a stark opposition between these two approaches. I have set them out here schematically in order to illustrate the point that without a theory of capitalism that inquires into the histories of agrarian change, the measure of livelihood changes and different modes of interventions is caught up in its own specific objectives and timescales. The main risk here is that the broader, longer-enduring, and structural

[19] Robert Chambers, *Putting the Last First* (1983).

[20] In this sense, the smallholder/livelihoods approach to agricultural development seems like the progenitor to the capabilities approach.

transformations within agriculture are not centrally addressed. Furthermore, recalling the dynamic interactions between the constructions of the empirical and the deeper realities of social life, we should recognize that our selection of analytical nomenclature is a significantly political choice. It would be a gross misrepresentation to argue that smallholder research is 'neoliberal' or somesuch, but it is more amenable to a naturalization of market social relations and a set of modalities of development intervention that do not challenge prevailing social relations of production.

A brief and analogous second example makes this point more forcefully. Throughout this book, we will use the terms capital and capitalist. Within the development literature, this is not fashionable. The more common terms are entrepreneur and businessperson. Again, as with peasantry/smallholder, ostensibly these two definitions focus on the same thing and they replicate the ontology of a 'real' categorization and an 'empirical' one. If one speaks of 'capital', one speaks of a historically informed and real social relation; and if one discusses a capitalist, one connects the ownership of private property with a deep understanding of the social relations of capitalism. The entrepreneur appears, again, as a most readily apparent and real-time agency. If one wishes to generate growth through the flourishing of small businesses, one can imagine ways of supporting entrepreneurs through loans, training, certification and standards, infrastructure, and contracts. There is no need to consider what happens to a society's deeper transformations in property, labour, and accumulation; there is only a need to make empirically-rich real-time calculations of cost–benefit and growth. And, more clearly than in the example of smallholders, it is to make an ideological point about the nature of capitalism which is that it is nothing more than the actual and empirical surfaces of the market.

Conditioners and Drivers: Capitalist Development

To summarize briefly, we have made a case for a theorization of development as capitalist development and therefore we need to embed our theorization of development in a theory of capitalism that identifies its essential developmental properties. We will do this by making a core distinction between the phenomenal observations of development and a deeper set of social relations which allow us to access a historicized and transformative notion of development. We will proceed in this direction within a tradition of Marxist political economy.

We have emphasized the deep conditioning factors of capitalism, mapping this onto the Critical Realist categorization of 'the real'. These are the essential or generic properties of capitalism that condition both the endlessly complex manifestations of a political economy and the ideas and techniques that we deploy to discern these manifestations. In relation to the capitalist real, this book will make a distinction between conditioners and drivers. The reason for this is that in developing countries, capitalism is not the dominant and totalizing system that it is in developed countries; if it was there would be no need for the theories of development that were distinct from theories of capitalism. Indeed, the historical co-ordinates of the global political economy of capitalism are that some spaces have full-fledged capitalist social relations, while some have partial and hybrid forms of capitalism, and within this constitutive unevenness, the project of capitalist development lies.

The term 'driver' is analytically distinct from 'conditioning factors'. The distinction is between those properties of capitalism that might be associated with its reproduction as a systemic totality (conditioning factors) and the properties within capitalism that generate social transformation (drivers). There is an implied sense that drivers do more transformative work than conditioners because they characterize situations in which capitalism is present but not universal and fully realized. In those countries, mainly in the post-colonial world, the social relations of production are most assuredly capitalist, but they are unable to sustain a political project of mass material well-being which might flatter capitalism with the epithet 'developed'. As a result, a major political and strategic problematique in the post-colonial world is identifying and executing a project to drive a weak capitalism into a more developmental condition.

To make our argument in bare bones here for the purposes of clarity: the deep realities of capitalism are both generic and differentiated. The differentiation that we are interested in is between those countries in which capitalism is self-expanding[21] and totalizing ('dominant' for shorthand) and those in which capitalism is present, combative, or driving, but not dominant ('ascending'). In the former reality, the social relations of capitalism are based on a near-total wage labour relation in which there is a sufficient degree of economic productivity, dynamism, and complexity to make the notion of a general material security for all a real and present political possibility within that country. In the latter, the political economy is focused centrally around the political project of transformation towards this state: ongoing restructuring of

[21] On this term, see Ben Fine and Alfredo Saad-Filho, *Marx's Capital* (2004): 33–6.

property relations, sectoral/technological change, expanded accumulation, and profound changes in the nature of labour. Inasmuch as this transformation is developmental, it is as a result of its successes in securing a basic material well-being for all and some level of universal social support. The varied ideologies and techniques of development politics are based on this 'driving' to transform capitalism into a developed state. Developmentalism is a drive towards dominance broadly in the name of commonwealth. But let us start by considering what are the essential properties of capitalism dominant that enable us to describe it as developed.

Capitalism Dominant

A Marxist understanding of capitalism must theorize capitalism as a complex and integrated whole. This is the fundamental premise that enabled Marx to write *Capital*. Through a range of closely connected concepts, Marx treats capitalism as a 'completed' political economy.[22] It is only by treating capitalism as a systemic whole that we might explore its internal dynamics, core properties, and means of reproduction and expansion. Herein lie capitalism's real. Let us take the cardinal terms Marx uses to identify these factors. This will allow us to move towards an understanding of how capitalism dominant generates the conditions of possibility for a commonwealth.

Marx starts *Capital* by asserting that capitalism is 'an immense accumulation of commodities'.[23] This might at first blush seem like an empirical observation, one that fits in with a range of critiques of capitalism. This statement is in fact a rather opaque signalling of the core conditioning reality of capitalism. Capitalism is a political economy in which the constant and universal circulation of commodities is the necessity for the realization of surplus value. As John Weeks so acutely demonstrates,[24] commodities are produced within capitalism as embodiments (Marx likes to say congealed) of the surplus value of labour, and the primary motive of the capitalist who owns the commodities is to realize that surplus labour through exchange, creating the possibility for further rounds of production and investment. In this way, Marx understands commodities as phenomenal manifestations of a real social relation, and this

[22] We do not need to insist that capitalism is fully universal to recognize plainly that the social relations of capitalism are both pervasive and dominant.

[23] Karl Marx, *Capital* (1995): 13.

[24] John Weeks, *Capital, Exploitation, and Economic Crisis* (2010): 15–19.

makes commodities within a capitalist political economy distinct from the history of goods exchange which is millennial.[25]

Thus, the phenomenal serial production of commodities and the relentless extension of markets is also a manifestation of the deep and complete marketization of social relations which involves the 'commodification' of labour through the wage-relation. Marx uses the term 'abstract labour' throughout *Capital* to ensure that the meaning of surplus value generation, expansion, and competition are framed not in broadly Smithian and Ricardian terms but rather as based on a general and fundamental social relation of labour in which capital owns the means of production and workers labour to generate value through their employment by capital. Absent this general condition and one cannot theoretically identify capitalism's immanent property towards expansive accumulation and growth.

It is the systemic and relentless drive to realize surplus labour, invest, compete, expand, generate efficiencies, and improve productivity that makes capitalism's universal social relations of the market distinct from societies 'with markets'. And it is this that gives developed capitalist societies their historically unprecedented dynamism and ability to generate massive amounts of wealth: 'capitalism is always about growth'.[26]

The immense accumulation of commodities also provides an 'actual' situation in which it is possible to imagine a good condition of material existence for everybody. Indeed, capitalism dominant also has this tendency within its real conditions. Capitalist production seeks not only to realize surplus-value, but also to maximize it—not once but constantly, restlessly. One might explain this through market competition: 'buying low and selling high'. But truism though this is, it does not identify the underlying reality of competition within a capitalist society. The deeper social relation is the seeking and securing of greater amounts of surplus labour. This might most obviously involve pushing workers to work harder and/or longer. But there are limits to this which are both physical and political. Overwork (however defined) depletes workers' ability to continue and it generates increasing risk of rebellion. As a result, capital balances a temptation to both 'squeeze' workers in their conditions of work and innovate the technologies of production in order to increase productivity. The use of technology to improve productivity can increase

[25] Marx characterizes the rise of capital as a process within which it makes the generality commodities its own.

[26] Harvey, *Companion*: 259.

surplus value and keep the conditions of work broadly similar, or moderately improved.

Marx refers to the general imperative to improve productivity through the term 'relative surplus value'.[27] The core point is that labour has become entirely dominated by capital, and through a range of processes (that Marx aptly characterizes as despotism) labour is constantly refashioned to generate improvements in productivity. These are not discrete productivity gains, but systemic ones. Productivity gains are embedded in new technologies of production which are socialized through competition, in cheaper commodities, and in changes in the nature of work. It is the shift towards relative surplus value over absolute surplus value and the actual rather than formal subsumption of labour that serves as the real conditioning factors in which productivity gains are both relentless and systemic.

To summarize, capitalism is a systemic political economy in which social relations come to be fully dominated by capitalism. Capitalism is not simply more trade and output; it is a deeper structural transformation. Among these deep and distinct properties lie two pivotal things: a relentless drive to produce and circulate commodities and an equally hard-wired imperative to employ labour and generate increases in productivity. Herein lie the historically specific preconditions for any politics of commonwealth.

We need to take care in how we present these claims. It is important to stress that the argument is not to set out a model of 'proper' capitalism for other countries to emulate. The sketch above of marketized social relations, relative surplus value, and the growth imperative is an identification of conditioning and underlying realities of capitalism. It is not an unqualified celebration.[28] It in no way precludes an acknowledgement of the ways in which *absolute* surplus is extracted; large numbers of people can be made unemployed; competition can lead to oligopoly, corruption, or a stagnation in technological change; and capital can push heavily against labour to maximize profit over relative gains in people's wages.[29] It is simply that the properties prioritized here are what give capitalism—both in terms of theorizing its properties and in terms of its histories—the possibility of generating a commonwealth for previously impoverished masses. And, as we shall go on to see, there is very strong historical evidence that capitalism has done precisely this.

[27] Marx, *Capital*: 191. [28] Recall the 'two cheers' coinage from Chapter 1.

[29] A concise summarization of all of this can be found in Barbara Harriss-White, 'Poverty and Capitalism' (2005).

Marx characterizes capitalism in Britain as tending towards equilibrium in reaction to the 'constant upsetting of this equilibrium'.[30] Capitalism is, in Marx's figurative, like a spiral,[31] ceaselessly and unstably generating growth in order to maintain itself. Each movement from capital in the form of money into capital necessarily has to produce more money and so on. And this value generation requires the putting to work of labour not as a single act of employment but as a relation in which capital seeks always to reorganize work and the technologies of production to increase profit. These 'spirals' never cease. The notions of both a stable and ungrowing capitalism are oxymorons. It is within the forging of the social relations that all of the countries we consider in Section 2 have developed. In Marx's phrase, the capitalist development is the achievement of 'self-expanding surplus'.[32]

Driving Capitalist Development

Throughout the developing world, myriad capitalist political economies are dynamized by not only the immanent expansive instabilities of capitalist social relations as set out above but also the connections and transformations between capital and what Henry Bernstein calls classes of labour.[33] As a result, the real nature of capitalism in developing countries is defined by—to use a stylized term—a kind of weakness. Capitalism is present; it pervades social relations of production; but it does not fully remake them in its own image. Rather, the condition of development is one in which capitalism encompasses and interacts with peasants and other producers who are not fully dispossessed of their productive property or are not in large numbers regularly employed by capital for wages. Capital has not (yet) generated a process of sustained and expansive accumulation of a kind that might generate a broader transformation into a capitalist political economy. As a result, markets are shallow and not strongly integrated into strong circuits of commodities, full-time wage labour is a small proportion of the workforce, and capital is only strongly present in specific sectors. The surplus generated by capital and the mass of wages earned by workers are too small to create the fiscal revenues to enable a government to provide material well-being for all, secured through pensions, effective universal healthcare, some minimal wage and working conditions legislation, income transfers, and so on.

[30] Marx, *Capital*: 219.

[31] Marx, *Capital*: 326. This is the chapter where Marx emphasizes the endless compulsion for accumulation thus: 'Accumulate! Accumulate! That is Moses and the prophets!': 334.

[32] Karl Marx, *Capital III*, (1992): chapter 24.

[33] Bernstein, *Class Dynamics*.

None of this connotes stasis or backwardness; it simply identifies how weak capitalism fails to provide the conditions of possibility for a generally shared decent material life. This is not a modernization argument about how developing countries need to catch up and copy the examples set by others. It is an argument that capital is not (developmentally) 'performing' in large parts of the world. It is present and weak. Consequently, the major political and strategic imperative is not to seek out a 'western' model of the right capitalism; it is to devise contextually specific[34] projects of transformation which have as their overarching aim the achievement of an ascendant capitalism moving towards a dominant one.

These conditions—extremely varied in reality—make a qualitative and analytical difference to the way we can conceive of capitalism's 'real'. There is no spiral of sustained growth, accumulation, and productivity improvement. These social relations exist as a tendency, but not within a fully realized capitalism. They interact with markets generated by low-productivity and partially independent livelihoods. Capital does not systemically invest in new areas or technologies of production that might secure increased surplus value. Generally, for the majority of people, work is extremely hard, precarious, and unrewarding, defined by a state of partial capture by capital. The reality of capitalism within developmentalism is its positioning as ascendant. This ascendance might be fragile and halting, but the underdetermining strategic question will remain: capital's weakness poses the possibility and even necessity of its dominance. Thus, the reality of capitalism within development is its insurgence within conditions over which it has incomplete control.

Consider any country one might define as developed. Its history will be one in which an emerging capitalism was driven by its own expansive dynamics and a political project to expand, increase its accumulation and investment, compel more people into wage labour, seek out productivity and technology gains, and out of this process generate the conditions of possibility of state forms which have as a realistic goal mass material well-being. Capital did not simply dominate at some datum point; it was a latent property whose tenacity and energy depend on state strategy, the technologies and organization of production, particular and historical endowments of resource and population, and the propitiousness or otherwise of global markets and investment.

Capitalist development is, then, a historically specific reality of capitalism. It is defined by both some generic 'deep conditioning factors' of capitalism and some more specific 'drivers' that derive from the historical condition of weak

[34] On the meaning of context within critical realism, see Sayer, *Realism and Social Science* (2000): 115–17.

Table 2.1 Capitalist development and levels of change.

	DOMINANT	ASCENDANT
EMPIRICAL	Mass social provision, support, or insurance. Poverty deemed as exceptional, requiring effective state action.	Mass poverty, inequality.
ACTUAL	Universal commodity production, generalized wage labour, universal private property.	Diverse classes of labour, low productivity, shallow and low diversity markets.
REAL	Capitalism dominant: conditioning the actual and empirical.	Capitalism weak/emergent: potentially driving transitions towards developed capitalism.

capitalist social relations (Table 2.1). It will be the burden of this book to explore the conditions of capitalist development in some detail. It suffices here to emphasize that there is a qualitative difference in the features of capitalism within different nation-states and that those countries we commonly call 'developing' endure patterns of capitalist production that offer very slender possibilities for the construction of a sustained improvement in the conditions of life for the masses of poor people. 'Development' is the strategic possibility of driving capitalism towards this condition.

Marxism and Development Theory

So, what does it mean to theorize capitalism in ways that cannot assume the self-expansion of capital as a generalized tendency? We shall proceed in three stages: first, to consider the existing ways in which Marxist theory has understood developing countries; second, to pay attention to the concept of primitive accumulation which has served as the main point of reference in discussions of capitalism's origins or even pre-history; and third, to set out an original conceptualization of capitalism in developing countries as a set of interconnected drivers.

Dependency Theory

We will not spend a great deal of space on this genre because in important ways it does not cleave to a Marxist methodology, although it is commonly seen as *marxisant*. Dependency theory's political economy is based on the following key co-ordinates: first, an understanding that western capitalism has become highly concentrated, globally dominant, and strongly backed by state power;[35] second, that its main mode of exploitation in the non-western/peripheral countries is through unequal exchange in various forms of trade;[36] and third, that this leads to weak, distorted, incomplete, and 'blocked' political economies in peripheral states.[37]

The core *problematique* of dependency theory is how trading and investment relations between core and periphery countries structurally subordinate the latter.[38] In peripheral countries, non-capitalist classes are maintained in poverty in order to reproduce the accumulation of monopoly capital in the West in the form of transnational corporations. Local capitalist classes are barely existent, 'lumpen', or 'comprador'. These two phrases suggest that capitalist classes in the periphery are structurally located in a world-system as historically ineffective[39] as classes and sociologically oriented towards enrichment, consumption, and integration into the West.

Although peasants are identified as exploited through surplus extraction, the concept of surplus extraction is largely 'mercantile', that is, it derives from the price exchanges between peasants and other classes. This is not Marx's understanding of surplus extraction that derives from the way in which capital employs labour in production.[40] Nor does dependency theory leave much space for the possibility that actually existing national capitalisms might grow and transform. The transformation towards capitalism dominant is always blocked: uneven, distorted, and impoverishing; conditional on the requirements of core economies.

The sense of being locked into a world-system dominated by western core economies is extremely powerful, and not without a certain intuitive truthiness. Global capitalism can seem globally hard-wired into a dichotomous spatial allocation of core and periphery in which poverty is seen as structurally determined rather than dialectic and relational. And capitalism at the national level in peripheral states is seen as a blocked and distorted political

[35] A key text here is Paul Baran and Paul Sweezy, *Monopoly Capital: An Essay on the American Economic and Social Order* (1966).

[36] The term 'unequal exchange' is here treated as a general and mainly descriptive term. Its mechanisms and theoretical expression have been less easy to settle. See for example Arghiri Emmanuel, *Unequal Exchange: A Study of the Imperialism of Trade* (1972); John Smith, *Imperialism in the Twenty-First Century* (2016).

[37] Fernando Cardoso and Ernesto Faletto, *Dependency and Development in Latin America* (1979).

[38] Andre-Gunder Frank, *Dependent Accumulation and Underdevelopment* (1978).

[39] Hardly Marx's more graceful term, and not one he uses with much conceptual weight, lumpen infers a social collectivity that is not politically organized or active.

[40] Robert Brenner, 'The Origins of Capitalist Development: A Critique of Neo-Smithian Marxism' (1977).

economy in which non-capitalist classes are integrated into capitalism through exploitative terms of trade. Relatedly, dependency theory does not allow for much of a theory of political change. The leitmotifs of dependency theory's political analysis are lumpen, comprador, sub-imperial... national elite manifestations of global structures of power.

Dependency theory does not base itself on Marx's analysis of capitalism and its recombinations of development and exploitation. Inasmuch as it has 'classic' origins, they derive from a selective reading of Lenin and his theory of imperialism. It is not suited to engage with the historic possibility of capitalist development in the post-colonial world.

Modes of Production

The conceptual tools of dependency theory do not offer us a strong consideration of the developmental dynamics of capitalism. They focus instead on trade, structural location, and external dominance. Emerging out of Marxist anthropology, a more theoretically sophisticated and empirically rich literature emerged roughly contemporaneously with dependency theory which came to be labelled as the modes of production (MOP) approach. The core insight of the MOP approach was that as capitalism expanded during colonialism, it did not simply destroy other social relations. Rather, it 'articulated'[41] them into a subordinate position. Focusing especially on Africa,[42] the MOP approach claimed that peasant societies[43] were modified by the emergence of capitalism and then connected into its circuits of production and exchange. In this sense, peasant modes of production could be reproduced within and in combination with fully capitalist modes of production.

Thus, the MOP approach identified concrete aspects of the social relations of production and recognized the hybrid nature of capitalism in developing countries. The most important of these articulations was the way in which peasant societies reproduced labour which would then be involved in temporary wage work for capital.[44] Many aspects of the reproduction of labour—as individuals and as families and communities—were undertaken by women using the family's fields and property, and as a result capital could employ

[41] Harold Wolpe, *The Articulation of Modes of Production: Essays from Economy and Society* (1980).
[42] Bill Freund, 'The Modes of Production Debate in African Studies' (1985).
[43] Commonly defined as a 'lineage mode of production'.
[44] Claude Meillasoux, *Maidens, Meal and Money: Capitalism and the Domestic Community* (1981).

migrant labour at wage levels well below the basic minimum to ensure that labour remained able to survive.

Marx and Marxist writers have generally denoted slave, peasant, tributary, and other modes of production as pre-capitalist.[45] What makes the MOP approach relevant for our purposes is that it is not a concept denoting a historiography of—to use Marx's phrase—'pre-capitalist economic formations'.[46] MOP's core concern is the way in which capitalism in developing countries conditions and modifies peasant societies rather than destroys them. There are a range of modes of livelihoods that can be maintained in a 'modern' condition by and through their connections to capital. What the MOP approach does is open up the conceptual possibility of a dynamic capitalism and a dynamic set of non-capitalist social relations in recombinant form, driven by capitalist processes but not entirely determined by them.

'Classical' Marxism

In *Imperialism: Pioneer of Capitalism*,[47] Bill Warren argued that capitalist social relations are developing throughout the post-colonial world. In a subversion of Lenin's well-known coinage 'Imperialism, the Highest Stage of Capitalism', Warren aimed to reclaim something of the sense of historical progress as capitalism expands and deepens throughout the world. There are two strands to Warren's work. In the first place, he argued (and rallied considerable statistical evidence) that national bourgeoisies were emerging throughout the post-colonial world. These bourgeoisies were forging processes of accumulation that would, it is implied, lead to nationally self-sustaining transitions towards capitalism. Second, he allowed for the possibility that foreign direct investment might also play a progressive role by supplying capital and technology. In other words, transnational corporations were not only the institutionalization of unequal exchange but also the vehicles of capital and technology, the two inter-related phenomena that lead Marx to be so equivocally

[45] The interplay between Marxist theories of social change and modes of production is meticulously discussed in Aidan Foster-Carter, 'The Modes of Production Controversy' (1978). For a strong critique, although not one generally in keeping with this book's approach, see Jairus Banajee, *Theory as History. Essays on Modes of Production and Exploitation* (2010).

[46] See especially Karl Marx, *Pre-Capitalist Economic Formations* (1964).

[47] Bill Warren, *Imperialism. Pioneer of Capitalism* (1980).

impressed by capitalism even as it disrupted, exploited, and impoverished.[48] In this framing, capitalism's expansion is both exploitative and progressive inasmuch as the latter generates an expansion of wage-labour and a capitalist class (national and foreign) willing and able to invest in a national economy. Where this dynamic was absent, 'capital created underdevelopment not because it exploited the underdeveloped world, but because it did not exploit it enough.'[49]

Marx's core insights remain extremely important. The insistence of a progressive property within capitalism not only makes a correction to the dour and pessimistic *marxisant* writing in which all is extraction, exploitation, and stagnation. It also is a way to recoup a scope of ambition for development in an age in which the small-scale, grassroots, and 'authentic' are celebrated[50] in ways that render development a process of extremely moderate change in the lives of the extremely poor. If capitalism is to earn its 'development' adjoinder in countries with mass poor populations it needs to do more than provide them with a corrugated roof and access to micro-credit. It needs to fulfil its historic promise of giving people wages, opportunities, and a social infrastructure that looks something like this—an income per person of at least $12,000, a dwelling with water and electricity, a public system of support for familyhood, unemployment, illness, and elderliness, some form of dynamic and complex economy within which there is some degree of social mobility, and forms of governance within which the politics of a commonwealth can flourish. This is not a perfect state of affairs; it is not easily achieved; and capital does not automatically achieve these things, but therein lies the development challenge.

Primitive Accumulation

The Constitutive Violence of Capitalism

Marx understood that capital's expansion required considerable political effort, a consideration that has been largely discussed in a voluminous

[48] Kevin Anderson, *Marx at the Margins. On Nationalism, Ethnicity, and Non-Western Societies* (2010): Chapter 1.

[49] Geoffrey Kay, *Underdeveloped and Development. A Marxist Analysis* (1975). Relatedly, see also Gavin Kitching, *Seeking Social Justice through Globalization* (2001): Chapter 9.

[50] Tom Brass, 'The Agrarian Myth, the "New" Populism and the "New" Right' (1997) is a brilliant rebuttal of the romantic neo-populism of this worldview.

literature on primitive accumulation. More than any other concept, primitive accumulation has been the focus of research on the ways and means through which capital has generated histories of development through political projects of dispossession.

Marx accounts for primitive accumulation thus:

> The so-called primitive accumulation, therefore, is nothing else than the historical process of divorcing the producer from the means of production. It appears as primitive, because it *forms* the prehistoric stage of capital and of the mode of production corresponding with it.[51]

Marx's usage of the term primitive accumulation aims to reveal the ways in which capitalism did not emerge through the metaphysical or natural processes of marketization, economic and technical change, or the realization of the human spirit. Rather, he sees it as the 'original sin'[52] of capitalism in which its foundational social relations of property are forged. Marx uses the qualifier 'so-called' in order to render the notion of primitivism ironic: not so much a pre-capitalist accumulation but rather a foundationally capitalist accumulation through which people 'are suddenly torn from their means of subsistence'.[53]

Marx understood capitalism as due to the outcome of a sustained and brutal campaign by emerging bourgeoisies and states to dispossess independent producers of their material autonomy. The classic point-of-reference here is the Clearances throughout Britain from the sixteenth to the nineteenth centuries.[54] Since then, the notion has been applied to other evictions of peasants, colonizing settlement, enclosure, and privatization of common land and resources.[55]

Although Marx did not make primitive accumulation a mainstay of his theorization, it does raise important questions for our purposes. The most obvious starting point is to recognize that capitalism does not emerge naturally out of immanent properties of human sociability. Nor is its genesis certain, stable, or predictable. It is violent or at the very least it requires systematic and imposed reallocations of property rights. Recognizing this constitutive property in capitalism brings us close to our understanding of developmentalism as a political economy of capital ascendant. It instructs us that capitalist

[51] Marx, *Capital*: 364. [52] Marx, *Capital*: 363. [53] Marx, *Capital*: 365.

[54] On the importance of England in particular to Marx's *Capital*, see Alex Callinicos, *Deciphering Capital. Marx's Capital and its Destiny* (2014): 33.

[55] These processes have been broadened most ambitiously by David Harvey in 'The "New" Imperialism: Accumulation by Dispossession' (2009).

development requires the imposition of property relations, the political reordering of labour within the wage relation, and the possible deployment of violence when these changes are resisted.

Marx's writings on primitive accumulation have attained prominence in part because this is a part of *Capital* in which he allows himself more than his usual ratio of rhetorical flourish. The acute insight that Marx suggests does not, as a result, figure an understanding of the use of political power, even though it would seem that primitive accumulation—or accumulation by dispossession—represents an especially 'political' facet of capitalism. Marx's point was that the 'secret' of primitive accumulation was not the generation of capital through thrift or market incentives but rather through forcible state action.

Coercion, Capital, and the State

Marx's writing on primitive accumulation recognizes that capitalism emerges through processes of changing class relations and patterns of state action.[56] The emergence of capitalism is always a story of asserting command over markets, property, and people within changing forms of governance. There is no sense to be made in an understanding of the rise of modern states which is not fundamentally connected to the emergence of capitalism. The state is not 'epiphenomenal' or 'super-structural' to the political economy of capitalism; it is part of it.[57] This is not an argument to include the state within a conceptualization of capitalism; it is to understand the nature of the capitalist state.

To put the point directly, primitive accumulation's distinctive contribution is to bring the state centrally into the forging of capitalist social relations. Capitalist development is driven by a class project which is intrinsically a political project:

> [Primitive accumulation] employ[s] the power of the State, the concentrated and organized force of society, to hasten, in hothouse fashion, the process of transformation of the feudal mode of production into the capitalist mode,

[56] Ellen Meiksins-Wood put it thus: 'The very structure of the argument suggests that, for Marx, the ultimate secret of capitalist production is a political one' in 'The Separation of the Economic and the Political in Capitalism' (1981).

[57] Marx's words have been slightly distorted here: he titled one of his works *A Contribution to the Critique of Political Economy* (1987), not critical political economy, and the import of this was that Marx wished to remove the formal distinction between state and economy (or civil society). On this, see Peter Burnham, 'Open Marxism and Vulgar International Political Economy' (1994).

> and to shorten the transition. Force is the midwife of every old society pregnant with a new one. It is itself an economic power.[58]

If we take development to be a social transformation driven by sustained capitalist accumulation from a point of weakness, then a key strategic property of the state is its ability to incentivize, create infrastructures, allocate property, and discipline societies into the service of expanded accumulation.

Historiographies of Capitalist Development

If the concept of primitive accumulation enables us to understand capitalist development as a political project for the ascendance of capital, it is already evident that we are describing both a constitutive historical moment and a generic tendency. Capitalist states discipline, regulate, enforce, and adjust patterns of accumulation and they do so with the intention of making the economy grow and remain stable. There is no moment at which point states stop enforcing and reinforcing the accumulation that is essential to capitalism. The art of capitalist governance is to keep the exercise of power as non-coercive as possible and to maintain as much of a formal separation of politics and the workings of the market as possible.[59] But the historic possibility that the state deploys violence in the pursuit of maintaining capital's ascendance or dominance remains.

The definitive work here is David Harvey's research on accumulation by dispossession. Harvey argues that primitive accumulation is not a stage but a core component of capitalism under all conditions. He connects this especially to the rise of neoliberalism in which the property rights of capital are expanded into areas previously understood as state-owned or commons.[60] He emphasizes the dispossession process as one executed through different kinds of political action: bare coercion, law, and macroeconomic policy. Privatization and 'land grabs' are the epitome of accumulation by dispossession.

Indeed, our list might expand outwards in other ways. The global economic crisis of 2008 resembles accumulation by dispossession: massive asset

[58] Marx, *Capital*: 376.

[59] On this separation, see Ellen Meiksins-Wood, 'The Separation of the Economic', and *Democracy Against Capitalism: Renewing Historical Materialism* (2016). The latter focuses on the erosion of democratic citizenship under capitalism.

[60] Massimo de Angelis, 'Separating the Doing and the Deed: Capital and the Continuous Character of Enclosures' (2004).

destruction of the poor and even more massive government-financed bail-outs for large financial organizations;[61] also new regimes of 'intellectual property rights' which define genetic information through patents; and the wide varieties of unfree labour.[62] We can readily recognize these forcible extractions and alienations as politically enforced intensifications of capital's reach. But we do lose something in this recently set consensus that primitive accumulation is an ongoing 'ordinary' part of capitalism.

What Marx argued most centrally was that primitive accumulation was something epochal. The separation of labour from any independent means of production under its direct control is the basis for the expansion of capitalism as a mode of production. This is not natural, as we have readily recognized; it is defined by the enclosure and dispossession of those with livelihoods not fully reliant on capital. This divorcing of labour from property is a condition for the ascendance of capital. As capital establishes greater control over a political economy, it does not relinquish a range of political involvements to impose and enhance its degrees of freedom or assets. But these involvements are analytically and historically subsequent to and enabled by the kind of primitive accumulation Marx focused on. They are sins, but they are not original.[63]

This distinction is most clearly put in *Grundrisse* where Marx distinguishes between capital becoming and capital being:

> The conditions and presuppositions of the *becoming*, of the *arising*, of capital presuppose precisely that it is not yet in being but merely in *becoming*; they therefore disappear as real capital arises, capital which itself, on the basis of its own reality, posits the conditions for its realization.[64]

It is not that Marx does not recognize how expanded accumulation relies on a constant reassertion of the property relations of capital, but he does insist on a precondition for these more quotidian separations or dispossessions.[65] In essence, the land grabs, capitalist cronyism, privatizations, and so on are only so systemic and totalizing because they are as a result of the imperatives expansively to accumulate generated by the separation of labour from the

[61] Saskia Sassen, *Expulsions: Brutality and Complexity in the Global Economy* (2014).
[62] Tom Brass, *Labour Regime Change in the Twenty-First Century* (2011).
[63] The translation 'primitive' is not definitive. The word Marx used, *urspriingliche*, might better be translated for our purposes as 'original' or 'primary'. Primary connotes something establishing but without precluding subsequent forms of 'separation' enabled by it.
[64] Karl Marx, *Grundrisse* (1973): 392.
[65] Gregor McLennan, *Marxism and the Methodologies of History* (1981): 162.

means of production and the subordination of the former to capital. Just before Part VIII of *Capital* in which Marx discusses primitive accumulation, he makes the point plainly: 'It may be called primitive accumulation, because it is the historic basis, instead of the historic result of specifically capitalist production.'[66] Separations, dispossessions, and thefts certainly pervade capitalism across its history, but the basis of these ongoing privations is on a transition—by no means fully perfected but epochal—towards a dominant capitalism.

This point is not simply about the way we conceptualize primitive accumulation. It is also a historical orientation. For those writers for whom primitive accumulation is in some form ever-present and therefore not 'original', meaning having an 'epochal' character, the history of capitalism is ever-present. If primitive accumulation is present in the emergence of capitalism and continuous in various forms thereafter, then it is difficult clearly to make a distinction between capitalist ascendant and capitalism dominant, as we aim to do in this book.

Conclusion

'Original' primitive accumulation is an unpleasant process, but we have posited that it is a necessary one for the forging of capitalist social relations, a set of social relations that we have argued are uniquely dynamic and which underpin all of the successful development experiences in the world. This is not an easy argument to justify in normative terms. Are we content to resign ourselves to a consequentialist history in which bad things with good outcomes can be called progress? Marxist and other modern historiographies can tend towards a kind of tragic imagery of history in which the great achievements of a present age belie the immense suffering of previous generations.[67] But this does not offer up many options to understand contemporary development or to understand that capitalist transformation is not destined to generate the absolute penury of the masses. That depends on the politics of development. What matters a great deal is context: the nature and extent of dispossession and its effects on social relations; the political contestations

[66] Marx, *Capital*: 345.

[67] There are many examples of this historic aesthetic, but as is often the case, Nietzsche perhaps has the most florid: 'how much blood and suffering lie at the root of all "good things"!' Freidrich Nietzsche, in Terry Eagleton, *Materialism* (2016): 112. Walter Benjamin declares that 'there is no document of civilization that is not at the same time a document of barbarism.' Walter Benjamin, 'Theses on the Philosophy of History' (1969): 256.

that accompany dispossession. As we have argued, it is within transition itself that normative contestation emerges. Recall the point made earlier that primitive accumulation is not unimodal and therefore its social effects are varied—even if always destabilizing. It is not forbidden to entertain the possibility that dispossession creates opportunities for some—something that seems fairly easy to imagine for some groups of women when patriarchal systems of tenure and inheritance are broken down.

One argument in this chapter is that countries go through stages to achieve development. Without primitive accumulation, there can be no self-expanding capitalist accumulation. But this book is emphatically not a stagist historiography. We do not assume any *necessary* causation at all. Drawing on the analytical language of critical realism, we conceptualize capitalist development as a transformation within which different conditions of possibility are generated by deeper processes. All that we can suppose is that because capitalist development is understood as an integrated system of change, there are predispositions for different kinds of change to co-determine each other. In other words, various facets of socio-economic change are not autonomous from each other or contingent in their effects; they have systemic properties even if they don't have strict causation. But possibilities are not certainties. Indeed, it is a core argument of the book that capitalist development is extremely difficult to achieve and it is as likely to fail as succeed. Capitalist development remains the exception, not the rule. There is no deterministic and linear capitalist development: if there was, perhaps more countries would have achieved it.

We have argued that development is best understood as capitalist development. As such, we insist that a deep theorization of capitalism's essential properties is necessary to understand the scope and dynamics of social change. This leaves us with a transformative understanding of development in which we are attentive to the political economy of changes in property, labour, and accumulation. We have suggested that capitalist development is based on 'deep drivers' within capitalism that are instantiated in countries in which capitalism is 'weak'; and we have distinguished this from capitalism dominant in which growth, accumulation, and productivity are such that political economies are characterized by a more direct concern with mass material well-being rather than mass poverty and associated major-order social suffering. We have considered the historiography offered by the trope of primitive accumulation and made a case that capitalist development is not—cannot be—normatively pleasing, and we have suggested some ways in which this calibrates the kind of normative thinking that we can perform. It is in this context that we can complete the portrayal of capitalist development offered in this chapter.

The next chapter (Chapter 3) considers an approach to development that is considerably more popular than the one set out in this chapter. We need to engage with it not simply because it enjoys the attention of many academics and development practitioners but also because it identifies key limitations in the liberal approach to development and reinforces some of the strengths in the approach that we adopt. Once we have done this, Chapter 4 will complete this section by setting out a political theory of developmentalism, including some co-ordinates for a normative discussion of development.

3

Capabilities and the Limits of Liberal Development

Introduction

The capabilities approach (CA) has risen to a position of generally approved centrality in the study of development. Although not exclusively an approach dedicated to development research, the relationship between capabilities and development is pivotal to any understanding of the former's rise. The key property that the CA offers to development research is a strongly foregrounded normative affirmation of agency. This is one of the reasons why we consider it here: it poses a more normatively 'pleasing' approach to development than the one we outlined in Chapter 2. The CA is also of interest for us because its understanding of socio-economic change fits within a liberal tradition in which economic growth and improvements in material well-being can be achieved through individual agency, socially harmonizing processes, and stable forms of change. We will argue that the CA is an effective way to understand well-being and agency within the livelihoods of the poor, but it is far less well equipped to move forward our understanding of the politics of structural transformation and mass poverty reduction.

Framing Development as Capabilities

The CA is precisely that: an approach, not a distinct theory. It is used in an ever-broadening fashion and has experienced an 'explosion' of academic interest.[1] It has been integrated into global development metrics; it has been used to generate research methodologies; it has been used to introduce new forms of normative political theory, connecting with ongoing conversations about rights and justice; it has been attached to the vision-statements of

[1] Ingrid Robeyns, 'The Capability Approach: A Theoretical Survey' (2005): 93; Sabina Alkire, 'Using the Capability Approach: Prospective and Evaluative Analyses' (2008): 27.

Developmentalism: The Normative and Transformative within Capitalism. Graham G.M. Harrison, Oxford University Press (2020). © Graham G.M. Harrison.
DOI: 10.1093/oso/9780198785798.001.0001

official development agencies and NGOs; and it has been deployed in an expanding research remit which is about not only 'development' but also well-being, quality of life, human rights, livelihoods, and emotional/psychological condition. The CA has enjoyed a remarkable ascendancy, partly driven by an intellectual advocacy which aims to promote the concept. In this context, it is fair to say that capabilities talk has become the foundation for a humane, broadly liberal, and inclusive development worldview.

The CA has made a claim to understand development in better ways than existed previously. There is commonly a claim that the CA goes beyond 'narrow' economistic approaches to poverty and poverty reduction and that this means that the CA is a better means to understand and reduce poverty. The CA aims both to give greater value to the individual and to be more inclusive in how development is measured, compared, and assessed. The canonical text of capabilities is Amartya Sen's *Development as Freedom*, which argues that 'development consists of the removal of various types of unfreedoms that leave people with little choice and little opportunity of exercising their reasoned agency'.[2] Martha Nussbaum[3] has presented her conceptualization of the CA in more detailed fashion as a way of thinking and doing development, offering ten 'central capabilities'. These include sense imagination and thought, emotions, and play. Issuing from these cardinal contributions, a range of researchers have used capabilities to understand development and global poverty in various ways. At the heart of all the CA work on development is the premise that poverty is centrally a rights or agency issue and that development is therefore a process of expanding individual agency of the poor.

Capability is the freedom that people have to improve their lives, to achieve the things that they have reason to value. Capability is an ontology of being and doing, constructed out of functionings which are, in essence, a set of possible actions that one might realistically take.[4] Capability is a term used to encapsulate the degree of agency or freedom that an individual has to realize different functionings. A CA concerns itself with progress in the sense of individuals having an expanded 'space' or freedom to make effective choices to improve their lives—effective in the sense that capabilities are pragmatic not ideal.[5] Capabilities are about the 'freedom to' only if those freedoms are exercised through a range of actual practices.

[2] Amartya Sen, *Development as Freedom* (1999): xii.
[3] Martha Nussbaum, *Creating Capabilities: The Human Development Approach* (2011): 33.
[4] Sen, *Development as Freedom*: 75.
[5] On this distinction, see Amartya Sen, *The Idea of Justice* (2009), which is in part a reflection on the thought of John Rawls.

This core ontology is surrounded by closely associated terms and foci. Assets strongly affect the extent of one's capabilities: not only financial assets but also other resources such as knowledge (there is an emphasis on literacy and education), social networks, and mobility.[6] The practice-based interest of the CA orients it to opportunities and their enabling. Functionings encapsulate a range of actual practices that collectively realize capabilities such as attending school, borrowing money, investing in a kiosk or new fishing net, and so on.

Capabilities and Development Research

In development research, the CA to development has been used in four overlapping ways. First, and most prominently, it has served to generate a contribution to normative political theory, located within a tradition of liberal reflections on social justice. The main point of entry is Sen's phrase development as freedom. Herein, we find that development and poverty reduction are understood not primarily as a material issue (Sen spends a lot of effort critiquing utilitarian and orthodox economic approaches to poverty) but rather as an issue of unrealized freedoms to act in pursuit of a life that an individual has reason to value. This refocusing moves the ontology of development towards the individual or perhaps community group and seeks the value in the choices that these entities make in pursuit of expanded capabilities. Sen calls this an 'accomplishment theory of justice'.[7] This is not an absolute denial of what one might call the material or metabolic necessities of well-being, but rather a procedure in which discussion of development includes basic material necessities and in which the securing of well-being is principally a question of realizing agency through capability.

Second, the CA has been used to refocus the way we understand poverty and development. This has been done through its narration of poor people's lives and the possibilities that there are to escape poverty. The CA considers income poverty as a component in the development problematique but does not give it a special status. The capabilities vision is one of livelihoods, culture, and well-being, often focused on the subjectivities of life as an individual or small bounded community. Development and poverty reduction are seen,

[6] Again, there is a prefiguring of this in Sen's earlier work. See Amartya Sen, *Poverty and Famines. An Essay on Entitlement and Deprivation* (1981).

[7] Sen, *The Idea of Justice*: 18.

then, as, in part, questions of material scarcity and in substance driven by an expansion of individual agency and self-realization, not better material conditions of life.

Third, the CA has been used normatively and metrically to measure and compare communities. It generates its own techniques of that core feature of development thinking: comparative assessment. It does so with an explicit rejection of the abstracted procedures of gross national income (GNI) ranking, but it does encompass other quantitative measures within the Human Development Index. The CA (again as with all development thinking) wants to identify cases where some success can be seen, asking what that success might mean for other places. Perhaps the best example of this is the Social and Economic Rights Fulfilment Index.[8]

Fourth, the CA offers a 'toolbox' of interventions. There is within capabilities writing a respect for the grassroots agency of the poor and a meta-norm that the only good development is that largely authored by those developing. CA practice is localized and incremental: 'the most important thing is to take that first step, however small—since without that first step no future steps . . . will follow'.[9]

How does the CA derive from these properties a vision of development? The CA defines a remit of development intervention that might be best characterized as galvanizing or catalytic. That is to say, localized and bespoke interventions are considered as a means to promote or enhance what is already there in a latent or potential state. Interventions are small-scale and proximate. They are facilitating and mobilizing rather than 'top-down' and generic. Throughout all of the capabilities literature, there is almost nothing concerning macroeconomics. Rather, capabilities research includes things like the provision of small grants or loans, skills training, infrastructural investments in things like clean market places and primary schools, and the promotion of small-scale producer associations. More broadly, a national literacy and numeracy programme would be *au fait* for the CA because it might enhance certain functionings that likely increase individual capabilities. Resettling large numbers of people by state fiat, even through well-resourced and devised projects, would not be development within the capabilities perspective, even if it generated significant increases in people's incomes.

[8] Sakiko Fukuda-Parr, Terra Lawson-Remer, and Susan Randolph, 'Fulfilling Social and Economic Rights' (2015b).

[9] Ina Conradie and Ingrid Robeyns, 'Aspirations and Human Development Interventions' (2013): 566.

It is fair to say that the CA has enjoyed an ascendancy within development thinking quite unlike any other since the 1980s. There has been an expansion in capabilities-focused research since the late 1990s, and this genre of research now has a (renamed) journal to host its publications and sharpen its intellectual identity.[10] Capabilities talk has expanded into NGOs and intergovernmental development organizations, most notably the United Nations Development Programme (UNDP) but also the World Bank.[11] It has connected with other research agendas such as livelihoods and Quality of Life studies.[12]

The Capability Norm

At the heart of the CA's rising fortunes is its normative agreeability. It is difficult to imagine how a researcher at a conference might declare that they are taking a CA and provoke any consternation from an audience. The ethical focus on individual flourishing, choice, and freedom lends the CA a powerful epistemology in which incremental, localized, and day-to-day practices of expanding capabilities are the very focus of development.

The CA associates strongly with democracy and/or liberal political institutions. As such, it has emerged out of a tradition in which development is couched in the advocacy of empowerment, democracy, and rights.[13] These values work to construct a broad liberal narrative in which development is realized through individual agency, the broader synergistic effects of these agencies, and the supportive context of minimal and facilitative rather than directive governance. CA research is often presented through vignettes in which authors might give the name of an individual or community and say something about the experiences of life and thoughts for the future therein. The CA approach is respectful of the poor and predominantly committed to people as means not ends.

[10] *Journal of Human Development and Capabilities.*

[11] See World Bank, *World Development Report 2000/2001: Attacking Poverty* (2000/2001). Sen has also spoken at World Bank workshops and given podcasts hosted on the World Bank's webspace. 'While not intended by Sen, his ideas were increasingly enmeshed in a free market approach'—William Moseley, Matthew Schnurr, and Rachel Bezner Kerr, 'Interrogating the Technocratic (Neoliberal) Agenda for Agricultural Development and Hunger Alleviation in Africa' (2015): 4.

[12] See for example Ian Gough and Allister McGregor, *Wellbeing in Developing Countries* (2007).

[13] Two good overviews of this genre of development research are Peter Uvin, *Human Rights and Development* (2004) and John Brohman, Popular Development (2005).

Why, then, would one want to reject the CA and seek a normative framing of development through structural understandings of social change that have hardwired into them the possibility of political coercion and dispossession? Should we not seek out ways of defining and valuing development in which these kinds of processes are absent?

Losing Sight of Capitalist Development

The Pitfalls of Inclusiveness

Although there are a number of ways one might theorize development through the conceptual language of capabilities, there is no discernible theory of development as capabilities. Martha Nussbaum argues that capabilities sits within a political liberal tradition,[14] but in the current intellectual landscape this is hardly a major act of identification. Amartya Sen's work establishes a rather adroit balance of theoretical exegesis (especially in regards to justice and utilitarianism) and pragmatism in which more foundational specifications about what capabilities are and how one comes to establish relations between them are purposefully avoided. Most writers remain happy to speak of capabilities as if the conceptual status of the term is sufficiently self-evident and/or 'capabilities' can be maintained as an approach rather than a theory, deployed for various reasons and within various analytical frameworks. Capabilities, then, might be understood as a potential component of various theoretical analyses of social change.

Thus, the term capabilities is not fixed within exacting theoretical parameters. The outcome of this is that capabilities talk is remarkably expansive and fungible. This property might derive from the fact that 'capabilities' is taken as a term that might be deployed across and within different issue areas and analytical frameworks. But it is also a result of the fact that the term is always presented as offering broader and more inclusive understandings of development. Indeed, this is one of its declared advantages. In introductions to the CA, authors commonly juxtapose capabilities with 'narrow' economistic understandings, especially the bugbear of the income per capita measure which economists interested in large-dataset or country-comparative studies still rely on as a foundation. The CA, it is argued, involves a great deal more. It is also about the nature and extent of agency, the values of community, the

[14] Nussbaum, *Creating Capabilities*.

psychological or existential nature of being. It is about flourishing, meaning, esteem, aesthetics. In a phrase, it aspires to encapsulate the breadth of human experience.[15]

The question begged here is the extent to which the desire to be broad and inclusive in defining development through capabilities helps rather than hinders. Inasmuch as capabilities connects to more formalized theoretical thinking, it needs to define what it is not as much as what it is; what matters most and what might logically be argued to be contingent or dependent. These tasks are intrinsic to the nature of theory-making and abstraction. In the more proximate and everyday in which the CA is best deployed, the ability to discern one thing from another is far from self-evident or seems to vary in opaque ways from author to author. How does one measure, value, and make prioritizations when capabilities include 'inner peace' or 'freedom from a headache'?[16]

It is possible within development thinking to analyse the extent to which a person or a community has the freedom to live without high risk of catching malaria. It might seem cumbersome to formulate a concern to eradicate a disease that scourges the lives of millions of poor people in this way, but we do not stray from a commonly agreed agenda of development issues. However, how do we reconcile this with an analysis of CA in which the Rwandan genocide is seen as a capability failure in which Hutus were denied the freedom not to kill Tutsis?[17] In this case, we see clearly both how cumbersome the 'freedom to' prefix can become and how motile it can be: moving through such a diverse range of socio-political processes as to render the subject of development profoundly unstable.

The language of the CA enables cognitive expansiveness, most notably through its prefixing of diverse forms of action with 'the freedom to' or close analogies. Poverty concerns that have been treated as commonsensical by political economy for decades—lack of income is bad, poor health is bad, and so on—are rephrased in ways such as 'opportunity to avoid poverty',[18] or 'free of preventable ailments',[19] or have 'the capability to read and write'.[20] This terminology is clearly one that derives from liberal (positive) rights theories, and it is normatively appealing for that reason.

[15] Sabina Alkire, *Valuing Freedoms: Sen's Capability Approach and Poverty Reduction* (2002): 96.
[16] Alkire, *Valuing Freedoms*: 8, 96.
[17] Severine Deneuilin, 'Beyond Individual Freedom and Agency: Structures of Living Together in the Capability Approach' (2008): 116.
[18] Robeyns, 'The Capability Approach': 101. [19] Sen, *The Idea of Justice*: 226.
[20] Deneulin, 'Beyond Individual Freedom and Agency': 106.

The 'freedom to' can be associated with any capability set, a way to express the agency that makes a capability practicable. It is, however, remarkably fungible: all manner of practices can be positively valued through the 'freedom to' prefix. Thus, it is difficult to establish any framework of priority or causation beyond what might be most immediately possible for an individual or community. Furthermore, this rendering of agency does not give central attention to the possibility—or in this book's framework, inevitability—that agencies conflict and that, at an aggregate level, incommensurate 'freedoms' require structured political negotiation through policymaking, institutionalization, and the imposition of constraints on some. The point here is that the CA sacrifices a square engagement with the realities of development's conflicts and their structural repercussions in order to maintain its normative conflation of development, capabilities, and rights.

Methodological Individualism

The CA is founded on a focus on individual lives: '[t]he capability approach brings attention to individuals' freedom to choose the valued functionings of life as the parameter for assessing well-being'.[21] It does so through an 'ethical individualism'.[22] By definition, capabilities is a term that draws focus onto the ways individuals act or are constrained from acting. Once one starts to talk about capabilities being exercised by collectivities, its meaning starts to dissolve because the 'beings and doings' that are its focus are replaced by notions of collective and/or institutionalized agency. One has to imagine how the agencies of individuals are aggregated in some fashion or collectively affected by something else which is not the focus of the CA. The upward migration of capabilities into social choice—meaning the analysis of possibility and constraint within which collectivities act—stops at the level of 'community'.

The individualist vision derives from a shared ethical position which is that any good that comes from development can only exist—or be realized—within the conditions of the individual. There is a hostility towards aggregation and structure because of the possibilities that this poses to obscure or downgrade the value of the individual's agency. It is in the nature of collective action that individual agency is represented and aggregated with the purpose

[21] Ann George, 'Explicating the Capability Approach through the Voices of the Poor: A Case Study of Waste-Picking Women in Kerala' (2015): 33; Ingrid Robeyns, 'Capabilitarianism' (2016): 400.

[22] Pinar Uyan-Semerci, 'A Relational Account of Nussbaum's List of Capabilities' (2007): 205.

of achieving more potent political demands than would be possible from an individual's agency. Although the CA might conceptualize institutions or movements as aggregations of individual desires, this offers a limited understanding of political agency. Political mobilization requires the construction of leadership, ideological positions (or framings in the social movements literature), and all manner of advocacies, compromises, and negotiations when interacting with other political institutions. The CA does not offer any conceptual guide as to how these political processes behave.

Let us look in a little more detail at the methodological individualism of the CA and the kinds of agency conceptualizations it opens up. The CA is based on the importance of the reasoning of the individual. It is within this reasoning that all values are created and possibly enacted. This thoroughly agency-centred approach relies a great deal on the premise that capabilities only exist when they are realized through reflective individual reasoning. Indeed, such is the importance of individual reasoning that Sen argues that a list of core or priority capabilities cannot be performed without closing off the full property of individual reasoning. There is a two-fold and interconnected foundation to the CA's methodological individualism: an ontology of capability that can only be narrated through the freedoms and capacities of individuals, and a strong affinity with human rights traditions of normative thinking in which the reasoning individual is the source of all positively valued political phenomena. It is in this respect that the CA shows its strong affinities with liberal rights theories.[23]

This individualist starting point opens up different methods of procedure. One of these is to rely on thought experiments or scenarios in which poor individuals are narrated in the abstract and empathetic thought is given to what they might have reason to value. Ethical or reflective reasoning does a lot of ontological underlabour within the CA.[24] There is an assumption that reasoning solves concrete political problems, that strong deliberative and reflective reasoning by poor people individually or within small communities leads to a process of improved ideas, motivations, and agencies that open up possibilities for development. The focus is strongly on this kind of 'reasonable change' narrative.

[23] Uvin, *Human Rights and Development*; Philip Alston and Mary Robinson, *Human Rights and Development* (2005); Ian Fraser, 'Distant Voices: Amartya Sen on Adam Smith's Impartial Spectator' (2012).

[24] Alkire, *Valuing Freedoms*: 92.

The second way that the CA considers individual agency is through vignette evidence.[25] The livelihood of an individual might be presented in some detail to illustrate how capability might be expanded or constrained, how freedom and choice are realized. Sometimes the individual is presented with a name and short biography, bolstering the normative empathy with the 'grassroots' and an interest in specific human experience. It might also be construed as lending authenticity to the author's argument: how can one question the lived experience of someone so distant and poor? In other research, the focus is on small communities defined by their involvement in an empowering development project or a particular livelihood issue.[26] This mode of presentation can reveal detail and also humanize changes that might otherwise be presented as rather abstract or technical. But they also have their limits. It is difficult to derive much insight from a vignette because it is unclear what broader process of change it represents. 'Storifying' a person's life choices also leaves unclear what kinds of selection of evidence are being made, especially when there is a focus on the subjective reflections of an individual. Indeed, methodologically, it is highly questionable how one should treat vignette evidence threaded into strongly normative argument.

Capabilities, Agency, and Development

Furthermore, within this facet of the capabilities writing, there is some anxiety concerning the favouring of people's subjective valuation of their lives. The belief that individual reflective agency is the core value of development leaves a kind of indeterminacy concerning the possibility that people might see things in ways that do not conform to the developmental, optimistic, and justice-seeking episteme that the CA relies upon. In some cases, it leads to discussions about people being comfortable with very little, in which qualifications are added to allow the CA to downgrade this subjectivity in pursuit of expanded capabilities. 'There is an increasing awareness that low aspirations may in some contexts constitute part of what poverty is, and hence that working on aspirations of the poor can play an important role in an anti-poverty strategy.'[27] In other cases, the value of people's freedom is suspended in the name of improved prospective agency, a temporal vision which resembles the

[25] See especially Nussbaum's (2011) use of 'Vasinti'.

[26] Alkire, *Valuing Freedoms*: 86; Sakiko Fukuda-Parr, Terra Lawson-Remer, and Susan Randolph, 'Introduction' (2015a): 5.

[27] Conradie and Robeyns, 'Aspirations and Human Development Interventions': 559.

consequentialism that the CA is generally uncomfortable with.[28] For example, one author argues quite explicitly and with only weak caveats that sometimes people don't know what's best for them: 'It is entirely consistent for a capability theory to argue that we have strong reasons to protect people against their own systematic irrationalities'.[29]

The question of how one reconciles the overarching clarity of purpose immanent within development with real individuals' subjectivities is not especially difficult for liberal thinking. It is resolved within the CA in ways that resemble other development strategies that focus on the grassroots: the provision of education and training, the organization of deliberative processes with the aim of empowering, and the provision of resources through projects that mobilize new forms of social consciousness. In this way, the CA overlaps with a wide range of long-standing grassroots and participatory development strategies. Indeed, the ontology within each seems very similar: individuals making reflective judgements through deliberative processes to improve their communities. As such, the CA's value of individualism and its concern that individuals might not have the right aspirations or reasoning expose it to some of the trenchant critiques of participatory development. We will mention two of these here: first, that participatory development techniques commonly base themselves on disciplinary techniques and power relations which render them as a kind of social engineering.[30] The means through which participation, empowerment, and capabilities are realized is always through an external intervention which comes with its own teleology.[31] And second, that the practices of empowerment, participation, and capabilities largely fit within a broader neoliberal political economy that governs societies composed of resilient and/or entrepreneurial individuals.[32]

These two criticisms of the participatory approach to development—an approach that has close affinities with the way that the CA understands agency—are not only two of the most trenchant. They also signal ways in which considerations of social structure and conflict which are not strongly present in the CA are inescapably pertinent. In the first critique, it appears that the practices of *developing* capabilities is in itself power-laden; in the

[28] Alkire, *Valuing Freedoms*: 7. In Alkire's example, malaria reduction is used as an example. But if pesticides, drainage, or foliage clearance are used, then these projects will have impacts on other functionings.

[29] Robeyns, 'Capabilitarianism': 401. Robeyns goes on to acknowledge some 'modest paternalism' for policy purposes.

[30] Brian Cooke and Uma Kothari, *Participation: The New Tyranny?* (2001).

[31] David Mosse, *Cultivating Development* (2005).

[32] Jonathan Joseph, *The Social in the Global* (2012).

second, it is clear that there are no ontologies of agency innocent of the broader workings of a wider political economy.

For all of its normative desire to imagine how people can escape poverty and powerlessness, it leaves little room for a rich understanding of political economy and might—if one was adversarially minded—be construed as acting in some degree to depoliticize poverty.[33] This is so to the extent that one wishes to understand development as conditioned by large and generalized forms of power which derive from states, properties, classes, the social relations of capitalist markets, global production networks, and so on. It is also the case inasmuch as one assumes that development generates considerable contestation over wealth, property, labour, and other social phenomena central to people's well-being.[34] Valuing the individual's measured and moderate progress in realizing capabilities does not easily engage with these kinds of concerns.

In summary, the value-individualism of the CA leaves it with a constrained analytical remit in which major aspects of social transformation are all but absent beyond cursory mentions of government policy. It does not engage with the social relations of exploitation or the nature of power. The evidence it uses derives either from hypothetical individual choices in which people have reason to act, or from vignettes based on single individuals' lives, neither of which enables any social theorizing. Finally, when it faces uncertainty about actual individuals' agency, it moves towards quite familiar anxieties about how to incentivize people to act appropriately without violating the primary value of individual agency, an anxiety that has, in other sub-disciplinary areas, been subjected to strong critique.

Development and Structural Change

Structure as Context

The individualism of the CA establishes development as the localized and incremental expansion of capabilities through the agency of the individual. As such, structural change is all but ignored and the scope ambition of development is moderate. The CA celebrates 'small scale development

[33] Relatedly, see John Harriss, *Depoliticizing Development: The World Bank and Social Capital* (2002).
[34] Stuart Corbridge, 'Development as Freedom: The Spaces of Amartya Sen' (2002): 194; Rutger Claassen, 'The Capability to Hold Property' (2015).

interventions':[35] the creation of a small new income stream, the introduction of a new appropriate technology. It might analyse positively an expansion of capabilities that has extremely meagre income returns because of its impacts on happiness or self-esteem.[36] Capability stories of individual, local, and moderate change through expanded agency are normatively pleasing but barely offer a sense of connection to the global conditions of mass poverty as a condition shared by hundreds of millions. Nor, as we shall see in Section 2, do they help us understand how mass improvements in material well-being have been achieved historically. Seen within the perspective of global poverty, it is hard not to see the remit that the CA sets itself as constrained. It neither addresses *mass* poverty nor offers much in the way of analytical devices for understanding structural change.

One might argue that the CA is open to the integration of structural factors, but it is yet to be demonstrated how this is done and with what repercussions for the CA. What exists in the literature is a rebuttal of the 'astructuralist' charge, followed by some notes about how the CA might encompass structural concerns, before moving on to more familiar capabilities terrain. There is, then, an *en passant* character to the CA research's consideration of structural factors. In effect, the notion of structures is translated through the CA into something more akin to context: 'social and environmental factors that influence...functionings'.[37] No clear theorization of what structure means[38] is present in spite of the fact that there are a great many structural theories of development and equally numerous discussions in Social Science literatures about the epistemology of structure.[39] Structure is minimally considered as a set of external and contextual factors that cannot be straightforwardly reduced into the livelihoods of an individual or community. It becomes something like 'constraint' or sometimes a 'policy' but no more than that.

Capabilities and Capitalism

The CA offers a normatively rich focus on the well-being of individuals. It has emphasized the importance of agency, choice, and freedom and opens up

[35] Conradie and Robeyns, 'Aspirations and Human Development Interventions': 559.

[36] Alkire, *Valuing Freedoms*.

[37] Robeyns, 'The Capability Approach': 8. Alkire also argues that the CA has a specifically ontological individualism that is not opposed to social structure, but, while minimally correct, the rest of her chapter and indeed the large book it is situated in does not more than bring in structure as context in a way that is not theorized or based in a clear analytical framework. Alkire, 'Using the Capability Approach': 34.

[38] 'The existence of certain structures of living together which explain the successes and failure of countries to promote the capabilities that people have reason to choose and value.' Deneulin 'Beyond Individual Freedom': 113.

[39] Ben Fine, 'Economics and Ethics: Amartya Sen as Point of Departure' (2004)

research into a breadth of aspects of the human experience. It has been used to challenge the 'monoeconomics' and income-focus of orthodox economists, to bring 'voice' squarely into development concerns, and to explore new research procedures and methodologies. What it does not do is offer a theory of capitalist development.

We have argued that development is capitalist development: a structural transformation that requires systemic political effort and major reorganizations in the social relations of work, property, and accumulation. We will proceed in Section 2 to show how this framework accounts for concrete histories of development in that all of the countries that are considered part of the developed world have undergone some form of this transformation. One might call this genre of research 'structural' or 'unorthodox' economics because it is focused on economic growth and related aggregated measures along with a consideration of shifts in economic activity, technology, labour, institutions, and patterns of investment.[40]

None of the CA writing concerns itself with this structural–historical tradition of research even as it precedes, outweighs, and directly relates to the concerns of the CA as a way of understanding development. There might be two cardinal reasons for the 'mutual ignorance' between what we will shorthand as structural approaches to development and the CA. In the first place, the structural approach understands development as an epochal and large-scale kind of change that takes generations. It is far less interested in the setting up of an artisanal co-operative or an adult literacy project. It is more likely to be interested in the relative balance between agricultural and industrial sectors, levels of investment, technological change, a rise in wage labour, upgrading within a production chain, global patterns of trade and investment, and so on.

Second, the structural approach is not centrally concerned with individual agency. Indeed, a great deal of social disruption, coercion, and hardship innate in development can be hidden under the rubric of greater historical forces of change. This indifference to the value of the individual is complex: it is both a normative aporia in which a structural theory of progress might be based on a tolerance for social perturbation and even harm, and a theoretical orientation that fits well with the historical experiences of development.

[40] This is something that Sen broadly agrees with in an early work (Amartya Sen, 'Development Thinking at the Beginning of the 21st Century' (1997): 9), although its import for a CA is less clear both in Sen's subsequent work and CAs to development more generally. There is a chapter on this by Sanjay Reddy, 'Economics and Human Rights: A Non-Conversation' (2012), but it is by far the shortest and does not have space to do more than suggest that a stronger relation between the CA and economistic approaches might be useful.

As we have argued, the most compelling reason to take a structural perspective in regards to development is that the kinds of transformations it might set out raise the promise—no more than that—of large-scale and major reductions in material poverty. It is now commonly accepted that the most powerful engines of poverty reduction have been industrial and service sector expansion in countries with large numbers of poor people, notably China and India but also across other traditionally 'developing' countries as well.[41] Between the late 1970s and the mid-1990s, China's industrial workforce increased from 95m to 149m. Global poverty estimates in 2008 show that most of the world's poor live in South Asia and Sub-Saharan Africa. In contrast, in 1990 half of the world's poor lived in East Asia and the Pacific, mostly in China, but the proportion of the world's poor in China fell to an estimated 14 per cent by 2008.[42] Although South Asia contains more poor people than Africa (approximately 25 per cent of the below US$1/day poor lived in Sub-Saharan Africa in 1998), both the extent and severity of poverty have been decreasing in South and East Asia but increasing in Sub-Saharan Africa.[43] All of the brute statistics of large national comparison suggest that the world's major poverty reduction has taken place where capitalist development has been most successful, and that those areas of the world where aid, the development project, and the CA are most prominent—South Asia and Sub-Saharan Africa—remain those zones with the largest concentrations of severe poverty. In light of this, it remains to be seen how well the CA will fare as a medium through which to consider how effective global poverty reduction works.

Beyond its normative antipathy towards 'top-down' structural approaches, the capabilities tradition has another response to the characterization of development sketched above. This is to argue that development is not simply economic growth or increased income per capita. Thus, 'according to the capability approach, we could not say definitively that poverty reduction has occurred simply because income per capita had increased';[44] or 'the connection of poverty with lowness of income is only instrumental'.[45] Recall that capabilities have been elaborated in terms of a range of aspects of the human condition,

[41] Martin Ravallion, *The Economics of Poverty: History, Measurement, and Policy* (2016); Andy Sumner, *Global Poverty. Deprivation, Distribution, and Development since the Cold War* (2016).

[42] Andy Sumner, 'Global Poverty and the New Bottom Billion Revisited: Exploring the Paradox that Most of the World's Extreme Poor no Longer Live in the World's Poorest Countries' (2015).

[43] Jonathan Kydd et al., 'Agricultural Development and Pro-Poor Economic Growth in Sub-Saharan Africa: Potential and Policy' (2004).

[44] Alkire 'Valuing Freedoms': 2.

[45] Caterina Laderchi, 'Do Concepts Matter? An Empirical Investigation of the Differences Between a Capability and a Monetary Assessment of Poverty' (2008): 206

either under the rubric of well-being (which in turn has an association with the project to measure and compare happiness) or under some form of Aristotelian flourishing (eudaimonism). But there are good reasons to work from the premise that income is the difference that makes a difference: wealth, levels of consumption, savings, and the basket of commodities in the possession of a poor person are the absolute core and key to an understanding of poverty and its alleviation. Other factors identified by the CA are heavily conditioned by these economistic metrics, and in the final instance, 'deficits in well-being rather describe the immediate consequences of poverty than present a theory on the causes of poverty'.[46] Improvements in self-esteem or the freedom to express oneself within a context that is largely indifferent to material poverty once again stretches the meaning of development into something broader and more vague as to require a loss of focus on what development mean. There is, surely, something to be said for the parsimony of addressing global poverty principally as a problem for those with very low incomes and material wealth.

When analyses of structural transformation are properly situated within a methodology of historical change (as we have endeavoured to do), it is important to understand that processes of transformation have two salient properties: one is the contemporary opening up or denial of agency within change; the other is the creation of the conditions for the exercising of new or energized agency. In short, capitalist development creates new forms of agency and new conduits of mobilization, and these must be considered in conjunction with its impositions and coercions. The CA has an underdeveloped historical methodology, defined by the presentism woven into its vignettes and local stories and this leads it away from an interest in social mobilization, the social base of state forms, the institutions within which politics, law, and policy are contested, or the struggles of workers within the capitalist social relations of labour—all of which are only analytically visible over periods of decades.

It is important to clarify that the argument here is not that individual capabilities do not matter; it is to suggest that they matter in ways that are historically produced and underdetermined by structural change. The historical realities of changing political agency suggest that, if we are serious about development as a process of mass poverty reduction, we need to think more clearly about the interplay between structural transformation, the political agencies it denies and enables, and the contestations within these

[46] Sumner, Global Poverty (2016): 137.

transformatory processes. The CA's conflation of development and freedom seems to efface what is perhaps the most important and vexed issue in the politics of development: the social instability of structural transformation and the myriad collective political contestations within and around that process.

Conclusion

The artist Renzo Martens has an installation which has toured through the Democratic Republic of Congo under the title 'Enjoy Poverty'. Although provocative and unstable in its meaning, the phrase does seem to encapsulate something of the credo of the CA. Largely focusing on the lifestory, the proximate and the incremental, the CA desires to tell stories of how poor people can find in moderate increases in income streams, socio-cultural empowerment and affirmation, and in the realization of agency, better ways of living largely untransformed lives—that is, some enjoyment within lives defined by poverty, moderately relieved. Exploring practical ways to make people's lives better and to do so with a primary respect for their own agency is a laudable project. More ambitious strategies of poverty reduction connected to broader possibilities of agency require a different set of theories and analyses.

The CA offers a broad and fungible set of categories and norms to explore the interplay between well-being and agency. It does not concern itself with mass poverty reduction based on broad structural change in spite of the historical evidence that this kind of change is what generates mass poverty reduction. Structural approaches to poverty reduction are hardly unproblematic in terms of their ability to value the rights of people or calibrate strategies of transformation against the agencies of the objects of development. But if one is interested in global poverty reduction, it is clear that it is within this framework that normative thinking would be best placed. In Chapter 4 we shall consider in some detail how this might be done.

4

Realism, Values, and Development

Introduction

Rights and Development

In Chapter 1, we set out a model of developmentalism that was based on two key foundations: that there is a particular species of capitalism which generates the growth, wealth, and dynamism that makes development possible; and that this kind of capitalist transformation is enacted through a politics in which successful capitalist transformation becomes the primary demand on governance. It is this state of affairs that I define as developmentalism. In Chapter 2, the theoretical basis for this understanding of developmentalism is set out through an engagement with Marxist theorizations of social transition, historical methodology, and an epistemology in which structural change and agency interact. Chapter 3 critically engages with the predominant liberal understanding of development in which—through a range of devices—development is understood as rights-conforming. Taken together, one striking point emerges: that development is not a process that easily cohabits with human rights norms. Indeed, capitalist transformations are intrinsically coercive or at the very least severely disruptive in ways that make it extremely difficult to suppose that the vast majority of people have given any kind of reasoned consent to the changes that they are living through.

This position is normatively troubling. One might suppose that an advocacy for capitalist transformation is an apology for—or a denial of—rights in the name of development. One might even construe that it enables all manner of dispossessions and violence by states that claim to be custodians of a well-planned programme of development. Does our understanding of developmentalism necessarily base itself on a materialist consequentialism that balances a Benthamite pain and pleasure over some 5- or 10-year plan? This would enable a defence of rights violations in one time period by reference to greater benefits in a subsequent time period. Or it might justify the extreme suffering and even death of some in the name of the benefits delivered to a

Developmentalism: The Normative and Transformative within Capitalism. Graham G.M. Harrison, Oxford University Press (2020). © Graham G.M. Harrison.
DOI: 10.1093/oso/9780198785798.001.0001

greater number?[1] For those who believe in the intrinsic value of human rights in all people, this sort of calculation is anathema.

Post-colonial states tend to use the language of development to legitimize state projects that deny or erase the rights of the mass poor. This violence might be implicit in the very episteme of technocratic development, embedded in the data that show 'numbers of people relocated' rather than the experience of forced eviction, for example. But, perhaps even more normatively troubling, governments might use discourses of ordered progress to obscure their endeavours to control populations or enrich elites. Development practice might violate rights through 'collateral damage' during a project, or it might purposefully violate rights and use development discourse as a smokescreen.

This is the kind of understanding of development that provoked the concerns of Amartya Sen and a community of researchers into capabilities and rights. As we have seen, these writers have sought to re-define development away from the tensions between development and rights as values that awkwardly cohabit the realm of development practice. They do this through what one might describe as a tautology-resolution: rights are part of development because that's what development is, and therefore anything that seems like development but is not rights-enhancing isn't. Capabilities approaches do not recognize how development has happened in all real historic examples; they do not acknowledge how radical and disruptive development is, and they do not identify a clear and convincing understanding of how capitalist transformation can generate mass poverty reduction.

We come to an apparently irreconcilable difference. Rights-based approaches to development cannot fully recognize that development involves major structural changes to societies that are top-down and disruptive. Structural approaches to development do recognize that development involves large-scale change but have weak tools to endow these changes with values relating to rights.

Normative Political Theory

This kind of normative difference can be connected to a broader contrast within normative political theory. A deontological tradition seeks normative

[1] This calculus of suffering led Bentham to support exemplary corporal punishment as a means to make a significant net reduction in overall crime, an argument that remains the mainstay of defences of the death penalty as a 'deterrent'.

justification in the degree of consonance an agent has to their duty to respect others' rights, interests, or self-determination/autonomy. Contrastingly, consequential approaches seek justification in the outcomes of an act. The normative framework established by a deontological conceptual orientation is Kantian: it identifies the value of a person metaphysically in an *a priori* discussion of human consciousness and the duties that emerge therefrom. A metaphysics of the moral, deduced through reason, commands how people are to act, a pure ethical structure not present in reality but amenable to be applied to political situations.[2] This basis for normative thinking has become immensely influential within political theory, especially since John Rawls published *A Theory of Justice* (1971). In this book, Rawls stipulated that justice required a complete ethical theory based on exhaustively deduced logical principles.[3] The Kantian–Rawlsian approach has also underpinned a great deal of writing on human rights: it has articulated rights as pre-political absolute values[4] of the human condition rather than historically specific and socially constructed political identities, practices, and claims. In the majority of human rights literature, the latter become imperfect realizations of the former, and the former enjoy the status of perfect ethical truth.[5]

The effects of this framing have been profound. The pre-political status of rights enables the construction of a deduced logic of justice that derives from abstract ethical thought. As a result, politics is framed by a set of ideal assumptions about what is morally right, just, and 'reasonable'. One starts with rights and justice as fixed abstractions and then proceeds to analyse politics in relation to the former. This is what Bernard Williams calls political moralism, a way of understanding politics through a pre-established moral framework. This generates strong and appealing normative statements[6] up front in which it is claimed that in some fashion or other all people have value

[2] This is culled from Immanuel Kant, *The Metaphysics of Morals* (2017): 12–13.

[3] This is a paraphrase of John Rawls, *A Theory of Justice* (1971): 10, and it is the basis for the rest of the book's now well-known and -discussed original position, veil of ignorance, and difference principle.

[4] Rawls' primary right to liberty closely matches a liberal understanding of human rights. He explicitly gives this priority over material poverty and inequality through what he calls 'lexical order' (Rawls, *Justice*: 61–3). Towards the end of the book, he briefly mentions that 'a certain level of wealth has been attained' (542), but this is not integrated centrally into the preceding 500 pages.

[5] This follows a Kantian procedure in which ethical purity is the primary virtue of moral thinking. Contrastingly (and more convincing) is Waldron's view on rights in which their value derives not only from their ethical virtue but also from the political disagreement about what they are. Jeremy Waldron, *Law and Disagreement* (1999): 10–13.

[6] One of political realism's source authors, Max Weber, is especially caustic and germane here: 'that unspeakably philistine softening of sensibility, however much it may command affect and respect in human terms, which believes it is possible to replace political with "ethical" ideals, and ingenuously to identify these in turn with optimistic hopes of happiness'. Max Weber, *Political Writings* (2010): 27.

and as a result all people and institutions should have a duty to value that value. This is, in a crude fashion, what a deontological approach must do. To reconnect with our interests here, the deontological approach asserts as an *a priori* that development should be rights-conforming or -enhancing or it will be unjust and therefore worthy of condemnation, no matter what kind of development is taking place. What justice demands of development supersedes all; it is a trump card.

The consequential normative approach is, in the eyes of a Kantian deontologist, no normative approach at all because it does not start with a theory of rights and justice. Nevertheless, in its own terms, it does treat with moral issues, and indeed more or less well-delineated versions of a consequentialist approach can be found in most texts of nineteenth-century European political economy. Consequentialism relies on a moral calculus derived from considerations of the pleasure and pain, harm and benefit, or utility and disutility (to use a more contemporary language) generated by acts of government. Within these terms, then, it is possible to justify a rights violation if it is perceived that the violation is part of a measure that generates more benefit for others than the harm committed to the rights-violated person or persons. The internal working of a consequentialist normative system is a Benthamite utilitarianism in which the good and bad of a policy are articulated in a more scientific language of (dis)utility. This approach is easily seen in a great deal of development policy-making, most obviously because of utilitarianism's foundational role in modern economics.

Deontology and Development

Valuing Institutions

The playing out of the broad rivalry between deontological and consequentialist modes of normative thinking depends in large part on the nature of one's inquiry and the object of one's study. Ideal normative theory often uses individualized thought experiments. The ethical tensions might look more stark when rendered through thought experiments of a child imprisoned in a cellar for the well-being of a village or the way a doctor communicates with a terminally ill patient. Most ideal theories of rights consider as their context what Rawls called 'well-ordered societies'[7] that allow theorists to assume

[7] Rawls, *A Theory of Justice*: 4–5. How these might be distinguished from other societies is set out by Rawls in *The Law of Peoples* (1999).

certain levels of stability and predictability that one is unable to assume prevail during development transformations. We are interested in capitalist transformations: the nature of institutions, collective agency, and the social relations of production and so on—all undergoing considerable and turbulent change. And, although, of course, all of these social categorizations are themselves filled with individuals interacting with others, it is not at all easy to deduce a clear value judgement of an institution, property regime, or social movement from the ethical decisions of an individual, real or imagined.

How does one deduce a duty for an institution? One can only do so metaphorically, supposing that an institution has a coherent and distinct moral compass through a framing of that institution as a single being. The connotations of dubbing the state a Leviathan imply a normative judgement both of overwhelming power and of a danger that states might suppress rights. In many African public cultures, states can be symbolized as Fathers with certain social responsibilities of patronage and discipline.[8] In western political cultures, there are categorizations of 'rogue' and 'failed' states, each with its own normative diagnostics. But no matter how technically sophisticated the endeavour, each of these is a stylization of the state-as-normative-agent which does not allow any clear and reliable way to assess the nature of human action in a way that would satisfy the methodological individualism of a deontological point-of-view.

Herein, in relation to development, the deontological and consequential become blurred. If bad institutions are those that do bad things, that is a consequential argument. It might well be the case that some people in those institutions do good things or fully believe that they are doing good. Connections between any discrete action and outcomes are analytically extremely difficult to identify when thinking about social change, and within the context of development, the connection between acts and outcomes is especially difficult and unstable. While political theorists' work uses individualized examples of actions to highlight a moral argument, cause and effect in relation to development are multivalent. That is, the devising of development actions and their execution are generated through protracted and complex interactions between many individuals, all of which will be in some degree working within a prevailing discourse of development or governance and defined to some degree by their socio-institutional location. This means that the actions of development—say the execution of a new rural development programme or a series of macroeconomic reforms—are not suitably thought

[8] Michael Schatzberg, *Political Legitimacy in Middle Africa* (2001).

of as 'actions' in the sense of an individual who assesses the value of that action in relation to a set of alternatives.

Briefly, there are three ways in which rights-based normative thinking addresses the difficulty in imputing moral agency to states or agencies within it. One is to deduce the conditions of law under which states might act morally. This is an approach strongly favoured by some cosmopolitans and which those writing in a broadly Rawlsian tradition take. In this instance, law becomes the pre-political mode to address institutional change, an intellectual realm in which judges advise legislators on moral reason.[9]

Second, writers might establish the conditions within which states become infused with a moral content by virtue of their democratic characteristics. It is, of course, a foundation of almost all western political theory that democracy is the foundation for the good behaviour of a state. However defined, democracy both makes states accountable for their actions and provides checks and balances to the remit of state action. Simply put, if a government embarks on a development programme that has many harmful effects and is imposed on people without their involvement, that party will be elected out of power. In effect, normative assessment of states is articulated through measures or assessments of the democratic performance of government.

Third, states' normative merits are understood through the consequences of their actions. Although the consequentialist metric is generally eschewed by normative political theory, a great deal of applied political theory considers the impact of policy on the rights, agency, or capabilities of a community or citizenry. In this sense, the duty to govern in a rights-congruent fashion is rendered not so much in the assessment of the merits of the governing but rather through the effects of state action on the governed.

So far, we have identified a constitutive difference in the way development is understood, between a position that development should be rights-enabling and one that sees development more structurally as principally a social reordering that will prospectively create widespread benefits. We have traced the outlines of the former approach as a deontological normative framework and considered how this approach maps onto the development project specifically. This has involved a transposition and adaptation of a broadly methodological individualist approach to states and the development projects and programmes that they pursue. One might consider that between the legislative, democratic, and rights-impact criteria, we can assess development in ways that cleave to a rights-based norm. If a government has a constitution

[9] Waldron, *Law and Disagreement*: 22–4; Jeremy Waldron, 'Judges as Moral Reasoners' (2009).

and legal system that affirms the rights of citizens, and is a signatory to a range of rights-based international protocols, then one would expect the business of development to conform to this framework. If a state holds regular elections, has opposition parties, a free press, and so on, one would expect development to be respectful of citizens' rights. If specific development actions take place within this legislative–democratic framework, one can concomitantly assess the extent to which those actions respect the rights of the subjects of development and suggest ways in which those actions might be improved from a rights-based perspective. Where the constitutional rights are violated and judiciaries are ineffective, where elections are manipulated or civil society suppressed, or where projects are imposed rather than negotiated, one can use stylizations of the state as normatively problematic in its development efforts, regardless of whether the actions generate improved economic performance.

Ideal Rights Theory and Development: A Partial Match

The focus on constitution, legislation, and democracy can generate quite formalized understandings of the state. There is a tendency within ideal liberal theory to deduce the rights and responsibilities of states to their citizenry and then to consider questions of implementation through institutional and legislative design. This is more or less the normative underpinning of the enormous global development project of good governance. The analytical direction of flow here is from abstract principles towards the rules and regulations within which states work and then the degree to which the latter conforms to those regulations. If the constitution is the autobiography of the state, the editing of this autobiography to make it conform to deduced standards of rights can lead analysts to imagine that a kind of substantive progress is being made.

The primary focus on establishing the logically consistent and defensible rights and duties of states has its limitations. It tends to frame politics as a task of implementation. This is a point made forcefully by contemporary realists. Put simply, for realists, a focus on matters of institutional conformity to *a priori* demands of justice and rights starts in the wrong place. It treats politics as a technique for the realization of deduced normative codes. For realists, politics is a more concrete and limited phenomenon in which any values one might identify and advocate necessarily must derive from the study of actual practices of power. As such, political norms are contextual, imperfectly expressed through political action, and not necessarily destined to ascendance because they have some kind of metaphysical property. There is, then, a substantially contrasting epistemology at work here.

In essence, the point here is that implementation-focused approaches are not well suited to understand the normativity of capitalist development. Capitalist development involves a transformation in a political economy that encompasses both the state and other agencies. States do not implement development, they are themselves immersed in it. Agencies are driven by a variety of norms in contexts of uncertainty, and neither the state, business groups, mass organizations, nor individuals can know the effects of their actions. Within this *mêlée*, rights values cohabit and combine with many others, and without the pre-political insistence that rights-based justice is superordinate, we should consider human rights as one among a bundle of desiderata articulated by numerous agencies, all of which advocate their norms politically. It is, then, extremely difficult to take the rights-justice *a prioris* that might work when considering the value of the individual in 'well-ordered' societies and transpose them to a valuing of state institutions during development.

Consequentialism and Realism

Does consequentialism offer a more 'real' way to understand the value in development? Even if we exclude what might arguably be extreme cases of harm from the consequentialist remit, the consequentialist position faces important limitations. Throughout this book, we have stressed the totalizing nature of capitalist development: it is neither linear nor monocausal in its trajectories of change, and, furthermore, the nature of change itself changes as crises are faced and reorientations managed. Capitalist development is far too complex to be rendered through the metrics of cause and effect. Moreover, the interactions between acts and outcomes are not easily embedded in a theory of agency that satisfies the requirements of consequentialist ontologies. Most especially in states where development is happening, projects can fail because they are badly designed and/or they are badly executed. It is reasonable to question whether the state had the capacity to effect change because its 'presence' in some parts of a national society is partial.[10] If the policies of that

[10] Sara Berry, *No Condition Is Permanent. The Social Dynamics of Agrarian Change in Sub-Saharan Africa* (1993).

state are likely to be socially deleterious, the outcome of weak state power is likely to be to reduce social harm. In any case, all manner of development endeavours in developing societies encounter all manner of adaptations, capture, and resistance when they are realized. Indeed, this is intrinsic to the notion of realization. It is unclear under what conditions the problem is too much or too little development. Unintended consequences prevail.

The multifaceted and uncertain totality of capitalist development makes both idealist and consequentialist normative analysis extremely difficult. In one case, the assumption that individuals or institutions can be evaluated according to their rights-conformity requires an *a priori* understanding of justice that renders development a question of implementation. In the other, apart from a utilitarianism that degrades all political values, the notion (sometimes seen in the conceits of the economist's plans) that cause and effect can be stably connected is untenable because capitalist transformation is intrinsically 'chaotic'. Realism's signal virtues are its willingness to identify values where they exist in context and to be open to the political vicissitudes of change. In this sense, realism is more richly political, unencumbered by deduced value systems that are necessarily imposed on realities, and attentive to the 'dirtiness' of politics. For this study, then, it lends itself well to the historic realities of development.

Political Realism and Human Rights

Rights and Legitimacy

The realist tradition has experienced something of a resurgence within political theory, deriving mainly from Bernard Williams' writing. This 'new' political realism has shown little interest in a transhistorical realism that might be found in Classical European or Renaissance city states, absolutisms, or empires. It concerns itself more with the modern[11] conditions of sovereignty and especially the underpinnings of liberal states and politics.[12] Williams argues that politics is best understood in its foundations as a project by states to ensure a social order that has within it some form of legitimacy. How this might be achieved is important in at least two respects. First, the construction of stable and legitimate rule has no telos; there is no equilibrating or

[11] Politics 'now and around here' in Williams' phrase.
[12] Matt Sleat, *Liberal Realism. A Realist Theory of Liberal Politics* (2013).

perfected state but rather iterations through history. States may be more or less stable and legitimate, but they do not necessarily progress irrevocably, nor do they have Archimedean goals towards which to strive. Second, the substance of normatively evocative terms like legitimacy is not determined through any kind of deductive, *a priori*, or idealist process but rather through an understanding of the context within which the politics of legitimacy emerges.

A realist approach to legitimacy starts with the concrete practices that create normativity within the political sphere. Legitimacy might be attained through the ascendance of rights norms or it might be secured through the emergence of others. How different norms emerge as political vectors for legitimacy is an outcome of politics itself: historical context, relations of power, ideological dynamics, and chance. There is no previous manoeuvre in which a justice meta-norm is stipulated. Thus, a realist approach is not indifferent to norms and values. It is not simply that power matters and ideas and morality arrange themselves contingently and largely valuelessly around *realpolitick*. It is rather that norms and values exist fully within the realm of the political.

This means that a realist approach is not necessarily a dour one, but it is a more exactingly and full-bloodedly a political one, open to its tragedies and progress. We have already averred to this in Chapter 1: capitalist development tends to generate new, intensified, and normatively charged political identities and associations around class, labour, and a sense of commonwealth. The politics and ideology of democracy, workers' rights, nationalism, or whatever do not exist ideally or abstractly, connecting like an enzyme to all actual political mobilizations. The broader meanings of rights, democracy, equality, and justice emerge historically out of the politics of these movements and the politics of the state. In a phrase, 'politics is thought and fought'.[13]

Rights, Disenchanted

So, human rights norms are not negated by political realism; they are just situated differently to the predominant idealism within which rights discourse is framed. The standard way to commence a discussion of human rights is to aver that all humans have certain innate rights as human beings. The fundamental articulation of the notion of human rights is ideal, derived from an

[13] Goran Therborn, 'Into the Twenty-First Century' (2001).

a priori reasoning that human rights exist before the political realities into which they are interpolated. In the liberal account, to use the vernacular, all people are born equal and consequently share a common humanity which imposes rules upon politics, especially the behaviour of government. Once discovered and articulated as a singular truth, the human rights norm remains forever: revealed and indefeasible. As Geuss argues, ideal theory tends to take the intellectually sophisticated coinages of human rights and remain 'relatively unreflective' of the diverse, hybrid, situated, antagonistic, and unstable notions of rights held within a general population.[14]

But if we consider human rights as a political phenomenon, two things readily occur. First, the politics of human rights is socially and historically specific.[15] The Jacobin–republican coining of the Rights of Man was in many ways very specific: it emerged out of the multiple currents of rebellion against the monarchy; it cohabited easily with violence; and it was of course heavily gendered and nationalistic. In post-revolutionary America, rights were racially exclusive.[16] By the early twentieth century, understandings of human rights (and indeed the coining of the term within the political lexicon) became socially embedded in Protestant–liberal Europeanness—again very much a product of a specific historical moment. More recently, the discourse and practice of human rights has persisted through considerable change, coded into a discourse of citizenship, the market, military intervention. and so on.[17]

A realist approach would take these concrete instantiations of human rights practice and content itself with understanding their dynamics, limitations, and prospects. It would not wish to identify specific forms of rights politics and consider them as instantiations of a grand historical realization. Arguably, it would trivialize human rights less by treating them as fully present political phenomena. It would be interested in the cultural hybridities and variations in rights-speak and practice, not as imperfect versions of a universal but as entities in their own right that may or may not succeed, may or may not converge with other rights practices. Human rights, like any other political phenomenon, are historically and socially contextual. Inasmuch as rights matter, it is because they matter politically.

And the politics of human rights is—for the realist at least—where the value lies. The abstracted *a prioristic* perfection of a rights statement is vastly

[14] Raymond Guess, *History and Illusion in Politics* (2001): 9.

[15] Samuel Moyn, *The Last Utopia. Human Rights in History* (2010); Stephen Hopgood, *The Endtimes of Human Rights* (2013).

[16] On liberalism and race, see Charles Mills, *The Racial Contract* (1997).

[17] A broader realist argument that supports this point is provided by Guess who states that concepts are 'historically accumulated constellations'. Guess, *History and Illusion in Politics*: 8.

less significant than the practices through which people come to 'bear' human rights. Although natural or idealized understandings of human rights start from the basis that rights are in some fashion innate as a result of being human, it is closer to a fair representation of the history of human rights that they emerge out of processes of socio-political change and the politics that these changes might variously generate. This procedure, both realist and not connected to ethical abstraction, arguably values human rights more richly: as 'thick' embodied values.[18] Having human rights is a political identity. There is broad consensus that social identities such as citizenship, gender, ethnicity, or class are historically constructed and contextual, changing in combination with other political processes. It seems odd to treat human rights as in some sense removed from similar kinds of causative relations, especially when the modern politics of human rights behaves in very similar ways to these other facets of identity: interfacing with governance regimes, political–economic change, ideological contestation, and so on. The glossing that needs to be done to render human rights a single universal and irrevocably expanding realization of an innate personhood would be treated as highly problematic if applied to, say, gender or class.

In summary, this section has argued that realism takes rights more seriously than idealism as a political phenomenon. It sees human rights as one important value among others in the constitution of a legitimate political order. It takes the values of human rights as a political phenomenon from beginning to end and seeks their value not so much in abstract justice procedures but rather in the political work that they do, whether that be in social mobilization, legislative change, social policy, or any other facet of governance. Realism is open to a consideration of human rights, but it does not wish to demand from a political case a correspondence to an overarching ethical framework.[19]

Political and Critical Realism

Realism's Weak Materialism

Realism's core features fit well with our understanding of capitalist development. It allows us to focus on context. It is open to an interest in popular

[18] A concise and eloquent version of this argument, focused around the critique of the 'contentless human', is given by Anne Phillips, *The Politics of the Human* (2015).

[19] What Williams calls 'political moralism'. Bernard Williams, *In the Beginning Was the Deed* (2003): 2.

agency but not in a way that expects certain rights or justice metaphysics to be enabled. But it is not possible to transpose an existing formulation of contemporary realist political theory to our analysis of developmentalism. Recent realist political theory offers something of a paradox. It consistently makes a case that we should start with the concrete political terrain and ask questions about power, but it does so in a way that is—so to speak—insufficiently real. Realists focus on the state almost exclusively and do not consider the ways in which much of the material power of states is produced through the social relations of production. The relation of states to classes, patterns of accumulation, forms of exploitation and resistance, and the nature of structural transformation is vital to any rudimentary understanding of the way states produce and exercise power and to the kinds of political challenges that states face. These phenomena are, analytically, at the heart of how state power is formed, shaped, and reproduced. They affect a state's ability to organize its revenue raising; they affect the nature and strength of opposition to a state or a ruling party; they create major-order challenges to social stability and order of the state.

Let us consider a specific example that draws from realist political theory. One of the best-known conceptual innovations in contemporary realism is Bernard Williams' basic legitimation demand (BLD).[20] The BLD serves as the only universal[21] for Williams' political realism and it claims that all states must secure for themselves a constitutive legitimacy by being able to ensure 'order, protection, safety, trust, and the conditions of co-operation'[22] in order that authoritative politics of any kind may take place. This encapsulates a core concern for realists in defining what the political is. It leads to a focus on law and order and political systems that manage plurality and disagreement. These aspects of governance are, of course, central to the establishing of conditions for a minimally legitimate politics to take place: one in which almost everyone accepts[23] the authority of the state and as a result practices politics within a certain set of social institutions. But any establishing of even rudimentary state authority over a territorially defined population that accepts that state's authority is a *material project*. Basic legitimacy is a product of the

[20] Williams, *In the Beginning Was the Deed*: 4–6.

[21] Derived from his universal definition, the 'universal material of politics'. Williams, *In the Beginning Was the Deed*: 59.

[22] Williams, *In the Beginning Was the Deed*: 62.

[23] Realists go no further than 'accept' because they reject the contractarian premise that some form of agreement to be ruled is exchanged by a commitment by the state to perform certain social goods. The social contract tradition tends to rely on idealized or imagined moments of consensual quid pro quo.

generation of surplus, the organization of property, the ability of the state to generate revenues for itself and to deploy these revenues. It is impossible to imagine even the most rudimentary basic legitimacy without these considerations.

In developed capitalist states, one might assume that questions about taxation, surplus generation, poverty and inequality, and patterns of property ownership are all basically conducive to statehood. But a realist should respond to this assumption by asking if this is the case in all states, if this was the case in developed capitalist states in their origins, and what are the prospects for these conditions to endure. Not to ask these questions is to assume that there is something natural or transhistoric about developed capitalist states, an assumption that would require an abstracted and idealistic notion of political history. It is also far from self-evident that all contemporary states endeavour to construct a basic legitimacy in broadly similar material circumstances. Some states do not fully control their territories; some states control their territories but face strong socio-cultural resistance to their actions. In both of these situations, states exist but not in conditions in which their actions are authoritatively seen as securing the conditions for politics, and in that sense even the minimal universal legitimacy of the political realist is not fully present. In a post-colonial setting, politics does not commence on the basis of the basic legitimacy demand; it commences within states seeking that legitimacy.

It is likely that a major reason why the material conditions of statehood are not integrated into the core universal of realism is its Hobbesian provenance. Hobbes is a key theorist for realists. His understanding of sovereignty as a resolution to the (danger of) violence of life in the absence of an overarching power is clearly the inspiration for realism's focus on politics as the management of disagreement and the securing of a life without generalized fear.[24] But Hobbes did not consider the nature of state power as a product of the social relations of production. Hobbes' *Leviathan* concerns itself with the sensory nature of the human condition, the interplay between religion and state authority, the social contract between fearful individuals and a state, and the philosophical reasoning behind the rise of highly concentrated sovereign power. As such, it bequeaths a realist agenda that concerns itself with violence, ideology, and political interest, the acceptance of authority by citizens, and the effects of fear and insecurity on order. Hobbes does discuss the role of private property within the rise of the state—something that leads some to

[24] On fear, liberalism, and politics, see Judith Shklar, 'The Liberalism of Fear' (1989).

understand his work as proto-bourgeois[25]—but his legacy for political realism has been not so much to consider the material conditions in which the modern state emerges as much as it is to define certain kinds of states outside of what politics is because of their failure to secure the basic legitimacy demand and as a result to endure forms of violence and instability within their statehood.

Materializing Legitimacy

We have argued that realism does not centrally concern itself with something that is fundamental to our concern with the authoritative construction of political power: its integument in social relations of production both in its origins and constantly throughout the political project to maintain basic legitimacy.[26] As a result, realism's attention to context, power, and legitimacy is constrained by a rather narrow definitional focus on the nature of political power. This might be a result of the different disciplinary remit of political theory and political economy. It might also be a result of realism's concern parsimoniously and clearly to define the specific nature of the political in contrast to other spheres of social practice. Be that as it may, there remains a lacuna in the political theorizing of realism in that it neither integrates a materialist line of inquiry into its analyses, nor sets out why it does not do this. This matters for us because capitalist transformation—and the ways in which we assess it—is fundamentally about establishing the basic conditions of legitimacy within the throes of major social change.

Our argument is that material structures do matter at the profoundest level in an investigation into the construction and maintenance of the BLD. In order to move our realist account towards a recognition of this, we can draw together what have been up to now two contrasting usages of the realism epithet: realist political theory and critical realism. Recall that critical realism was set out in Chapter 2 as an epistemology that enabled us to establish a way of understanding capitalist development as a process that has certain 'real' characteristics in its patterns of change. The 'real' in critical realism is an external property that social science can (partially) understand and in doing so construct theories of causation, the patterning of social relations, and

[25] C. B. McPherson, *The Political Theory of Possessive Individualism: Hobbes to Locke* (2010).

[26] Relatedly, see here Benno Teschke, *The Myth of 1648: Class, Geopolitics, and the Making of Modern International Relations* (2009).

critical evaluation of empirical case studies. The 'real' in realist political theory is a signal that politics is non-ideal and fundamentally concerned with power, legitimacy, sovereignty, and the authoritative management of disagreement.

We have, then, two distinct understandings of 'the real' here. One refers to the underlying processes and relations that generate social phenomena; the other refers to the conditions within which politics takes place. What both approaches share is an acceptance that certain real and concrete (not ideal and deduced) conditions produce the social and the political. Between these two understandings of the real, we have already concluded that capitalist development requires expanded accumulation through transformed social relations of production and that the politics of this process exerts demands on states to construct a basic legitimacy rather than realize justice or the flourishing of human rights. What we have at this point is an affinity between two non-idealist theories that acknowledge external conditions within which socio-political change takes place. But we do not yet have a way of unifying the two.

In order to do this, let us return to the basic legitimacy demand. Williams defines this as a requirement that states minimally but universally justify their authority to the population within their territory. By doing so, government and political contestation can exist without substantial fear of violence or a breakdown in law and order. States should enjoy a 'roughly equal acceptability to all', an acceptability that must include the 'radically disadvantaged'.[27] As already noted, this is a minimalist theory of the political and Williams is constantly careful to avoid expansive and moralized political universals. As a result, he does not need to explore the nature of radical disadvantage. The coining of this term largely serves to set a condition of material inclusivity in the state's basic legitimacy.

For Williams, the first political question is how to sustain the conditions within which fear of violence is abated and as a result politics can take place.[28] This seems reasonable, but it does raise a question about the categorical status of a fear of violence. Might it not be equally primordial of politics that all citizens do not endure a fear of hunger? Hunger has an equally unmediated and visceral effect on the possibility of political agency as does 'raw' violence.

[27] Williams, *In the Beginning Was the Deed*: 5.

[28] Williams, *In the Beginning Was the Deed*: 3. Williams argues that 'first' means principal, not first-stage. The conditions upon which politics is practiced remain a historically 'active' consideration for all states. This is in fact in keeping with the generally mis-represented 'state of nature' in Hobbes which is also not presented stadially but as a way of explaining how politics under sovereignty is possible historically. Also, for clarity of analysis, and in case it seems that we are blurring concepts, the first political question is, for Williams, 'answered' by meeting the basic legitimacy demand. Certainly in *In the Beginning Was the Deed* the two are very closely intertwined.

Hunger's metabolic effect is to induce severe physical discomfort; the malnutrition that constant hunger generates means that one is innately vulnerable to disease and illness, which intensify suffering and severely constrain agency. And constant hunger kills through either attrition or a famine event. It is this analogy that serves as the title for one of the best case studies of famine: Michael Watts' *Silent Violence: Food, Famine, and Peasantry in Northern Nigeria*.[29] Hunger is understood as a form of violence, replete with effects that are closely analogous to physical violence—pain, suffering, and death—which causes radical disadvantages that render state rule inexplicable. In a brute phrase: how can a 'basically legitimate' government let some of its citizens starve?[30] There are broader connections here. Johan Galtung's concept of structural violence is based on the argument that some property and wealth relations can be entirely lawful, enforced, and stable, but also reproduce extreme penury among some groups, say those in rural areas without land or those living in extreme squalor in slums. Galtung distinguishes structural violence from the 'direct violence' of assault or arbitrary detention, but also identifies the similarities between the two in that they generate a kind of systemic and extreme suffering and fear of death. In his words, structural violence occurs 'when human beings are being influenced so that their actual somatic and mental realizations are below their potential realizations'.[31] This is, surely, 'radical disadvantage'.

If we allow some minimal but essential consideration of material hardship into the basic legitimacy demand and its first political question—the constitution of authoritative power in the absence of radical disadvantage—then we identify an analytical connection between our two realisms. Critical realism's interest in the deep drivers of capitalism concerns itself with the social relations of production, and these crucially underdetermine the extent and ease through which a basic legitimacy-seeking state might produce the conditions within which stable and authoritative governance and politics might happen.

In summary, we have identified a connection between political realism and critical realism which is that the basic legitimacy demand includes within its imperative to ensure a social order free of fear of violence and suffering a material condition which relates to radical disadvantage. We do not have to specify what this is exactly to recognize that intense physical suffering as a result of poverty and overwork qualify for the BLD. For post-colonial

[29] Michael Watts, *Silent Violence: Food, Famine, and Peasantry in Northern Nigeria* (2013).

[30] On this question, see Alex de Waal, *Famine Crimes. Politics and the Disaster Relief Industry in Africa* (1997).

[31] Johan Galtung, 'Violence, Peace, and Peace Research' (1969): 168.

countries (and arguably all others) this makes the nature of capitalist growth and accumulation directly pertinent. It is, in fact, the principal instance through which the possibility of a commonwealth is constructed through capitalist development.

Developmentalism and Realism

We have argued that a realist approach to politics is better suited to an understanding of capitalist development because it does insist on an *a priori* and abstract valuing of universal rights or justice. Having this kind of *a priorism* forecloses what is the most important and interesting feature of capitalist development: its recombinations of progress towards mass material improvement (something that is surely 'good') with all manner of disruption, dispossession, and exploitation (things that are, for all but the most hard-headed utilitarian, 'bad'). We have insisted that realism is not amoralistic but in fact well purposed to make moral judgements that are contextual and attentive to the ways in which social change generates political mobilizations to justice, rights, and so on. Realism rejects moralism but not the morality of politics.[32] It seeks to develop critique through an empirically attentive inquiry into the content of political practices and the extent to which these realities meet their declared aims.[33] We have sought to integrate a realist understanding of politics with critical realism, a tradition that shares a premise that there are concrete external conditions to politics. Critical realism serves a specific purpose: it provides a lucid way to situate our understanding of the political in relation to capitalist development whose essential features foundationally condition the possibilities for legitimate authority in any modern context. We can now move on to set out the ways in which this analytical framework provides an enrichment to our conceptualization of developmentalism in ways that seek to provide a normative orientation to the governance of capitalist development.

States do not promote capitalist development because it is right, but because it is necessary. The forging of a capitalist development transition is extremely difficult and most of the time it fails. Capitalism is not innately 'developmental'; it is *potentially* developmental. Capitalist development is not

[32] Sleat, *Liberal Realism*: 21.

[33] Broadly culled from Bernard Williams, *Truth and Truthfulness* (2002), and the critical theory principle.

rights-affirming; it is not predictable; it is not positive-sum. Capitalist development has, historically, clearly demonstrated its ability to generate mass improvements in material well-being and no alternative political economy recently in existence has come close to capitalism's ability to generate growth and increased productivity; nor are there any robust alternatives to capitalism in the present-day. It is, therefore, fundamental to recognize that developmentalism is extremely hard to sustain and in no way guaranteed success.

Efforts to sustain capitalist development more often than not fail and might do so in ways that make it hard even to identify any residue of improvement in people's lives. Development requires governments to allocate both benefits, opportunities, hardships, and dispossessions as property regimes and expanded accumulation are realised. Development itself is complex, unstable, and unpredictable, which means developmentalism is the art of governing within concrete contexts that are unmanageable and not under any single institution's control.[34] Indeed, at the heart of developmentalism resides a fundamental agony, which is that capitalist growth destabilizes, threatens to exacerbate inequality, and is prone to crisis.

At first blush, then, realism is fit for purpose if we are to take capitalist development seriously. It does not expect virtue in the politics of adverse circumstances. In the rest of this section, we shall identify some more specific ways in which we can use the conceptual language of realism as we have set it out above in order to establish some purchase on how we might normatively evaluate developmentalism.

Coercive Governance

Capitalist development is coercive. It necessarily involves a systemic reorganization of the social relations of property and work. These reorganizations—which can appear historically in very different forms—are imposed and enforced through the exercise of political and economic power by the state and capital. The more rapidly a country aspires to develop, the more likely it is that coercion will be intense. Any project to coerce large numbers of people into different livelihoods will be both contested and unstable, and as a result capitalist development can generate intensified violence even to a degree that

[34] On realism's affinity with politics as art, see Raymond Guess, *Philosophy and Real Politics* (2008): 15–16.

it undermines accumulation. Thus, we need to take coercion seriously as an immanent component of developmentalism and not simply condemn all rights violations as categorically wrong according to an ideal value.

States might exercise coercion simply to stay in power. They might detain journalists, assassinate political opposition leaders, round up a specific group of people considered a threat and put them into camps, use secret police to create a network of spies, construct an infrastructure of torture centres, or make the law a device to criminalize certain groups of people for their social identity or political beliefs. These practices are all clearly rights-violating and they do not connect with developmentalism.[35] Not all states in poor countries are embarked on programmes of capitalist development: many are ensconced in political projects to maintain power, cow opposition, and generate wealth-through-pillage. These kinds of practices can easily be condemned. They do not generate any requirement that they be considered as components of a programme to forge processes of accumulation and growth, far less as part of an ideology of commonwealth. Governments might claim that they are protecting national interests by arresting opposition leaders who supposedly might upset the orderly nature of progress, but one can likely look at the circumstances of these cases and conclude that this kind of narrative is both massively overblown or that there are many more convincing reasons available to explain a person's detention which relate simply to the concentration of power. In a nutshell, the normative consideration of state action in the name of development requires detailed empirical study and this study does not automatically offer some justification for coercive state actions; on the contrary—bearing in mind how rare capitalist development is—it expects otherwise.

Capitalist development involves reorganizations of property. This might be realized through land tenure law which can affirm the state's legalized capacity to use coercion to protect property, to remove secure ownership from others, or to facilitate the emergence of a new class of property owners. Governments might also deploy the state's ability to 'create facts on the ground' through extraordinary measures—possibly legalized—such as rezoning land, resettling people, or funding large civil engineering projects such as dams, new mining ventures, or the 'fortressing' of conservation areas for the tourist industry. These kinds of measures constitute major exercises in coercion

[35] Or if they do, the connection is weak and therefore open to challenge. As we insist throughout the book, our normative thinking is not guided by the seeking of clear categorizations and hierarchies of rightness.

that are justified in terms of a more or less distant future improved condition. These kinds of actions might be developmental and therefore might require more 'agonistic' moral discussion.[36] We would require more contextualized inquiry which is attentive to the coercive nature of capitalist development. There is a considerable amount of moral distinction within the ways in which projects are governed: for realists, herein lies the normativity.

Although qualitatively different from, say, the targeted assassination of opposition politicians, grandiose projects of social engineering might indirectly cause deaths through the destruction of livelihoods. Reorderings of this kind are often done with an authoritarian contempt for the people whose lives are disrupted. People's existing ways of life are defined as obstacles or problems within the development vision and, as a result, it is likely that the reorganizations devised by the state will be imposed. Resistance to the project might well be taken as ignorance or trouble-making. In this antagonistic political relation, it is very possible that the state will deploy coercive force to ensure obedience. This might involve using the army to move people from one place to another or the destruction of residual property to enforce change. If people openly resist through protest, perhaps by the cutting of newly installed fencing or the breaking of property, this might provoke a police response. In that eventuality, governments might respond by increasing the police presence in expectation of renewed protest; they might change aspects of the execution of the programme; they might use resources in an attempt to mollify opposition. They might also introduce practices of 'participation' and consultation, co-opting local leaders into discussions with government offices, representatives of capital, and amenable peacekeeping or community development NGOs. Violent resistance to the project might intensify or dissipate; the intensity of coercion by the state might intensify or dissipate. As these conditions develop, the threat of violence will also condition the possibilities of resistance and oppression. In any situation in which violence becomes increasingly common, people are more likely simply to wish for a return to a more peaceable normalcy.

Capitalist development involves reorganizations of labour. The ascendance of a capitalist class always involves the putting of people to work in new and intensified ways, a transformation that is achieved through myriad rebalances against independent livelihoods and a growing demand for cheap and

[36] I take the meaning of agonism loosely from Mouffe who argues for 'the necessity of the political and the impossibility of a world without antagonism'. Like all realists, she is concerned that ideal ethical thinking denudes politics of its specific properties. Chantal Mouffe, *The Return of the Political* (2005): 4, see also 139–41.

disciplined wage labour. There is in the midst of the reorganization both coercion and opportunity: a sense of disruption and destabilization and mobility and acquisition. How these reorganizations play out is an empirical question, shaped by political context. In concrete situations, gender and ethnicity very often become integrated into the social dynamics of change in ways that might be characterized as adverse incorporation. Developmentalism involves authoritarian labour regimes: suppressing independent labour organization, legislating minimal rights for workers, supporting extended and intensive working days, moving labour in ways that generate insecurity and an excess supply of workers, infusing workplaces with spies, and deploying the police during strikes and lock-outs. Within all of this, the possibility of new forms of production, increased productivity, and an increase in wage labour are possible.

We have noted how developmentalism requires of states the use of coercion to create and enforce changes in property and labour in the hope of creating expanded and transformative accumulation. Governments also have to make decisions about the ways in which they relate to the ongoing deleterious effects of capitalist transformation. As capital ascends, its power to make societies in its own image consolidates. The forging of new regimes of labour and property generate instability and penury for some and maybe many. This might be a result of dispossessions of one kind or another, of increased stress on households and individuals as work is intensified, and/or it may generate new forms of migration. It might also be the result of the 'externalities' of capitalist production in which pollution, waterway modification, or deforestation create public health problems and environments central to livelihoods are degraded. Uprooted, exhausted, or chronically ill populations might experience comparatively high rates of mortality, a process that clearly fits with the silent/structural/slow characterization of violence, as set out in the section 'Materializing Legitimacy'.

A major decision facing states is, then, how to respond to these harms. Formally speaking, the state here is not directly the commissioner of violence, but there is a normative question to be answered in relation to omission. It is the difference between making people suffer and letting them suffer. The strength of the state's efforts to rescue people from extreme hardship are, again, profoundly context-specific. Some public emergencies can be genuinely unexpected—a result of companies hiding the nature of their operations or a result of an unexpected environmental disaster. Some states do not have the capacity to deal fully with the social hardships generated by expanded accumulation. The relationship between the state and capital is, of course, a political one: one in which certain factions of capital easily exercise power[37] and certain forms of state struggle to regulate capital at all. It is also the case that not all coercion is the monopoly of the state, even if it is the case that the state must legislate and regulate the exercise of coercion. Private security companies protect and enforce the boundaries of property. Governments in these situations have to consider how effectively to assert political power in order to rescue desperate populations and to implement laws, contracts, and institutions to ensure that certain kinds of extreme social damage are not allowed in the future. Or, governments might judge that it is more expedient to let those people live or die as they see fit.

The account of state coercion offered above is a sketch of the practices of violence available to the state during capitalist transition. We shall see in Section 2 how these have been realized in some detail. What matters here is firstly to notice that coercion is variegated and politically contextual. Coercion is realized by different kinds of states and institutions in different circumstances. In this sense, we need to calibrate normative assessment of state actions that supress agency, impose hardship, or physically coerce with the transition possibilities within which they are embedded. This task is imperfect in that it is open to contention and debate; it is agonistic in that it will not lead to resolution or harmony in moral thinking; and it is 'tragic' in that it contains some collation of suffering, hubris, and progress. These considerations seek not to excuse coercion as much as differentiate its dynamics as a tense reconciliation of incommensurate political demands: sovereignty, legitimacy, and progress within a capitalist transition. This is not an amoral position as much as a more pluralistic and imperfect one. Developmentalism's coercions are themselves norm generating: they commonly rest on some evocation of the rightness of stability, national esteem, and security. These political goods can be immensely important for legitimacy.[38] It is perhaps a manifestation of what Kukathas calls 'justicitis'[39] that we tend immediately to think of human rights and justice as the meta-narrative for all normative thinking.[40] Developmentalism's basic legitimacy demand is often addressed through the construction of politics as stability, security, and nationhood

[37] Typically, very large transnational corporations with strong connections to their host government, the latter being accustomed to projecting power overseas.
[38] Bruce Gilley, *The Right to Rule. How States Win and Lose Legitimacy* (2009).
[39] Chandra Kukathas, 'Justicitis' (2018).
[40] A short vignette by way of personal illustration. In my PhD fieldwork I interviewed about 200 peasant farmers in Mozambique on their attitudes towards democratization. No-one much cared for the idea of open political debate or considered the new freedoms they had as especially valuable because the prices of basic goods had gone up and because multiparty politics had made village life less stable.

and that capitalist transformation becomes inextricably intertwined with these political imperatives.

Section Summary

This section has set out a theoretically informed analytical framework to understand development. Developmentalism is understood as the political–economic project of creating a capitalist transformation. The real underpinning of this political economy is economic growth, expanded accumulation, and increased productivity. Only these real structural processes contain the potential to generate massive increases in material well-being. We have based these co-ordinates on a Marxist political economy that understands capitalism's dynamism, maintains a strong sense of its exploitations and violence, and historicizes capitalist development as a turbulent global system. We have proceeded to explore the major political issue generated by capitalist development: the fact that it is inescapably defined by coercion, the suppression of resistance, and dispossession, and that this makes it difficult to take capitalist development as a normatively desirable phenomenon. We have seen that this trepidation has been strong enough to generate a development tautology in which 'if it's not freedom it's not development'.

Rather than seeking a way of escaping the agonistic normativity of capitalist development, we have endeavoured to embrace it, but without expectations of resolving anything. Instead, we have drawn on political realism to make two claims. One is that capitalist development is intrinsically 'dirty': normatively, it presents empirical case studies in which specific acts of governance might be more or less harsh, more or less well intentioned, more or less effective, and informed by different *techne* of action. We argue that it is within this morass that normativity is generated—without any seeking of moral correspondence to an idealized justice or rights framework. Second, we have argued that the basic legitimacy demand of developmentalism is distinct in some ways from the kinds of broadly developed–liberal modelling that political realists have habituated themselves to. We have argued that basic legitimacy derives from the construction of some kind of minimal commonwealth which allows us to speak reasonably about an absence of extreme physical suffering not only from state violence or civil conflict but also from poverty, hunger, and overwork. It is within this basic legitimacy demand that norms of security, stability, and nationhood might cohabit with rights and justice in the moral universe. In Section 2 we shall see how developmentalism has been realized in actual histories.

SECTION 2
CASE STUDIES

5
Britain

Introduction

In Section 2, we shall review the histories of capitalist transformation in selected countries, some originary, some successful, and some in progress. The general aim is to develop a 'thick' and empirically substantiated sense of capitalist development in which the themes elaborated in Section 1 become discernible in history. We shall see how capitalist transformation is holistic. It involves changes across various sites of political economy in ways that are broadly mutually enabling. It involves different political projects to support, prosecute, discipline, and consolidate economic growth and increased productivity. It involves the emergence of various forms of political ideology in which development becomes conflated with major-order political challenges of statehood. It involves transformations in the nature of agency and normative discourses of right and wrong. It involves an ability to not only endure crises but also subsequently renew processes of accumulation. It involves some progress in the construction of a commonwealth. And it involves evidence of major increases in material wealth that are broadly shared. Within these interconnected axes of change, states establish a legitimate authority which in itself opens up possibilities for further progress in the achievement of equitable increases in standards of living. Although these themes are present in almost all of our cases, the specificities of each case do not offer strong opportunities for model building. What they do is provide a wealth of actual and empirical material of the realities of capitalist development. We start with Britain.

Capitalism in the Countryside

Consolidating Landlordism

The Mediaeval period was, in all of its complexity and violence, one of expanding landlordship to a degree that, by the end of the 1400s, rural societies were characterized by estates, (declining) serfdom, demesnes, cottages,

Developmentalism: The Normative and Transformative within Capitalism. Graham G.M. Harrison, Oxford University Press (2020).
DOI: 10.1093/oso/9780198785798.001.0001

commons, and open field systems within villages. The latter two forms of land use were eroded as landlordism expanded. The fourteenth and fifteenth centuries witnessed impoverishment, declining population, famine, and plague. All of these dynamics played themselves out within a system of landlordism which was significantly varied but also persistent throughout England's regions. Landlordism does not simply mean landowner and serf. Indeed, it is notable that much of the debate about the nature of the enclosing and landlordism in this period is based on what insights historians derive from regionally specific work—the specific marginality of the Fens, compared with the more strongly commercialized Home Counties, the relative poverty of Yorkshire, and so on. For our purposes, what matters is simply a recognition that the direction of change—*mutatis mutandis*—is towards a consolidating landlordism that led to about 45 per cent of England's rural land being enclosed by 1500.[1] What also matters is to note that the content of landlordism changed considerably throughout this period. Serfdom ceased to exist by the end of the 1400s, and tenure on lordly estates was increasingly defined by the desire to increase revenues from allotted lands.

The sixteenth century is often the place that writers start when narrating the agrarian origins of capitalism in England. The Tudor state became the first centralized and effective English state, a project established by the relatively unknown but historically highly significant Henry VII.[2] Tudor records of taxation, the survey of Crown and landlordly property, registers of population and Priory all provide historians with strong evidence of a state that was endeavouring to survey and assay its people and property in centralized and/or regular ways.[3] This was also a period in which serfdom ended, a state-driven system to allocate lands to a nobility and gentry emerged, and in which the seeds of a more commercialized agriculture might be identified.

Under Henry VIII, and mainly through the work of Thomas Cromwell, the Tudor state 'suppression' of Church property dispossessed lands, retaining lands for the Crown as a source of revenue and largesse, reallocating them to a nobility and gentry that was politically aligned with the state, but also to merchants and tenants. The sale of lands was often motivated by the need to raise revenues for war in Europe. By the mid-1500s the Catholic church

[1] Spencer Dimmock, *The Origin of Capitalism in England 1400–1600* (2014): 134.

[2] Thomas Penn, *Winter King: The Dawn of Tudor England* (2012). The notion of the Tudor monarchy as early modern is based on a mixture of both reforms to the state and an increasing rigour in the pursuit of pre-existing reforms. As is always the case with histories based on monarchical succession, there can be quite cumbersome explanations as to how continuity and change accompany 'regime change'. This suggests that kingly historiographies tend to reify politics.

[3] Gordon Batho, 'Landlords in England, 1500–1640' (1990): 23.

owned about 10 per cent of the agricultural land but was subjected to an increasing degree of taxation and dispossession.[4]

Landlordism was maintained through an established nobility and a rising gentry.[5] The nobility was based on Crown-endowed peerage, a system that was in fact dynamic rather than strongly hereditary. The gentry were formed out of more diverse patterns of enrichment: through mercantile wealth, industry, and the legal profession, for example. The gentry tended to occupy territorialized positions of authority: Justices of the Peace, sheriffs, subsidy commissioners, and so on. It continued to be the case that the nature of landlordism varied considerably. In different places and periods, landlords might loosen ('commute') labour or rent obligations but at the 'grace' of the landlord and still embedded within the same overarching property relations that constrained peasant socio-spatial mobility. Some landlords were absent from their property. The scale of lands owned varied a great deal as well.

Enclosure took place at this time but was kept in check by a state that understood the socially damaging possibilities of enclosure in the countryside. Cardinal Wolsey undertook numerous Commissions into illegal enclosures for this reason.[6] This caution can be identified throughout the Tudor and early Stuart periods.

Smallholding agriculture was defined by access to fields within a landlord's property, access to commons, and customarily derived rent obligations towards a landlord, although it must be stressed that the variety of livelihoods sustained under this general disposition was extremely broad. Customary tenure was based on specific local conditions generated from inheritance and use of the land. Access to land for smallholders was also set through copyhold in which long-standing use of land was written into the manorial rolls and copied for the smallholder. There was also some freeholding and cottage farming in garden plots. The social conditions of smallholding were defined by a kind of mutual responsibility: of landlords to respect farmers' access to land; and of farmers to pay fines and a fee for tenancy of the land. As such, smallholders were not 'free' independent farmers (of a kind sometimes defined as yeomen) but nor were they subjected to the same levels of direct physical coercion, fines, and restriction of movement that one finds in feudal

[4] Robert Tombs, *The English and their History* (2015): 167.

[5] Batho, 'Landlords in England, 1500-1640': 50 *et seq.*

[6] Enclosure was, formally, something that required the agreement of all parties up until 1740, when parliament arrogated the right to enclose with a lesser degree of consensus. In practice, landlords had various ways of putting immense pressure on smallholders to leave the land, most notably by increasing rents when copyhold terms were expiring.

agriculture. Agrarian historians have been troubled by the sixteenth century as one in which smallholders were neither fully serfs nor peasants. One might view this period as a 'rupture of the old system and the beginnings of something... different'.[7] This removes the retrospective temptation to speak about transition in a way that makes certain changes necessary; but it remains the case that this period contained within it properties that made a capitalist transition in the countryside possible.

Enclosure, Tenancy, and Profit

Throughout the seventeenth century, processes of commercialization and enclosure expanded and intensified. Large-scale sheep grazing by landlords led to the enclosing of commons or the reclaiming of marginal lands. Landlords increasingly allotted land to relatively capitalized farmers under tenancy, a key development that led to a gradually increasing concern with 'improvement' and engrossment in the countryside. This involved some brute force, legal manoeuvres, and the raising of fines or rents to push less-productive or smaller-scale peasant farmers off the land. Landlords received an increasing proportion of their revenues from commercial farmers' rent rather than the more static fees derived from less-capitalized peasant farms.

One would not want to overplay the sense of emerging class distinctions in the seventeenth century. The increasing scale of farming did not necessarily connote a degree of commercialization or capitalization, and all farms remained subject to the caprice of both weather and price fluctuations, so that the consolidation of fields might give way to some breaking down of farming units. There was a great deal of regional variation.[8] The social relations of production were often complex *in specifica*: different kinds of tenure, upwardly and downwardly mobile yeomanry, landlords who farmed, different traditions of property based on copyhold and other kinds of lease, and all manner of commons. The point here is that, although the English countryside was changing in ways that with hindsight seem very significant—more commercial farming, enclosure, and the rise of capitalized tenant farming—the social relations of production in English agriculture remained extremely diverse, complex, and subjected to contestation and contingency.

[7] Michael Zmolek, *Rethinking the Industrial Revolution. Five Centuries of Transition from Agrarian to Industrial Capitalist in England* (2013): 27–8.

[8] Martin Daunton, *Progress and Poverty. An Economic and Social History of Britain 1700–1850* (2013): 26–9.

Nevertheless, it is also clear that throughout the seventeenth century, the tenure relations established within estates were increasingly defined by competitively allocated capitalist farming. Landlords employed managers to allocate land; the legal status of tenure was devised in ways that became aware of capital stock and improvement on the land; the scale of farming in general increased; and commercial farmers with tenure employed larger numbers of workers on their farms. This was an age when some villages and hamlets would be left to rot as they sat in consolidated units of agricultural land. These changes were accompanied by increasing landlessness and growing rural industry that required agricultural inputs, especially wool for the cloth industry. Strong supporting evidence for this characterization can be found in the development of public discussions about agriculture which were increasingly framed in debates about enclosure, landlessness, depopulation, and improvement. Herein lie the origins of capitalism in England and, with due respect for the detail and nuance of historical work, one can say that this political economy was underway by the beginning of the seventeenth century and in full force by its end.

During the eighteenth century, the capitalist tenant farming system consolidated itself through continued enclosure and increasing commercialization. Seventy per cent of rural land had been enclosed by 1700[9] and processes of enclosing continued throughout the 1700s and indeed intensified by the end of that century as a result of Parliamentary Enclosure Acts, meaning that 85 per cent was enclosed by the end of this century.[10] Peasants were by and large transformed into a rural proletariat: 'commoners into labourers'.[11] The social nature of enclosure during this period continued to shift from one in which a landed nobility coercively asserted rights over land, towards one in which the law asserted commercially minded gentries' rights over enclosed land.[12]

The size of estate farmholdings increased, as did productivity, in ways that generated clear distinctions with the rest of Europe.[13] Agriculture was driven

[9] Dimmock, *The Origin of Capitalism in England 1400–1600*: 153.

[10] Joyce Burnette, 'Agriculture, 1700–1870' (2014): 92. There was a final high-point in enclosure during the 1770s. There were over 4,000 Enclosure Acts between 1750 and 1850. Boyd Hilton, *A Mad, Bad, and Dangerous People? England 1783–1846* (2006): 9.

[11] J. Neeson, *Commoners: Common Right, Enclosure, and Social Change in England, 1700–1820* (1993): 18, although full destruction of the commons in all forms (apart from residual leisure and walking areas not used for agriculture) occurred at the end of the 1800s.

[12] Philip Corrigan and Derek Sayer, *The Great Arch. English State Formation as Cultural Revolution* (1985).

[13] Robert Brenner, 'Agrarian Class Structure and Economic Development in Pre-Industrial Europe' (1976); Robert Brenner, 'The Agrarian Roots of European Capitalism' (1982).

by competitive profit-seeking, based on capitalized farms and a rural wage labour force. The 1700s was also the period within which an ongoing formalization of the status of property was stepped up through the rise of leasehold (in place of customary and copyhold tenure) and myriad court actions which did not always decide in favour of estate consolidation but did serve to create saleable land through contract. A generalized wage labour system replaced a more complex set of customary rights to a garden plot and payment in food and lodgings.[14] One result of this was that capitalist farming tenancies became increasingly competitive and based on shorter periods of time, both of which put a strong incentivization on profit margins. Another was the securing of a source of revenue for the state through land taxes, although there was always countervailing pressure from the gentry in relation to rates set.[15]

It was also during the 1700s that the landed class systemically purchased property in cities, a process that leaves its imprimatur on contemporary British cities' squares and listed buildings. Furthermore, revenues generated from land ownership were internationalized throughout this century as Britain asserted naval and mercantile dominance throughout the world. The landed gentry of the eighteenth century was a global imperial class, not simply a national one.[16] A core part of this process of enrichment was the Atlantic slavery–plantation system. The Utrecht Treaty (1713) in which Spain gave Britain the *Asiento* to trade slaves in the Spanish colonial realm made Britain *primus inter pares* in the Atlantic system.[17]

It is worth noting that the processes of change were uncertain, incremental, but also broadly 'sedimentary'. This latter characterization connotes that the nature of agrarian change reinforced a shift towards capitalism, most clearly from the 1650s when—and provoking much discussion—the English state underwent a series of revolutionary changes that issued in a definitive end to a post-feudal 'interregnum' and created a stronger parliamentary system or constitutional monarchy.[18]

A key outcome of the increasing productivity of agriculture, the deepening of wage labour in the countryside, the generation of larger amounts of profit and capital, and an increase in disposable income is that it provides something of an 'organic' enabling context for Britain's industrialization, a process

[14] These changes were in part driven by ongoing enclosure which reduced cottaging rights and rising food prices which made payments in crops appreciate in relation to rural wages.
[15] Phyllis Deane, *The First Industrial Revolution* (1979): 51.
[16] This point is made meticulously in A. G. Cain and Peter Hopkins, *British Imperialism* (2016).
[17] Philip Curtin, *The Image of Africa: British Ideas and Action, 1780–1850* (1964): 6.
[18] A detailed discussion which is both theoretical and historiographic is given in Neil Davidson, *How Revolutionary Were the Bourgeois Revolutions?* (2012).

that, although more condensed than the agrarian transition we have just characterized, was also initially gradual and piecemeal, as we shall see in the next section on 'Capitalist Industrialization'. The core point—and one that allows us to escape some of the irreconcilable debates among historians about principal cause and definitive moments of change—is that what we are witnessing is a complex and integrated single process of capitalist transition.

Capitalist Industrialization

The Slow and Uncertain Rise of Industry (1700–1780)

The notion of an industrial revolution is both insightful and misleading. There was clearly a remarkable transformation in the British political economy from the late eighteenth century. If one looks at the British economy in the mid-1700s and compares it to the mid-1800s a great deal has changed in terms of the criteria by which we measure industrialization, and latterly economic development: urbanization, population growth, economic output, growth in industry and especially manufacturing, the application of new technologies to production, the emergence of large-scale units of production, the rise of exported manufactures, and the broadening and deepening of consumer markets. This is what gives this period its revolutionary image. But, on the other hand, it is difficult to identify a revolutionary moment, a conjuncture in which certain conditions were triggered or a specific event changed everything. Although there was sustained growth over this period, there wasn't rapid growth. If the 'revolution' might be better understood as a transition rather than a rupture, one might question the specifically industrial nature of change. As we shall see, agriculture, finance, and services grew during this transition. Industry remained pivotal, but its sustained growth and broader impacts were crucially a product of its embedding in social relations of capitalism. Thus we take the main import of Britain's industrial revolution as its capitalist transformation which also incorporated other sectors.

The construction of a capitalist agrarian system in the 1700s took place during a period when England was undergoing the early stages of its urban industrial revolution. In crucial ways, this agrarian transition underpinned and conditioned Britain's prospects for industrialization.[19] There was no schism between rural and urban or agrarian and industrial but rather a

[19] Colin Mooers, *The Making of Bourgeois Europe* (1991): 168.

bundle of inter-relations between the two which in retrospect can be characterized as the relative rise of industry over agriculture. We can sketch the main ways in which this interplay worked.

The consolidation of capitalist agriculture created increases in agricultural output[20] which were pivotal for industrialization. Raw materials (especially wool) and staple foods (especially wheat)[21] fed into industrial production.[22] The slow but steady increase in output and market orientation of agriculture was a product of the rise of competitive tenancy within a consolidating landlordism.[23]

The movement of people from the countryside as a result of the diverse and complex processes of enclosure also generated a surplus labour force in cities and towns, evident in the rise of migration to cities and itinerant poverty (vagabondage) in the 1700s, although it is important to point out that this was not a process of depopulation in rural areas. This was a process keenly identified by Marx and his epigones as the creation of a reserve army of labour, although the nature of change in the labour force was more complex. Growing rural industries[24] had generated a demand for skilled labour throughout the 1700s,[25] and this sector did not rapidly disappear. In fact, the association of the industrial revolution with 'dark satanic mills' and factories is rather partial. In its infancy, Britain's industrial sector was strongly characterized by small-scale manufacture into the mid-1800s, often along river courses.[26] There was something 'organic' about industrialization in which new technologies and innovations spread fairly slowly through different sectors working on different scales.

Capitalist agriculture has also bequeathed a broader and deeper domestic market. The creation of commercial lease farming and a large rural proletariat created rising demand for consumer goods throughout the country, not just in the cities where urbanization and the rise of a middle class were very visible. Historiographies of Britain's consumer society tend to focus on London and the 'nation of shopkeepers' image (most especially during the Victorian period), but a fuller understanding of rising demand would recognize how consumption in rural areas and small towns had changed as well. The persistence of small-scale manufacture which emerged in rural areas and small

[20] It is worth noting that smallholder agriculture was also capable of generating increases in outputs through innovation, but this was not a 'path' that was strongly pursued in Britain.

[21] Commonly known as 'corn'.

[22] Burnette, 'Agriculture, 1700–1870': 114.

[23] Brenner, 'Agrarian class structure': 61.

[24] Deane, *The First Industrial Revolution*: 50–1.

[25] Brian A'Hearn, 'The British Industrial Revolution in a European Mirror' (2014): 21.

[26] Edward Royle, *Modern Britain. A Social History 1750–2011* (2012): 43.

towns along with the growth of effective demand in the countryside suggest that industrialization was in crucial part a progeny of the rise of capitalism in agriculture.

Landlords themselves commonly had one eye on urban society and wealth, the most affluent keeping a *pied à terre* in London, and looking for ways to invest or consume there. Recall that the social origin of the 'modern' gentry was as urban and 'professional' rather than peer-based and manorial. As commercial farm leases generated more income and it became easier to raise mortgages on property,[27] landlords were a source of capital for financial, real estate, and industrial investment. It is clear that agrarian capitalism had an intimate and positive relationship with the early emergence of industrial capitalism.[28]

Capital Ascendant: Industrial Transformation (1780 to the mid-1800s)

The emergence of capitalism is a social transformation that is broad-ranging and systemic. It is also based on the rise of industry and services—not as discrete developments but as the drivers of integrated and sustained economic expansion. We shall see how this happened in Britain, albeit in sketch form. Industrial transformation took place over about a century (1770–1870), during which the agrarian and imperial changes of previous centuries fed into a historically definitive capitalist transition. The processes that define this transition hardly offer a model, far less an easily celebrated one. Much of the change that took place was unstable, unpleasant, and unplanned. But much of the change also generated growth, investment, technological progress,[29] and increased mobility.

One might characterize the origins of capitalist industrialization in a rather modest set of changes that took place in a fairly diffuse and labour-intensive fashion: the mines and cottage industries that emerged throughout the 1700s in cities and towns located near waterways. 'Traditional' skills remained important, and outwork remained common rather than relocation to towns and the scaling-up of production. Nevertheless, within these myriad and

[27] Daunton, *Progress and Poverty*: 75.
[28] Brenner, 'Agrarian Class Structure and Economic Development': 66–7.
[29] Note the phrase 'technological progress', not necessarily innovation. There is a lot of debate about who originally invented what, which for our purposes is less important that how technologies were put to work and put people to work.

localized transitions in work emerged small capitalists who employed workers and took an increasing interest in the changing organization of production. They also had capital to invest.[30] From the 1780s onwards, cautiously and selectively, the scale and productivity of industrial production increased in a sustained fashion. Indeed, the rate of productivity growth itself increased significantly from the late 1700s to the mid-1800s.[31] The industrial revolution involved expanding regimes of wage labour, the application of new or applied technologies into production, increases in scale, and the intensification of work and exploitation.

The introduction of steam-powered technologies in weaving increased labour productivity drastically. This is not to make a claim that cotton manufacture was transformed through drastic advances in science. In fact, technologically speaking, new machines for weaving and looming were not drastically new or scientifically sophisticated. The core concern was productivity and this was addressed by constructing greater scale of production and introducing power looms, technologies that were gradually implemented and were based on existing machinery but which had significant effects on productivity, driving the unit price of printed cotton from three shillings and seven pence in 1818 to just over two shillings in 1830.[32] The kind of innovation alluded to here resides in how technology was drawn into the imperative to increase outputs and profits.[33] This was an endeavour based on generating investment capital, building factories (of varied sizes), and allocating labour to make most profitable use of the machinery. It was not simply the iconic technological innovations such as the Spinning Jenny but a more diverse, incremental, and pragmatic set of micro-inventions.[34] Much of this technological innovation was based in moderately scaled factory-shops in provincial towns. Also, at the heart of this increase was intensified work. Industrial labour forces were far more diverse than the term 'industrial proletariat' suggests: the sons and daughters of farmers working in small and medium-sized workshops or 'sheds'.

In retrospect more significantly, it also led to the construction of large-scale factories in growing cities—especially Manchester with its apocryphal 'dark satanic mills'. In the large cotton textile factories, labour became specialized

[30] Eric Hobsbawm, *Industry and Empire* (1999): 7.

[31] Patrick O'Brien, 'Modern Conceptions of the Industrial Revolution' (1993a): 13; Emma Griffin, *A Short History of the British Industrial Revolution* (2010): 18–19.

[32] Richard Evans, *The Pursuit of Power. Europe 1815–1914* (2017): 133.

[33] G. N. von Tunzelmann, 'Technological and Organizational Change in Industry during the Industrial Revolution' (1993).

[34] Robert Allen, *The British Industrial Revolution in Global Perspective* (2009): 149 *et seq.*

and transformed by the application and adaptation of existing technologies to the large-scale working of machinery that ran for 12 hours according to regimented output schedules. Britain urbanized rapidly and chaotically, and urban spaces became increasingly oriented around new and large-scale manufacturing. The new urbanization focused most notably on Lancashire, followed by Yorkshire, the West Midlands, South Wales, and the Scottish central belt. Port cities such as Bristol and Portsmouth also grew. The upwardly mobile gentry consolidated their power through the construction of townhouses. Dense and poorly sanitized workers' housing also emerged.

The period from 1770 to 1830 is generally considered as the 'first industrial revolution'. It was focused on a specific set of manufactures based on textile production and the application of machinery based on steam power. Large factories co-existed with smaller ones, each defined by an expanding process of intensified wage labour, investment, and profit. During this period, manufacturing expanded, but it did not generate what one might characterize as a transformational effect, something that belies the notion of 'revolution' in some degree.

Furthermore, the social effects of the early rise of manufacture were disruptive and deleterious. It was not the case that industry absorbed those moving from an enclosed and capitalizing countryside, and those who did find manufacturing employment were thrust into conditions of work that were far from a clear improvement, either materially or in terms of intensity of work. By the early 1800s there was no mass male industrial workforce with regular employment in a factory. Wage labour was growing, but it was commonly unstable, involved men, women, and children and it produced a marked increase in migration.[35] This was a period of major social anxiety, narratives of declinism, and hardship as well as technological progress, mobility, and periods of growth.

Although the British economy was growing, exporting more manufactured goods, and asserting a naval supremacy, it was also the case that by the 1790s, the economy's growth was slowing considerably. The British state was centrally concerned with its military conflicts with France and related economic exactions. By the end of the eighteenth century, one might characterize the British political economy as being in a state of expansive flux rather than having undergone a revolution. In the contemporary writings on Britain's growth and industrialization, there was certainly no clear and certain sense

[35] Carol Morgan, *Women Workers and Gender Identities, 1835–1913* (2001).

that growth would continue or that the rise of manufacturing would continue and set the tone for the next two centuries.

Nevertheless, the flux of this period went beyond discrete spurts of growth or the discovery of a new market; this was an intensified period of capitalist transformation after a more protracted set of agrarian changes. It was defined by venture capital investment in the adaptation of technologies to production. It was also a period in which incorporated and share-raising capital was invested heavily in canals (1790s) and turnpikes,[36] intensifying the market infrastructures bequeathed by capitalist agriculture and mercantile port cities. The 'turnpike revolution' that left Britain with the densest road infrastructure in Europe by the mid-1700s was underpinned by the fiscal transformation of the state. The same applied with railways a century later. Revenues from colonial investments—often pursued by the gentry[37]—also fed into these 'prospective' capital investments, as we shall see in the section on 'The Nineteenth Century'. Industrial capitalists themselves emerged from a varied social base of yeoman farmers, small-scale producers, adventurous merchants, and the middle classes. In his study of the emergence of textiles in Oldham, Foster mentions cola-owners, bankers, merchants, wholesalers, and yeomen—all people with a relatively substantial capital base.[38] Partnerships between ambitious capitalists, scientists, and investors often underpinned the scaling-up of production.

Capital Dominant

The industry that most clearly moved towards a factory system of production was cotton, but from 1815 (after the end of the final war with France) there was a marked scaling-up and concentration of industrial production especially in the coal–metallurgy industrial complex.[39] By 1850, manufacturing had become Britain's dominant economic sector,[40] after the complex and protracted shifts from commercialized farming, cottage industry, and demographic and settlement change throughout the earlier decades of industrialization. In metallurgy, pottery, and textiles one can identify the large-scale industries that defined towns and cities, especially in northern England. The growth of

[36] Christopher Harvie, 'Revolution and the Rule of Law (1789–1851' (1988): 85.
[37] Eric Evans, *The Forging of the Modern State. Early Industrial Britain 1783–1870* (2001): 135.
[38] John Foster, *Class Struggle and the Industrial Revolution* (1979): 9.
[39] Daunton, *Progress and Poverty*: 134; Hilton, *A Mad Bad and Dangerous People?*: 2.
[40] Hobsbawm, *Industry and Empire*: 50.

industrial cities during this period was unprecedented: Manchester rose from 17,000 people in 1760 to 237,000 in 1831, and by that latter date over 40 per cent of the working population were employed in manufacturing.[41] Large-scale manufacturing had become the dominant sector in the British economy, and it would continue its expansion into the 1940s.[42] This domination expressed itself in the emergence of new and more complex manufactures: investments in the production of new commodities embedded in upstream and downstream component manufacture, maintenance, warehousing, and retail. Nevertheless, it is important to remember that the social relations of capitalist production were not simply about the rise of the factory. Capitalist production, wage labour, and competing capitals also pervaded agriculture and within manufacturing generated a massive profusion of small-scale workshops, the latter being the source of a concern over 'sweated' labour well before contemporary global value chains.[43] In any case, the industrial wage labour force almost doubled between 1780 and 1820.[44]

From the 1830s onwards, industrial production was diverse, networked, and complex. Although there is an aesthetic focus on Lancastrian textile mills, Midlands metallurgy, and coalfields, we should not be entirely convinced of an image of industrialization as an outcome of changes in technology and resource use. Capitalist social relations became universal in an increasingly diversified and networked economy that was not simply based on the mass employment factory. Rather, it spanned workshops, medium-sized industries, all manner of services, and mass-production factories. It sought to diversify, invest in new technologies, and to reorganize its labour.[45] It was about shipbuilding, weaponry, pottery, glass manufacture, furniture, clothing, tool-making, and so on, all at varied scales but also 'socialized' through purchasing contracts, connections to retailers, the use of patents, and collusion.[46] London was in fact the largest industrial city within Britain until the mid-1800s, housing as it did (with some exceptions)[47] a remarkable range of flexible and medium-sized capitals.[48] Although major technological developments in steam and textiles, and later coal and metallurgy, are seen as

[41] E. K. Hunt and Mark Lautzenheiser, *History of Economic Thought. A Critical Perspective* (2011): 43.
[42] David Edgerton, *The Rise and Fall of the British Nation* (2018).
[43] Gareth Stedman Jones, *Outcast London. A Study in the Relationship Between Classes in Victorian Society* (1971): 106.
[44] Foster, *Class Struggle and the Industrial Revolution*: 19.
[45] Peter Mathias, *The First Industrial Nation. An Economic History of Britain 1700–1914* (1969): 253.
[46] Priya Satia, *Empire of Guns. The Violent Making of the Industrial Revolution* (2018): 20.
[47] The main one being armouries.
[48] John Stevenson, 'Social Aspects of the Industrial Revolution' (1993): 236.

iconic of industrialization, a far greater number of patents for innovations in production were filed in a wide range of other areas.[49] Capital markets deepened. Metallurgy and engineering diversified to provide components for other industries, large and small. Relentless economic growth which one can identify statistically from the mid-1800s—with all of its moments of crisis—is nothing other than the manifestation of this complete and vibrant dominance of capital which is at once focused within the British nation-state and also global in its field of operations, as we shall see in the section 'The Fiscal–Military State'.

A capitalist class had fully established social dominance. It was forged out of a comingling of landed property,[50] industrial capital, and finance, each of which had substantial shared interests as well as differences in worldview, and also in practice flows of finance and political lobbying often overlapped.

The effects of this were to create a historically unprecedented economic dynamism and growth. Put simply, capitalist transformation towards industrialization and more capital-intensive forms of production created the historic possibility of a profound and widespread improvement in the material well-being of the majority of the people. This is the *leitmotif* of many of the social histories of the Victorian era: the cohabitation of immense social hardship with such profound transformation in the productive economy. It is noteworthy that, although the immiseration generated by capitalism ascendant is well recognized in fiction and government and charitable surveys of conditions of life, there was also a distinct tendency for people to struggle against these conditions and to achieve improvements in their prospects and conditions of life.[51]

A revealing facet of Britain's dominant capitalism was that it transformed and continued to transform not only industry but also services and agriculture. Capitalist agriculture throughout the nineteenth century (and beyond) is best seen not as a separate sector but as part of a single political economy, generating wage labour, connected to upstream and downstream industries and services, and connected to various technological innovations.[52] Overall, agricultural output increased throughout capitalist industrialization, as did land under cultivation and numbers employed in agricultural wage labour.[53]

[49] Griffin, *A Short History of the British Industrial Revolution*: 89.

[50] The aristocracy and gentry have proven remarkably enduring. See Chris Bryant, *Entitled. A Critical History of the British Aristocracy* (2017).

[51] Emma Griffin, *Liberty's Dawn. A People's History of the Industrial Revolution* (2013).

[52] Michael Turner, 'Agriculture 1860–1914' (2004): 134.

[53] Burnette, 'Agriculture, 1700–1870': 100.

In spite of the common modernization theory expectation that agriculture declines as a non-industrial and/or 'traditional' sector of the economy, agriculture in Britain maintained output levels both before and after the repeal of the Corn Laws, and it continued to maintain employment levels in rural areas. From the 1850s, new technologies developed by manufacturing and chemical companies created new regimens of fertilization and drainage that improved agricultural productivity. Some landlords invested in these technologies, some farmers borrowed, farmers bought out their tenancies, and—depending on the region—some farmlands consolidated into large enterprises that resembled industrial companies. There was—again for many but not all parts of the countryside—a marked diversification and flexibility in cropping in order to respond to market signals.[54]

By the late 1800s, the rather amorphous categorization of services became the largest employer. In 1871, 1,341,000 people were employed in services.[55] This encapsulated finance, domestic work, retail, and myriad other labour activities. As with agriculture, it is unclear the extent to which this categorization illustrates rather than obscures. The generalized structural shift towards a manufacturing economy is, as we have argued, a crucial component for a country's possibilities to develop. But this in itself is also a story about agriculture and services. Agriculture was, as we have seen, a terrain upon which capitalist social relations were forged.[56] Industry did not invent itself. And services also and in varied ways 'served' capital through the socialization of information, the provision of credit, and the organization of consumer markets.[57] The early twentieth-century interest in the leisured class, conspicuous consumption, and domestic service is one manifestation of a service sector inextricably interlined with sustained accumulation and growth.

In services, as well as textiles and less visibly within family-owned firms, women participated significantly in wage labour, albeit commonly at lower rates of pay. As heavy manufacturing, labour unionism, and Christian norms of familyhood and social provision consolidated in the second half of the century, women were pressured more exclusively into the role of domestic work and found their possibilities of securing wage work more regimented. Herein, capitalism and patriarchy worked together.[58]

[54] Turner, 'Agriculture 1860–1914': 145.
[55] Eric Evans, *The Shaping of Modern Britain: Identity, Industry, and Empire 1780–1914* (2011): 241.
[56] Zmolek, *Rethinking the Industrial Revolution*: 399–400.
[57] Gary Magee, 'Manufacturing and Technological Change' (2004): 96–7.
[58] Hobsbawm, *Industry and Empire*: 96.

Not only did capitalist transformation generate a fluid and expanding wage labour force across all sectors of the economy, it did this within a process that was liable to crisis. In 1802, war and social dislocation in the countryside created widespread hunger.[59] There was a severe recession in 1830, pushing industrial employment below that of agriculture.[60] From 1837 and into the 1840s,[61] international trade fell, a phenomenon that contributed to the liberalizing force of the Anti-Corn Law lobby.[62] In 1848 there was a financial crisis, one of many that were generated by bubbles of financial speculation and poor regulation. There was a depression in 1885–6, a result of severe winters making food scarce and outdoor labour impossible, the result of which was that unemployment and food prices rose, a shift that led to the end of the 'high farming' era. And between 1873 and 1896 there was a protracted depression, arguably the first fully capitalist one. By this I mean that it was an outcome of a loss of market and technological advantage to rival national capitals that manifested itself in a shedding of labour and a repression of wages. Previous crises had resulted from adverse weather, speculative bubbles bursting, war, and industry-specific instability. The notion of capitalist crisis—and especially its overcoming—is a key consideration throughout this book.

Between 1780 and 1860 the economy doubled in size.[63] Between 1760 and 1860 agricultural productivity doubled and industrial productivity trebled.[64] Between the 1750s and 1800 the average worker could produce 100 lb of cotton in 50,000 hours and 300 hours respectively.[65] Between 1780, 1820, 1870, and 1913 income (£) per person rose respectively as follows: 1,806, 2,121, 3,191, and 4,921. Over the same periods, life expectancy shifted as follows: 34, 39, 41, and 53.[66] By the 1840s Britain produced two-thirds of the world's coal, half its iron, five-sevenths of its steel, and half its cotton.[67] By 1900 the mass of the British population 'enjoyed a standard of living and rich diet... that would have astonished their parents and grandparents'.[68] It is a plain fact that capitalist ascendance in Britain generated improvements in people's material well-being in a sustained and systemic

[59] Derek Fraser, *The Evolution of the British Welfare State* (2009): 44.
[60] Daunton, *Progress and Poverty*: 134.
[61] A period characterized by Anti-Corn Law advocates and the 'hungry forties'.
[62] Mathias, *The First Industrial Nation*: 297.
[63] Zmolek, *Rethinking the Industrial Revolution*: 261.
[64] O'Brien, 'Modern Conceptions of the Industrial Revolution': 19.
[65] Griffin, *A Short History of the British Industrial Revolution*: 91.
[66] Incomes measured in international dollars at 1990 prices. Nicholas Crafts, 'Long Run Growth' (2004): 6.
[67] Hugh Cunningham, *The Challenge of Democracy. Britain 1832–1918* (2001): 70.
[68] Frank Trentmann, *Free Trade Nation. Commerce, Consumption, and Civil Society in Modern Britain* (2008): 36.

way that is historically unprecedented and based on the productivity and growth effects of expanded capitalist accumulation.

In broad brush, expanding capitalist accumulation in Britain was characterized by tendencies to generate economic expansion and sudden and unstable intervals of crisis as a result of bubbles bursting, markets collapsing, and new waves of innovation and investment within and between nations. This is a salient feature of capitalism everywhere and it identifies a key property of developmentalism: the ability to 'push through' crisis. In the discourse of the contemporaries who lived through Britain's many crises, there was nothing inevitable about recovery—indeed, there were always voices openly mooting the possibility of systemic collapse. Nor was there a clear sense of a plan to overcome crisis; there was as much experimentation and contingency, generated out of the complex lobbies of parliament and the intellectual fervour of the age. We do not seek to generate models of certainty out of this history; we simply need to recognize that crisis is an immanent feature of capitalist accumulation and it poses a major-order political challenge: how to deploy the institutions of the state to adjust and reinvigorate processes of accumulation?

By the early 1900s, capitalism was both dominant and dynamic in Britain in a fashion not found in other countries. It remained driven by competitive accumulation and drives to increase productivity, and this lent Britain's social history throughout this period a remarkable changeability: enclosures, innovation in agriculture, growing towns and cities, massive investment in infrastructure, new forms of industrial production, the rise of the factory, the near-universalization of wage labour, and the profusion of commodities and consumerism—by any measure a remarkable century from 1750 to 1850, made all the more remarkable because this was a century that consolidated a 'change to change': all of Britain's capitalist history from thereon has been nothing more than the restless political economy of accumulation.[69] Relatedly, it is worth bearing in mind that, despite the rise of Germany and America, Britain remained globally dominant or a considerable peer of these two right up to the First World War.[70] In 1860, with two per cent of the world's population, Britain accounted for up to 45 per cent of the world's industrial production.[71]

[69] Between 1760 and 1860, capital investment increased throughout this period and the percentage invested in industry, trade, and transport increased from 5 per cent to 26 per cent (Evans, *The Pursuit of Power*: 130).
[70] Roderick Floud, 'Britain, 1860—1914: A Survey' (1994).
[71] Kees Van der Pijl, *Transnational Classes and International Relations* (1998): 66.

This is the basis for capitalist development in Britain and it is what marks Britain out as historically primordial.

Governing Capitalist Ascendance

The Law

A core part of the agrarian origins of capitalism in Britain was the changing property rights that it produced. Although a full-blown 'private' or freehold system of property did not exist until the mid-1800s, from the late 1600s onwards a property regime based on enclosure, landlordism, and commercial leasehold evolved. Wealthy merchants and gentry purchased land in towns and cities. Investments in land by mining companies (most often under leases from landlords), the gentry themselves (for example in canal systems), and capitalist tenants endowed this regime of property with a capitalist ambition to generate revenues from property through investment, either individual or joint-stock. This property regime was enforced by localized state power—country magistrates and others—as well as by parliament which used enclosure and trespass acts to enforce these rights. This was not a 'top-down' and centralized state project but rather one that built on localized assertions of property rights by the gentry through a combination of parliamentary act and localized juridical enforcement. Enforcement was not only penal but also 'theatrical': asserting the symbolism of the sanctity of property through judicial and police power with the threat of fines, whipping, or worse.[72]

The late 1700s ushered in a century of draconian legislation which had at its heart a desire to enforce and clarify property rights and criminalize any organization or violence against these rights. One aspect of this was the 'bloody code' which endured into the early 1800s and made petty theft and trespass offenses that merited corporal punishment or detention. During the wars with France, the government enacted laws that made a wide range of political organization and discussion criminal. After Waterloo, the government legislated 'Six Acts' which suspended *habeas corpus*, censored the press, banned protest gatherings, and allowed imprisonment without trial.[73] Anti-union legislation was a key part of the legislative 'political economy'

[72] Peter Linebaugh, *The London Hanged* (2003).

[73] Evans, *The Pursuit of Power*: 78.

of the 1800s: parliament 'enacted no less that forty statutes prohibiting unions...before it passed the Combination Act of 1800'.[74]

One of the mainstays of narratives about the industrial revolution is that it was based on the putting into production of new technologies.[75] The late 1700s onwards was a time of increasing technological innovation and adaptation and there was a considerable increase in the submission of patents. The patent office of the government was small and unequipped to give proper assessment of submissions. Furthermore, patents were commonly ignored by other industrialists, leading to long legal processes. There was a great deal of copying and adaptation, and the government did not and could not enforce the kinds of strict intellectual property rights that serve as the premise for the exacting and scientifically complex work of contemporary patents offices. As with land tenure, the transformation of production techniques into capitalist proprietorship was effected through a combination of some governmental regulation that interacted with competition and conflict between the 'hostile brothers'[76] of different capitalists, each wanting to defend their own innovations (especially if they had invested a great deal in bringing them to fruition) and to appropriate what worked in other factories and workshops.

In general, capitalist property relations were the outcome of a protracted and interlinked set of changes. Capitalists asserted their ownership of land and technology with increasing muscularity through a centralized and authoritarian state. The multi-level and complex institutions of law shifted towards more systemic and universal property rights, deploying a considerable amount of coercion in the process. And individual firms constantly sought to borrow and adapt technologies in the name of competitive advantage in ways that made proprietary rights over productions technologies hard-won.

The Fiscal–Military State

The seventeenth century witnessed a process of incremental state centralization that arguably had been going on for some time but was distinguished in

[74] Patrick O'Brien, 'Political Preconditions for the Industrial Revolution' (1993b): 131. In the early 1800s, political economy became the vernacular for the paradigm that government should conform to the rules of the unconstrained market, an ideology based most fundamentally on Adam Smith and David Bentham.

[75] Relatedly, see E. A. Wrigley, *Energy and the English Industrial Revolution* (2010) and Joel Mokyr, *The Enlightened Economy: Britain and the Industrial Revolution, 1700–1850* (2011).

[76] Karl Marx, *Capital III* (1992).

this century by the Absolutist ambitions of the Stuarts, the civil war, Restoration, and Glorious Revolution. This was a century of construction and reconstruction, of selective forgetting and remembering in which an idea of the English state as a historic artefact was used to build itself. It relied on myths of monarchical continuity, of parliamentary representation of 'the country', and of ultimate jurisprudence in the central courts.

Strictly speaking, none of this is to say that a modern Weberian nation-state was forged in the 1600s. A great deal of power remained localized and 'relatively autonomous'. And, of course, the English state was unstable and crisis-prone. But from the 1690s the template of a state was in place which would, over the coming century, provide the underpinnings for Britain's capitalist transformation. After 1688, the English state might be characterized as a combination of permissiveness and effectiveness.[77] That is to say, it did not have powerful institutions or revenue-raising ability, but it consolidated a sovereignty based on a combination of monarchical nationalism balanced by parliamentary autonomy and revenue-raising power. By the early 1700s, parliament had become a regularly convened institution to produce legislation underpinned by the social power of the gentry (the Commons) and especially their ability to raise revenues during a period in which the rents and sales of royal property were unequal to the challenges of statehood.

And challenges there were. The period 1688–1714 was one of continuous warfare with France. During this period, a remarkable 75 per cent of expenditure by the British government was allocated to war-making: personnel, capital, and ordnance.[78] The financing of war was the imperative of sovereignty in a period in which inter-state rivalries were immediately present. The English state was, like all European states during this period, a product of European warfare and intervention to an extent that barely a single British monarch could claim not to have ascended to the throne without at some point having gone through a European war.[79]

More broadly, the British government and polity was riven with a politics of insecurity, in regards to both external threats of invasion and its own internal stability and unity.[80] This created a situation within which the construction of an effective state was centred around the construction of a robust

[77] Corrigan and Sayer, *The Great Arch*: 90; Daunton, *Progress and Poverty*.

[78] John Brewer, *The Sinews of Power* (1989): 137.

[79] A historical pattern—French, Dutch, Prussian—that gives the British royal family a remarkably European genealogy.

[80] Jonathan Scott, *England's Troubles. Seventeenth-Century English Political Instability in European Context* (2000).

military, something that was achieved by the end of the first quarter of the eighteenth century and led England (then Britain) to become a European and then imperial power. By the mid-eighteenth century, Britain had achieved a dominance of the oceans that was vital to its capitalist transformation, a dominance forged over the previous century's European wars between absolutist monarchs.

The centrality of war and military capacity continued into the eighteenth century and therefore into the industrial revolution. By the 1780s, expenditure on the army, navy, and ordnance was still two and a half times expenditure on civilian matters.[81] Events such as American Independence and the French Revolution had profound effects on the British state, not only in terms of creating major war and security issues but also in infusing parliamentary and royal debates about British statehood.[82] After 1815, military expenditure continued to constitute the heart of the British state's material concern. The Royal Navy ensured the pre-eminence of British shipping and enforced its own network of imperial preferences through the Navigation Acts. It also deployed to protect or advocate on behalf of companies close to the state, most notoriously the East India Company. The British military was permanently using force of arms throughout its expanding empire.

Revenue-raising for war involved some major changes to the British state. In the first place, from the early 1700s the fiscal structures of the state shifted from rents, land sales, and duties towards the accrual of long-term debt and excise revenues.[83] Excise was raised on commodities, mainly agricultural goods.[84] As such, a crucial basis of the 'fiscal–military state'[85] was the increasing productivity of capitalist agriculture. The social basis for this consolidating revenue stream was the increasing power of parliament, an institution that ensured the power and representation of the gentry.[86] From 1688, parliament wrested financial authority away from the Crown, and it did so not only through a simple assertion but also through a transformation of the way that revenues were raised, from 'demesne' to 'tax'.[87] This meant more transparent financial management—this was the period in which annual

[81] Evans, *The Pursuit of Power*: 35.

[82] To pick out the major effects here, the American War of Independence created a strong push for a more efficient and rationalized British government; the French Revolution generated a pervasive securitization of governance of a kind that could—again to borrow from contemporary concepts—be described as authoritarian.

[83] Scott, *England's Troubles*: 401 *et seq*; Linda Colley, *Britons. Forging the Nation 1707–1837* (2005): 65.

[84] Brewer, *The Sinews of Power*: 99; Gary Cox, *Marketing Sovereign Promises. Monopoly Brokerage and the Growth of the English State* (2016): 32.

[85] Corrigan and Sayer, *The Great Arch*.

[86] Corrigan and Sayer, *The Great Arch*: 93.

[87] Cox, *Marketing Sovereign Promises*: 31, after Schumpeter.

budgets with data on revenue and expenditure were first created[88]—and more secure and transparent forms of credit.

The fiscal infrastructure was consolidated through the eighteenth century. This was the century in which a permanent and professionalized state administration was created, a cadre whose first task was to raise revenues for the state in ways that were regularized and systematic.[89] Tax officers worked indefatigably, moving throughout the country, taking inventories of goods, and assessing for tax. The British became the second highest taxed economy in Europe,[90] mainly through land taxes (which the gentry accepted begrudgingly in times of war and resisted in peacetime) and duties on imports and exports.

The monopoly brokerage of parliament on public debt[91] allowed the British state to accrue and manage debts on a long-term basis, a mechanism that allowed it to maintain Europe's most powerful military. As long as state debt remained credible and the government could service the debt, indebtedness was a political asset rather than a liability. Throughout the eighteenth century the British state regularly dedicated 30 per cent of its revenues to debt service.[92] This unique global positioning as sovereign debtor was underpinned by the ascendance of the Pound Sterling as global currency.

The nineteenth century witnessed a steady increase in tax effort and a consolidation/universalization of the state's extractive architecture. From the late 1600s to the early 1800s, tax yield had increased sixteen-fold.[93] This would increase drastically with the final Napoleonic war, which also left the British state with substantial international debt.

Britain's capitalist transformation was vitally underpinned by 'protectionism, coupled with a powerful navy, a strong state, and the funding to prosecute war'.[94] But all of these key features of state power do not in themselves give a full explanation for the sustained social transition within Britain itself. It is the strength of the connections between this global power projection and the ascendance of capitalist social relations that provides the core of any explanation of this small and fairly peripheral country's global power. And these interconnections become especially visible when we review the ways in which Britain's imperial project generated a global political economy of accumulation.

[88] Hence the creation of the science of statistics—derived from the exigencies of statehood.

[89] Brewer, *The Sinews of Power*: 89.

[90] After the Dutch. See Kenneth Morgan, 'Mercantilism and the British Empire, 1688–1815' (2002): 173.

[91] Cox, *Marketing Sovereign Promises*.

[92] Brewer, *The Sinews of Power*: 116.

[93] Cunningham, *The Challenge of Democracy*: 6.

[94] Morgan, 'Mercantilism and the British Empire': 165.

The Imperial State

Empire and Capitalist Development

Thus far, we have sketched the contours of Britain's capitalist transition. We have noted the transformation of its political economy: new property relations, the accumulation of capital, and the changing modalities of state action. This account shows how—as argued in Section 1—capitalist transformation is an innately systemic phenomenon. It is neither a new technology, the emergence of a new industry, the rise of the market, a state project, nor any other discrete social change. It is—and must be—all of these things to qualify as transformation, a multifarious social transformation generated by the causal efficacy of the real properties of capitalist development. This is innate to our understanding of capitalism, something that Marx recognized as he spent his best efforts trying to reveal the essences and connections of the system that was consolidating around him.

This point is recapitulated here in order to set up a discussion of the effects of imperialism on Britain's capitalist transition. A great deal of the writing on empire and capitalism in Britain (especially more recent writing) has focused on the ways in which imperialism was responsible for Britain's capitalist development.[95] We shall see how a range of international flows established by Britain served to generate processes of accumulation and address major socio-economic problems within Britain's economy. But we shall not be making an argument that resembles the dependency theory tradition mentioned in Chapter 2. In other words, we will not be aiming to make an argument about how imperialism was the most important reason for capitalist industrialization or to try to make a balance sheet of 'internal' against 'external' causes of successful industrialization. Rather, we will be treating imperialism as 'systemic' in the same way as the rest of this account. This means that our concern is with the interplay between imperial and endogenous processes of change not as in some way separated into internal and external but rather as parts of a complex whole in which a nationally located transformation remains predominant. After all, many modern European empires made heavy extractions on other parts of the world and did not industrialize.

[95] A detailed and strong case that slavery was crucial to industrialization is made by Inikori, who sets out the main connections convincingly Joseph Inikori, *Africans and the Industrial Revolution in England* (2002): 8.

There are dangers and limitations with an approach in which the analytical aim is to show how important imperialism was to industrialization. In the first place, the rise of capitalism in Britain was intrinsically transnational. The emergence of a solidly British-national political economy with clear boundaries from an 'overseas' was in fact a fairly recent phenomenon, identified by Edgerton in the early twentieth century.[96] The rise of industrial capitalism in Britain was not a national project as much as a class one that involved the construction of a global project and frequent associations between the 'black' peoples of empire and the 'dark' peoples in the impoverished cityscapes.[97] It was constructed on a landlordism that squeezed rents from tenant farmers and plantations in the Americas that extracted surplus from enslaved and indentured labour. In summary, the ascendance of a capitalist class in Britain was *ab initio* global in scope and concerned itself with the putting to work of peoples within the core and frontier of the nation-empire.

It is important to bear in mind two aspects of empire in Britain's capitalist transition. First, exploitation—even extremely harsh and violent exploitation—in itself is not a sufficient relation to generate the kind of broad and sustained transition that Britain endured from the late 1700s. The dynamics of this transition were mainly nationally based and it was the tenacity and complexity of this sustained accumulation, investment, and flexibility in the British political economy that pushed what ostensibly look like bare-faced dispossessions and exploitations into resources that contributed not only to enrichment but also to the generation of capital. Related to this—and secondly—the various conduits of extractive imperialism that Britain imposed were not always easily seen as 'good' for the national economy. The importation of precious metals in the late 1600s and early 1700s generated an early 'resource curse'; speculation and dependence of re-exports made the British economy resemble something of an entrepôt or windfall economy.[98] There was also a period when the British current account relied overwhelmingly on coal exports. These ostensibly 'dependent' or 'extraverted' patterns of global relations have to be understood as components of a national capitalist transition which overcame all of these patterns through flexible investments, changed imperial relations, and the exercise of new forms of globalization.

[96] Edgerton, *The Rise and Fall of the British Nation*. See also Julian Hoppit, *Britain's Political Economies. Parliament and Economic Life 1660–1800* (2017) on legislation and empire. See Duncan Bell, *The Idea of Greater Britain. Empire and the Future of the World Order 1860–1900* (2007) on political ideas and ideologies.

[97] Robbie Shilliam, *Race and the Undeserving Poor* (2018).

[98] Comparatively, one might consider imperial Iberia in the sixteenth and seventeenth centuries.

The Eighteenth Century

Britain's early industrialization ran roughly from the 1680s to the 1760s. During the period, as discussed earlier, small-scale manufacture, commerce, and agrarian change generated intensified commercializations and improvements in agricultural productivity. Markets in the colonies allowed Britain's early manufacturers to expand beyond their domestic demand base. This was most salient in woollens, linen, and a range of artisanal manufactures such as metalwork and stationery.[99] About half of the increased manufacturing output during the seventeenth century was exported, and the bulk of those exports went to Africa, India, and the Americas.[100]

In the early eighteenth century, Britain's imperial project was diverse and piecemeal, prosecuted through its naval dominance, privateering, a range of private trading, and chartered companies, the most prominent of which was the East India Company (EIC). The EIC enjoyed the legislated monopoly on the import of commodities from India into Britain and as such was the vehicle through which Britain secured textiles, some spices, silks, and potteries.[101] At its peak, the EIC imported up to 750,000 pieces of Indian textile to the British market and managed up to 15 per cent of Britain's total imports.[102] In the latter half of the 1800s, the EIC deployed British government and its own military forces to secure territorial control over large parts of South Asia.[103] Nevertheless, it did not have a monopoly over trade in India; its merchant fleet was used to carry commodities from the 'private trade' that coursed through India.[104] The EIC served as a source of credit for the British government and as a joint-stock company also generated a large mercantile capital base for itself that allowed financiers and the imperially minded gentry to seek fortunes.[105] As the company shifted from a chartered trading institution

[99] Robin Blackburn, *The Making of New World Slavery: From the Baroque to the Modern, 1492–1800* (1998): 373.

[100] Patrick O'Brien, 'Inseparable Connections: Trade, Economy, Fiscal State, and the Expansion of Empire 1688–1815' (2001): 53–4.

[101] This monopoly was the reason why the company was subjected to critique from Adam Smith—although he did apply for a post with the EIC before he wrote *Wealth of Nations.*

[102] P. J. Marshall, 'The British in Asia: Trade to Domination, 1700–1765' (2001): 487; Nick Robins, *The Corporation that Changed the World: How the East India Company Shaped the Modern Multinational* (2012): 32.

[103] The 'East Indian' toponym derived from the infamously erroneous nomenclature endowed to the Caribbean as the 'West Indies'. As the EIC moved its trading focus eastwards towards China, the geographical signalling only became more bizarre.

[104] Emily Erikson, *Between Monopoly and Free Trade. The East India Company 1600–1757* (2014).

[105] Relatedly, see Catherine Hall and Sonya Rose, *At Home with Empire. Metropolitan Culture and the Imperial World* (2006) and Leonore Davidoff and Catherine Hall, *Family Fortunes. Men and Women of the English Middle Class 1780–1850* (2002).

into a colonial agency, it used force to pillage and extract tax from indigenous populations.[106] Towards the end of the century, the EIC moved its trading efforts towards the export of tea from China, a commodity that, like sugar at the same time, provided cheap sustenance to the growing population of wage labourers in industrializing British towns and cities. This generated a structural trade deficit with China, sustained by silver from the Americas. By the 1800s, the EIC's solution to this haemorrhaging of a strategic and precious metal was to manage the growth in opium production in India and export this into China's entrepôts: opium imports into China doubled from 1800 to 1820.[107]

It was, of course, slavery that underpinned the emergence of an integrated Atlantic system in which Britain established dominance. From the 1720s, Britain became the dominant Atlantic trader, and by 1775, Britain's slave colonies were producing over half of the Atlantic's trade in tobacco, sugar, and rice.[108] During the 1700s, British ships carried an unsurpassed three million enslaved Africans to its plantations in the Americas.[109] The Navigation Acts established a navally enforced trading monopoly to Britain's mercantile dominance in which all commodities and enslaved people were legally obliged to use British ships, ports, and seamen, serving British economic interests either in Britain itself or in its colonies.[110] This generated considerable duty revenues for the British state right through to the mid-1800s, a period during which there was no income tax and the fiscal demands of warfare were overbearing. Thus the Acts secured access to both foodstuffs during warfare in Europe and revenues for the massive expenditures on the military (especially the navy). Beyond the considerable commodity trade and productive advantages that were generated by Britain's Atlantic dominance, the slave trade itself generated at least a 10 per cent return on investment.[111]

The plantations of the Americas generated massive cheap imports of sugar, rice, tobacco, indigo, and cotton. Sugar was destined largely for the British mass consumer market, contributing to the nutritional needs of a growing urban wage labour class. Sugar consumption per person per annum rose from

[106] Robins, *The Corporation that Changed the World.*

[107] Julia Lovell, *The Opium War* (2011): 25.

[108] Blackburn, *The Making of New World Slavery*: 381; Seymour Drescher, *The Mighty Experiment. Free Labour Versus Slavery in British Emancipation* (2002): 24.

[109] Kenneth Morgan, *Slavery, Atlantic Trade and the British Economy 1660–1800* (2000): 10.

[110] The Acts were repealed in 1849 during the liberal reforms of the second half of that century.

[111] David Richardson, 'The British Empire and the Atlantic Slave Trade' (2000): 460. Like many aspects of the accounting of the slave trade, estimates are keenly contested. The highest estimate I have found is 50 per cent (Inikori, *Africans and the Industrial Revolution in England*).

6 lb in 1710 to 23 lb by the 1770s.[112] Rice and tobacco were major parts of the British re-export trade to Europe, a component of the former's trade structure that ensured its currency and current account remained stable at a time when Britain was not an exceptionally strong economy and in which it needed to import semi-finished goods from Europe.[113] Indigo served as a vital dyestuff for woollen and later cotton textile production: the value of dyestuff imports from slave plantations rose from £226,000 in 1700 to £506,000 in 1774.[114] Cheap imported cotton was the mainstay in the textile industrialization of Lancashire, a process that also relied on the destruction of textile manufacture in South Asia. By 1787, slave labour produced 70 per cent of the cotton for Britain's textile industry, rising to 90 per cent by 1838 when apprenticeship ceased.[115]

The ascendance of commercially minded landlordism was not only an outcome of enclosure, improvement, and the consolidation of large farms under pressures to achieve economies of scale. It was also a result of the revenues generated by investments in slavery plantation in the Americas.[116] Younger sons of gentry families sometimes ventured into the 'new world' of the Americas, seeking their own fortunes and an opportunity to reproduce the gentry life elsewhere.[117] They were accompanied by a rising merchant and finance class[118] which aspired to make money and also to establish a social standing in the global-imperial Britain that was difficult to achieve within Britain itself.[119] Institutionally, this coalition of properties and interests was expressed through the rising interest of joint-stock companies in the slave trade which collected investment capital together and managed the complexities of trade, which, although ostensibly 'triangular', involved 2-year or more journeys to multiple destinations. Under the mantle of British trade protection, plantation owners maintained opulence while also accruing debt to merchants.[120]

112 Blackburn, *The Making of New World Slavery*: 382.

113 Morgan, *Slavery, Atlantic Trade and the British Economy 1660–1800*: 18; Patrick O'Brien, 'Inseparable Connections: Trade, Economy, Fiscal State, and the Expansion of Empire 1688–1815' (2001): 55.

114 O'Brien, 'Inseparable Connections': 82.

115 Seymour Drescher, *Capitalism and Antislavery. British Mobilisation in Perspective* (1987): 7.

116 Drescher, *The Mighty Experiment*: 122. The London Stock Exchange was established in 1773.

117 Blackburn, *The Making of New World Slavery*: 220, 313; S. D. Smith, *Slavery, Family, and Gentry Capitalism in the British Atlantic* (2006).

118 Cain and Hopkins, *British Imperialism*: 74; O'Brien, 'Inseparable Connections': 60; Richardson, 'The British Empire and the Atlantic Slave Trade': 447.

119 Indeed, a constant motivation for non-landed classes' participation in empire was to achieve a social standing that made them 'peers' to Britain's gentry. See Eric Hobsbawm and Terrance Ranger, *The Invention of Tradition* (1992).

120 David Davis, *The Problem of Slavery in the Age of Revolution, 1770–1823* (1999): 52–3.

From the middle of the 1700s, plantations in the British Caribbean established regular regimes of labour and technology. They were integrated into circuits of credit and aware of markets in Europe. In spite of the long journey times from West Africa to the Americas and from the Americas to Europe, the plantation became powerfully integrated into an emerging single modern Atlantic political economy.[121] Gang labour, work specialization, and the deployment of machinery made the plantations 'machine-like' in their work, consuming the bodies of Africans and purchasing more at slave markets in ways not dissimilar to raw materials.[122] Indeed, some have argued that the techniques of exploitation in the plantations fed back into Britain's own early industrialization.[123]

It is important to note that after the abolition of the Atlantic slave trade by Britain in 1807, British traders continued to purchase slave-produced cotton and sugar. Slavery itself was abolished in 1837, although it was replaced by an apprenticeship system which committed slaves to work on plantations until 1838. Indebtedness and indenture continued to coerce former slaves to remain on the plantations and also to bring in new unfree labourers from Africa and India.[124] The abolition of slavery was passed with a discernible anxiety concerning the status of the plantation owners—who were still British citizens and well represented in parliament. As a result, a massive state subsidy to those planters was allocated, one that generated a spike in real-estate development in Britain itself, as well as all manner of other projects.[125] This, abolition was very much a 'capitalist' affair, principally attentive to the property rights of plantations owners and the continued control of labour.

The abolition of plantation slavery in British colonies took place not as the system was in decline. Indeed, plantation slavery in the Americas generally flourished after the abolition of slavery by Britain.[126] Although there were intense debates about slavery and political economy, there was no crisis in productivity. Abolitionism was driven by a religious–moral campaign which was thoroughly bourgeois, involving as it did middle-class unorthodox Protestants, a dominant parliamentary group (together appropriately dubbed

[121] James Dunkerley, *Americana: The Americas in the World Around 1850* (2000).

[122] Blackburn, *The Making of New World Slavery*: 332 *et seq*. For most of the 'modern' plantation slave period on the Caribbean islands, the slave population depleted and needed to be replaced with new purchases. This was less the case in the Chesapeake.

[123] Matthew Parker, *The Sugar Barons. Family, Corruption, Empire, and War* (2012): 34.

[124] Drescher, *Capitalism and Antislavery*: 10.

[125] Nicholas Draper, *The Price of Emancipation. Slave Ownership and British Society at the End of Slavery* (2010). For example, the Royal National Lifeboat Institution.

[126] Davis, *The Problem of Slavery*: 59; Drescher, *Capitalism and Antislavery*: 4.

'the saints'), and a working-class movement to promote freedom for workers (a less considered aspect of abolitionist historiography). The prospective of a post-slavery world was effectively based on a controlled social experiment in which the British state did its utmost to support plantations' transition into a 'free' labour market.[127] Former slaves were neither listened to nor compensated.[128]

It is impossible to imagine early British industrialization without empire and slavery. The early industrial process in Britain was intrinsically an imperial one, and within the complex and wide-ranging networks generated by British empire, plantation slavery was pivotal for the securing of cheap raw materials and consumer commodities for Britain's industrializing cities. Imperial networks also went well beyond Atlantic slavery throughout the eighteenth and early nineteenth centuries, most obviously in relation to India and to some degree China. Along the coast of West Africa mercantile entrepôts served as the destination for British exports and the evacuation of the British trade in slaves. All of these links generated capital for a merchant class, based increasingly in London, Bristol, Glasgow, and Liverpool. It generated revenues for landlords who had invested in plantations. It balanced British trade with Europe through re-exports—effectively making Britain an entrepôt. Re-exports nearly doubled from 1750 to 1800.[129] All of these patterns of trade, production, and investment were, as we have seen, based firmly on the ascendance of the British state as a globalizing military and trading power.

The Nineteenth Century

Britain industrialized into a turbulent world. The 'first empire' and early industrialization of the eighteenth century which combined the Atlantic slave trade with the rise of merchant finance and trading and the supply of specific commodities to the British economy did not at any point establish a stable state of affairs. As Britain went through its protracted and unstable industrialization, the patterns of dynamics of empire changed considerably.

[127] Drescher *The Mighty Experiment.*

[128] The notion that abolitionism was in some sense anti-racist is a fantasy. Slaves were never listened to and were represented as beseeching children, and after abolition a good number of abolition campaigners went on to promote the civilization of Africans in Africa.

[129] Deane, *The First Industrial Revolution*: 55.

From the early 1800s until the 1840s, Britain became a major exporter of manufactured goods, initially and most notably textiles. In the 1850s, 93 per cent of British exports were manufactured goods and British commodities constituted 40 per cent of global manufacturing trade.[130] This shift is remarkable, and all the more significant when set in the context of a marked export boom from 1840: by the 1860s, export values had increased by over 110 per cent.[131] Within the manufactured exports category, there was a strong shift away from textiles towards a broader range of metals and engineering goods.[132] From the 1840s onwards, Britain also increasingly imported manufactured goods from its competitors, notably Germany and America where major 'second revolution' industries such as chemicals and metallurgy were driving processes of accumulation.

Capitalist industrialization generated economic growth and a clear uptick in population growth. As a result, by the early nineteenth century, Britain's broad self-sufficiency in food production was lost and merchants sought sources of grain from colonies and other countries with strong links to the British economy. Britain's net food importing balance of trade was based mainly on imports from North America: in the later 1800s, up to half of Britain's wheat imports derived from America.[133] Grain imports were destined to supply the growing populations of wage labourers in cities.

The imperial nature of Britain's capitalism served as a vital technique to regulate and discipline labour. The emergence of a mass population of unemployed or underemployed people served to both repress wages and pose major problems for the British state in terms of social provision and security. From the 1830s onwards, major emigrations to the 'white' colonies and America reduced the surplus populations in Britain[134] and generated a new facet to the burgeoning system of carceral discipline for the poor: transportation.

The great emigrations of Britons in the latter half of the 1800s were accompanied by a migration of capital.[135] As Britain's industrialization was fully consolidated from the mid-century, returns on investment within Britain levelled off and investors saw more lucrative frontier investments. This investment went into colonial productive enterprises such as farming, mining

[130] Mathias, *The First Industrial Nation*: 250; A'Hearn, 'The British Industrial Revolution in a European Mirror': 3.

[131] Evans, *The Shaping of Modern Britain*: 242.

[132] Evans, *The Shaping of Modern Britain*: 239.

[133] Turner, 'Agriculture 1860–1914' 4: 134.

[134] Cain and Hopkins, *British Imperialism*: 36.

[135] Hobsbawm, *Industry and Empire*: 96.

(during the various 'rushes' in the American western frontier, Australia, and southern Africa), and other geographically specific manufactures.

Much of the investment in the colonies was financed and insured by Britain's dominant financial sector, based in the City of London. These investments were not entirely colonial but also focused on Europe, America, China, and South America. The nature of British imperialism shifted towards capital export on a massive scale. Foreign direct investment went into projects to construct railways in what was, between 1840 and 1900, a remarkable international project of rail construction.[136] It also went into the forging of large-scale commercial farming in a period during which Britain's agriculture no longer managed to provide grain for its people. Investment also sought out mineral supplies for industry. British finance developed a massive portfolio of foreign lending which generated an inflow of income on capital lent sufficient to ameliorate the economy's structural imbalance on the current account. Britain also generated invisible exports through shipping and insurance, considerable sources of revenue in a world where trade was increasing and becoming more complex, and supported by metal ships, steam power, and the telegraph.

These patterns of investment in the late 1800s have been understood within international political economy as the international regime of British predominance or hegemony. The regime was underpinned by global sterling linked to gold as well as a colonial/imperial state. More detailed work on the nature of this imperial regime looks at the way it transformed productive relations in other parts of the world through investment and a dissemination of capitalist social relations, this being most prominent in settler agriculture.[137] If the eighteenth century might be roughly characterized as a century of British imperialism based on slavery and mercantilist strategies of trade advantage, the nineteenth century might be (again roughly) painted as a century of capital export and global integration through transformed production and trade. All was focused around the relentless requirement of British capital to accumulate through its putting to work of labour in Britain and its integration into global circuits of capital, a large proportion of which it controlled. This generated a certain degree of liberalization in the second half of the century.[138]

Not that more bare-faced state projects of imperialism were ushered out by an 'informal empire' of market power. Mid-century, the British state used its

[136] Evans, *The Shaping of Modern Britain*: 241; Mathias, *The First Industrial Nation*: 253.

[137] Harriet Friedmann, 'International Regimes of Food and Agriculture since 1870' (1987).

[138] Anthony Howe, 'Restoring Free Trade: the British Experience, 1776–1873' (2002), Trentmann, *Free Trade Nation*.

military power to enforce what were effectively illegal smuggling rights for British traders of opium in China. The opium trade generated revenues for an ailing East India Company which organized opium production in India. It also addressed a chronic trade imbalance with China based on Britain paying for China's tea with silver mined from South America, the latter being part of the capital export mentioned above.

From the 1880s, Britain's imperial geography changed as it incorporated large areas of Africa under its control. African colonies were subjected to imperial 'preferences' that locked exports into the service of the British economy. West African palm oil was the major import of importance. In the early twentieth century (mainly from the 1920s), investments in cocoa, coffee, sisal, and tea served British consumer markets and were promoted by the Empire Marketing Board. The extent to which African colonies 'paid off' for the British economy after 1885 has been extensively debated. There were certainly major investment opportunities for some British companies in tropic crops—tea, coffee, and cocoa—which were increasingly lucrative for a growing British consumer market. Colonialism also allowed British mineral companies security to seek out sources of diamonds, gold, aluminium, and copper—especially in southern Africa. British colonial exports to America helped address Britain's structural imbalance in trade with America.[139] Throughout the continent—and in a diversity of often coercive ways—peasant smallholders were integrated into global markets for tradeable crops.

More generally, it is important to note a vital context within which these imperial articulations of capitalism developed. As capitalist development emerged in Germany, America, and France between about 1840 and 1880, global trade increased massively, as did the complexity of international trade. British imperialism was, then, changing with and in relation to a transforming global economy, one in which rivalries with European capitalisms were intense. The infrastructures of communication and commerce were changing with the emergence of steam-powered metal ships and telegraphs. A profusion of international regulation took place at this time to ensure that investment and trade were subjected to standards and basic contractual obligations.[140] Britain's Victorian imperial high-point in the second half of the 1800s when its monarch became an empress was also a period in which Britain became one capitalist power among others and a global order was being forged in

[139] Mathias, *The First Industrial Nation*: 319.

[140] The Sterling Gold Standard (1819), Paris International Property Union (1833), first Most Favoured Nation Treaty (1860), and Berne Copyright Convention (1886) were the main laws regulating the globalization of industrial capitalism.

which multilateral order of capitalist nation-states managed investment and commerce. By the 1880s, Britain was fully ensconced in a tripolar global industrial capitalism with German and America, experiencing a major recession as a result.

The relationships between Britain, Germany, and America might be characterized as rivalrously interconnected. Each country connected to Britain through investment, trade, and technology, but each came to perceive of its own national standing in competitive economic relations to the other two. This was an issue at the heart of debates about the repeal of the Corn Laws, in which those defending the Corn Laws would sometimes rely on stereotypes of German bread flooding into British shops, for example.[141] America involved itself in the Napoleonic War, severing trade with Britain. Indeed, after the Napoleonic War, mainland Europe suffered a century of war and instability which created a 'constant motif' of military threat in Britain.[142]

In conclusion, then, we should recognize both the vitality of empire for British capitalist development and the fact that its importance was about not only the extraction of various forms of values from plantations, trade deals, and military dominance but also—crucially—how these served a dynamic and complex national economy. To put it brutally, it is one thing to exploit a hinterland and get rich doing it; it is another to exploit a hinterland in a variety of ways to sustain processes of expanded accumulation over 200 years or so.

Developmentalism

From the 1780s to the mid-1800s,[143] we have seen how the British state and economy underwent a turbulent but also discernible capitalist transformation. This involved changes in the social relations of production, shifts in the nature of state power, the resolution of major-order security threats through military build-up, and an imperial project. By the end of this period, Britain was a different country to that which emerged out of the seventeenth century. It was industrialized, enclosed, governed by a centralized national government,

[141] Trentmann, *Free Trade Nation*.

[142] Bell, *The Idea of Greater Britain*: 38. The dynamics of military and economic rivalry in this period and their impact on state-building are fantastically set out in Evans, *The Pursuit of Power*.

[143] I acknowledge that my periodizations throughout this chapter (and all subsequent chapters) are rather vague. This is because historic change is 'vague' in the sense that when multiple and connected changes take place, any identification of a specific year looks like ostensible clarity and precision but loses the sense of what was actually happening.

and exercising power over great swathes of the rest of the world. It became Europe's unequivocally dominant power.

But it had not yet constructed a form of developmentalism, as defined in Chapter 1. This was because it had not yet fully connected the political economy of capitalist growth to a national project of commonwealth. Nor had it yet displayed an overarching political goal of ensuring sustained growth. This might seem odd for a period in which economic growth was in a very concrete sense the underpinning of so much of Britain's political economy, but it is worth remembering that economic growth was not the political meta-norm that it later became; it was, rather, a more delimited amateur science pursued by intellectuals.[144] Growth was a component of discussions about inter-state rivalry, about the prospects for empire, or an implied factor in discussions about debt management and revenue raising. It was the outcome of proprietary society. It is in fact only in 1934 that gross domestic product (GDP) accounting—and therefore a sustained metric of economic growth—became standard practice within government.[145] The core notion of growth as political legitimacy which is at the heart of developmentalism was not present throughout Britain's capitalist transition.

From the 1830s, one can discern an embryonic developmentalist politics, in the 1834 Poor Law and its subsequent development.[146] Although it would be a misrepresentation to argue that the Poor Law Amendment Act ushered in a new regime of social provision, it did provide a distinct reference point for a more systemic and universal response by the state to mass poverty. The Act replaced the parish-based 'Elizabethan' provision which had generated very variable geographies of social support based on the assumption that people supported those from their own parish.[147] The Poor Law established a system of provision which was more apt to the conditions of an urbanizing and proletarianizing capitalism.[148] Before the 1830s, there was no coherent nationally articulated anti-poverty discourse or project.[149] From the 1830s until the early twentieth century, social provision under the Act was defined

[144] As noted in Chapter 1 in the work of Paul Slack.

[145] Richard Peet and Michael Watts, *Liberation Ecologies: Environment, Development and Social Movements* (1996): 19–20.

[146] As with almost all aspects of social reform throughout the Victorian era (and beyond), the subject of intervention was the male head of household. In regards to the Poor Law, it was assumed that single women were vulnerable or delinquent and that married women assume their husbands' identity (Cunningham, *The Challenge of Democracy*: 75).

[147] See Jonathan Healey, *The First Century of Welfare. Poverty and Poor Relief in Lancashire* (2014).

[148] Although it is noteworthy that the initial focus of concern was rural poverty before the focus moved towards the cities.

[149] Stevenson, 'Social Aspects of the Industrial Revolution': 229.

by the workhouse, means testing, and charity.[150] At the heart of this was the Charity Organization Society. This society attempted to identify a categorization of deserving and undeserving poor as well as a 'casual' and 'respectable' working class.[151] Based on stout Benthamite political economy of deterrent, it aimed to reduce pauperism and put people to work rather than improve the working conditions of the proletariat, an objective that it had some success with.[152] The core imperative of the new Poor Law came to be a fear of mass poverty concentrated in cities and a desire to discipline the poor into the kinds of orderly behaviour that matched the models of political economy that had flourished as capitalism ascended.[153] As such, the Law cannot be seen in isolation. Its logic was supported by other acts such as the Vagrancy Act (1824), Poor Removal Act (1846), and the Casual Poor Act (1882). Various projects, the Cholera Act, 'Improvements', and Sanitary Acts sought to provide public health infrastructure[154] out of a concern with the productivity of the labour force.[155]

In a sense it seems perverse to consider the Poor Law as a 'developmental' programme. One of the salient concerns that drove the implementation of the Poor Law was a desire to *reduce* expenditure on social support. Furthermore, as sketched above, the Law was sustained by a mixture of fear, Christian philanthropy, narcissism, and paternalism towards the poor rather than a clear and unadulterated intention to reduce mass poverty.[156] And the workhouse system itself was nothing less than a social disaster, based as it was on a strict carceral labour system. But it set in place the beginnings of a systemic state-based infrastructure to provide support to those considered to be below the poverty line. Indeed, the notion of a poverty line derives from precisely the sensibilities of the Poor Law, the phrase being coined by Charles Booth in the 1880s.[157] It developed to allocate support to the working poor as well as 'paupers', and it interconnected with discussions that emerged in the latter half of the century concerning the urban environment.

[150] It would be an interesting research project to explore the ideational and strategic parallels between the nineteenth-century Poor Laws and overseas development assistance.
[151] Gareth Stedman Jones, *An End to Poverty? A Historical Debate* (2004): Chapter 2.
[152] Fraser, *The Evolution of the British Welfare State*: 58.
[153] A concise summary of all of this can be found in David Englander, *Poverty and Poor Law Reform in Nineteenth Century Britain, 1834–1914* (1998).
[154] In the early 1800s, public health science did not understand the causal mechanisms of water- or air-borne diseases, instead cleaving to theories of good and bad air. In an imperial setting, this explains the etymological origins of the name for malaria.
[155] Fraser, *The Evolution of the British Welfare State*: 76.
[156] Gertrude Himmelfarb, *Poverty and Compassion. The Moral Imagination of the Late Victorians* (1991); Hobsbawm, *Industry and Empire*: 66.
[157] Fraser, *The Evolution of the British Welfare State*: 163.

By the 1880s, urban poverty was seen not simply as a moral failing or a property of those who were infirm or insane. It was also seen as a product of disease-ridden and unsanitary housing, as well as a condition suffered by the working classes when work dried up or economic crises occurred. The political economy of free market utilitarianism remained but was tempered by a 'new' liberalism of state intervention and even at its margins a socialism of state responsibility for poverty. Thus the Poor Law and associated laws, inquiries, and discourses generated a political project of 'commonwealth': elitist, top-down, disciplinary, and incomplete.

The Education Act (1870) initiated a process that made primary education universal and compulsory. Education for the poor had been expanding throughout the age of the Poor Law as religious charitable organizations provided basic schooling within the Victorian tradition of philanthropy. The 1870 Act generated a structure through which the government made it compulsory for children to receive a basic education and to pay schooling institutions per child.[158] The deep logic of universal education was similar to that within the Poor Laws: a form of social provision that was both a more inclusive commonwealth (literacy is seen generally as a basic skill required for citizenship and agency) and a means to discipline and maintain order through an extremely regimented didactics and the metaphysics of Christian obedience to God's plan.[159]

The other important legislative and programmatic aspect of the construction of a basic capitalist commonwealth was the increasing regulation of the working day and the conditions of work. In the early 1800s, a working day in a growing industry might involve over 12 hours, danger, ill-health, and exhaustion. Children were commonly used in factories and mines. 'Sweated' labour was not a term invented to describe the factories of East Asia's export processing zones but rather the workshops and factories of Victorian capitalism. Organized labour consistently challenged the penuries of unfree, poorly paid, and excessive work, through unions and other less formal organizations.[160] Strikes in demands of better conditions and pay and also more secure employment were a constant feature of Victorian industry. In part as a result of this, the British government enacted Factory Acts which limited the use of children in wage employment, and subsequently set maximum hours of work

[158] Much of the struggle over expanding basic education was filtered through an Anglican Dissenting Protestant rivalry.

[159] Fraser, *The Evolution of the British Welfare State*: 96.

[160] The latter were necessary to allow labour mobilization in the teeth of Combination Laws.

for all in specific industries and then more generally.[161] A system of inspectors audited factories, retaining the ability to fine factory owners, although in practice this happened sporadically. Slowly, haltingly, and unstably, the pay and conditions of wage labour in large industries improved in the second half of the nineteenth century and into the twentieth, leading to a gradually declining income inequality, even in a context of an expanding share of income retained by capital.[162] Incomes for the working classes grew in the later nineteenth century.[163] In 1908, the Pensions Acts was passed and in 1911 National Insurance was introduced. The National Grid was completed in 1926. After about 120 years, British capitalism had created the conditions of possibility for mass material well-being.

Labour, Struggle, and Commonwealth

The emergence of a basic and patrician system of social support was not simply the outcome of a set of elite calculations concerning social stability and basic well-being. They were also driven—often chaotically—by the social mobilizations of the working class. Indeed, from the 1830s, Lancastrian textile workers—men and women—had been organizing and agitating for representation, and better wages and working conditions. These mobilizations expanded into other industries against the teeth of a state that sought to criminalize labour organization. The Chartist movement mobilized over 300,000 working people to push for male franchise in the core belief that this basic property of a fully democratic state would open up the possibility of more or less radical redistributions of wealth.[164] The rise of large and politically engaged labour unions supported 'radical' Whig MPs as the franchise gradually expanded in the late 1800s, putting forward issues relating to democratization and conditions of work to a factious parliament. Workers would also riot[165] or march, generating fears concerning public order, a phrase strongly ensconced in the desire to maintain secure property rights, desires that led to the establishment of police forces in urban areas and

[161] Fraser, *The Evolution of the British Welfare State*: 27.

[162] Gregory Clark and Neil Cummins, 'Inequality and Social Mobility in the Era of the Industrial Revolution' (2014): 211, 230.

[163] Stevenson, 'Social Aspects of the Industrial Revolution': 241.

[164] Chartism itself had 'democrats' and socialists within it, cohabiting uneasily with reform-minded middle-class groups.

[165] For example, in London in 1848, 1852, 1886, 1888, and 1889. Outside London, notable examples were the Plug Riots (1842) and Aberdare strike (1857–8).

eventually nationally.[166] Specific factory or industry grievances developed into broader trades unions[167] and trades union committees, some of which promoted the representation of labour interests in parliament.[168] Working-class activism also generated its own ideologies of decent work, trade policy, arguments for land reform, utopian futures, and internationalism. These cultures of politics or moral economies[169] were enabled and constrained by the ascendance of industrial capital.

In essence, the sustained expansion of the working classes throughout the 1800s generated a broad, tenacious, and unstable politics of justice that put immense pressure on the government and industry to reduce hours, improve working conditions, and open up government to the popular vote.

Britain's democratization is commonly told as a rolling out of the Reform Acts in which parliamentarians manage their own convictions with their party positions and their sense of pressure for an expanding franchise from the masses. But a close look at the discourses around the Acts and, indeed, their textual content suggests that 'reform' was principally articulated as a way of avoiding democracy as much as expanding it through careful reform.[170] There was, consistently, a commonly held belief across parties that reform was an alternative to democratization which was often associated with the tyranny of the masses and a fear that property relations would be overturned. The Revolution and Commune in France and the rise of Marxism sharpened the intellectual climate significantly. The mechanics of reform were entirely based on considerations of allowing a broader constituency of property owners to vote and there was almost no consideration of women voting: even wealthy and educated women were assumed to have the same political preferences as their husbands. After three reform Acts, no women had the vote and about 40 per cent of men did. Much else in reform concerned constituency design, MP eligibility, and cycles of parliament. Inasmuch as the British government expanded the franchise, it did so substantially in response to pressures from middle-class and especially working-class mobilization.[171]

[166] The 1856 County and Borough Police Act.

[167] The Trades Unions Congress was created in 1868.

[168] The Independent Labour Party was created in 1893.

[169] E. P. Thompson, *The Making of the English Working Class* (1980).

[170] Cunningham, *The Challenge of Democracy*: 32.

[171] Cunningham, *The Challenge of Democracy*; more generally, see Dietrich Rueschmeyer, Evelyn Stephens, and John Stephens, *Capitalist Development and Democracy* (1992).

Emergence of the Developmentalist Episteme

Government itself became thoroughly embedded in ideas of progress, discipline, and order—ideas increasingly articulated through metrics rather than rhetoric. Knowledge became centralized in government offices that were now, in a sense, machines to generate evidence.[172] The Chancellor of the Exchequer only becomes the *primus inter pares* of the Ministries in the mid-1800s.[173] The legal system for companies and finance is only fully established in the 1830s,[174] and even then did not lock in what most see as the basis for the legal entity of a firm. Statistics on the provision of education and sanitation (two recognizably central components of contemporary developmental legitimacy) can just be discerned in the mid-1800s.[175] And it is not until the 1870s that we can identify an expanding state expenditure on national well-being of a kind that seems analogous to other developmentalisms in more recent times.

From the 1830s onwards, mass material well-being started to increase in a secular fashion, even in the context of a relatively rapidly growing population. Generally stagnant wages started to increase.[176] Per capita income rose from £12 in 1801 to £49 a century later, a four-fold increase.[177] The shift to coal-based manufacturing with more complex chains of production generated a qualitative shift in capitalist industrialization.[178] In spite of a trebling of the population in the nineteenth century, by the last quarter of that period incomes were discernibly increasing for the working classes.[179] The state also commenced a social project to secure a minimal material provision to its population and to do so in ways that were heavily moralized and therefore infused with legitimacy claims. Recombinations of utilitarianism and Protestant values created a protean sense of an 'unjust' poverty that required a 'just' state for its remedy. Although there is of course complex and debated evidence, from the mid-1800s onwards, people's lives tended to become defined by both an intense working life and a greater material prosperity and social mobility, not least through emigration.

[172] The term statistics is etymologically historically derived from the notion that governance requires numbers. Census-making, taxation, balances of trade, and so on were all the province of the state.

[173] Evans, *The Forging of the Modern State*: 19.

[174] Corrigan and Sayer, *The Great Arch*: 121.

[175] Corrigan and Sayer, *The Great Arch*: 129.

[176] A'Hearn, 'The British Industrial Revolution in a European Mirror': 4.

[177] Mathias, *The First Industrial Nation. An Economic History of Britain 1700–1914*: 243. There are varied cliometric methods that contest the degree of increase, but they all concur on the core trend of increased income per capita. Nicholas Crafts, 'Long Run Growth' (2004): 6.

[178] Griffin, *A Short History of the British Industrial Revolution*: 125.

[179] Stevenson, 'Social Aspects of the Industrial Revolution': 241.

Capitalism's expanded accumulation was now articulated to a political project in which growth, mass welfare, and national planning were major-order concerns. This required a science of governance increasingly concerned with economic growth and the art of economic policy. The repeal of the Corn Laws and full abolition were major instances of a political economy of experimentation in which politicians, civil servants, and intellectuals came to believe that they could deploy state power to make predictable and major changes to the patterns of accumulation within Britain's capitalism.

By the 1890s, mass hunger had been eradicated in Britain[180] and, politically, became almost unthinkable. The state had taken on responsibility for a basic pension, and the bare bones of a welfare state were in fact constructed in this period. The notion that the performance of the British economy as a delineated space was the primary concern of statehood emerged in this period and was crucially and constantly connected to a sense of competition in which Germany, America, France, and later others were rivalling Britain for markets, technological innovations in production, resources in various parts of the world, and more generally influence and grandeur. In short, Britain only became developed at the end of the nineteenth century.

It would seem, then, that our understanding of developmentalism as both a successful political mechanism to ensure the expanded accumulation of capital and to forge a legitimacy claim for government out of the translation of sustained growth into common wealth only appears in Britain after a sustained period of capitalist transition. And, finally, and crucially, this change takes place at the point at which Britain's global ascendancy starts to decline as Germany, America, and shortly afterwards France develop rapid economic growth on the basis of industrialization. This is pivotal because it introduces the final component of our modelling of developmentalism: national economic rivalry. Successful development is always both internal or unit-specific and comparative or framed within a society of states.

Conclusion

The argument of this chapter is that Britain's developmentalism spanned a period roughly from the mid-eighteenth century to the late nineteenth century. During this period, an emerging agrarian capitalism and imperial mercantilism provided the possibility for industrialization, which commenced

[180] James Vernon, *Hunger. A Modern History* (2017).

on a small and dispersed scale before urbanizing and concentrating (unevenly) into factory systems. Throughout all of this complex change, labour productivity and expanded competitive accumulation drove the process, tenaciously and unstably. These processes generated considerable political challenges which the British state met as it elaborated governance practices of security, nation-building, and the legitimation of its authority. By the late 1800s, capital is dominant, the politics of commonwealth established, and—warts and all—Britain is a developed capitalist political economy.

The British case fits well with our model of developmentalism. We see massive systemic coercion, an increasingly powerful state that advocates for expanded accumulation. We also see the rise of capital through industrialization, competition, and the seeking out of productivity gains. We see new political forces contest the social effects of change, and we see the beginnings of a welfare state. Generally, incomes increase, people consume more, and hunger is largely eradicated. We might, then, treat Britain as the 'original' developmentalism case. But for all of its developmentalist properties, conceptually, there are two distinguishing features.

First—and precisely because of its original historical definition—Britain's capitalist transition was very gradual, arguably over centuries, or even if one starts with early industrialization over nearly 150 years. For most of that time, the material well-being of the masses was worsened or marginally improved. Second, Britain's capitalist transformation was intrinsically global, and as a result it endeavoured to create an imperial network in which accumulation was sustained through differentiated zones of trade and labour. A major effect of this globalization was that—for all of their variability—many parts of the world saw their own political economies in relation to Britain's. This meant, third, that Britain bequeathed to other parts of the world the key development challenge: how to forge economic growth through capitalist transformation in a world defined by preceding capitalist transformations. Developmentalist ideologies emerged in the late 1800s as a result of this historic situation. Thus the British case both shows us how uniquely powerful capitalist industrialization can be as a motor for development, and remains somewhat unique for having undergone this transition in a world not already dominated by the capital of other nations. We will develop this theme in Chapter 6 when we explore the American experience of capitalist development.

6

America

Introduction

Colony, Settler State, Nation

As we saw in regards to Britain, the question of origins is contentious. When does one start an account of the development of capitalism, bearing in mind that this development is always 'organic' in that it emerges from non-capitalist social relations and 'carries forward' through various transmutations features of what went before. In relation to England/Britain, the debate revolves around the post-feudal agrarian question in which landlordism and tenancy generated enclosing, competitive, and productivity-enhancing agricultures. In relation to America, we need to address its colonial and slaveholding origins.

Following from the conclusion of Chapter 5, the British[1] colonization of North America establishes a major consideration for capitalist development: that all development projects take place in a world that has been powerfully shaped by capitalisms already established. Although Britain was constantly besieged by major-order security threats which fed into the construction of the modern state and the national economy, it did not face a world in which a more advanced capitalist economy that generated a global political economy existed. Indeed, a key reason for its pre-eminence over France was its ability to manage its national debt and military expenditures in a more sustainable fashion, something that generated no little vexation within French intellectual circles[2] who saw a tiny island to their north which maintained dominance of the Atlantic. America was in a sense the first exemplar of post-colonial capitalist development: liberated from colonial rule, America sought to forge a national capitalism in order to remove its dependence on Britain.

Seen from this perspective, American development might raise questions familiar to dependency theorists about both the damage done by European

[1] France and Spain also colonized North America, but we will focus on Britain as the main and victorious colonizer.

[2] 'I am completely astounded that England, which is a very tiny bit of Europe, is dominant,' said Louis XV's foreign minister, in David Reynolds, *America. Empire of Liberty* (2010): 52.

Developmentalism: The Normative and Transformative within Capitalism. Graham G.M. Harrison, Oxford University Press (2020). © Graham G.M. Harrison.
DOI: 10.1093/oso/9780198785798.001.0001

empire and the distortions, limitations, and extractions exercised by the metropole over the periphery—in this case Britain and North America, respectively. Until America's independence, Britain maintained a trade and tax regime that locked it into a role of providing a limited number of primary commodity exports to service its own industrialization and to maintain a strong current account vis à vis its European trading partner-rivals through re-exports.

But one cannot take the colonialism–dependency categorization very far. European settlements were afforded considerable self-government in a way that contrasts with subsequent colonial projects in Asia and Africa. This is in no small measure a result of the fact that colonization established large white settler populations that erased or displaced indigenous peoples. In that sense, America, Canada, and Australia seem distinct: dominions with extensive self-government. Indeed, in the thirteen states, most ordinary people participated in polities far more extensively than ordinary people in Britain. British colonialism in North America was, then, defined both by a core–periphery structuring of the Atlantic and a mass settlement project of racially exclusive self-government.

The colonialism–dependency relation also fails to capture the political economy of slavery in the colonies. As European settlement pushed indigenous peoples away from the coast, Africans were drawn into plantation economies mainly in the South. The rice, tobacco, and indigo plantations that consumed millions of African bodies generated the exports that fed into British industrialization. Plantation slavery became a systemic feature of the southern colonies and it generated a powerful planter class that commanded labour and land, even if they were obliged to sell to British merchants and often maintained relations of indebtedness to those merchants or creditors from the northern colonies. The place of plantation slavery in America's capitalist development has been subjected to considerable debate. Plantation slavery generated agrarian and mercantile classes and it transformed massive stretches of the South into commercial agriculture. But it did so through a system of exploitation based on unfree labour.

We need to make sense of the fact that major social transitions in eighteenth-century and nineteenth-century America were forged through slavery, not the expansion of wage labour. In Chapter 2, we have argued that a core driver of capitalist development derives from wage labour. It is the putting to work of wage labourers that sets the imperative for capital relentlessly to seek both to push wages down and to find ways to enhance productivity. Workers themselves have mobility and collective agency that also pressures capital to seek to invest to achieve greater productivity. The wage–labour relation is a constantly contested and unstable negotiation between labour and capital that is reproduced through the rebalancing of downward pressure on wages and innovations to generate higher productivity. This is also the foundation of the construction of an ever-expanding system of commodity production and the generation of surplus value that might be captured by governments for the purposes of basic material well-being.

Slavery systems in the Americas did not contain these dynamics. Nevertheless, plantations throughout the Americas demonstrated an ambition to increase productivity, change systems of labour, introduce new technologies, bring in new crops, and reorganize regimes of unfree labour. Plantation slavery was neither static nor removed from the competitive pressures of the modern Atlantic trading system. And historiographically, plantation slavery intimately fed into America's capitalist transformation: it was part of the early rise of industry in America and it profoundly shaped the way in which a development strategy emerged from the 1870s onwards. A separation of plantation slavery from America's capitalism would, then, need to be based on a high degree of formalism in the categorization of social relations, which might logically enable a sense of distinctiveness in historical change but also require a substantial cleansing of the empirical details of history. Thus we will discuss plantation slavery while also making some distinctions concerning its relation to capitalist transformation.

American Developmentalism

In Chapter 5, we argued that Britain's industrialization was profoundly based on the imperial networks it forged throughout the Americas, India, China, and Africa. But we also made two points that calibrated the extent to which these myriad exploitations could explain Britain's transformation. In the first place, the capacity of Britain to coerce large swathes of the world to serve British capital was itself an outcome of this national economy's power, both militarily and commercially. In the second place, the inflow of cheap goods into the British economy did not just make a difference to the enrichment of government, mercantile capital, or workers in search of cheap staple goods. It also fed into Britain's already-established circuits of expanded accumulation. It was argued that empires generally draw in surpluses from the societies they conquer, but these extractions commonly generate enrichment rather than transformation. A close example in terms of European modernity would be the Iberian empires which shaped mercantile national economies (based on gold and silver and then slave-produced crops) that did little to transform agriculture or generate capitalist industrialization. In a nutshell, capitalist development requires at its heart an expanded accumulation that generates a mass wage labour force, out of which the specific dynamics for growth and increased productivity emerge, but in any historically concrete example, these dynamics are organically interconnected with a range of other social relations of production that often manifest through differentiated geographical space. *Mutatis mutandis*, one might consider the role of the slavery plantation system in a similar fashion: defined by its own dynamic and egregious social history, but for our purposes relevant especially in its interconnections to the development of a capitalist industrialization.

In this chapter, we shall explore the American case similarly to the British one. We will attempt to provide as detailed as possible a historic sketch of the political economy of capitalist transformation, picking out the themes that pertain to our developmentalism analytic framework: primitive accumulation, the nature of transformative accumulation, the combination of major-order issues of statehood with economic growth, and the extent to which a general improvement in material well-being was achieved. America's capitalist transformation discernibly commenced in the mid-1800s, and it did so through a political economy of northern industry and frontier expansion. If developmentalism requires a major-order political imperative that goes beyond the ambition to improve people's lives, for America it was nation-building.

Colonial America

The South

The colonization of America by England started through the Virginia Company in the early seventeenth century. As a private corporation chartered by the Crown, the company succeeded in little more than establishing a single settlement and killing nearby indigenous people. Initially, settlers under the company's remit were obligated to supply staple crops to the company.[3] It was taken over by the Crown in 1624, becoming a colony of the English state and was effectively contracted out to Lord Baltimore—a particularly vainglorious

[3] James Parisot, *How America Became Capitalist* (2019): 26.

example of the Jacobean patronage system. The Virginia Company established agricultural colonial settlements throughout the Chesapeake Bay. These settlements were initially based on a model of landlordism and tenancy, but this tenure system was undermined by the ability of farmers to establish their own farmsteads. The colonial state did not exercise the kind of political strength to compel farmers to adhere to tenancy. Those who established smallholdings were strongly aware of their release from the prevailing landlord tenancy relations prevailing in Britain, and this contradistinction served in part to infuse early settler cultures with ideals of autonomy and self-reliance.

As a Crown company, Virginia under Baltimore sought to generate revenues for the English state. It did this by introducing new strains of tobacco into areas where tobacco was indigenous but more bitter. Tobacco production by smallholders connected the colony to England: it was relatively cheap to produce and could be subjected to heavy taxes by the state. Throughout the seventeenth century, a class of tobacco plantation owners emerged, relying on indentured immigrant labour from Britain. The colony of Maryland[4] was chartered by the Crown for the purpose of expanding tobacco. By the end of the century, the demand for labour on tobacco plantations had outstripped the supply of indentured labour. A further colony to the south of the Chesapeake colonies—Carolina—used Caribbean money to establish plantations using slave labour. Carolina received investment from the British Caribbean planter class, exporting not only tobacco but also rice, cotton, and indigo. By the 1740s, South Carolina had twice as many enslaved black people as it did white planters and farmers.[5]

Throughout the period from the mid-1600s until 1865, planation slavery expanded constantly. In the colonial period, this was driven by planters who immigrated from Britain and the Caribbean and who fully settled in the South. Although backed by a colonial power, the plantation-owning class established a sub-regional hegemony:[6] the conditions of life for other classes were defined by the plantation; government was controlled by planters; and independent smallholders were connected to plantations which traded and processed the surpluses that those 'upcountry' smallholders produced. Each southern state had a well-specified 'slave code' that effectively legislated the right of slave owners, even to the degree of exonerating owners who killed

[4] Both Maryland and Carolina were also initially 'proprietary' colonies, effectively contracted out to British members of the aristocracy.

[5] Reynolds, *America. Empire of Liberty*: 28.

[6] Indeed, the drive to establish slavery plantations was, in the case of Georgia, pushed by planters and resisted by the British government.

their slaves. But it is important to note that the large-scale plantation owners were a minority within the slave-owning class. As a result, there was an exceptionally high concentration of wealth and power in a group of families that owned close to one hundred slaves or more.

Whether in the 'middle' or 'deep' South, slave labour was based on highly coercive labour regimes—mainly gang work enforced by overseers and 'drivers'. There is a wealth of historical material gleaned from slave narratives as well as commentary from plantation owners that relates the racialized violence exercised on slaves in the pursuit of constant disciplining and extraction of work. Slaves also constructed, cooked, cleared land, maintained drainage, worked processing machines, and portered. Enslaved women were subjected to the sexual violence of their owners.

Concentrated in the more remote areas around the southern Appalachians, independent smallholder farmers established freehold field systems based on mixed agriculture and family labour. The main commodities sold were animal skins and livestock.[7] These farmers were strongly oriented around self-provision but also sold, bought, and processed crops at plantation-controlled markets. Sporadically, this might have generated some credit relations between plantation owners and smallholders.

The North

Contrastingly, in the North, there was a far stronger drive to expand smallholder farming inland as far as the Great Lakes. Slave ownership and plantation agriculture was not prevalent.[8] Smallholders came *en masse* to the American North through transportation schemes managed by the colonies in which people either paid their travel and as a result received freehold rights to land, or had their transport paid and then committed themselves to indentured labour for a period (usually 7 years), after which they could move in search of land. The purchase of land for the latter often involved taking on debt from the North's network of local banks which issued their own paper money in a pre-dollar economy.

[7] Benjamin Marley, 'The Coal Crisis in Appalachia: Agrarian Transformation, Commodity Frontiers and the Geographies of Capital' (2016): 232.

[8] It is noteworthy that this did not connote a general hostility towards enslavement, far less a less racist culture. The agricultural–environmental conditions for plantation crops were not amenable in the North. But, generally, northern states permitted slavery and there were regular racist invectives and physical attacks on black people.

The North received a far larger number of immigrants and from more varied backgrounds, mainly through the port of New York. In the mid-1600s, New York state accommodated Dutch landlords who gleaned income from tenant farmers, generating a Dutch business class that survived the end of tenant farming. But, beyond this, Protestant English, Scottish, Irish, and Germans immigrated in pursuit of freer conditions for religious expression which they aimed to achieve by creating largely autonomous smallholding farming communities. On the eve of the War of Independence, the North had a population of about 1.5 million.[9]

For the bulk of the colonial period, settlement was scattered and focused on New England. Smallholdings were forged out of a constant clearance of forest and evacuation of indigenous peoples from the land. As Terence Byers notes, there was a cruel irony in Scottish settlers who took refuge from the Highland Clearances commandeering land from those who previously worked, moved through, and lived on it.[10] Into the eighteenth century, settlement took diverse forms. Colonial governments issued land grants, parcelling out land for household smallholding settlement. This was funded by government and colonial merchants, both of which wished to generate colonial agricultural outputs to fuel mercantile ambitions (and associated tax opportunities in a situation where no income or value added taxes existed). From the 1750s, land companies, funded by merchants, purchased tracts of land to parcel out to tenanted farmers, but this was not widespread. Additionally, settlers simply squatted on the land, aiming to stay on the land for long enough to establish a customary and then legal right to the land. This was done by individual households or organized communities.

By the end of the colonial period, these forms of clearance and settlement had remade the northern colonies as freehold agrarian smallholder colonies, socially diverse and expansive. Surpluses were regularly sold at local markets, in addition to artisanally produced cloth, leather, wood, and metalware. These goods were not traded internationally but served markets in northern towns and also the demands of plantation owners.

In summary, colonialism was underpinned by an imperial state that contracted settlement and the forging of new relations of production to clients of Crown patronage. Colonial settlements were patchwork and diverse. In the seventeenth century, settlements achieved a considerable degree of self-governance and, locked as they were into an Atlantic system dominated

[9] Reynolds, *America. Empire of Liberty*: 42.
[10] Terrence Byers, *Capitalism from Above and Capitalism from Below* (1996): 88.

by Britain, they were both sustained and limited by the British state. The Navigation Acts meant that the British government commissioned exclusively to British merchants the right to buy and sell tobacco, sugar, cotton, and so on. These British merchants also dominated the credit system which integrated many planters into the Atlantic mercantile system. Beyond the commissioning of authority to colonial states and the control of the Atlantic trade, the British state had very limited power, largely relying on the social and political dominance of the varied state elites which ensured that assemblies judged and ratified patterns of settlement. Force was exercised by militias and settler farmers were often armed and ready to protect their property from others. The further inland one went, the less stable even this process became. Regular British troops only arrived in America in 1754.[11]

The political economy of settlement agriculture came to be defined by three spatial patterns: a smallholder North with some slavery and tenancy, an expansive western frontier into which immigrants sought individual or communal autonomy, and a South in which slave plantations dominated over peripheral smallholding.[12] All of these changes were imposed upon the indigenous peoples of America. Each facet of colonization was centrally defined by efforts to displace, undermine, and kill indigenous people. This was the beginning of a primitive accumulation that could, by the mid-nineteenth century, and would reasonably be defined as a genocide. As is often the case within colonial settlement projects, sustained acts of aggression against incumbent peoples were represented as problems for *settler* security in which the resistance or mere presence of indigenous peoples was seen as a security threat. This political disposition underpinned a growing militarized and bonding colonial state project. During the Seven Years War—which was not simply a European war—this sense of insecurity at the borders was intensified as French–British military rivalry was played out through the co-option or destruction of indigenous American communities and the expansion of British colonial territories into the Great Lakes region. There was, then, a strong colonial state underpinning to settlement in which each state's army and militia constantly exercised violence to enforce the property claims of settlers at their expanding frontiers.

[11] Charles Post, *The American Road to Capitalism. Studies in Class Structure, Economic Development and Political Conflict 1620–1877* (2012): 465.

[12] This is a simplification. Any detailed study of American colonial development would make distinctions between New England, the middle states, midwestern frontier, and southern frontier zones. Nevertheless, the simplified distinction does capture the essential differentiations generated throughout the colonial period.

Independence *Ante Bellum*

The War of Independence emerged out of multiple causes. The highly extractive duty regime on exports, the restriction of export markets exclusively to Britain, and the imposition of a stamp duty each fed into a strong resentment that Britain was acting as an egregious external power. This was connected to ongoing complaints about a lack of representation of the Colonies in parliament,[13] and a diverse set of religious cultures that placed heavy emphasis on self-determination, localism, and a republican affirmation of non-domination. Also, the British government was intransigent in responding to the demands of colonial elites.

Independence created the conditions for the construction of a nation-state. Ratifying the constitution and defining the ways in which the federal state would tax, maintain a military, and legislate required constant, intense, and contentious political effort for the rest of the century. The War of Independence itself initiated political and economic changes that we see in other examples of capitalist development. The insurgent American state endeavoured to purchase greater amounts of crops from smallholders for the war effort—a productionist imperative generated through a security imperative.[14]

After independence, the federal government constantly faced security threats, each of which incentivized government to combine state-building, nation-building, and economic expansion. This imperative was driven not only by a concern with the actions of imperial Spain and France, but also in relation to the resistance of indigenous people and the fealty of its own westward-facing settlers. The newly independent American state existed in the midst of major internal and external insecurity. Its leaders perceived the American state as both decolonized and imperial[15] and, very much aware of the rise of European capitalist economies, it saw its national project as bound up with the prospects for capitalist development in America: 'not only the wealth but the independence and security of a country appear to be materially connected with the prosperity of manufactures'.[16]

Before the civil war, independence might be characterized as a period in which a national capitalist project was impossible because of the distinct

[13] It is important to note that the 'no taxation without representation' aphorism was articulated by a colonial elite that was engaged in British political matters. There was no desire within this elite to see a popular democratic revolution in America. For some 'founding fathers', democracy was seen as potentially disastrous.

[14] Post, *The American Road to Capitalism*: 476.

[15] Daniel Gaido, 'The American Path of Bourgeois Development' (2002).

[16] Alexander Hamilton, in Reynolds, *America. Empire of Liberty*: 86.

and in some degree conflicting political economies of North and South, and their projects of frontier expansion. As is well known, the thirteen states shared little beyond their desire to rid themselves of British over-rule. In both constitutional design and political practice there was a strong affirmation of state over federal government and no attempt to question slavery.[17] Indeed, the Congress barely functioned as a national government in the 1780s. It had an army and a loose collective leadership constructed out of the representation of states. It began its existence as a 'waterfront state', taxing commerce at the port cities but largely absent from the lives of ordinary people.[18] But, as the legislative, judicial, and executive machinery of the American state was constructed, salient characteristics of a national development strategy emerged. As it did so, strongly contrasting models of national development flourished in ways that generated such oppositions as to create the conditions for a civil war.

The Growing Plantation System

The slave plantation system did not look especially dynamic towards the end of the colonial period. In the late eighteenth century under British rule, plantation agriculture relied on a heavily taxed and fairly static demand for tobacco, indigo, rice, and smaller amounts of sugar and cotton. These served consumer markets in Britain and assisted Britain's current accounts vis à vis the rest of Europe through re-export. From the 1790s, plantation agriculture was re-energized, importing more Africans, expanding its territory, and most crucially developing the Deep South's cotton belt from Georgia through to Mississippi. Cotton came to be America's major export: up to 58 per cent of total export value.[19] The principal cause of this expansion was the powerful increase in demand for cotton from Britain which, from 1783, recognized American sovereignty and reconstructed close trading relations with it until the British–American War of 1812. The securing of cheap and regular cotton imports from America was pivotal to early British textile industrialization.

The expansion of plantation slavery through cotton was not simply the expansion of a colonial plantation system. It also involved significant changes

[17] The governing elite meticulously avoided bringing the 'negro question' into the sphere of public deliberation, no matter how much angst they expressed in private letters.

[18] Brian Balogh, *A Government out of Sight: The Mystery of National Authority in Nineteenth-Century America* (2009): 80.

[19] Gaido, 'The American Path of Bourgeois Development': 63.

in the techniques of production within the slavery regime. Cotton plantations were larger, incorporating larger numbers of slaves. There was an intensified and constantly coercive drive to produce more cotton. Gang work was organized and reorganized to expand cotton yields. The first mechanized separation of cotton from the seed in the boll came from the plantation system's need for faster production of clean unspun cotton. Gang work was set up with production targets and forms of competition between different gangs or task groups.[20] Structures of (meagre) reward and (visible) punishment for 'hard work' and 'laziness' were introduced.[21] From 1808 when the importation of Africans was banned, plantations increasingly reproduced their own slave populations, setting up family barracks with small plots of land. After the Louisiana Purchase of 1803, there was the possibility that westward expansion would lead to a massive growth in plantation slavery: by the time of the British–American War, large areas had been cleared of indigenous peoples in order to set up cotton plantations. New states from Georgia to Texas brought massive tracts of land under American sovereignty and also into the remit of the slavery plantation. Thus, after independence, the large-scale cotton plantation owners established a remarkable social, economic, cultural, and political dominance of southern states. The accumulation by dispossession of westwards expansion was accompanied by—and interlinked with—the primitive accumulation of absolute surplus value of enslaved black people, ultimately driven by the demand for cotton in Lancashire's textile mills.

There is a need to understand post-independence plantation slavery as both expansive and generative of considerable wealth for the plantocracy, but also as extremely limited in its developmental potential. We have focused on capitalist development as a historically unique expansion of accumulation, productivity, and innovation. It would be a stretch too far to characterize slave plantations with these properties. Within our framework, capitalist development derives from wage labour, competition, and a restless imperative to produce more and more diverse commodities. The plantation system most certainly accumulated wealth, but it did so through an 'absolute' extraction of work from slaves who were not paid and in no sense—even an ironic one—free. There was also most certainly a commercialization in plantation agriculture, but in a mercantile sense rather than one defined by the capital–labour relation. As a result, few commodities were produced in the South, there

[20] On the most technically sophisticated plantations, younger men would lead a series of task-specific gangs, enforcing an extreme productivity on others.

[21] The notions of work and laziness in the plantation South were heavily racialized.

was a stagnant consumer market, credit markets were extremely shallow, infrastructures were rudimentary,[22] and almost no industrial activity emerged off the back of surpluses accrued to plantation owners. Charles Post summarizes the contrast between plantation slavery and the developmental properties of capitalism excellently:

> By contrast, there is little evidence of gains in productivity through replacing labour with new and more complex tools and machinery, the increase in *relative* surplus labour extraction that typifies capitalist agriculture and industry. While capitalists continuously attempt to increase absolute surplus labour extraction by increasing and intensifying the pace of work (speed-up), it is relative surplus labour extraction through mechanization that distinguishes capitalism from all previous forms of social labour. The capitalists' ability to introduce, in a relatively continuous manner, labour-saving tools and machinery is the basis for capitalism's unique capacity to shift labour progressively from agriculture to manufacturing and services.[23]

This is not to say that plantation slavery was undynamic; it is rather that its dynamism was not driven by competitive accumulation within the social relations of wage labour. Plantation owners sought to organize slaves to produce more work,[24] and they aggressively expanded cotton production into the southern frontier. They also reorganized plantation work and the conditions of slaves after imports of slaves were banned.[25]

The Rise of a Northern Elite

After independence, in the North, smallholder farming continued to expand into the Midwest. Agriculture was largely based on household labour, mixed farming, some livestock, craft industry, and a basic set of assets such as a plough and a weaving machine. Although there was some differentiation

[22] River transport remained the main way to evacuate cotton throughout the ante-bellum period and even beyond.

[23] Charles Post, 'Plantation Slavery and Economic Development in the Antebellum Southern United States' (2003): 295. See also Byers, *Capitalism from Above and Capitalism from Below*: 238; Daniel Gaido, 'A Materialist Analysis of Slavery and Sharecropping in the Southern United States' (2000).

[24] Ralph Anderson and Robert Gallman, 'Slaves as Fixed Capital. Slave Labor and Southern Economic Development' (1977).

[25] Eugene D. Genovese and Elizabeth Fox-Genovese, 'The Slave Economies in Political Perspective' (1979): 19.

between farmers, there was no broad-ranging employment of farm hands, and crops and livestock products were sold as surplus rather than as dedicated cash crops.

Canal systems and turnpike roads were constructed, funded through joint-stock companies. Market towns connected farmers more closely and regularly to merchants who had their warehouses on the coast (and usually in New York City). The densening of market infrastructures in the North was accompanied and facilitated by a federal state that increasingly controlled access to land and formalized property rights. Smallholders found themselves having to purchase land and as a result were increasingly likely to take on loans or mortgages. The disruption brought about by the War of Independence and the spreading of debt into rural households compelled farms to dedicate more land and labour to selling cash crops to merchants for cash income. In short, independence created the political conditions for the 'capture' of smallholder farms by merchants and lenders.[26] By the 1840s, expansion into the Midwest, the introduction of new technologies, and the growth of a large-scale global market for wheat led to a sustained increase in output and productivity in northern agriculture. Between 1840 and 1860 agricultural output doubled in value.[27] New technologies for ploughing, harvesting, and threshing allowed large plots to be farmed with the same labour; European (and especially British) demand for wheat increased annually, creating buoyant prices; and farmers with enough capital or the wherewithal to take on debt[28] could set out larger farms in the Midwest. Northern agriculture might be characterized in this period as expansive, improving, but not highly differentiated with an emerging wage labour force. This condition was what allowed the Jeffersonian–Republican image of the autonomous and self-improving smallholder to persist.

Around New York and Boston, a merchant class emerged. This class generated its capital through international trade, some industry, and income from tenant farming. The northern capitalist class was closely connected to the federal state, and as the latter established the sinews of national government, its policies aspired to support this class. The clearest instantiation of this was the introduction of tariffs on imports—sometimes very high tariffs.[29]

[26] Post, *The American Road to Capitalism*.

[27] Bruce Levine et al., *Who Built America? Working People and the Nation's Economy, Politics, Culture, and Society, Volume 1* (1989): 222.

[28] Associately, this was a period in which literacy rates in the North diverged positively from the South.

[29] The Tariff Act (1816) imposed 20–25 per cent tariffs on manufactured goods. Walton and Rockoff, *History of the American Economy* (2014): 181.

The aim here was clearly to generate a protected market for nationally produced manufactures. The North's emerging manufacturing economy was based on the relatively simple processing of raw materials and low-capital-intensity investments such as textiles,[30] but also including a quite diverse bundle of other activities.[31] The government created the Bank of the United States in 1791 which served as a vehicle to pump money into industry through contracts and bonds. The government also established a gold–dollar link which ensured both stable international prices for trade and a secure investment environment for international capital.

As in the South, there was a constant drive to expand westwards. Here again, the national state played a crucial role as it commenced a massive cadastral survey of land, partitioning land into parcels that could be purchased individually or *en bloc*. This act was in effect a legalized means to dispossess indigenous people of access to land, coercively moving them further west or into reserved areas. From the 1810s, settler farmers themselves also asserted claims on land through claims clubs.[32] However, the state's effective presence at the frontier remained limited or even non-existent, and, in this context, groups of farmers set out property boundaries themselves which they protected from indigenous people and the instruments of the state. Commonly, this protean Lockean statehood worked to transform 'claims' into legalized property, although from roughly the 1840s onwards the state developed more systemic and effective ways of parcelling out land.

From the 1840s, the Midwest was settled and wheat agriculture consolidated itself. As with cotton, the wheat frontier was dynamized by increasing demand in Britain,[33] a result of industrialization and also the Great Famine which led to a precipitous decline in wheat imports from Ireland. Some mechanization of reaping and threshing was also present but not widespread. A little later, the Great Plains were commandeered for cattle ranching—the source of the emergence of massive cheap beef markets in Chicago.[34]

The frontier became a *leitmotif* of America's national ideology, an ideology propounded by the political elite. The government used its military and militias to enforce the expansion, but, in practice, frontier expansion was as

[30] Douglas North, *The Economic Growth of the United States 1790–1860* (1966): 159–61.
[31] Francois Weil, 'Capitalism and Industrialization in New England, 1815–1845' (1998).
[32] Ilia Murtazashvili, *The Political Economy of the American Frontier* (2013).
[33] Also relevant in terms of changing demands for imports from the Americas, in the early eighteenth century, the first slave-produced mass consumer item in Britain, sugar, became the focus of abolitionist campaigning.
[34] Joshua Specht, *Red Meat Republic. A Hoof-to-Table History of How Beef Changed America*: Chapter 1.

chaotic as it was ordered. And it was consistently extremely violent. Furthermore, it was not only focused on farmstead construction. There was also the exploitation of natural resources, first timber and, especially from the 1840s, gold. Both the commercialization of timber and gold also generated claims clubs.[35] But, in regards to gold, there was a more speculative, violent, and unstable expansion westwards.[36]

The value of land rose around rivers and lines of rail, both of which became the focus of speculation as northern coastal elites (industrial and mercantile) purchased land in expectation that leasing or parcelling out for sale would generate income. By 1848, the American military had supported American settler encroachment into extensive parts of Mexico, going to war to attain Texas and forcing Mexico into an agreement to relinquish its north American seaboard in the Treaty of Guadeloupe Hidalgo. Through a combination of settler militia violence and an increasingly strong-armed national army, the American government expanded from its original thirteen states to a continent-wide dominion, even if much of the space to the west of the Rockies was yet to be effectively occupied. The project to expand the American frontier westwards was centrally motivated by a desire to construct a large national market—not only for American manufactures but also for investment in infrastructure. Expansion was driven by capital in search of property, bounty, and speculative profits. Combinations of investors gained contracts from government to construct railways to the Pacific Coast. These were political projects dedicated to the construction of a single continental national economy.

America's independence was defined by a project of nation-building. But because of the high levels of autonomy by the original thirteen states and the fragility of federal state power, considerable political autonomy and difference remained. Nation-building aspirations were expressed through the expansion of the westwards frontier, something that the British colonial power had always been more cautious about. However, this expansion did not escape the structural differences between North and South as slave states expanded towards Texas and homestead farming expanded into the Midwest. Two economically incompatible models of America from the Atlantic to the Pacific had emerged[37]—one that could only continue to grow if it expanded its essentially non-dynamic plantation economy, and one that saw the frontier as a

[35] Murtazashvili, *The Political Economy of the American Frontier*.

[36] Clifford Trafzer and Joel Hyer, *Exterminate Them: Written Accounts of the Murder, Rape, and Enslavement of Native Americans During the California Goldrush* (1999).

[37] The northern states had ended slavery by 1804. Hugh Brogan, *The Penguin History of the USA* (1999): 280.

means to generate a market economy of smallholder agriculture integrated into a nation-state with a mercantile elite and emerging industrial class. It was this incompatibility that underpinned the civil war. The federal state's power had grown over independence, increasing southern concerns about their own state autonomy. And a stronger abolitionist politics had emerged in the North, although this was by no means dominant.[38] The first half of the nineteenth century had come to be defined by the desire for unalloyed economic growth: average incomes doubled over this period and GNP doubled every 15 years.[39] But the distinct regional political economies of North and South posed different modes of frontier conquest and statehood.

Civil War and Post-Bellum Reconstruction

Civil War

The civil war's outcome was in part driven by the ability of the North to purpose its agriculture and industry to the war effort. The increasing commercialization of smallholder agriculture, the relatively dense market infrastructure, and the existence of a government that could co-ordinate and enforce the war effort ensured that soldiers were provisioned and armed better than the Confederate army. In the North there was—as is often the case at some point during capitalist development—a military Keynesianism. The national government grew to become the largest employer in the Union.[40] It also repurposed as a war-making state: contracting firms to manufacture ships, materiel, and railways for the Union army. Individual farmers and 'sewing women' were tasked with supplying crops and clothing, respectively, to the army through government purchases. It was war demand that generated the rise of the meat-packing industry.[41] Pork and grain wholesale markets were generated through the war effort.[42] Mustering an army depleted the supply of labour in agriculture, which intensified the adoption of labour-saving machinery. The loss of male labour to the war and the expansion of production brought increasing numbers of women into wage labour. Especially after

[38] Slavery remained in the North, but not on the plantations, and Lincoln did not declare the war's aim as abolishing slavery.

[39] James McPherson, *Battle Cry of Freedom. The Civil War Era* (1988): 7, 10.

[40] Some historians characterize the state during this period as a rising 'Yankee Leviathan'. Richard Bensel, *Yankee Leviathan: The Origins of Central State Authority in America, 1859–1877* (2008).

[41] Eric Foner, *Reconstruction. America's Unfinished Revolution 1863–1877* (1988): 18.

[42] Richard Bensel, *The Political Economy of American Industrialisation 1877–1900* (2000).

1863, the North's economy grew, industry and agriculture displayed considerable dynamism, and the balance of the war moved consistently in the North's favour. By this time, there were already 1.3 million industrial workers in the North.[43]

In the South, the horrors of the slave plantation became impossible to maintain as the war continued. Slaves left plantations and headed north or simply away from the plantation.[44] After 1863, former slaves joined the Union army. The quotidian violence and brutalization that sustained plantation society was substantially weakened. The war effort left the Confederate states and plantations with debt, very unstable social relations of labour, and substantial damage to urban buildings. Once the Union army occupied areas around the Mississippi, the core of the plantation economy was lost to the Confederacy.

We have argued that the war was driven very centrally by a contestation concerning the development of the frontier and the remit of the national state.[45] From this perspective, the ending of the war was nothing so much as a reconciliation of a single future direction which itself had to be put into practice: an integrated national development strategy, increasingly dominated by a national state, in which the frontier would be consolidated through the tandem processes of commercialized smallholder farming and the relentless dispossession of indigenous peoples (forcing them into reservations and/or social death). It was, then, a boon to the North, although to represent 'the North' as a single constituency with a single ideology would be to oversimplify. It was, most profoundly, a victory for the American state which ended the war with a national military and a massively expanded federal budget.[46] Thus, we will proceed to highlight how America's political economy after the war was defined by intensified pre-bellum trends, considerable change in the South, and a remarkably intense capitalist transition—one that left America as the world's leading industrial capitalist nation by the end of the century.

The Rise of Agrarian Capitalism

In the North, after the war, smallholder agriculture was fully 'captured' by commercial markets and the state. Within long-settled areas, farms regularly

[43] Levine et al., *Who Built America? Vol 1*: 440.

[44] On this, see especially John Franklin and Loren Schweninger, *Runaway Slaves. Rebels on the Plantation* (1999). The migration exploded after Lincoln's Emancipation proclamation in 1863.

[45] It is worth noting again that this is not to say that slavery was unimportant but rather that the origins of the civil war were not oriented around slavery and its abolition.

[46] Foner, *Reconstruction*: 23.

provided cash crops for merchants, took up mortgages, abandoned their diverse labour practices in order to specialize, and progressively tended to purchase farm implements and consumer goods. Outside of the frequent economic crises of this period, farming households became more productive, generated more commercialized outputs, and bought more goods. From the 1850s, America's growing and increasingly productive agriculture generated major export revenues which, after the civil war, helped balance a current account that was defined by a massive influx of indirect foreign capital through bond issues in London.[47] Between 1870 and 1900, wheat production doubled and the number of cattle nearly tripled.[48]

After the war, the question of the frontier was settled in favour of continued smallholder expansion. As a result, the federal state parcelled out land through the Homestead Act: 160 acres of free land to anyone who could work it. Between 1862 and 1913, the government granted 2.5 million homestead claims.[49] More land went into cultivation in the thirty years after the end of the civil war than had done in the 250 years before.[50] Throughout the American prairies west of the Mississippi, a 'second empire' emerged in which ranching and wheat prevailed. This homestead-driven expansion was in practice riven with sharp practices: land speculators would use individual homesteaders (always men) to purchase blocks of land that would then be sold to speculators and resold to larger commercial ranchers and farmers. In the final third of the nineteenth century, the massive expansion of railway abetted settlement as rail companies (who were concessioned land along the line of rail by the government)[51] sold off parcels to settlers and developers. The availability of land for settlement continued to attenuate differentiation within agriculture and also to make shortages of labour a constant concern for capital. Nevertheless, in densely populated agricultural areas, considerable investment was put into machinery as well as new chemical fertilizer products, and as land became more expensive in 'core' agricultural areas, tenancy became more common.

Although the frontier was 'closed' by the end of the 1840s, the full continental space of America was only fully surveyed, settled, and committed to clear property rights by the end of the century. At this point, American

[47] Thomas Cochran and William Miller, *The Age of Enterprise. A Social History of Industrial America* (1949): 137.

[48] Reynolds, *America. Empire of Liberty*: 261.

[49] David Gordon, *The Rise and Fall of American Growth* (2016): 261.

[50] Eric Foner, *Give Me Liberty. An American History, Vol 2* (2012): 485.

[51] Over a hundred million acres of cheap land. Murtazashvili, *The Political Economy of the American Frontier*: 72.

agriculture was universally defined by private property farmsteads, either bought outright or mortgaged. Farms were intensively integrated into commercial networks which facilitated both the sale of cash crops and the purchase of a large basket of consumer goods and capital goods such as machinery and chemicals. The commercialization of farming also generated regional specialization as farmsteads ceased their auto-provisioning strategies and identified the most productive crops for sale. This shift in the last quarter of the century was crucially supported by mass transit rail lines which made it cost effective to move agricultural produce throughout the country. Nevertheless, it is important to note, agriculture was by-and-large defined by the social relations of the farmstead: labour and resource management relied on family labour even if considerably enhanced by machinery.

Reconstruction

Thus, the post-civil war period witnessed an intensification and expansion of commercial homestead agriculture. But the major agrarian question facing the post-bellum government was how to manage the transition away from the slavery plantation. The Reconstruction period (1965–1977) aimed to assert federal government authority and to restabilize the agrarian South. We should note the following salient features of Reconstruction. Most importantly, there was no widespread and systemic reallocation of plantation property. Former slaveholders became plantation owners.[52] Formerly enslaved workers faced difficult choices, one of which was to continue to work on the plantations where they were formerly slaves, but now as wage labourers. Understandably this was unpopular, but there was no concerted state project to provide any restitution to former slaves. Plantation owners attempted to re-impose the same working conditions on their wage labour by pushing up the hours of work, keeping back wages, and attempting to integrate 'paternalistic' conditions into work contracts. Ex-slaves often preferred to seek independent means of livelihood in order to ensure that 'freedom' had enduring social meaning. For some, this was achieved by moving and settling elsewhere, but more commonly black families took up farming on plantations with

[52] The ratification of plantation property was part of a broader politics of racially oriented reconciliation in which white planters and politicians declared themselves pro-Union and the federal government sought political allies in a South it had previously been at war with. The result was a pervasive and continued racial hierarchy in all aspects of social life, perhaps best encompassed in the Jim Crow laws and the rise of the Ku Klux Klan.

smallholder allotments as sharecroppers: access to the land was exchanged for the provision of a share of the crop to the landowner. As a result, Reconstruction became a moderate adjustment for the agrarian South: plantations remained, ex-slaves often ended up either working for or tenanted to plantation owners, and the government made no effort to recompense ex-slaves or implement property relations that would enable a substantive social freedom for them.[53] State power remained in the hands of the plantocracy. It is also important to bear in mind that not all whites in the South were wealthy slave-owners. Two-thirds of whites did not own slaves[54] and most were poor underemployed farmers.[55]

Slowly, the South and North became integrated into a national economy. We have noted the emergence of manufacturing industry in the northeast from the 1940s, based mainly on workshopping and textiles. As noted at the beginning of this section on 'Civil War and Post-Bellum Reconstruction', the war had generated a government-driven scaling up of the production of staple commodities such as foodstuffs, textiles, and shoes. After the war, industry continued to grow and it did so through various means which we can only sketch here. The commercialization of agriculture was crucially focused on the repurposing of agriculture towards industry not export. Cotton production recovered in the South,[56] and it focused increasingly on domestic supply rather than Atlantic trade. Northern capital flowed into the South and a relatively modest industrialization occurred, mainly in textiles.[57] There also emerged a sheep farming sector in the North that supplied woollens for cloth manufacture when cotton output was destabilized. Increasingly cheap and plentiful foods fed into the expansion of foodstuff manufacturers. The increasing productivity, expansion, and commercialization of smallholder agriculture generated a large market for manufactures, a market protected by government tariffs and the 'natural tariff' of the Atlantic Ocean.[58] The expansion of the railways drew capital unevenly into the newly forged national market. From the 1840s, the American government imposed tariffs on imports. After the civil war, the purpose of tariffs shifted from 'waterfront'

[53] The most extreme example of this continuity is the use of black prison labour on plantations, which was effectively indenture.

[54] Howard Zinn, *A People's History of the United States* (2015): 236.

[55] On the historic origins of this class, see Kerry Merritt, *Masterless Men: Poor Whites and Slavery in the Antebellum South* (2017).

[56] Zinn, *A People's History of the United States*: 88.

[57] Foner, *Reconstruction*: 391.

[58] The use of faster metal steamships, the telegraph, and a general increase in oceanic traffic significantly reduced the costs of trade from the 1950s onwards, generating price convergence and responsiveness between America and Europe.

revenue-raising purposes towards support for industry and the consolidation of a national market. The demand for increases in tariffs often came from business, and it directly related to the competition faced by the flourishing industrial capitalisms of Europe.

After Reconstruction (1880–1920s)

National Development

In the period after Reconstruction, the industrial sector became increasingly concentrated in large and networked businesses. These businesses benefitted from the considerable economies of scale that derived from having a protected and well-integrated expanding national market. They developed what would now be called supply chains which connected them to major agricultural and resource regions. They often emerged having benefitted from government support, and they were not shy to use graft and covert deals to carve out markets and contracts. They also colluded in various ways to dominate and manage markets, most (in)famously through trusts or other more or less formalized agreements. The late 1800s witnessed the rise of the American corporations that would, in the next century, become the largest concentrations of capital in the world.[59] The base of the large-scale industrial sector was very clearly an expression of America's expansive and colonizing project: coal, timber, railways, meat packing, and then oil all connected to the purloining of land and natural resources, not simply in a westward expansion but also through spikes of interest in more specific zones within.

Industrialization during this 'second revolution' witnessed a shift away from textiles and agricultural produce towards machine manufacture, construction, infrastructure (especially rail), and into the twentieth century mass commodity production on an unprecedented scale. This system was based on the vertically and horizontally integrated corporations that emerged in the late 1800s in steel, oil, tobacco, and processed foods. The use of coal and then oil in production processes that were continuous and organized through scientific management generated a national capitalism in which increasingly differentiated labour forces served the 'continuous flow' machinery to

[59] Seen in an American context, the rise of the American corporation has always been an image of national esteem and concern, the latter provoked by the oligopolistic nature of corporations. Throughout American political history there has, as a result, remained a virulent anti-corporation ideology on the libertarian Right.

assemble, disassemble,[60] and package commodities for a mass market and into the twentieth century increasingly for export. There was—as there was in Britain and in other cases later—a virulent wave of innovation. This was not only about new inventions but more importantly about inventiveness, adaptation, and the application of technologies to production.[61]

Industrialization benefitted from a continental market and a productive and commercialized smallholder agriculture. It also enjoyed the benefits of a constant influx of cheap labour and the maintenance of tariffs. These tariffs were designed to protect local manufacturing through impositions on imported consumer goods but not capital goods.[62] Labour scarcity was a constant issue for capital in America. The homestead frontier removed the strong compulsion to sell one's labour for wages, and the pool of labour was in any case relatively small. Throughout this period, about 20 per cent of wage workers were women.[63] As a result, labour supply was strongly influenced by the ingress of labour from Europe and China.

The full-blooded ascendance of capital in post-Reconstruction America was vitally a product of a consolidating national government forging an alliance with business through a strategy of national development. Indeed, the core political imperative of the American state in this period was to realize a 'development vision'.[64] From the 1840s, consolidated through war, and fully fledged after Reconstruction, a set of policies emerge that can be understood collectively as a development strategy based on promoting the ascendance of capital. We can set these core policy areas out.

The government directly supported some businesses that were considered strategically important. The railway network was supported through bond issues and land concessions which effectively gave the railway companies land and capital to underpin their own investments. The federal government gave land concessions to rail companies to sell, and it issued government bonds to rail companies that it could also sell on. In some states, rail companies were paid by mile of track laid, leading to a 'rail rush' in which companies would lay down shoddy track as fast as possible in search of income. Rail companies were also financed through investments from East Coast capital and Europe, based on the expectation that revenues from the railways would be high and

[60] This is the rather dark term used to describe the industrial manufacture of meat from animal corpses.
[61] Cochran and Miller, *The Age of Enterprise*: 181.
[62] Peter Lindert and Jeffrey Williamson, *Unequal Gains. American Growth and Inequality Since 1700* (2016): 170.
[63] David Kennedy, *The American People in the Great Depression: Freedom from Fear* (1999): 27.
[64] Balogh, *A Government out of Sight*.

steady. From the end of the civil war up to 1893, 150,000 miles of track had been paid.[65] As a result, by the 1860s, transport costs had been halved compared with the beginning of the century.[66]

Railway expansion created the physical infrastructure for a national economy and the Supreme Court created the legal infrastructure for it. The Supreme Court was one of the busiest bodies of the state in the final third of the nineteenth century, addressing a raft of specific cases in which state assemblies established differential treatment within their territories and the Supreme Court judged whether these differentiations were unconstitutional. The constitution served as a point of reference to render it illegal to stymie the flow of goods and capital between states.

In the late 1800s, the federal government tried to create a national currency out of a dollar whose value depended on the price of silver and gold and the extent to which state banks issued their own currency. In 1879—for the first time after the war—the government created a single national dollar in paper connected to the gold standard. This had two major effects. In the first place, it stabilized a single currency as a means to deepen capital markets. Investors and creditors could be assured that large and unpredictable changes in currency value would be controlled. Second, it encouraged foreign direct investment into America's large and rapidly growing national economy. This was the period in which the Sterling Gold Standard was strongly ensconced in the international system. The Federal Reserve System was created in 1913 as a single board that managed twelve reserve banks,[67] which would manage the creation of currency, its relations to reserves, and the maintenance of national banking standards.

In sum, the post-civil war government persistently and systemically pursued a national development strategy with the core aim of creating an integrated single nation. Capitalism and nationalism were profoundly integrated. Of course, a great deal of debate coursed through the political elite throughout this period, but there was also a stable core coalition around the Republicans and business that supported the central aspects of the development strategy set out above. Indeed—and again to use a contemporary phrase—there was a strong political settlement around the American development vision.[68]

[65] Cochran and Miller, *The Age of Enterprise*: 131.
[66] McPherson, *Battle Cry of Freedom*: 12.
[67] Walton and Rockoff, *History of the American Economy*: 359.
[68] Bensel, *The Political Economy of American Industrialisation.*

But, of course, policy is not politics. The ascendance of capital was replete with corruption, secret deals, fraud, and venal speculation.[69] The rise of a systemic corruption—one that was in some degree innate to governance rather than singular and exceptional—can be found in the war economy,[70] but corrupt practices most certainly did not fall away after the instabilities of war. There are many examples of this. The railway companies gained concessions of land along the lines of rail that were subject to immense speculative attention. Land companies would buy up 'rail land' either directly or through proxies, then sell to smallholders. In general, when there were spikes of land grabbing[71] in the frontier, speculation would be rife. In the post-bellum South, northern businesses moved in to acquire assets at low prices before selling on or moving on to other opportunities, a practice that was not illegal but was generally seen as immoral, as one can see from the caricatures of 'carpetbaggers' in the 1860s. Larger businesses readily exercised political pressure to gain favour, made secret deals, and constantly attempted to control markets, giving us another pejorative: the robber baron.[72]

And, again, it is important to note that the consolidation of a national military and a nationally controlled militia enabled the final destruction of the indigenous peoples of America: fully settled in reserves or socially traumatized into the margins of American citizenship. As capital ascended after the civil war, it also gave immense effort to the exploitation of natural resources in a way that was largely unregulated. Great swathes of forest were cut for timber and mountainsides blasted in search of coal.

Commonwealth

New Mobilizations

The post-Reconstruction period was one in which capitalist transformation was prosecuted forcibly, leading to a sustained period of economic growth,

[69] For brevity of exposition, we shall generally gloss these practices as 'corruption' unless there is a need to be specific.

[70] Cochran and Miller, *The Age of Enterprise*: 118.

[71] The alienation of land to freehold homesteading did not occur smoothly but rather in concentrated spikes of speculative activity, a process sometimes described as a land rush.

[72] See especially Matthew Josephson, *The Robber Barons: The Great American Capitalists, 1861–1901*(1962) who captures the criminal and progressive nature of industrial magnates, and Zinn, *A People's History of the United States*: Chapter 11. In keeping with all instances of what would now be called 'grand corruption', robber barons flourished because of rather than in spite of state regulation. See Richard White, 'Information, Markets, and Corruption: Transcontinental Railroads in the Gilded Age' (2003).

rising productivity, increasing wage labour, the emergence of new industries, and a gradual decline in the importance of agriculture. Technological sophistication increased, work intensified, and governance became squarely focused on the management and support of a capitalist political economy. Amid all of this, benefits to labour and the poor more generally were extremely limited. Although income inequality did not rise, nor did it fall significantly.[73] Wage labour was characterized by insecurity, physical danger, and overwork. By 1864, 200,000 workers were unionized—although much labour organization was racially and ethnically exclusive. In the 1880s, the Knights of Labor organized strikes and public assemblies, and sought members throughout the industrial labour force. In 1886, mass demonstrations at Haymarket Square, Chicago created the impetus for demands on limits to the working day. In 1877, there was a 'great uprising' in which unions throughout the country protested the austerity effects of the economic crisis of 1873.[74] In the 1890s, the People's Party (or Populists) generated a policy platform based on economic equality, support for indebted rural farmers, and workers' rights.[75] And all of this mobilization was articulated to the sense that the American economy was growing and transforming and therefore greater rewards were due to labour.[76]

In these crucial respects, we can see how America's capitalist transformation was analogous to Britain's: creating the conditions of possibility for the construction of a commonwealth in which people's material lives are generally improved. As with Britain and indeed all of our case studies, there are three cardinal facets to an investigation of the extent to which a commonwealth is realized through capitalist transformation: the ability of capital and state to endure crisis; the extent to which expanding accumulation is contested by labour in order to secure benefits; and the degree to which the state acquires revenues from expanded accumulation in the pursuit of social provision. We shall look at each in turn, focusing broadly on the post-Reconstruction period.

Crisis

It is difficult to identify a more violent, unstable, and crisis-prone capitalist transformation than America's. Indeed, it is tempting to see the entire

[73] Lindert and Williamson, *Unequal Gains*: 173.

[74] Roy Rosenzweig et al., *Who Built America? Working People and the Nation's History, Volume 2* (2008): 18.

[75] The justice narrative developed by the Populists is encapsulated in a speech quoted in Zinn, *A People's History of the United States*: 288.

[76] Rosanne Currarino, 'The Politics of "More": The Labor Question and the Idea of Economic Liberty in Industrial America' (2006).

transformation period from the 1880s until the 1920s as one long boom and bust. There were crises, 'panics', and depressions in 1873, 1884, 1890, and 1894.[77] Between each downswing were periods of 'rush' and 'boom' in which speculation was rife. This was most strongly present in the 'Roaring Twenties', a period that ended with the dustbowl[78] and the Great Depression.

The causes of crisis were manifold, but might be characterized as different expressions of a rapidly expanding capitalism within a governmental regime of unstable and weak regulation. The rise of large consolidated companies, commanding extremely large amounts of capital from investment banks, with heavily overlapping networks of management and ownership between banks, rail, and manufacturing meant that any failure within this loose consortium could generate systemic exposure and vulnerability. In 1893, the failure of the National Cordage company created a stock market panic that led to a drying up of finance and the closure of around 500 state banks and 16,000 companies. Subsequently, small branch railway companies closed, undermining provincial companies that had relied on branch lines for their marketing.[79] The American government did not have the motivation or wherewithal to make systemic interventions to moderate any of the post-Reconstruction crises. The ideology of the self-correcting market and the dangers of state intervention were still powerful.

Crisis periods generally intensified throughout this period, and because people's well-being was concurrently becoming increasingly interlinked with capitalist growth, the social effects of crisis also intensified.[80] During the 1894 crisis, unemployment increased to 9 per cent and only went back to pre-crisis levels in 1901.[81] Although there were crises before the late 1800s,[82] it was broadly possible for most people to rely on the relative autonomy of the homestead in order to cope with downturns in industry and finance. As industrial capitalism generated larger proportions of wage labourers, crisis created a kind of unemployment in which people were more drastically impoverished and malnourished, and in which the social dynamics of that crisis focus squarely on the capital–labour relation. Cutting wages, intensifying work,[83] and laying people off who are urbanized and entirely dependent on

[77] So consistently unstable was the American economy that different economic historians have different accounts of when they began and ended. This account is taken from Walton and Rockoff, *History of the American Economy*: 356.

[78] Timothy Egan, *The Worst Hard Time* (2006).

[79] Rosenzweig et al., *Who Built America? Vol 2*: 126.

[80] Rosenzweig et al., *Who Built America? Vol 2*: 127.

[81] Until the 1930s, this period was known as the Great Depression.

[82] In 1819, 1837, and 1857.

[83] From the late 1800s, larger factories introduced 'flow' production which used conveyor belts to maintain constant and high rates of work. Walton and Rockoff, *History of the American Economy*: 176–7.

wage income meant that crisis was thoroughly 'capitalist'—as a contestation around the justice in the allocation of hardship within the capital–labour relation. The word 'tramp' emerged from the unemployment and poverty created by the economic crises of the 1870s and 1890s.[84] This was the period in which labour organizations mobilized against unemployment and increasingly severe working conditions. By the 1890s, labour organizations across workplaces were created that also engaged with issues of governance and policy—especially oligarchy in business. It became possible to discuss the need to secure standards or work and employment and the possibility that the government might have a role in balancing the interests of workers and business.

Capitalist Transformation and Material Well-being

As with Britain, sustained (and unstable) capitalist growth generated weak and delayed improvements to people's well-being. But bring them it did, albeit slowly from the 1880s to the 1920s. Generally, people's diet improved as a result of increased food production, storage (especially caning and refrigeration), and processing.[85] Death rates began a long decline from the 1870s, associated with gradual improvements in water supply, sanitation, and later electrification.[86] Real wages rose by 25 per cent between 1922 and 1929.[87] From 1900, life expectancy increased and the length of the working week decreased[88] and income per capita had overtaken Britain's.[89] By the end of the 1920s, half of all Americans owned a car,[90] 68 per cent of households had home lighting, 51 per cent indoor flush toilets, and 42 per cent central heating.[91] In every aspect of these metrics of progress, there persisted radical differences between white and black Americans.[92]

These broad indicators demonstrate a general material improvement in the majority of people's lives from the late nineteenth century. These improvements were the outcome of the interplay between the mobilizations of workers, the political dynamics of government, and the surplus generated by capital. It was the campaigns of labour that put pressure: to reduce the average number of

[84] Foner, *Give Me Liberty*: 483.
[85] Gordon, *The Rise and Fall of American Growth*: Chapter 3.
[86] Walton and Rockoff, *History of the American Economy*: 323.
[87] Foner, *Give Me Liberty*: 483, 614.
[88] Gordon, *The Rise and Fall of American Growth*: 248, Rosenzweig et al., *Who Built America? Vol 2*: 207.
[89] Lindert and Williamson, *Unequal Gains*: 171.
[90] Foner, *Give Me Liberty*: 613.
[91] Walton and Rockoff, *History of the American Economy*: 400.
[92] For example, see Walton and Rockoff, *History of the American Economy*: 321.

hours worked per week; to legislate some security for workers injured during work; and to reduce the extent of child labour.

It is important to recall here a recurring theme of the chapter which is the ongoing presence of structured inequalities between 'European' Americans, the descendants of African slaves, and indigenous peoples. Labour movements often considered workers' rights in racialized or ethnicized fashion, and employers commonly enforced informal colour lines in either employment or the allocation of different jobs.

Welfare Provision

If we take the middle of the nineteenth century as a period in which capitalism ascended, increasingly embedded in industry and asserting intensified controls over agriculture, then we should note that the federal state made very little effort to set up an infrastructure of social provision. Although we have seen that, post-bellum, the federal state made considerable efforts to construct an integrated and open national market and to construct a regime of protection, patronage, and coercion in order to allow capital's ascendance, we cannot identify anything like a public welfare project.[93] From mid-century until the early 1900s, social support was focused on groups who were portrayed as exceptionally vulnerable and the paltry support that they received was delivered through private voluntary organizations or small-scale state-based projects. Private voluntary organizations resembled those that emerged in Britain (and especially London) in the preceding 50 years: middle-class, paternalistic, sourced from Christian philanthropy, and as keen to reform the poor as help them. Compared to Britain, there was less vexation around the moral–utilitarian boundary between the deserving and undeserving poor. The assumption that poverty was the lot of those who had not worked or had a moral weakness that was their own business was more pervasive. Social support was focused on children and single mothers—categories more easily identified as morally deserving and also as exceptional. The notion of exception was important because it ensured that the transformation that America was undergoing was not understood as in any way systemically generating mass privations, but rather groups of highly distressed women and children

[93] After the war, pensions for veterans took a considerable chunk of government expenditure (up to 37 per cent), to the extent that some have called this America's first welfare state. But this social support was neither universal nor based on some measure of need/poverty.

who had been met with the human tragedy of losing a husband. Everyone else justifiably owned their poverty. In any case, the social support offered by private voluntary organizations was scanty and unco-ordinated. It relied on the beneficence of the relatively wealthy. In no way could it be seen as a universal 'safety net' even for specific 'tragic' groups. The efforts of private voluntary organizations were more dedicated to instruction and correction than the transfer of resources. And some of the larger organizations were vehicles for the emerging industrial class to demonstrate their philanthropy as they bribed, broke unions, and squeezed surplus for their workers. For larger businesses, the provision of social welfare was also a means to ensure industrial peace.[94]

As private voluntary organizations expanded, greater efforts were made to portray them as a 'sector' that did 'social work' rather than as an amalgam of separate organizations. The template of the Charity Organization Society (COS) (see Chapter 5) in Britain served as the inspiration through which COSs were formed in America.[95] As with the British COS, the American COSs articulated a social project in which charity became a strategy to discipline groups of poor and to correct what were seen as social delinquencies. There was, as mentioned earlier, a stronger sense in America that providing resources to the poor and desperate would generate 'dependency' which would undermine the virtues of the free making of the self which is still so clearly at the heart of American national ideology.[96] But in any case, social provision was paltry and localized.[97] It was only in the final years of the century that discussions around mass poverty and the nature of capitalist transformation emerged. This was provoked by the 1894 economic crisis mentioned in the section 'Crisis' which generated mass unemployment and protest. These events made it difficult to cleave to 'a failure of the individual' premise in which social provision should be minimal and accompanied by disciplinary correction.

Into the twentieth century, the federal government gradually shifted towards a politics of universal provision and an acceptance that poverty was social. The ground shifted in part because of the obvious public health problems in America's expanding cities and the protests of workers against

[94] Gerald Zahavi, 'Negotiated Loyalty: Welfare Capitalism and the Shoeworkers of Endicott Johnson, 1920–1940' (1983).

[95] Walter Trattner, *From Poor Law to Welfare State. A History of Social Welfare in the United States* (1989): Chapter 5.

[96] 'Nature's remedy: work or starve.' In Trattner, *From Poor Law to Welfare State*: 89.

[97] Jacob Hacker and Paul Pierson, 'Business Power and Social Policy: Employers and the Formation of the American Welfare State' (2002).

severe hardship. It was also constructed through White House-funded research which effectively created the intellectual base for 'social work' in its modern sense.[98] Although perceived in terms of universal provision to address systemic problems, social provision was focused on children and single mothers as specific 'safety net' groups that needed exceptional help.[99] It was only from the 1910s that labour unions and some politicians argued that labour itself required social support. Between 1910 and 1920, forty-three states implemented some form of workers' compensation.[100] Workers' compensation was legislature that compelled companies to contribute to an insurance scheme that would pay out if workers were injured through work. In those states that implemented workers' compensation there was commonly support from larger businesses that saw a government-supported regularization of the protest and legal actions from workers after injury as disruptive to business.[101]

Throughout the late 1800s, American capitalist transformation generated little social protection and—as is well understood—compared unfavourably with European welfare regimes during the same period. There was no (near) universal social protection in terms of healthcare, unemployment, or pensions. Patchy state projects were accompanied by patchy private organizations, both of which feared that social support would disincentivize work and create moral turpitude.

During the Great Depression and the 'dustbowl' agrarian crisis, government was effectively compelled to expand into social provision by the drastic increase in poverty and joblessness and the social disillusion and political protest that this generated. Under President Truman, a series of temporary but country-wide mass assistance programmes were rolled out to provide support for the unemployed. These schemes relied on cofunding by state governments and took various forms: cash transfers, food redistribution, and paid public work. Although these measures have been seen as progressive and to some degree radical, they barely dealt with the deep mass unemployment of the Great Depression, nor did they amount to anything more than measures to deal with a specific and major crisis. Indeed, the language of social

[98] Trattner, *From Poor Law to Welfare State*: 217 *et seq*.

[99] Social provision is always gendered. The heavily gendered nature of America's protean social support is termed 'maternalism' by Theda Skocpol, *Protecting Soldiers and Mothers: Political Origins of Social Policy in the United States* (1995).

[100] Previously, workers had to sue individually against employers, an arduous task in which businesses could claim that the risks of the job were evident when the employment contract was drawn up.

[101] Additionally, workers' compensation did not encompass chronic illnesses developed through work, but rather specific 'accidents' that created injury.

policy during the Great Depression was of security: social security and economic security combined as a major matter of state.

It was only in 1935 that the skeleton of a universal and comprehensive social security infrastructure was created through the Social Security Act (SSA). This Act was the policy foundation of the Roosevelt New Deal. The SSA provided basic unemployment insurance, old age pensions, and federal money for relief projects.[102] It was implemented as the economy gradually recovered after The Crash and it inaugurated a transformation in the federal state's fiscal governance in which it dedicated larger proportions of its revenues to social support. But the Act did not cover all people,[103] and it did not cover healthcare. It was only after the New Deal that inequality levels started to fall in a sustained manner.

Conclusion: The Beginnings of (Comparative) Development

American capitalist transformation commenced in the early nineteenth century as the independent government collated a set of policies to nurture industry and expand its western frontier. It also allowed the southern states to expand the slave plantation system, supplying cotton to industry in the North and generating export revenues. However, changes in the ante-bellum period were limited: industry was nowhere near as important as agriculture and agriculture was based largely in smallholdings with loose market connections. The civil war generated a 'productionist' imperative in the federal government which boosted military-related industries such as textiles, metallurgy, and preserved foods. As with many countries, 'total war' bequeathed a renewed socio-political project of economic resurgence.[104]

After the war, the use of state power to generate a single market, a systemically protected industrial sector, and a macroeconomic framework based on the management of the dollar created a 'development vision' which had not existed previously. The federal government made little attempt at restitution or reallocation of property in the South, leaving a fragile recovery based on labour tenancy, plantations, and some industry. The frontier was aggressively pursued through railways, speculation and fraud, and settlement until its

[102] Kennedy, *The American People in the Great Depression*: 271.

[103] Agricultural labour and workers in small companies were altogether excluded from unemployment insurance.

[104] We shall see this very clearly in Chapter 7 which looks at Japan.

official 'closure' in the 1890s. By this time, a unified continental capitalism was being forged through mass production, technological advance,[105] and a massive proletarianization that involved millions of immigrants as well as a rural–urban migration. The American economy experienced capitalist transformation from the late 1870s until the 1910s and this was—as with Britain—a period of sustained economic and productivity growth that generated all manner of social hardship and new forms of inequality. However, it did also create the conditions of possibility for the construction of a broadly shared and profound improvement in people's lives. Generally, people's lives improved, even in the context of sustained inequality and considerable economic instability. It was only after the Great Recession and the New Deal that a basic universal system of social welfare was created and it was only after the Second World War that the 'great levelling' took place in which one could reasonably say that a commonwealth was realized. Throughout this transformation, America's allocation of progress and pain was profoundly racialized, even if black people's incomes and social mobility did increase throughout the developmentalist period.

But it is important to note—as with Britain—how drastic and encompassing America's capitalist transformation was. By 1893, 'New England alone was producing manufactured goods more valuable per capita than those of any country in the world'.[106] Steel output had increased ten-fold between 1877 and 1892[107] and nearly 1,500 factories each employed nearly 20,000 people.[108] In the late 1800s, levels of industrial investment were higher than anywhere else in the world[109] and the value of manufactures had increased from just under 2 billion dollars to 11 billion dollars between 1865 and 1900.[110] From 1900 to 1910, the economy's output increased by 85 per cent.[111] By the 1920s, American companies produced 85 per cent of the world's automobiles and 40 per cent of its manufactured goods. Agricultural production also increased by 50 per cent between 1900 and 1930.[112] Between 1870 and 1910, America grew almost twice as fast as Britain and 0.5 per cent faster than the European average.[113] From the 1920s, the American economy, fully capitalist, grew and

[105] Walton and Rockoff, *History of the American Economy*: 302.
[106] Cochran and Miller, *The Age of Enterprise*: 136.
[107] Rosenzweig et al., *Who Built America? Vol 2*: 31.
[108] Rosenzweig et al., *Who Built America? Vol 2*: 168.
[109] Bensel, *The Political Economy of American Industrialisation*: 4.
[110] Trattner, *From Poor Law to Welfare State*: 81.
[111] Foner, *Give Me Liberty*: 545.
[112] Kennedy, *The American People in the Great Depression*: 20.
[113] Lindert and Williamson, *Unequal Gains*: 169.

sustained a productivity boom until the 1970s, and during this period mass material well-being improved unprecedentedly for millions of people.[114]

Capitalist transformation is always different and always the same. There is a great deal of specificity in America's experience. Capitalism's expansion was both extensive as the frontier moved westwards and intensive as the industries in the northeast grew, differentiated, and dominated. America's capitalist project involved a massive space with relatively minor geopolitical rivalry in comparison with Europe. America's capitalism—like so many—realized itself through racialized hierarchies which served to exercise downwards pressure on labour and maintain rivalries and prejudice within working-class organizations. In this regard, America was/is more extreme than exceptional. Capitalism in America was also forged through immigration to a degree and in a way that is unique.

Each case study of capitalist development looks more unique the more detail one brings into accounts of its history. The most densely analysed capitalism in the world—Britain's—is often narrated through a trope of originality and uniqueness. But, from our point of view, there are realities to capitalism which are generic. This means that the actual and empirical facets of American capitalist development should connect with Britain's preceding but overlapping transformation. In Chapter 2, we set out a Marxist theory of capitalist development in which we argued that the 'real' in capitalism—that is, its deep generic causative features—is conditioned in the actual and empirical worlds along a fairly simple distinction between developmentalism and a subsequent developed capitalism. The former condition relates to both our British and American cases and therefore we would expect to identify 'deep' features that both share and will manifest themselves in historically and contextually specific ways in the actual (processes and relations) and real (empirical) phenomena of their political economies. Let us recapitulate the core real features of capitalist development and connect these very briefly to aspects of the detail offered in this and Chapter 5.

Primitive Accumulation

Capitalist ascendance in Britain was based on a range of social dispossessions. Most notably, the long and variegated process of enclosure removed customary or long-held tenancy land from smallholders. The commons were also

[114] Details of this period can be found in Gordon, *The Rise and Fall of American Growth*.

alienated from rural communities through engrossment and pasturage. In America, primitive accumulation involved the removal of indigenous people from almost the entire country, so that by the early 1900s, a few 'reserves' remained.[115] The Indian Allotment Act depleted indigenous people's land from 138 million acres in 1887 (when the Act was passed) to 78 million acres in 1900.[116] This alienation in pursuit of the establishing of private property was warlike in a way quite different to Britain. In both America and Britain, capitalism's ascendance relied on an extreme exploitation of labour—what Marx called the extraction of absolute surplus value. Child labour, 12-hour days, minimal safety, and absolute poverty wages characterized Britain's labour from the late 1700s and America's from the early 1800s. In both cases, clearly, capitalist development was based on the mass systemic squeezing of surplus value out of workers in a way that involved removing livelihoods, overwork, and penury.

Nation-Building

Both the British and American states governed their capitalist transitions while also facing major-order challenges to shore up their sovereignty. The social transitions that capitalism requires are not easy to secure. Rebellion, the instability of change (such as mass migration, rapid impoverishment, urbanization), and the imperatives to construct and regulate a capitalist economy required both states to grow, exercise more authority, and construct nationalisms in which capitalism became geopolitically fixed within a discrete territory. In Britain this was done over a longer period and within an imperial project. In America, this was done rapidly and through the expansion of a frontier. Both projects were highly militarized. Both involved the establishment of cadastral, fiscal,[117] and financial instruments of power previously unseen in their bureaucratic and informational sophistication. Both involved the construction of a legislature and judiciary to define and regulate property and contract. It was through these processes that the British and American states enjoyed extensive periods of primacy in a world of modernizing nation-states. And, vitally, these projects of state construction were only

[115] Zinn, *A People's History of the United States*: Chapter 7.

[116] Rosenzweig et al., *Who Built America? Vol 2*: 59.

[117] Although there is a general understanding of America as a light tax state, it would be more accurate to say that it has a complex and extensive fiscal infrastructure with no single 'high take' tax. Sven Steinmo, *The Evolution of Modern States. Sweden, Japan, and the United States* (2010): 152 *et seq.*

possible as a result of the resources governments could purloin from expanded accumulation through the taxation of revenues, trade, and workers' wages.

Capital Advocacy

Both states elaborated a range of institutions and policies to promote expanded accumulation and advocate the transition of industry into more complex and productive assemblages. In both cases, this involved systemic patronage: the allocation of property and resources to businesses with close connections to government and which were expected to generate growth, employment, armaments, or new industrial activities which were seen as 'in the national interest'. It also involved the construction of policy regimes that were increasingly oriented around the idea of the national economy and its growth. Both governments started to generate statistical measures of economic change—in Britain in the 1830s, in America in the 1870s—which resulted in a conflation of growth, accumulation, and national progress more generally. As a result, policies and institutions were oriented towards the promotion of industry through subsidies, the disciplining and training of labour, and an everyday overlap of business and government.

Legitimacy and Commonwealth

Both countries' governments promoted capitalist ascendance as a means to galvanize economic growth and a nation-building project, and to consolidate strong sovereignties. As these projects were pursued, both states worked hard to associate these extremely demanding transitions with a legitimacy of governance. This legitimacy was 'basic' or—perhaps better—fundamental. It was not (only) a legitimacy that enabled the state to attain a consensus of its governed peoples. It was also that the state was absolutely necessary to the project of capitalist transformation. It was—to recall the arguments of realists—the conditions upon which capitalist transition could be socially possible. If politics is in its essence a means to ensure people live together in conditions of radical disagreement, political economy is in our view about the conditions under which people can live together within the throes of a capitalist transformation that is destabilizing, extremely exploitative, and unequal.

For the state, capitalist ascendance was the engine of national grandeur; economic growth would generate greater wealth for all; and the market—properly and minimally regulated—was the most just disposition of wealth and opportunity. American developmentalism 'bound individual liberty to the prospect of enhanced economic opportunity through nationally enforced public policy'.[118] But both states—no matter which party governed—increasingly saw their main legitimacy claim through their role in serving as custodian to national economic growth. As both economies grew, both states were subjected to pressures to ensure a commonwealth: some form of social provision in terms of healthcare and education; some form of insurance against deep poverty; some measures to restrain the social harms of capitalist accumulation in terms of safety at work, standards of production, child labour, and so on. Later, both states would roll out social insurance to mitigate unemployment and old age.

America's developmentalism was comparative, competitive, and integrated. It received investment from Britain in its own industries, it traded with Europe, it borrowed and adapted technologies from industries that emerged in other countries, and it saw the world as a series of trade and investment opportunities defined by the geopolitics of capitalist nations. This was about not only Britain, but also Germany and France. By the late nineteenth century, global capitalist political economy had been constructed. For the rest of the world, this structure constrained the possibility of both non-capitalist development and capitalist development. In Chapter 7, we shall explore the first country in the twentieth century to make a success out of these inauspicious circumstances.

[118] Balogh, *A Government out of Sight*: 58.

7

The Post-Imperial Era and Japan

From Capitalist Growth to Development

The Colonial Origins of Modern Development

The capitalist development that took place in Britain and America was not called 'development' in the contemporary sense. As we have seen, the process of capitalist transformation was understood as a matter of constructing a national space, securing authoritative state rule, being militarily powerful, maintaining social peace, promoting growth, providing the conditions for capital to thrive, and resourcing the provision of social infrastructure. It was only from the 1840s that American governance became centrally oriented around the ideology of the economic growth of a single national economy.

The development of industrial capitalism in Britain and America was not only a transformation within these two countries; it was also a *global transformation*. From the mid-1800s, a global political economy was made by the capitals of these two countries in which minerals, agrarian economies, systems of migration, communication, governing organizations, and metrics were constructed. It was within the construction of a global capitalist political economy, driven by Britain, other European capitalist economies, and America, that the term 'development' in its modern sense emerged. In the late 1890s, a final wave of colonial expansion took place (mainly in Africa) in which colonies were not only possessions of imperialism but also 'development' concerns.[1]

Colonialism in the late colonial period[2] was strongly connected to the endeavour to make colonized spaces safe for capital. Indeed, colonial states understood quintessentially late nineteenth century terms like 'effective occupation' and 'Afrique util' in relation to the concerns of capital. Effective

[1] Michael Cowen and Robert Shenton, 'The Invention of Development' (1995); James Ferguson, 'Anthropology and its Evil Twin: "Development" in the Constitution of a Discipline' (1997); Vernon Hewitt and Mark Duffield, *Empire, Development and Colonialism: The Past in the Present* (2013).

[2] Roughly from the 1880s to 1945.

Developmentalism: The Normative and Transformative within Capitalism. Graham G.M. Harrison, Oxford University Press (2020). © Graham G.M. Harrison.
DOI: 10.1093/oso/9780198785798.001.0001.

occupation meant imposing institutions to define private property, tax, invest in infrastructure, and put people to work. 'Afrique util' refers to the ways in which colonial surveys and zoning forged geographies of economic opportunity for capital, separating space according to its climate, minerals, waterways, and various unproductive spaces. The racialism of the time also imposed 'tribal' separations on Africans in which some were seen as more 'civilized' than others. Colonial states considered their main purpose after the imposition of formal dominance to be the promotion of colonial economies that served their home countries. This was not simply about pillage and exploitation—although it was certainly about those things. It was also about managing the transformations taking place within colonized societies which required a balance between promoting changes that enabled accumulation and restricting processes that challenged accumulation or generated the expansion of autonomous 'indigenous' property-owning classes. It involved the integration and disciplining of labour—as peasants, mine workers, plantation workers, stevedores, factory workers, construction workers, and so on.[3] In all these areas of proletarianization, colonial states endeavoured to constrain union formation, maintain low wages, and enforce colour bars. Throughout these profound changes—which intensified after the 1920s—women were barely noticed, although they were fully integrated into these changes. The nature of 'domestic' work changed in relation to the dynamics of proletarianization, and women sought opportunities to become more mobile or secure their own income sources.[4]

In summary, it was the remarkable power generated by developed capitalist economies in Europe that created a global political economy in which the rest of the world was organized according to its relation to industrial and financial capital. The ideological effects of this were very varied, but the various discourses on colonialism took place within an overarching framing which was that the zones of the world were seen in terms of their prospective possibilities of transforming into capitalist political economies. This framing delimited debates about the rights and wrongs of colonialism, the judgements made about peoples in 'distant places', and the progressive or exploitative nature of capitalist states.

[3] Fred Cooper, *On the African Waterfront: Urban Disorder and the Transformation of Work in Colonial Mombasa* (1987).

[4] Janet Bujra, *Serving Class: Masculinity and the Feminisation of Domestic Service in Tanzania* (2000).

The Rise of Development as Sovereignty

A protean development project emerged in the late 1800s, and it became an explicit part of colonial politics after the 1920s. But *developmentalism* emerged after the Second World War. Developmentalism was an ideology born out of resistance to imperialism and a struggle for decolonization and/or full sovereignty. It was structured as a politics of nationalism within a global capitalist society of states. As argued in Chapter 1, developmentalism conflates the ambition to generate capitalist transformation with the foundational task of establishing and reproducing statehood. In this sense, developmentalism can only manifest itself within nation-states. This is a point worth further attention because the direction of travel in theories of development since the rise of globalization studies has been to emphasize the global nature of development.

Globalization studies have encouraged us to understand the world's poverty and inequality at both a supra- and sub-national level. It has also suggested that the project of promoting development can only make sense as a transnational or intergovernmental project. Concepts such as value chains, the international financial architecture, and of course neoliberalism portray development as a series of processes that work through states but are only coherent when understood at the global level. Discourses within the global social movements and cosmopolitan traditions see development as something transnational, multi-scalar, and universal. Concrete development practices have hardly abandoned the notion of state sovereignty but nor do they take it very seriously. And, as we saw in Chapter 3, the capabilities approach gives scant recognition to the nation-state.

If the direction of travel in development studies is towards a more richly global framing of development and a relativization of state sovereignty, it is worth recalling that, historically, all development projects have been national projects. And this is not incidental, a product of those times when the state was taken more seriously. Rather, it is constitutive of development itself. Capitalist development in the way we understand it cannot happen globally. One might borrow from the language of Lefebvre and say that developmentalism produces the national space.[5] Developmentalism requires a state that has a national zone of operation; it requires a population that occupies that space and is therefore able to manifest a politics of commonwealth. And, in

[5] Henri Lefebvre, *The Production of Space* (1984). 'No space disappears in the course of growth and development' (86).

some form, capital needs to be bounded: that is, there needs to be a set of conditions imposed upon the entry of capital and a set of conditions imposed upon capital within the national space. None of these political practices and processes—authoritative political action, a commonwealth, or the nuanced and dynamic regulation of capital—makes sense when set within a global context. The political sophistication and effort required to generate a capitalist transformation requires a national government, which is to say, a potentially authoritative, legitimate, effective, and regulatory government. Once one looks towards global social movements, international organizations, and the global market, the politics palpably thins out into notions such as 'norm cascades', intergovernmental regimes, and idealized understandings of justice.

This is not to say that the global does not matter. Indeed, the Marxist tradition that this book cleaves to has always set considerable store in understanding capitalism as intrinsically global. But the broad and encompassing truism that capitalism is global does not so much refute the methodological nationalism adopted here as much as highlight how exacting development is. Developmentalism does indeed work against the international, although this 'against' does not mean Manichean opposition. Rather, developmentalism is the political art of resisting the global in some circumstances and opening up to it in others while maintaining a nationalist strategic perspective in relation to both. Simplistic 'open' and 'closed' narratives about national economies will not do. If there is a single globalization then development requires many recipes,[6] and the notion of many 'recipes' only makes sense within the spatial container of the nation-state.

International Development

The term 'development' only entered common parlance in the institutions of states and intergovernmental organizations in the 1950s as the post-colonial state system emerged. Historical accounts of international political economy commonly note that the Bretton Woods global architecture was based on a regulatory regime that identified development in the post-colonial world as a key part of its business. This is essentially the story of the rising importance of the World Bank, International Monetary Fund (IMF), and development-dedicated specialist United Nations organizations, especially the UN

[6] Dani Rodrick, *One Economics, Many Recipes: Globalization, Institutions, and Economic Growth* (2008).

Development Programme.[7] By the 1960s (a Decade of Development), development discourse had been mainstreamed into global intergovernmental practices, most centrally through the provision of aid and loans to the post-colonial world and the emergence of an epistemic community of economists and policymakers who attempted to develop models for countries to follow.

The underlying structure that enabled the profusion of development practices was the global political economy forged by developed capitalist Britain and America. Without these concrete historical processes and their impacts on the relations between economies throughout the world, the entire cognitive structure of international development would make no sense. Industrial capitalism in Britain, America, and of course other European states (most notably France and Germany) created the 'great divergence' that identified countries both as increasingly unequal and potentially converging. It is this couplet that underpins practically all orthodox development thinking from the 1960s to the present-day. Closely related, the fact of capitalist development's emergence in a small number of countries—and its dominance globally—established a metanorm for the entire world in which the desirable telos of development was to approximate the conditions prevailing in these countries.

But the rise of development discourse and practice was not simply a global order of power in which the West imposed itself on the South. Post-colonial governments identified within the development promise a fundamental claim to sovereignty and legitimacy. As we argued in Chapter 4, the basic legitimacy demands faced by post-colonial states involved a qualitatively more fundamental consideration of mass poverty than did those in modern western states. In a nutshell, the full sovereignty of post-colonial states revolved around the claim to legitimacy made through development performance.

In the late 1950s and early 1960s, development became the metanorm of post-colonial sovereignty. It was structured within the simple categorical dichotomy of developed and developing countries, with the former serving as a telos for the latter; it was actualized through the rise of an international development 'community' which managed aid, lending, research, and policy advice; and it infused the diverse ideologies of sovereignty that emerged throughout the post-colonial world as independence was won.

This matters a great deal in relation to how we proceed with the rest of our case study material. We have derived from our examples of Britain and

[7] Richard Peet, *Unholy Trinity: The IMF, World Bank and the WTO* (2003).

America a clear empirical account of how capitalist development worked as a project of transformation underpinned by state action. Recognizing that these experiences of transformation were global as well as national and that a core outcome of this was the rise of the politics of international development requires us to understand how development as an explicit, powerful, and fungible ideological symbol infused itself into many states' attempts to prosecute capitalist development within their territories. We have defined the politics of developmentalism as ideological. It requires strongly established and interconnected norms and values that are shared within elites. Any project of national capitalist development must take place in a world made by already-developed states that have attempted to make the world serve their own purposes. Developmentalism is in some degree an adversarial project that seeks convergence: within and against.

Developmentalism in Imperial Decline

We have seen how—in very different circumstances—Britain and America did this through violence, concerted state action, the rise of capital, and the intensified exploitation of wage labour. Both, of course, also drew upon broader networks or trade and labour, networks in which pillage, enslavement, and coercion were prevalent. In both cases, economic transformation gradually generated an expanding commonwealth; and there was considerable lag between the amassing of wealth by capitalists and the provision of social security and improved consumption for the mass population, but this should not surprise us. Broader social benefits from capitalist development are the outcome of class struggle—expressed both in the contentions between capital and labour and within the state itself, and there is of course a considerable amount of political contingency in all of this as ideologies, ruling elites, and specific political events impact the nature of governance. But there is an irrefutable historical stylization that Britain, America, and shortly afterwards other core European economies all underwent capitalist transformations that had as their outcome in the early twentieth century a historically unprecedented situation in which it was politically possible to imagine nations in which all people enjoyed a basically decent material livelihood.

The reality of capitalist development in Britain and America generated not only its own transformations but also a global transformation. As a result, 'actual' capitalist development elsewhere and subsequently has taken place in relation to these already completed developments, and in a world substantially dominated by the latter. This has generated a range of political effects which endow post-imperial developmentalism with certain key properties. We will sketch these below and then explore how they have manifested in concrete situations as we return to our case studies.

Urgency

Although it would be erroneous to argue that Britain and America did not consider economic expansion as an extremely serious matter, post-colonial developmentalism (from hereon simply developmentalism) contains an urgency that is considerably greater. Developmentalism commonly contains within it an understanding of political time perhaps best represented by a generation. That is, the prospective vision of developmentalism is that of a 20- or 30-year period in which a society will have transformed into a developed capitalist one. Historiographically, the British and American timescapes of layered and complex change over centuries have been replaced by the ideal of a single and integrated process of change that can be completed within decades. An empirical manifestation of this is the profusion of rolling Three/Five/Eight/Ten Year plans throughout the post-colonial world. Within each of these plans resides an expectation that transformation can be achieved extremely rapidly and through a directed process that involves co-ordinated changes in social, agrarian, industrial, and technological facets.

The political impetus for urgency derives from the immediate need to establish legitimate conditions for post-colonial sovereignty and to meet the equally immediate challenges of retaining statehood within a global political economy that is made in the image of other countries—countries that might well be formed colonizers. Within these conditions, a slow 'organic' process of development is politically unthinkable. States and the political economies within which they are situated are themselves very often a legacy of imperial imposition and, as a result, their transformation is an immediate and politicized strategic issue. Independence itself allows a momentary popularity, but post-colonial states face populations whose relations to the state are far from settled.

Rivalry and Insecurity

The urgency of developmentalism is not only energized by the post-colonial nature of statehood or the adversities of existing in a global capitalist economy historically constructed by other powerful states. It is also driven and sustained by a political insecurity generated by the fact that the post-colonial condition was faced by many states. As we have argued, developmentalism is based on a comparative episteme in which metrics of progress between nations serve as the primary means of establishing relations between states. Of course, British and American development was galvanized by inter-state rivalry, but these rivalries were significantly distinct. Post-colonial rivalry has particular *systemic* properties in which a large number of countries with undeveloped political economies cohabit the post-colonial space of development ambition.

This post-colonial condition is shared by many states and it is not in itself sufficient to underpin a developmentalist project. Developmentalism emerges in situations where insecurity is more profound and systemic. Doner et al. set out the meaning of systemic insecurity as follows: 'the credible threat that any deterioration in the living standards of popular sectors could trigger unmanageable mass unrest; the heightened need for foreign exchange and war matériel induced by national insecurity; and the hard budget constraints imposed by a scarcity of easy revenue sources'.[8] This definition is very pertinent to our purposes because it suggests that the kind of insecurity that might provide the political conditions for developmentalism is existential. In others words, the threats to sovereignty and basic civic stability are clear and present in a way that is qualitatively distinct from what one might call the pedestrian governance of post-colonial states. In a phrase, capitalist transformation becomes about survival in specific situations of intense and directly threatening insecurity.

Nationalism and Nation-Building

We have noted how a certain kind of spatial 'fixing' is needed for capitalist development which is the nation-state. The nature of post-colonial nationhood was often that it was legislatively present but more substantively provisional. The institutional reach of the state was questionable. The extent to which peoples within national boundaries acceded to state power was equally uncertain. Colonialism left a legacy of cultural antipathy towards the state

[8] Richard F. Doner, Bryan K. Ritchie, and Dan Slater, 'Systemic Vulnerability and the Origins of Developmental States: Northeast and Southeast Asia in Comparative Perspective' (2005).

which—although mollified by the accession to power of a 'national' elite—did not entirely dissipate.

As a result, post-colonial politics has been about nation-building. This has taken many forms: the universalization of fiscal regimes, the imposition of a single national language and education, the construction of national myths of origin and unity, or membership of a political party or state-affiliated organization. Again, these were common state projects throughout the post-colonial world, but they are not sufficient to drive developmentalism. In some countries, the national project has been realized through the construction of a national economy that is highly integrated and—when growing rapidly—conducive to the consolidation of national state power. In this respect, very practical aspects of governance such as the universalization of fiscal infrastructures, regimes of property rights, and investment in transport and communication are germane. Beyond this, the expansive accumulation of capital integrates provincial markets more intensively and makes labour more mobile. Frontier zones (perhaps also insecure zones) can be re-ordered by states as investment zones. None of this has necessarily to be equalizing, but it is integrative. Capital's loathing of a vacuum might serve the purpose of forging a national space.

This chapter has established a relative distinction, rather than an absolute and categorical one, between 'original' capitalist transformations and those that have taken place in a world created by these 'originals'. It has done so by establishing a fairly well-used historiography of development in which its emergence is a post-Second World War affair, derived by the decline of empire. Post-colonial national sovereignties have been situated in adverse global circumstances and faced the challenge of attempting to engineer a capitalist transformation. As a political project, we have taken the features of developmentalism set out in Chapter 1 and added some distinctions that are either more prominent or distinct within the post-colonial period. These are: urgency, rivalry, and nationalism. These stylizations will help us identify the ways in which developmentalism is driven by powerful political imperatives that have considerably greater muscularity than the desire to promote economic growth or reduce poverty *sui generis*; and they will help us set out some categorizations for the case studies in Chapters 8 and 9. This is a graded distinction. It is not meant to separate 'original' from 'late' but rather to make the historical point that capitalist transformation *became development* as a result of the global capitalist economy constructed by Britain and America.

Japan

Japan might be seen as the last of the cases of first-phase capitalist developers or the first of a second phase of post-imperial developers.[9] Japan was the first country to achieve capitalist development as the age of empire was in decline. Although not colonized, its developmentalism was profoundly imperial and post-imperial. As we shall see, Japan's developmentalism emerged out of a politics of antagonism towards western powers and it was realized through its own colonizing designs. Its success has undoubtedly served as an inspiration or even model for other countries.

Preliminaries

In development studies, there is a predisposition to focus on Japan's post-Second World War 'miracle' development from the late 1950s until the mid-1970s. This is understandable, and indeed it is Japan's unprecedentedly (at the time) rapid growth during this period that has substantially defined its development success and status as a model for others. Policymakers and development researchers have commonly aimed to derive models, lessons, and contrasts from Japan. Japan's recovery from extensive American firebombing and nuclear war to a wealthy industrial capitalist nation is surely one of the most remarkable instances of the potential progress capitalist development offers, and as a case study it has become the foundation for a considerable theoretical and policymaking literature on how successfully to develop. But Japan's capitalist transition did not commence after 1945 but rather in the early 1800s, or the late Tokugawa period. As with Britain and America, it is important to understand how capitalism emerged out of prevailing social relations and how its ascendance was coloured by a range of coercions and dispossessions.

During the early 1800s, Japan's political economy was defined by a 'feudal'[10] *daimyo* landlordism oriented around a dominant lineage that exacted tribute from farmers within the *han* territories over which it had near-absolute

[9] It is included in both 'models of capitalism' and 'newly industrializing' research.

[10] There is considerable contention concerning the appropriateness of the term 'feudal', but for our purposes it works well enough in that it distinguishes between the localized concentration of political, coercive, and economic power in the samurai landlord, whereas during the Meiji period landlordism transforms towards something more akin to commercialized tenancy.

political and economic control. Small-scale farmers gave a portion of their crops and performed services to their landlord in the form of tribute, and each landlord passed tribute to the Tokugawa lineage which reposed above each 'fief'. These levies were extracted at the level of the village, not individual farming families. Within the village, different households would offer different forms of surplus produce. The resources of woodlands, water, and land might be divided or redistributed in varied ways.[11] The loyalty of the *daimyo* to the Tokugawa lineage was maintained through a system in which all landlord families had to maintain a house and family in Edo, the capital city, and to attend court for half of the year.

We start our analysis at this point because generally throughout the Tokugawa period, agricultural output and the population grew steadily as a stable political order, infrastructural development, and land reclamation extended throughout the realm.[12] There was also an expansion in artisanal mining. In the eighteenth and first half of the nineteenth century, population growth slowed, and although agricultural output continued to grow, it did so at a slower pace. Japan remained a predominantly agricultural country throughout the Tokugawa period, but there was a marked increase in trade and traffic, the reclamation of land, and intensification of work. All this took place within a static set of social relations in which landlords extracted rent and gave tribute within a centralized system. Although the government promoted all manner of agrarian good practices, such as the introduction of new seeds, better implements, and of course more frugality and hard work, Japan's agrarian social relations were constantly defined by the constraints of a domineering, hierarchical, and non-competitive landlordism.

During the early 1800s, a mercantile class consolidated itself in Edo, which was, at the time, the largest city in the world. Additionally, trading houses emerged in other parts of the archipelago that were often in tense cohabitation with the ruling dynasty. Indeed, the major concern of the Tokugawa government was to maintain authority over what were independent fiefdoms, some with independent socio-political traditions and samurai-based militaries.[13] It was this desire to consolidate state power that led the Tokugawa regime to invest in transport infrastructure: canals and roads. There was also state investment and ownership in a limited number of industries identified as

[11] These are very general characterizations. There was considerable complexity and regional variability within Japan. A detailed and meticulous account is given in Thomas Smith, *The Agrarian Origins of Modern Japan* (1959).

[12] Andrew Gordon, *A Modern History of Japan* (2003): 29 *et seq.*

[13] Conrad Totman, *A History of Japan* (2005): 229.

strategically important: metallurgy, shipbuilding, and armaments.[14] The other industry of note that emerged towards the end of the Tokugawa period was textiles. As a result, by the time of the Meiji 'restoration',[15] Japan had established a market infrastructure, a small mercantile class,[16] and a cluster of primary industries.

The Origins of Developmentalism

It was the persistent threat posed by the extra-territorial rights of European powers that generated rebellion against the Tokugawa regime and which led to its overthrow. Nevertheless, the core domestic logic of government strategy—asserting authority throughout the national territory and imposing stability and through the construction of a national economy—remained.[17] What made the difference was the means and forcefulness through which this strategy was achieved under the Meiji and subsequent imperial rulers, most notably its integration into a military–imperial system.

The restoration of imperial power was less of a restoration than a transition towards a more centralized state that replaced the provincialized despotism of *han* rule with a more institutionalized oligarchy of landlords: military and economic elites who ruled in the name of the Emperor. During the period of imperial rule (1868–1945), gradual and 'organic' growth, nation-building, and expansion of infrastructure were succeeded by a developmentalist project from around 1910.

The Japanese Meiji state was initially composed of a council of Samurai from western Japan[18] who effectively ruled as an oligarchy, formally advising the Emperor.[19] The major political and strategic motivations of the oligarchy were nation-building and security. These were the two concerns that led to the downfall of the Tokugawa government and drove its ouster.[20] The late Tokugawa regime was unable to break the 'unequal treaties' signed with western powers in the 1850s which gave some foreign citizens extra-territoriality

[14] Thomas Smith, *Political Change and Industrial Development in Japan: Government Enterprise 1868–1880* (1965): 4.

[15] The notion of restoration was largely mythical.

[16] Penelope Francks, *Japanese Economic Development. Theory and Practice* (1992): 22.

[17] David Flath, *The Japanese Economy* (2000): 26; Carl Mosk, *Japanese Economic Development. Markets, Norms, Structures* (2008): 101.

[18] Gary D. Allinson, 'The Structure and Transformation of Conservative Rule' (1993): 124.

[19] The power of the Emperor was largely symbolic, most effective through his declarations and edicts. Policies and strategies were largely the business of the oligarchy.

[20] Totman, *A History of Japan*: 289–96.

and constrained the Japanese government's abilities to set its own tariffs. Discontent with the foreign power these treaties allowed generated the Meiji regime's modern Japanese nationalism.[21] At the same time, western powers—not only Britain and America but also France and Germany—were actively colonizing and going to war to establish control in northeast Asia, most notably through the 'opium wars'. It is not an exaggeration to say that, by the 1860s the Japanese government considered itself to be facing an existential threat from an industrializing Europe, as well as an expanding Russian state and a Chinese dynastic state. Indeed, after an extended period of exclusion from international influence,[22] Japan re-engaged in the 1850s into the world system of states and markets as one of the few entirely uncolonized and imperially dominated spaces left in the world.

The Meiji Restoration was motivated by a desire to escape unequal treaties and construct a robust national project during a period of exceptional threat to sovereignty. Furthermore, the Meiji government had come to power effectively through a kind of occupation-coup. The armies of the Chosun and Satsuma *daimyos* (along with smaller allies and a general but cautious support from peasant farmers) had occupied Edo. Other parts of the country had not rebelled and the general population in part perceived the new regime as alien. Other *daimyos* were potential warlords. The sense that Japan was ruled by 'occupiers' remained in some parts of Japan after power was consolidated.[23] The Meiji government saw economic growth and modernization not as ways to improve the lot of Japanese people but as the means to consolidate state power throughout the territory and to secure an improved material well-being for the general population.

Thus the first major effort of the state after pacification was to invest in the infrastructure of governance and a national economy: a structure of systemic local government and taxation, a massive increase in the amount of road and rail,[24] and conscription. From the 1890s, the government undertook a far more ambitious programme of transformation than simply state consolidation, and this had a number of interlinked components, which we can sketch here.

[21] Gordon, *A Modern History of Japan*: 50.

[22] Throughout the eighteenth and early nineteenth centuries, intercourse with other parts of the world did exist, notably with China and the Netherlands. It is also the case—as with China and other historic states in northeast Asia—that they were all strongly 'regionalized', that is, integrated into trading, cultural, and diplomatic relations with each other. The 'isolated Japan' image has been used in ethnocentric accounts of the country's history. The point for our purposes relates specifically to relations with western imperial powers.

[23] Totman, *A History of Japan*: 309, 325.

[24] Flath, *The Japanese Economy*: 39.

In 1871, the decentralized 'feudal' concentration of power in the *daimyo* was abolished and replaced by a state that retained absolute coercive power for itself. The localized *noblesse oblige*, rice tax rates, village loyalties, and the remains of the retainer armies were abolished in the first 10 years of the Meiji state. Samurai bureaucrat-soldiers had their payments from the government commuted into single severance payments, leaving them to seek employment.[25] A wide-ranging cadastral survey transformed land tenure from village-based customary allocations under the feudal ownership of the *daimyo* into individualized and legally identified land tenancy.[26] Now tenants paid for their lease in cash at a government-controlled rate.[27] These reforms galvanized an agrarian transition within which tenants could pursue more stable strategies of improvement. Productive activities outside of sharecropped rice were free from the exactions of the landlord and tenants could work towards purchasing their land outright, a possibility that eroded the property of landlords. Agricultural productivity increased and rural manufacturing expanded, especially in sericulture but also food processing.[28] Feudal agrarian sharecropping relations were being replaced by tenancy, and this became the basis of a new fiscal infrastructure.[29] As a result, new seed and farming techniques emerged and spread more rapidly, processes supported by government through extension services.[30] The expansion of commerce, monetized tenancy, and rural industry and wage labour all generated considerable pressure/incentive to seek out productivity-enhancing activities within peasant agriculture.[31]

From the 1910s,[32] the imperial state expanded its transformative ambition. The government implemented a set of policies to promote industrial capital. This was the period in which a set of diversified large companies emerged—the zaibatsu. These companies dominated large-scale industrial activities and

[25] Gordon, *A Modern History of Japan*: 64–6.

[26] Mosk, *Japanese Economic Development*: 103.

[27] Flath, *The Japanese Economy*: 73.

[28] Francks, *Japanese Economic Development*. Household brewing of sake, miso, and soy. Penelope Francks calls this 'pluriactivity'. Francks, 'Mechanizing Small-Scale Rice Cultivation in an Industrializing Economy: The Development of the Power-Tiller in Prewar Japan' (1996).

[29] Gordon, *A Modern History of Japan*: 95. Considerable effort was dedicated to making extension services work, which involved sustained and localized engagement. See Penelope Francks, 'The Development of New Techniques in Agriculture: The Case of the Mechanization of Irrigation in the Saga Plain Area of Japan' (1979).

[30] Francks, *Japanese Economic Development*: 120 *et seq*.; Mosk, *Japanese Economic Development*: 103, 109.

[31] Mark Cohen, 'Reforming States, Agricultural Transformation, and Economic Development in Russia and Japan, 1853–1913' (2018).

[32] From 1912, the Meiji emperor was replaced by the Taisho and then Showa imperial regimes. Generally, these three imperial regimes are seen as part of the same period. From 1912, the most distinct shift is less in relation to imperial rule and more in relation to the rise of military dominance in decision-making.

enjoyed strong support from government.[33] From the early twentieth century, some zaibatsu (sometimes called 'new zaibatsu') received contracts to expand Japanese economic power into China and Korea.[34] Some zaibatsu diversified and sought out new production technologies, allowing them to produce textiles, woven silk, higher-tech mines, and military goods. Outside of the zaibatsu, the stable, highly connected, and well-regulated trade and property system imposed by the imperial state enabled the emergence of small-scale 'workshop' firms[35] both in the expanding cities and in the countryside, the latter especially in the production of silk, sake, and soya. Within small-scale firms and within the larger textile factories, there was a substantial proletarianization of women. As cities expanded, almost as many women were engaged in sex work as were working in textile factories.[36] Within the towns, a mercantile class emerged that negotiated the export of silk and managed credit—especially with samurai who were seeking to maintain their grandeur and put their relatively diminished pay-offs to work.

Japan went to war with Russia (1904–1905) and China (1894–1895). It occupied Taiwan from 1895,[37] and projected itself into Korea, eventually occupying it in 1910. In 1937 it invaded China and occupied an area of northern China that it named Manchukuo. These military operations stimulated the Japanese economy. They also brought new resources within the Japanese economy's reach. This was especially the case in relation to food imports: by the early 1900s the Japanese food economy was essentially a regional–imperial one. The Japanese state also used Korean forced labour in its mines. From 1894, the government forced European powers to rescind the 'unequal treaties' of the mid-nineteenth century. It also more intensively occupied its own peripheral zones, seeking out new mineral and forestry resources.

There is of course a great deal of nuance and detail one could add to this sketch. But we do have a robust case that the Meiji state undertook the first developmentalist project, historically defined by the capitalist industrialization of Europe and its effects on Japan's place in the world, as well as its own historical–regional context. The industrial navies and weaponry of America, Britain, the Netherlands, and France, each seeking its entrepôts for the 'battering ram' of cheap exports, presented a novel threat. Japan's elite self-perception was of weakness and vulnerability in the face of peoples seen as

[33] Gordon, *A Modern History of Japan*: 97.

[34] Flath, *The Japanese Economy*: 46–7. A fact that fed into the American desire to dismantle zaibatsu. See section on 'Reconstruction'.

[35] Flath, *The Japanese Economy*: 49.

[36] Gordon, *A Modern History of Japan*: 104.

[37] Previously, Taiwan had been part of the Qing Chinese imperial state.

barbaric, and there was a very real sense that the country might be colonized by a western power.[38] The Meiji Restoration was a reaction to that. The new government also had to legitimize itself within its own territories, as an 'occupier'. It had to transform Japan rapidly in order to attain the wherewithal to maintain its sovereignty and it did this through an ideology of *fukoku kyōhei*—rich nation, strong army, and a desire to make Japan a 'great power', in order to be secure in a world that was now dominated by capitalist western states.

A further component of developmentalism was very present in Japan: the combination of hostility towards other countries and a desire to take them as models. Japan sought to import European technologies; it employed large numbers of Europeans in what would now be called 'technical assistance' roles.[39] It invested considerably in education and training in ways that sought to infuse in a broad population the ideas and techniques of the science and industry that had emerged from European and American capitalist industrializations. In terms of popular culture, Japan's cities became arenas of western–Japanese hybridity. There was a constant agonism in this 'hate–emulate' dynamic, and by the 1930s some within government also sought out rival models from, among others, Germany, France, and Turkey.

Insecurity, rapid capitalist transformation of the economy, the seeking of legitimacy through modernization, and inter-state rivarly: this was the essence of the Japanese developmentalist project.[40] And one can readily see the progress that Japan made in this period. There was steady economic growth from the late 1880s to the late 1930s.[41] By the 1910s, there were palpable signs that a systemic capitalist transition was under way, in part because of the effects of the First World War. By 1920, industry had overtaken agriculture in terms of gross domestic product (GDP) share.[42] This involved not only light 'first wave' industries but also shipbuilding and some motor vehicle manufacture.[43] Nevertheless, as we have already argued, developmentalism did not look much like it contemporaneously. Japan suffered bouts of inflation, recessionary deflation, a stock market crash (1920) currency crisis, and

[38] Bruce Cumings, 'The Origins and Development of the Northeast Asian Political Economy: Industrial Sectors, Product Cycles, and Political Consequences' (1984): 8.

[39] There are American examples of this as well in relation to textiles and metallurgy, although—as ever—there was also some competitively driven theft.

[40] Franks, *Japanese Economic Development*: 28.

[41] Kazushi Ohkawa and Henry Rosovsky, 'Postwar Japanese Growth in Historical Perspective: A Second Look' (1998): 88–9.

[42] Franks, *Japanese Economic Development*: 55.

[43] Closely related to the 'total war' industrialization of the 1930s and the second wave of zaibatsu.

food shortages. It also endured food riots, and peasant and wage worker protest. General indicators of social progress do demonstrate improvements in material life, however: income per capita increasing between 2 and 3 per cent, declining death rates, and increasing access to electricity.[44] As is the case as capitalist transformation takes place, more forceful political pluralities emerged, parties vied for position within the Diet, labour unions emerged, and socialist ideas have considerable force. Furthermore, factions within the military attempted a coup.

The prevailing ideas of this period were not of development but of national sovereignty, contested moral economies of nationalism, and injustice. Japan offers us the first case of what came to be called 'late development'.[45] It pursued the kind of capitalist transformation that we have identified in our model: expanded accumulation, the conflation of sovereignty and economic transformation, crisis endurance, and the rise of class politics of commonwealth. But it did so in a world substantially constructed by Britain, America, and indeed by the late 1800s Germany, France, and the Netherlands. The 'existential threat' response to this is what enables us to identify the striking urgency, rivalry, and nationalism in the Meiji state. This is why Cumings describes Meiji strategy as defensive industrialization.[46] The intensity of the conflation of an ideology of besieged national survival and state-driven economic transformation was encapsulated in the notion of total war: economic development to support military capability, and the deployment of military capability to secure resources and labour for the economy. This generated an imperialist and increasingly militarized governance whose conclusion was the Pacific War and eventual defeat after the firebombing and detonation of two nuclear bombs by the American military.

Reconstruction

The damage wrought by the American military campaign was immense. About a quarter of the housing stock was destroyed, along with much industrial plant.[47] The cost of physical destruction was estimated at double the 1948–9

[44] Mosk, *Japanese Economic Development*: 159.
[45] Cumings, 'The Origins and Development of the Northeast Asian Political Economy'.
[46] Bruce Cumings 'Japan's Position in the World System' (1993): 35.
[47] Tessa Morris-Suzuki, *The Technological Transformation of Japan. From the Seventeenth to the Twenty-First Century* (1994): 161.

national income.[48] Industrial output was about a sixth of that before the Pacific War.[49] But the Japanese state-elite was not destroyed and its agricultural and small business sectors recovered to some degree fairly rapidly.[50] The Diet continued to function through an elite more dominated by political party leaders and bureaucrats than military men. The state and economy was, of course, underpinned by the Supreme Command of the Allied Powers (SCAP) which oversaw government and also directed it in key areas, not least by writing a new constitution that institutionalized multi-party politics and free labour unions.[51] It also abolished landlordism entirely, replacing it with freehold peasant land tenure.

In the first few years after defeat, Japan's political economy was managed in a fairly chaotic fashion by SCAP. The zaibatsu were broken up and no clear strategy for economic transformation emerged. Industries associated with the build-up of military power were reorganized and prohibited from producing war materiel. Unemployment remained high.[52] A brief period of what might be called punitive occupation was succeeded by a reconstructive occupation, driven by an awareness that Japan was an important and vulnerable state that shared borders with Russia and Maoist China. As a result, SCAP slowed down its breaking up of industrial conglomerates and allowed the Japanese government some leeway in rebuilding its economy, so that, by 1951, industrial output and income per person had recovered to pre-war levels.[53]

Although the American policy orientation in Japan was towards liberal economic policy and a balanced budget, the Korean war generated a considerable military Keynesianism as Japanese companies received contracts to supply textiles and other goods to the American war effort in Korea after the Chinese supported North Korea.[54] Thus, in all, American occupation imposed a liberal political economy underpinned by the buoyancy effects of war contracts. With some historic irony, the militarism of Japan's capitalist industrialization before defeat to the Americans was re-introduced by America but this time through contracts for textiles and foodstuffs.

[48] G. C. Allen, *A Short Economic History of Modern Japan 1867–1937* (1972): 170.

[49] James Vestal, *Planning for Change. Industrial Policy and Japanese Economic Development 1945–1990* (1993): 14.

[50] Morris-Suzuki, *The Technological Transformation of Japan*: 184.

[51] The latter after a 'Red purge', although membership of labour unions did increase substantially: 56 per cent by 1949. Gordon, *A Modern History of Japan*: 235).

[52] Vestal, *Planning for Change*: 22.

[53] Allen, *A Short Economic History of Modern Japan 1867–1937*: 173, 174.

[54] Flath, *The Japanese Economy*: 85.

The Japanese government and its people exercised considerable agency in reconstruction. The land reform programme directed by SCAP abolished the vestiges of landlordism, transforming tenancies into freeholds and imposing a ceiling on the amount of land a large landowner could possess. The area farmed by tenants fell from 46 per cent to 12 per cent between 1945 and 1950.[55] Throughout the 1950s, this led to a sustained growth in agricultural output, especially of rice. Imports of rice were banned, generating a protected market for Japanese rice. Agricultural output increased by 4.3 per cent per year during occupation.[56] Japanese farmers continued as they had done before the war in using more chemical fertilizers and new seeds in their fields. By the 1960s, Japanese smallholder agriculture became increasingly mechanized as a result of the availability of relatively cheap machinery and the ability of famers to access credit on the basis of their freehold as collateral. As large-scale industrialization took off in the 1960s, men moved into factories and farming was increasingly undertaken by women. Outside of the large-scale industrial sector, men tended to farm and work for wages in varying combinations and with some flexibility. Women wage labourers—the mainstay of Japan's pre-war textile expansion—found themselves increasingly excluded from the newer post-war industries.

Miracle

By 1970, Japan's industrial production was approximately ten times that of 1936.[57] Between 1950 and 1973, the Japanese economy grew by an average of 10 per cent per year.[58] In the late 1950s, up to 30 per cent of national income was invested, and Japan continued to maintain exceptional levels of investment and accumulation.[59] From a country devastated by war and a collapsed empire, Japan was the world's largest shipbuilder by 1960. Life expectancy rose from 47 years in 1935 to 68 in 1960.[60] All of this was achieved through a sustained process of accumulation and investment articulated by a central government obsession with growth and transformation.

Throughout the late 1950s and 1960s, agriculture increased productivity, generated staple foodstuffs, and acted as a source for new labourers. Labour

[55] Totman, *A History of Japan*: 456. [56] Vestal, *Planning for Change*: 15.
[57] Allen, *A Short Economic History of Modern Japan 1867–1937*: 171.
[58] Gordon, *A Modern History of Japan*: 245.
[59] Allen, *A Short Economic History of Modern Japan 1867–1937*: 175.
[60] Totman, *A History of Japan*: 466.

productivity on farms was achieved through the deployment of machinery and improved seeds and fertilizers. This form of agrarian transformation did not require massive dispossession[61] through the rise in landlordism or through the destruction of indigenous people's ways of life and their replacement with frontier smallholdings and cattle ranching. The sustained increase in agricultural production[62] was also the result of both the protection and subsidization of production for the domestic market and the application of machinery to agriculture. One important facet of Japan's flexible industrialization was that medium-sized and large firms could produce affordable agricultural machinery that could be purchased by smallholders.[63] Nevertheless, there is some debate about whether a concentration of land into larger parcels (as took place in both the British and American agrarian capitalist transitions) might have made agriculture more productive still. But the maintenance of stable peasant tenure was seen throughout the transformation period as key to securing social peace.[64]

Although, as we have noted, Japan is substantially industrialized by the 1930s, the focus of attention in relation to Japan's capitalist development is the period from the early 1960s to the late 1970s. This is the 'miracle' that frames developmentalism throughout the Cold War period. We shall identify the key components of this political economy of capitalist transformation. There are two common points of departure that account for this remarkable transition: the emergence of a particular form of capital and the institutionalization of a particular kind of economic governance. We shall make a brief sketch of each.

Larger Japanese industries proactively sought to transform their production activities. They did so by seeking out new technologies internationally and adopting/adapting[65] them in order to move into new sectors.[66] This is part of the story of the development of Japanese automobile, machinery and electronics manufacture.[67] It is also a pivotal part of the development of precision tool manufacture.[68] Investments in these areas were secured through coalitions—more or less formalized—between leading firms and large banks,

[61] The qualifier 'massive' is salient. In Hokkaido from the late 1800s to the early 1900s, the Japanese state dispossessed indigenous peoples and settled 'modern' farmers from other parts of Japan. This process was key to reducing the food insecurity anxieties of the period as a new rice frontier emerged.

[62] Vestal, *Planning for Change*: 36.

[63] Mosk, *Japanese Economic Development*: 247.

[64] Allinson, 'The Structure and Transformation of Conservative Rule': 147.

[65] Morris-Suzuki, *The Technological Transformation of Japan*.

[66] Francks, *Japanese Economic Development*: 174; David Friedman, *The Misunderstood Miracle. Industrial Development and Political Change in Japan* (1988): 28.

[67] Ohkawa and Rosovsky, 'Postwar Japanese Growth in Historical Perspective'.

[68] A detailed account of the development of Japan's precision machine tool industry is provided by Martin Fransman, 'International Competitiveness, Technical Change and the State: The Machine Tool Industry in Taiwan and Japan' (1986).

a structure that was in some degree underpinned by the Japanese state. As the Americans halted their breaking up of zaibatsu,[69] some firms merged and established long-term connections with finance banks, known as *keiretsu* or 'systems'. And new large firms (such as Sanyo) emerged.

This strategy was achieved through proactive technological change underpinned by stable capital markets. It was also the outcome of the forging of a set of labour relations within larger firms in which the loyalty of the labour force was generated through structures of lifetime employment, promotion, and dedication. These firms enjoyed what might be called economies of expansion and scale in which growing to become mass-producer exporting firms generated efficiency gains.[70] It was also based on 'post-Fordist' production methods of flexible specialization and just-in-time production.[71] Labour in many large firms was constantly monitored and reorganized. Manufacture was based on quicker turnarounds of components and end products to suit specific orders. This reduced waste and warehousing. Quality control within manufacturing was enhanced through the mutual vigilance and monitoring of performance within different sets of workers. A form of labour unionism in which firms, government, and unions worked together in the pursuit of productivity gains was supported by firms and the government. Indeed, more radical labour unionism was heavily repressed by both American and Japanese governments.[72]

But it is important to note that the sustained accumulation and growth of the late 1950s to the early 1970s was not simply about the emergence of *keiretsu* combinations of finance and manufacturing or the formation of cartels and mergers. Indeed, the bulk of Japan's growth in its 'miracle' period derived from small and medium-sized enterprises.[73] Throughout the growth period, small and medium-sized enterprises contributed around 60 per cent of gross national product (GNP) and employed the majority of workers.[74] Nor did these smaller firms simply service larger firms upstream. In key sectors, they were dynamic and flexible in their production strategies, adopting and adapting technologies, seeking new markets, and upgrading the skills of workers.[75]

[69] Mitsui, Mitsubishi, and Sumitomo survived the war and occupation.

[70] Mosk, *Japanese Economic Development*: 245.

[71] The iconic example of this was Toyota's *kanban* system.

[72] SCAP initially supported new independent unions but subsequently changed tack when, in the 1950s, Marxist currents within mass unionism emerged.

[73] Vestal, *Planning for Change*: 47.

[74] Friedman, *The Misunderstood Miracle*.

[75] Morris-Suzuki, *The Technological Transformation of Japan*.

Large numbers of small and medium-sized firms emerged, producing primarily within Japan's domestic markets. Indeed, although some have identified Japan as the epitome of export-led industrialization, its transformation was substantially 'nationalist', imports being managed and exports remaining a comparatively small portion of GNP. Export success was considered vital as a way to protect the national economy from the effects of balance of payments problems and the possibility that foreign transnational corporations might bully national firms unless they achieved a scale and spatial reach to hold their own. Domestic markets were highly competitive, and this competitiveness pivotally fed into the levels of innovation and testing of export success.[76]

Nevertheless, it is certainly the case that export success underpinned the growth of the largest Japanese companies, especially from the mid-1970s. The Japanese transnational corporations that produced cars, computer technology, chemicals, musical equipment, and so on emerged through some combination of the factors noted above: dynamic appropriation and adaptation of technologies, new forms of labour organization,[77] a secure capital base generated through domestic market success and government support, and a network of equally dynamic and technologically adept medium-sized firms producing competitive-edge machinery and components up the supply chain. Japan's opening up as an export economy was a strategic move, based on a political view that some liberalization would maintain economic growth.[78]

The transformation of Japanese capitalism into a highly capitalized, technologically ambitious, and productive industrial sector has been narrated as much as a governmental success as a firm-based success. Indeed, the most prominent term in post-war development strategy debates emerges from studies of Japan's developmental state, a term used to highlight and emphasize the 'plan rational'[79] interventions of Japanese governmental institutions.

Japan's developmental state was intuitionally based on the Ministry for International Trade and Industry (MITI). MITI became a powerful and largely administrative body that provided three key strategic functions: identifying

[76] John Weiss, 'Japan's Post-War Protection Policy: Some Implications for Less Developed Countries' (1986). Early post-Occupation Japanese development strategy did involve a concern with 'excessive competition', but this was not meant in a pervasive way but rather in a strategic way relating to economies of scale and technology management.

[77] Labour was not cheap, but capital and skill-intensive. See Mitchell Kellman and Daniel Landau, 'The Nature of Japan's Comparative Advantage' (1984).

[78] Bai Gao, *Economic Ideology and Japanese Industrial Policy. Developmentalism from 1931 to 1996* (1997): 28–9.

[79] This term was popularized by Chalmers Johnson in *MITI and the Japanese Miracle. The Growth of Industrial Policy 1925–1975* (1982). This influential work has served as the foundation for a great deal of developmental state research. Much of the account of MITI here is derived from Johnson.

priority industries and advocating support for them through loans via the Japanese Development Bank and (for a time)[80] control over access to foreign exchange/import licences; organizing the consolidation of firms into larger single firms or co-ordinated coalitions; and supporting the procurement of new technologies and managing their dissemination throughout industrial sectors.[81] Overall, and in a more day-to-day fashion, MITI's planning and research personnel provided 'administrative guidance' to firms with a view to promoting protection, co-ordination, and the incentivization of firms to pursue new lines of production or new technologies. This also involved making strategic decisions about which industries are no longer 'developmental', a decision MITI made in relation to textiles. From the 1960s, MITI's power started to decline gradually as the economy liberalized. Its core function—and one that was seen as vital to ensuring that the economy's gradual opening up would not undermine the progress of the 1950s—was to promote exports.

There is considerable debate about the extent to which MITI successfully forged Japan's capitalist transformation. Competition rather than co-ordination as well as the ambitions of firms themselves (not all of which received much support from MITI) were certainly very important. Furthermore, not everything MITI did was successful, and the ministry suffered its fair share of accusations of inefficiency and cronyism. It also failed to impose its will on capital in many instances.[82] There is a tendency to endow institutions with a 'false prescience' when attempting to explain successful transformations.[83] But the political art of designing incentive structures, adapting to changed circumstances, and keeping in mind that capitalist development requires strategic thinking undeniably make MITI something of a loose genotype for many subsequent developmentalisms: an authoritative semi-autonomous government agency that uses various incentives and disincentives to forge structural change in capitalist accumulation towards higher-productivity activities. MITI identified a series of industries and industrial structures[84] that were considered nationally vital in order to secure Japan's besieged sovereignty:

[80] The control over forex and imports was liberalized from the mid-1960s and by 1973 Japan's international trade regulation largely conformed to the Organization for Economic Cooperation and Development/International Monetary Fund/General Agreement of Tariffs and Trade norms.

[81] Johnson, *MITI and the Japanese Miracle*; Vestal, *Planning for Change*: 32–3.

[82] Friedman, *The Misunderstood Miracle*: 204.

[83] Laura Hein, 'Growth Versus Success: Japan's Economic Policy in Historical Perspective' (1993): 99.

[84] By this I mean interconnected industries in which growth in one would stimulate growth in others (what was sometimes coined as 'investment creates investment') and the financing of expanded investments by closely connected financial institutions, whether government-managed or private. 'Systemic' thinking of this kind was prevalent in MITI and within large firms.

initially chemicals, coal, and steel, then synthetics and textiles, then transistor and processor technology.

This does not exhaust our consideration of government action, however. The Ministry of Finance's fiscal and financial strategy responded nimbly to the mini-recessions that Japan encountered during its capitalist transformation.[85] Education policy was strongly vocational, expanding the skill base of the population.[86] The Ministry of Education centralized the curriculum in order to disseminate a post-war narrative of Japanese national purpose and unity.[87]

Japan's developmentalism sought legitimacy in a stable and supported peasantry, near full employment, rising wages, and rising consumption. It relied on a regulated and productivity-oriented labour unionism which combined (at least in large firms) 'industrial democracy'[88] with employment and a career ladder at least until the age of fifty.[89] Indeed, the militancy of early post-war labour generated pressure on large firms (where unions were relatively large and organized) to institute security or work, a living wage, and clear structures of promotion and seniority.[90] The Japanese government committed to promoting minimum wages, improved working conditions, and social provision throughout the 'miracle'.

By 1960, average wages were about 50 per cent above pre-war levels; and by 1970 they had risen again by about 80 per cent.[91] More strikingly, the family income of an urban wage worker increased from an index of 11.7 in 1960 to 100 in 1980.[92] Throughout the 1960, Japan's developmentalism was oriented around the connection of growth, industrialization, and improved material conditions. There was a constant concern to ensure that the increasing cycles of investment, industrialization, and technological change did not generate massive unemployment.[93] There was a concern to keep real wages buoyant. An ideology of growth and national well-being was constantly propounded by the state, especially after the Income Doubling Plan. And there emerged

[85] There were recessions in 1957–9 and 1975.

[86] Allen, *A Short Economic History of Modern Japan*: 201.

[87] See the Japan case study chapters in Laura Hein and Mark Selden, *Censoring History. Citizenship and Memory in Japan, Germany, and the United States* (2000).

[88] Sheldon Garon and Mike Mochuzuki, 'Negotiating Social Contracts' (1993): 158.

[89] This labour regime existed in large industries and has been the centre of attention in analyses of the 'miracle'. But, as mentioned before, most work was done in smaller firms where labour was more fluid and also involved a more equitable balance of men and women. Throughout the increase in wage labour, women earned an average of 50 per cent less than men. Deborah Milly, *Poverty Equality and Growth. The Politics of Economic Needs in Postwar Japan* (1999): 11.

[90] Friedman, *The Misunderstood Miracle*: 135.

[91] Allen, *A Short Economic History of Modern Japan 1867–1937*: 194.

[92] Hein, 'Growth Versus Success': 101.

[93] Vestal, *Planning for Change*: 43.

a cultural political economy of mass consumption. It was through the government's ability to oversee sustained growth, manage crises, and ensure mass employment and consumption that Japan's politics enjoyed its greatest stability and legitimacy ever.

Conclusion

Japan grew faster than any economy in history during the period from the mid-1950s to the early 1970s. It had transformed from a war-torn political economy that had the vestiges of an early and imperially dependent industrialization into an economy with deep capital markets, sophisticated technologies, agile and efficient production systems, and a high material quality of life for the vast majority of its population. It had—in a way that was historically unique—undertaken capitalist transformation in order to catch up with an existing 'core' of developed capitalist states. Indeed, by many measures it had overtaken lots of them.[94] It has moved from textiles and metallurgy towards chemicals, precision machine tool manufacture, cars and transistor goods, synthetic materials, computers...and by the 1970s Japan's economy was so networked and diverse that it becomes difficult to identify a simple characteristic that it has within an international division of labour.

Economic growth was Japan's primary goal and it was pursued by government and capital fundamentally as a basic political exigency: growth would ensure social stability and national sovereignty.[95] The sustained accumulation and institutional design of the state largely worked to achieve this. As with Britain and America, Japan's political economy of capitalist transformation was fundamentally a sustained economic nationalism.[96] Japan faced fundamental political challenges of security, sovereignty, and legitimacy at least as intense as America and Britain: during the 1950s it faced an expanding communist China and an overbearing American patron, and it possessed a severely weakened economy.[97] The Japanese government addressed this situation through the pursuit of a strategy of capitalist transformation. A crucial and fairly specific difference—beyond the 'post-colonial' historical setting—was the prohibition of any large-scale military build-up after occupation. This led, quite explicitly,

[94] Japan's economy surpassed West Germany's in 1968. Michael Smitka, *Japanese Prewar Growth. Lessons for Development Theory?* (1988): x.
[95] Hein, 'Growth Versus Success': 108.
[96] Chalmers Johnson, *Japan: Who Governs? The Rise of the Developmental State* (1995): 103.
[97] Johnson, *Japan: Who Governs?*: 27.

to Japanese elites and major firms framing their developmentalism through a tenacious and determined articulation of economic growth with security in what was a geopolitically highly charged region. Those industries that grew, transformed, or emerged were seen not simply as competitive but also as strategic: domestic rice production, metallurgy and chemicals, and later technology, design, and brand-intensive exports as Japan liberalized.

Japan straddles two ages of capitalist transformation. Its earliest capitalist growth takes place in the late nineteenth century when a small number of countries sought to forge strong national economies through capitalist industrialization and within a specific historic context: a British-dominated global political economy. From the late 1800s until the late 1930s, Japan transformed gradually and under considerable state tutelage towards an industrializing and expanding national economy. Comparative to European experiences, writers speak of Japan's 'proto industrialization', its textile industry, its agrarian commercialization, and its imperialism. After occupation, in a decolonizing world, Japan's state and larger firms find themselves in a world of sovereign states in which colonization is no longer possible and in which there has emerged a moderately expanded 'core' of industrialized capitalist states. A world-region emerged for the first time that can be called 'developed', at least within capitalism's own historiography. As a result—although in no way inevitably—Japan's post-war politics focused around a developmentalist strategy in which national security, government legitimacy, and sovereignty served as major-order political imperatives for an urgent, flexible, tenacious, and (largely) effective cohabitation of industrial transformation under purposeful political guidance.

8

Taiwan and Israel

Introduction

Let us recap. We have set out a concept of developmentalism which has the following core features. We have identified a 'real' essence in capitalism which is its relentless imperative to accumulate through the generation of increasing amounts of value. This imperative is produced through the wage–labour relation and the competition between capitals. This core reality in capitalism is manifested in two sequential histories: one in capitalism's transformation (or ascendance) and another in its reproduction as a completed and universal political economy (or its dominance). We have argued that developmentalism is the strategy and ideology to complete the former. Without this project, most parts of the post-colonial world endure non-transformative capitalisms which do not generate sustained growth and which leave countries resembling adjuncts to processes of accumulation whose value is realized elsewhere. Developmentalism is a political ideology and strategy that is highly elastic and context-specific, but it does have a key identifying feature: it is driven by a major-order political imperative that relates to sovereignty and growth.

The possible benefits of development in itself are not sufficient to drive the kind of transformation that capitalism requires. We have argued that we can see developmentalism as a basic legitimacy demand within many post-colonial and poor states: the exercise of authoritative power not only to make politics possible but also to oversee and regulate an economic transformation that allows the basic commonwealth within which people do not fear the harms of extreme poverty. Within this context, we have set out criteria to identify and assess developmentalism: its inter-relations with processes of accumulation and especially its ability to promote expanded and productivity-enhancing forms of production; its ability to respond to crisis; the techniques deployed to ensure social stability during periods of contention and struggle; and its ability to transform the increased production of surplus into a commonwealth. We have also added that in a post-colonial period, developmentalism is defined by impatience, rivalry, and nationalism.

Developmentalism: The Normative and Transformative within Capitalism. Graham G.M. Harrison, Oxford University Press (2020).
DOI: 10.1093/oso/9780198785798.001.0001

In Chapter 7, we reviewed the first 'late developer': Japan. In this chapter, we consider Taiwan and Israel. Both of these countries went through capitalist transformations from the late 1950s. They exemplify the role that nationalism and insecurity play in compelling states to promote capitalist ascendance. They are coupled together in part because they share a socio-political property that fixes our interest on existential threat in a more specific geopolitical and historical fashion. Both countries have lacked the international legislative legitimacy of unquestioned statehood. Also, both countries' governments have been ruled by elites that are 'immigrated': that is to say, both states were commandeered by groups that moved into both government and the nation simultaneously. This mode of accession to power defines elites as in part alien to their own territories and, as a result, creating a national economy that legitimizes rule and unifies territory is essentially the be all and end all of government. In both cases, the failure of developmentalism might have meant the failure of the nation-state.

Taiwan

Taiwan's developmentalism occurred between the mid-1950s and early 1980s. The average annual growth rate of GNP between 1951 and 1955 was 9.7 per cent, between 1956 and 1960 7.0 per cent, and between 1961 and 1965 10.1 per cent.[1] From 1963 to 1972 the average rate of growth was 10.8 per cent. Between 1953 and 1982 industry grew at a rate of 13.3 per cent.[2] Over the full period of transformation, real GNP grew at 8.6 per cent between 1952 and 1994.[3] As with other cases, the 'miracle' period was a product of a longer set of changes in the political economy.

Colonialism

As with so many successful examples of capitalist development, the early forging of capitalist social relations was violent, alienating, and rights-denying. The imperial Japanese state occupied Taiwan from 1895, integrating it

[1] Shirley Kuo, 'Government Policy in the Taiwanese Development Process: The Past 50 Years' (1999): 54.

[2] Thomas Gold, *State and Society in the Taiwan Miracle* (1986): 4.

[3] Eric Thorbecke and Henry Wan, 'The Lessons from Taiwan: Relevance, Limitations and Transferability' (1999): 6.

(as we noted in Chapter 7) into a regional–colonial political economy of labour and primary production. Taiwan's political economy was engineered to provide sugar and rice for Japan. The colonial state imposed a labour regime on smallholders in which they were integrated into this production system. Some of the 'second-generation' zaibatsu invested in Taiwan during occupation, mainly processing agricultural produce. After the end of the First World War, Japan invested more concertedly in infrastructure and basic education. Almost no Taiwanese elite—political or economic—was permitted and as a result there was almost no secondary or higher education. The land tenure system was modified rather than changed. A form of hybrid landlordism and tenancy bequeathed by Taiwanese and Chinese systems was overlain with the establishing of smallholder rights to their fields but without any major eradication of landlords themselves.[4] The colonial government also pushed farmers to adopt improved seeds and intensify the use of fertilizers, the outcome of which was a gradual improvement in productivity.[5] These brief and externally imposed changes are noteworthy because in some degree they provide the context in which Taiwan embarked upon a sustained transformation. The decentralized nature of agricultural and industrial production, the dense infrastructure, and the expanding universal basic education all fed into Taiwan's post-war development, although, as ever, historians disagree about the extent of the significance of these factors.

Independence and Economic Growth

The first strategic priority of the Taiwanese government was to invest systematically in agricultural development.[6] Between 1949 and the mid-1950s, the government capped the level of rent on tenanted land and then redistributed public and private land to smallholders, so that by the end of this period 71 per cent of agricultural land was under smallholder tenancy.[7] The government capped rents, sold land it owned, and then compulsorily purchased land from landlords for bonds and stocks, subsequently selling purchased land

[4] Dubbed the 'one field two owners' system, this involved an overall owner and a renter who then leased land to tenant farmers. Japanese land reform abolished the upper tier of largely absentee ownership and worked through 'present' landlords.

[5] Raymond Myers and Adrienne Ching, 'Agricultural Development in Taiwan under Japanese Colonial Rule' (1964); Edgar Wickberg, 'Japanese Land Policies in Taiwan, 1895–1945' (1969).

[6] Thorbecke and Wan, 'The Lessons from Taiwan' (1999): 5.

[7] Land reform was mainly undertaken through the Land to the Tiller programme in 1953. Kuo, 'Government Policy in the Taiwanese Development Process': 56.

cheaply to smallholders. Agricultural output grew at 4.4 per cent per year between 1954 and 1967—the fastest growth rate in Asia at that time.[8] Indeed, it is common in accounts of Taiwan's development to speak of its first phase of growth as an agriculture-focused one in which increases in agricultural output were coupled with export success. The government prioritized investment in rural infrastructure: irrigation, electrification, transport, education, and other forms of rural construction.

It also committed heavily to the promotion of new agricultural techniques through the Joint Commission on Rural Reconstruction (JCRR) (1948)[9] which supported the creation of Farmers' Associations in each county. Farmers' Associations provided extension services, purchasing and warehousing facilities, and tax collection services to all farmers within their catchment area.[10] The JCRR undertook nearly 6,000 rural development projects between 1951 and 1965.[11] The outcome of this agrarian strategy was an equalization of property and an increase and diversification in agricultural output. Throughout this period, the fiscal relation between smallholders and the state was extractive. Controlled prices for rice were below their international market prices and this gave government-owned marketing institutions revenues when the rice was traded on. This 'rice tax' was never heavy and was balanced by the extensive investments in rural areas by the state, the latter financed substantially by American aid.[12] Beyond the political project to increase rice output for export, farmers were encouraged to produce raw materials for local industry. The increase in agricultural production was mainly a result of effective government support to promote productivity increases, not the incentives of high crop prices.

Taiwan's agrarian transition was accompanied by a fairly distinct industrialization in which capital was not heavily concentrated in a small number of urban areas and within large agglomerated units (as it was in Japan and South Korea). As many accounts of Taiwan's capitalist transformation attest, the early phase of growth was driven by small and medium-sized enterprises (SMEs) that were sited in towns throughout the island. These firms produced textiles, timber, glassware, and other commodities. This meant that industrialization was more embedded in the transformation towards smallholder

[8] Robert Wade, *Governing the Market. Economic Theory and the Role of Government in East Asian Industrialisation* (1990): 76.

[9] The JCRR was partly funded by America and it has American advisors.

[10] Tsu-tan Fu and Shun-yi Shei, 'Agriculture as the Foundation for Development: The Taiwanese Story' (1999): 209.

[11] Fu and Shei, 'Agriculture as the Foundation for Development': 210.

[12] American aid was ended in 1965.

commercial agriculture. Households would supply labour to industry without family members having to move to a city. Commonly, a bicycle or bus trip would suffice for a day-long wage labour. Smallholders could farm, earn money from selling crops, work for wages, and purchase goods in town. Agriculture grew, and the transfer of surplus from agriculture to industry also grew through trade taxes and savings.[13]

In 1949, Taiwan's industry was constituted by the remains of the Japanese colonial–industrial sector,[14] the capital imported by Chinese mainlander businesspeople,[15] and a small indigenous business sector. This was the basis upon which the *Kuomintang* (KMT) government sought to construct an industrial economy, and it pursued this transformation through a series of 5-year plans, each of which was realized through a range of interventions by the state.

In the early 1950s, the government set up a series of tariffs and quotas, the aim of which was to encourage import substitution, focusing on low-technology industries that produced commodities affordable to Taiwan's low-income population. A panoply of state agencies regulated, supported, and protected firms through controls on capital, export licenses, and the provision of subsidies.[16] In this period, export earnings were dominated by agricultural produce. The limits to this strategy were well understood. Taiwan's small domestic consumer goods market and pressure on its current account meant that this 'primary' import substitution strategy would not be sufficient to generate a sustained process of accumulation and growth. In this period (1952–8), manufacturing output doubled.[17]

Transformative Growth

From the early 1960s, with hyperinflation controlled and an expanding capitalist sector, the Taiwanese government planned to generate more capital and technology-intensive industrial sectors. This is the period commonly defined

[13] Penelope Francks, Johanna Boestel, and Choo Hyop Kim, *Agriculture and Economic Development in East Asia* (1999): 169–71.

[14] American bombing against Japan involved massive destruction in Taiwan as well.

[15] These might have moved to the island after the exit of Japan during which republican China had sovereignty over Taiwan, or it might have been after the 1949 revolution when much of the southern KMT elite fled.

[16] On this, see Stephan Haggard and Chien-Kuo Pang, 'The Transition to Export-Led Growth in Taiwan' (2015): 61–5.

[17] Wade, *Governing the Market*: 77.

as the Taiwan miracle, a second phase of transformation. The steady growth of the previous decade shifted towards a transformative growth in which technology, new forms of labour, economic diversification, and an ascending capitalist class distinctively energized Taiwan's political economy. This was in part a result of the increasing activism of a developmentally minded group of policymakers within the government. The leadership became increasingly aware that 'simple' industrialization and foreign exchange constraints[18] meant that Taiwan's growth was unlikely to last, let alone increase. The country's status and security remained unclear and America was signalling that it would cease aid transfers later in the decade. In short, the consolidation of a capitalist strategy of national security in the 1950s created the basis for a series of political–strategic decisions to transform Taiwan radically.[19]

The government maintained tariffs through this period, although they were reduced and used with more strategic nuance. Some firms were given export targets and made to pay penalties when these were missed.[20] It also maintained and set up state-owned enterprises.[21] It established partnerships between its own company and foreign and domestic private companies, and in 1965 an export processing zone was set up. These arrangements were underpinned by clear political support and subsidies. They were also set up to exert conditions on foreign companies to train, share technology, and purchase components from domestic suppliers. In other words, the state–private partnerships institutionalized a political device in which investment was purposed to enhance technological change, investment, and new production methods within Taiwan's own capitalist sector. All foreign direct investment (FDI) dedicated to serving the Taiwanese market had to have 50 per cent Taiwanese participation and a certain percentage of components had to be manufactured in Taiwan.[22] The government also gave preferential access to credit to selected companies. It introduced rebates on import taxes on condition of export success. It habitually scoped and researched firms (usually Japanese and American) and attempted to 'curate' investments in combination with local firms, technologies, and supply chains. In some cases, it directly subsidized research and development within firms.

[18] Haggard and Pang, 'The Transition to Export-Led Growth in Taiwan'.
[19] Details of these shifts are given in Tai-Chun Kuo and Ramon Myers, *Taiwan's Economic Transformation. Leadership, Property Rights, and Institutional Change 1949–1965* (2012).
[20] Haggard and Pang, 'The Transition to Export-Led Growth in Taiwan': 75.
[21] Alice Amsden, 'Taiwan's Industrialization Policies: Two Views, Two Types of Subsidy' (1999): 96.
[22] Murray Rubenstein, 'Taiwan's Socio-Economic Modernisation 1971–1996' (2007).

In the 1970s and especially after 1973, the government intensified its activities in developing larger-scale, more capital-intensive, and technologically ambitious production. Although Taiwan is known for its distinctively SME industrial structure (in comparison with the zaibatsu, keiretsu, and chaebol leadership in Japan and South Korea), there was a concentration of capital as the economy moved into larger-scale metallurgy, shipbuilding, semiconductor-based production,[23] and precision tool manufacture. In the late 1970s, the government increased investment in research and development, investing in research parks, making support to firms conditional on percentages of investment in research and development, and investing in technology-based vocational secondary education. It also dedicated expenditure to large-scale infrastructure projects, especially the flagship Ten Major Projects to which was dedicated US$8.8 billion.[24] By the early 1970s, Taiwan had an economy characterized by a diverse, integrated, technologically dynamic capitalism that provided the basis for generalized material welfare. Industry had risen from 16 per cent to 36 per cent of GDP between 1958 and 1973, and by that latter year, 85 per cent of exports were industrial.[25]

General social well-being improved throughout Taiwan's transformation. The government introduced compulsory free primary education in 1968 which led to a literacy rate of 89.3 per cent by 1979. Life expectancy improved throughout.[26] Income per capita increased from US$100 to US$12,500 from 1952 to 1994. Houses with electric lighting went from 33 per cent in 1949 to 99.7 per cent in 1994.[27]

Existential Threat

The Taiwanese government was subjected to a set of immutable and pressing circumstances within which development, sovereignty, and legitimacy became inextricably intertwined. There are few countries that have faced such immediate and pressing an existential threat as Taiwan, and it is this major-order political condition that underpinned the Taiwanese government's determination, flexibility, and authoritarianism, each and all focused on

[23] Constance Squires Meaney, 'State Policy and the Development of Taiwan's Semiconductor Industry' (2015).

[24] Rubenstein, 'Taiwan's Socio-Economic Modernisation': 373.

[25] Francks, Boestel, and Kim, *Agriculture and Economic Development in East Asia*: 162.

[26] Gold, *State and Society in the Taiwan Miracle*: 5–6.

[27] Kuo, 'Government Policy in the Taiwanese Development Process': 43.

capitalist development. Wade characterizes the Taiwanese government as an institutional combination of development, legitimacy, and security.[28] One can see this in a number of specific respects.

The Taiwanese government was a conquest government with 'virtually no ties to Taiwan'.[29] The KMT state occupied Taiwan and was staffed by refugee-emigres from the Chinese mainland after the revolution that brought the Chinese Communist Party to power. Although, after the Second World War and Japan's defeat, Taiwan was ceded back to China, the KMT's 'provincial' rule in Taiwan presaged the conquest logic that defined the period after 1949. The KMT considered the Taiwanese as secessionist and emerging from collaboration with the Japanese. Culturally, the KMT saw Taiwan as alien and/or backward.[30] The KMT's main endeavour between 1945 and 1949 was to repress and erase social opposition within indigenous Taiwanese to its rule. Up to 20,000 Taiwanese were killed in this process.[31] As a result, indigenous Taiwanese did not perceive the new 'nationalist' government as anything but an occupying force with a social base in the two million mainlanders that fled to Taiwan in the late 1940s. The government, for its part, maintained a strong bias towards former mainlanders for its personnel and most strictly for its core executive. In a nutshell, the KMT government in Taiwan was constructed out of an occupying elite and facing a nation that it was not socially familiar with and considered to be potentially insurrectionary and backward. It considered capitalist development as its high priority, as a means to create regime legitimacy.[32]

In its early existence, Taiwan was not seen by any other country as a going concern or a fully fledged nation-state. It was seen as a war-torn territory that had just lost its two main markets—Japan and mainland China.[33] It was left largely unsupported and, of course, it faced a very large and very close neighbour that officially saw Taiwan as an illegal secession that would, in time, be integrated into the People's Republic of China (PRC). The PRC briskly commenced navy manoeuvres in the Taiwan Straits. Chinese involvement in the Korean War provoked America to consider Taiwan as a strategically significant asset in the context of the Cold War, and from the mid-1950s, aid and preferential trade were crucial to Taiwan's survival. In the 1950s, China

[28] Wade, *Governing the Market*: 228. [29] Wade, *Governing the Market*: 75.

[30] Murray Rubenstein, 'The Taiwan Miracle' (1994).

[31] Gold, *State and Society in the Taiwan Miracle*: 51.

[32] Yu-Shan Wu, 'Taiwan's Developmental State: After the Economic and Political Turmoil' (2007).

[33] Ching-yuan Lin, *Industrialisation in Taiwan, 1946–74. Trade and Import Substitution Policies for Developing Countries* (1973): 39.

continued to carry out military manoeuvres and bomb islands that Taiwan considered part of its territory. American geopolitical support never fully mollified the sense of existential threat felt by the Taiwanese government, especially during periods of rapprochement between western states and China between the Korean and Vietnamese wars, then in the mid-1970s with Nixon's engagement with China. In 1971 Taiwan was derecognized as the 'Chinese government' state by the UN.

Taiwan maintained a large military. It did so with fulsome American support, but also by developing state-owned companies that produced military hardware and some weaponry. And it maintained conscription and a large standing army. This military force was both a deterrent against possible invasion by China and a preparation for 'unification' of the PRC with Taiwan. Until the late 1980s, Taiwan's militarization expressed a tense combination of defensive and offensive scenarios, both of which securitized Taiwan's centralized and undemocratic political system. The Taiwanese government also developed a formidable internal security apparatus.

As time passed, the KMT position that it was the government of mainland China temporarily exiled softened from a military strategy to a statement of principle. As a result, the KMT had to reproduce its authority in rather paradoxical circumstances. It could not construct the formal institutions of national politics, institutions that might have consolidated democratic and citizen-based political practices, without accepting the historical fact that its claim to be the Chinese government was largely an ideological one and that it was, in reality, the government of the island of Taiwan.[34] This disposition fed strongly into its emerging ideology of developmentalism from the mid-1950s. The ability of the Taiwanese government to generate legitimacy could not derive from a strong nationalism or democratic accountability. It could, however, derive from a strong sustained economic growth, the extra effect of which was to provide a (provincial) bastion of relative success vis à vis the PRC. Capitalist transformation was, then, a strongly governed political project to consolidate a kind of sovereignty peculiar to Taiwan's geopolitical and historical circumstances. It was achieved through a strategy of accumulation in which firms successfully grew and moved into high-value productive activities as a result of sustained investment within a supportive political context.

[34] From 1949 until the late 1980s, the Taiwanese government described itself as a provincial government, not a national one, in order to avoid a nomenclature that suggested it was not the Chinese government. This is also why it maintains its official name as a republic of China.

Israel

Achieving Statehood: Nation/Economy/Security

From the late 1800s until the end of the First World War, Palestine was an increasingly weakly governed part of the Ottoman empire. A Jewish population cohabited with a larger Arab population. The Palestinian political economy was constituted by Arab landlords,[35] tenant farmers, urban Jewish communities, some agricultural wage labourers, and merchants governed through a patchwork of political authorities which contained considerable self-governance and autonomy. The intensification of anti-Semitism in Europe and the pogroms against Jews in Russia from the 1880s generated a political project of 'return' to *Eretz Israel*, an imagined Jewish homeland free from the persecutions experienced by Jews in Europe. It was these political circumstances that created ideologies of Zionism[36] which were driven by the desire to repopulate Palestine with Jewish communities with a view to establishing a Jewish state in Palestine.

From 1919 to 1947, Palestine was mandated to the British. Waves of immigration of Jewish people from Europe continued, obviously intensified by the rise of Nazism in Germany.[37] The British government was generally supportive of Jewish immigration into Palestine. This enabling environment galvanized Zionist organizations to fund migration to Palestine and to set up a range of institutions and funds for Jewish settlement. Within Palestine, Jewish settlers were organized into farming communities. Mainly eastern European Jews who did not farm were trained, funded, and settled on purchased land to create the framework for a Jewish claim to statehood. Land was purchased from Arab landlords or the Mandate government. Funds from Jewish diasporas were allotted to farming communities through an increasingly well-organized set of quasi-governmental Jewish organizations. The broadly convivial Arab–Jewish societies of loosely governed Palestine were replaced by increasingly exclusive ethnic relations. Zionist projects aimed to construct Jewish-only urban spaces. Jewish agricultural settlements were instructed to

[35] In the 1920s, up to 23 per cent of the land was owned by Palestinian Arab landowners. Henry Rosenfeld, 'The Class Situation of the Arab National Minority in Israel' (1978): 375.

[36] As with pretty much everything relating to Israel, nomenclatures and historical accounts are controversial. Some argue that Zionism is intrinsically an ethically exclusive violent ideology and others argue that Zionism also includes more liberal political possibilities.

[37] It is worth noting that anti-Semitism between the World Wars was not only German but also present in many countries.

employ Jewish wage labourers and when this made poor economic sense, those farms were financed to do so. Jewish militias were set up in the 1930s.

The Histadrut, funded by diasporas, was created as an organization to fund Jewish businesses, organize Jewish wage labourers, provide healthcare and education, allocate people to farms and jobs, fund the construction of apartments, and set up institutions of representation and decision-making that brokered the power of emerging political parties. In essence, Histadrut became an embryonic state within the Mandate for Palestine, preparing to transform into a state based on an ethno-demographic project of Jewish immigration. We will come to see how this corporate labour organization played a crucial role in Israel's industrialization.[38]

Throughout the 1930s and early 1940s, the Palestinian economy grew at a considerable pace.[39] The Jewish settlement project was accompanied by some industrial investment, mainly at first in agricultural processing, then other small-scale manufactures,[40] and residential construction as more Jews immigrated. The Second World War boosted demand for goods produced in Palestine as the war moved into the Middle East and North Africa, and there was some import substitution as routine imports were stopped under conditions of conflict. By the end of the war, Palestine was the most industrialized country in the Middle East.

With the Mandate due to end in 1947, the British government became increasingly concerned with the stability of Palestine. Although there had been some cross-ethnic political mobilization in the early 1930s, the Zionist project relentlessly aimed to construct an ethnically exclusive political economy.[41] The British Balfour Declaration (1917) stated that the Jews had a right to a homeland in Palestine, although it also stipulated that this would only be possible through consultation with Arab Palestinian organizations and it explicitly stated that the civil and religious rights of Palestinian Arabs should not be undermined. The subsequent UN Special Committee inquiry concluded that post-Mandatory Palestine should be split into two associated states, one Jewish and one Arab, a proposal that the UN General assembly agreed. Arab leaders in Palestine and neighbouring states rejected this; Jewish organizations largely accepted it on the expectation that it would be rejected by Arab organizations. A roughshod coalition of Arab state forces entered

[38] A definitive account of Histadrut is Lev Grinberg, *Split Corporatism in Israel* (1991).
[39] Yair Aharoni, *The Israeli Economy. Dreams and Realities* (1991): 67.
[40] Perhaps most salient here was diamond polishing.
[41] Lev Grinberg, *Mo(ve)ments of Resistance: Politics, Economy and Society in Israel/Palestine 1931–2013* (2014): 64.

Palestine in 1948 and the Jewish military organizations quickly engaged with them, having been prepared for precisely this eventuality. Repelling the forces of neighbouring states, the Jewish quasi-state declared its independence as Israel, occupying an area considerably larger than the two-state map suggested by the UN. Throughout this turbulent end-of-Mandate period, Arabs were intimidated and pushed away from zones considered to be part of Israel. After 1948, the Israeli state consistently endeavoured to 'cleanse' Israel of Arabs through military operations, threats, the cordoning off of populations, and the construction of new Jewish settlements.[42]

Israeli statehood was forged out of a Zionist project, unrecognized by the UN. It generated a mass dispossession of Arab Palestinians,[43] a considerable amount of hostility from neighbouring states, and left Israel facing a constant and considerable threat to its existence. Israel was in a state of war with Egypt until 1979 and with Jordan until 1994 and remains in a state of war with Iraq and Syria.[44] Jewish immigration and Arab expulsion/fleeing created a Jewish-majority state. The fundamental political reflex that this situation generated was to treat the economy as a political resource for an ethnically exclusive nationalism. Indeed, the notion that 'the economy' had a distinct existence at all was entirely absent from Israeli governance in its first decade. 'In Israel, economic goals arise naturally from the general goal of the survival of the state.'[45]

In the years after independence, the Israeli government centralized political authority out of the vibrant, politicized Jewish civil society that had emerged under the Mandate. It then proceeded to use economic policy to create an Israeli economy. All labour markets were ethnically segregated, completing the exclusion of Israeli Arabs from almost all wage labour opportunities in order to consolidate a 'socialist' Jewish worker identity.[46] Arab wage labour was managed separately and as an auxiliary to mainstream Jewish wage labour. Immigrants were ordered to settle in new villages which were planned as a means to create national boundaries co-extensive with Jewish occupancy.

[42] There remains considerable debate about the facts of mass Palestinian displacement. See Norman Finkelstein, *Image and Reality of the Israel–Palestine Conflict* (1995).

[43] An estimated 700,000. Robert Blecher, 'Citizens without Sovereignty: Transfer and Ethnic Cleansing in Israel' (2005): 727.

[44] Perhaps the most detailed and balanced account of Israel's insecure sovereignty is provided by Paul Gelvin, *The Israel–Palestine Conflict. One Hundred Years of War* (2007).

[45] General Director of the Ministry of Finance in 1985, quoted in Jonathan Nitzan and Shimshon Bichler, *The Global Political Economy of Israel* (2002): 5.

[46] This social identity was at the heart of the political construction of Israeli nationhood out of what was a diverse set of Jewish communities, indigenous to Palestine, immigrated from Europe, and immigrated from Arab states in the Middle East and North Africa. 'Socialism' came to mean an ethno-corporatist nationalism.

The Israeli government systematically dispossessed Arabs of their land in order to achieve this. Government funded the kibbutz and moshav villages, provided services to farmers, and acted as a monopsonistic marketing board. The government constructed apartments for immigrants in increasingly exclusive urban spaces. These were also allocated by the government, not by a housing market. The government and the reformed Histadrut[47] provided employment through companies owned or controlled by these two institutions.[48] Infrastructural investments in road transport, energy, and water created the framework for a Jewish national economy. The Israeli state and nation were constructed together through the government's near-absolute control of the economy and its 'ideology of industrialization'.[49] In sum, between 1948 and the early 1960s, a highly statist economy had been consolidated on the basis of the Jewish nation/statehood, with a residual 'minority Arab' population whose mobility was restricted.[50]

1948–1973: Corporatism/Industrialization/Nation-Building

Israel's average annual rate of GNP growth was 9.1 per cent for 1951 to 1964 and 8.9 per cent for 1964 to 1972, the annual growth of GNP per capita for these periods being 4.9 per cent and 5.5 per cent, respectively.[51] Between 1968 and 1974, the Israeli real growth rate averaged near 10 per cent.[52] Between 1948 and 1958, industrial production doubled, doubling again between 1958 and 1964.[53] Between 1955 and 1965, industrial production increased by an average of 12 per cent per year, accompanied by a 5 per cent annual increase in employment, 10 per cent in capital reserves, and 20 per cent in exports.[54] Israel achieved near full employment by 1962.[55]

[47] On the dynamics of Histadrut's division of remit vis à vis the Israeli state, see Grinberg, *Split Corporatism in Israel*: 38–45.

[48] In the 1960s, Histradut-owned enterprises employed 24 per cent of the labour force (Gershon Shafir and Yoav Peled, 'The Socioeconomic Liberalisation of Israel' (2000): 6.

[49] Dov Khenin, 'From *Eretz Israel* to *Yisrael Hashnia*: The Social Discourse and Social Policy of Mapai in the 1950s' (2000): 65.

[50] Indeed, Arab areas of Israel were under military administration from 1948 to 1966.

[51] David Levi-Faur, 'The Developmental State: Israel, South Korea, and Taiwan Compared' (1998): 66.

[52] Ali Kadri and Malcolm Macmillen, 'The Political Economy of Israel's Demand for Palestinian Labour' (1998).

[53] E. Kleiman, 'The Place of Manufacturing in the Growth of the Israeli Economy' (1967): 227.

[54] Shafir and Peled, 'The Socioeconomic Liberalisation of Israel': 5.

[55] Grinberg, *Split Corporatism in Israel*: 122. For similar figures, see Gelvin, *The Israel–Palestine Conflict*: 170.

After independence, the core driver of investment, employment, and growth was the state. With considerable alacrity, the Israeli state built up the institutions to consolidate a national economy, centralizing resources, seeking capital from oversees, pressuring and organizing remittances from Jewish diasporas, and setting up a fiscal system within Israel. It also financed a project to accommodate millions of immigrants by providing employment, accommodation, and social provision. By the early 1950s, the Israeli state pretty much controlled the allocation of capital in the economy, excepting the small-scale movement of money within the country's small-scale enterprise sector.

Throughout Israel's history, the government has been financially underpinned by concessional transfers from abroad. These have come from Jewish diasporas, German state reparation payments, and most importantly the American government. From 1948 to 1988, Israel received \$4.5 billion from America and diaspora remittances.[56] It received a total of \$850 million from Germany up to 1964 when reparations payments ended.[57] Reparations transfers declined over time, but America has remained a constant support. The structural current account deficit (see below) that characterized the Israeli economy until the early 2000s was compensated by concessional transfers.[58] Military expenditure relied crucially on American aid. It is difficult to imagine how Israel could have sustained its investments in industry without exceptionally high levels of aid.

The government considered capital and expenditure as nation-building resources. After the 1948 war, the main focus was agriculture. Agrarian development was fundamentally based on the appropriation of Arab Palestinian land and property and the state-supported settlement of that land by Israeli Jews.[59] In 1952–3 agriculture and water took up 56 per cent of the development budget, and the water budget itself was oriented around the provision of irrigation for agricultural settlement.[60] Agriculture's share of the growing economy moved from 11 per cent to 15 per cent between 1950 and 1958, declining from this figure thereon.[61] Village and co-operative settlements were fundamentally about—to use a phrase which characterises Israel's entire history—creating facts on the ground. Moving immigrants into rural areas previously populated by Palestinians who had already fled or were removed

[56] Aharoni, *The Israeli Economy*: 4. [57] Aharoni, *The Israeli Economy*: 74.

[58] Compensated, not resolved. The Israeli government also had to take out loans from international creditors.

[59] 'The Israeli government took over approximately 94 per cent of the property abandoned by Palestinians' (Gelvin, *The Israel–Palestine Conflict*: 166).

[60] Aharoni, *The Israeli Economy*: 73. [61] Paul Rivlin, *The Israeli Economy* (1992): 7.

created a geopolitical securitization of Israel's rural areas. The new state also considered the distribution of newly immigrated Jews into rural work as part of its nation-building ideology: the Israeli social identity was constructed out of a connection to land and hard work.

This population–colonization policy was also driven by a need to ensure livelihoods, and this required strong state support. Thus the government did not simply subsidize settler farmers or the kibbutzim but also provided marketing and extension services and later research and development. It protected domestic agriculture from cheaper food imports and integrated Israeli agriculture into emerging industries which it largely controlled or strongly influenced. From 1948 to the mid-1950s, the Israeli state invested public resources in agricultural development as a means to establish a territorial presence of the state itself. In 1957, the government institutionalized Production and Marketing Boards[62] to support and plan the expansion and diversification of agricultural production. In the process, agricultural production grew remarkably: between 1948/9 and 1984/5 aggregate agricultural output increased sixteen-fold and the cultivated area expanded by 65 per cent.[63] Agriculture became more capital intensive as a result of various innovations in the use of hybrid seeds (adapted from the Green Revolution hybrids from Mexico),[64] fertilizers, and irrigation—all supported by government. If developmentalism is driven by security concerns, Israel's food security drove its agrarian development.

From the mid-1950s, the Israeli government shifted its strategic attention towards industry.[65] At independence, Israel's industrial sector was small and concentrated around the government, Histadrut, and a small number of private ventures from the Mandate period.[66] These three sectors habitually co-ordinated their actions, even if there were significant tensions between them. Industrial policy was initially based on a fairly standard import substitution strategy. Quotas and high tariffs severely restricted imports and import licences were granted carefully by the government, initially allocated to firms

[62] These were co-managed by government and farmers' associations.

[63] Rivlin, *The Israeli Economy*: 77.

[64] Yoav Kislev and Michael Hoffman, 'Research and Productivity in Wheat in Israel' (1978).

[65] Note the phrasing here—to say it shifted its focus *away* from agriculture would be misleading. The Israeli state was in construction until the late 1950s and part of this process was developing capacity to develop the economy. Agriculture was an overwhelming strategic priority that, from the mid-1950s, changed to a priority in a broader developmental project.

[66] The best-researched example of this is Palestine Potash Limited. Michal Frenkel, Yehouda Sherhav, and Hannah Herzog, 'The Ideological Wellspring of Zionist Capitalism: The Impact of Private Capital and Industry on the Shaping of the Dominant Zionist Ideology' (2000).

in the textile,[67] foodstuffs, metallurgy, and mining industries.[68] The government maintained import licensing and banned some imports altogether.

Behind these protective barriers, the government allocated capital through a range of measures: direct subsidies, the provision of subsidized credit, the direct ownership of companies that could then be run at a meagre rate of profit or loss through cross-subsidization, or the co-ownership of companies (commonly with companies also owned by Histadrut) that also sheltered firms from any imperative to maximize profits. Most crucially, the Israeli state dominated capital markets. It compelled banks and the industrial–finance complex Histadrut[69] to purchase government bonds with accrued pension and provident fund savings, and it then used these generated revenues to allocate capital to firms and projects identified within the national sovereignty remit.[70] It also only permitted banks to lend to selected firms, publically guaranteeing the loans.[71] In 1958, the Industrial Development Bank was created by government directly to fund firms identified as contributing to the economic construction of the nation. Throughout the 1950s, Israeli industrialization derived from the expansion of private companies that were integrated into a systemic state-based endeavour that sought to establish the conditions for self-provision during a period when the boycotting of Israel by neighbouring states had disrupted its normal trade flows. The state invested heavily in the industrial development of a network of 'development towns'. These were a kind of wage labour analogy of the kibbutz settlement strategy, located in strategic areas such as Negev and Galilee. From 1960 to 1965, investment in industry increased annually by 6.6 per cent.[72] Within all of these measures was a growing and heavily activist state that aimed to generate a national industry: by the end of the 1950s, the state undertook 55 per cent of industrial investment.[73]

There was another political imperative at work here. The government constantly sought to encourage Jews from other parts of the world to immigrate to Israel in order to fulfil the Aliya ideology. From 1948 to 1952, 1.2 million Jews immigrated to Israel, tripling its population.[74] From 1950 to 1967, the

[67] Levi-Faur, 'The Developmental State': 77.

[68] Arie Bregman, 'Government Intervention in Industry. The Case of Israel' (1987): 357.

[69] Daniel Maman and Zeev Rosenhek, 'The Institutional Dynamics of a Developmental State: Change and Continuity in State–Economy Relations in Israel' (2012): 348. Histadrut owned Bank Hapoalim and Israel's largest industrial conglomerate, Koor.

[70] Lev Grinberg and Gershon Shafir, 'Economic Liberalisation and the Breakup of Histadrut's Domain' (2000): 106.

[71] Yakire Plessner, *The Political Economy of Israel. From Ideology to Stagnation* (1994): 38.

[72] Plessner, *The Political Economy of Israel*: 17.

[73] Grinber, *Split Corporatism in Israel*: 50.

[74] Aharoni, *The Israeli Economy*: 15.

civilian labour force increased from 450,000 to 927,000.[75] The Zionist project that had led to the creation of Israel was one of 'labour Zionism' in which the national project revolved around work on the land and in the factory. The massive immigration into Israel required the construction of mass wage employment, without which the foundation of the nation would be jeopardized. Government and Histadrut investment in industry was driven by this imperative. Histadrut maintained an ethno-religiously exclusive worker employment agency.[76] The government bundled employment in industry together with social provision and the provision of housing. These measures were applied with considerable determination not only because of Israel's ethno-nationalist ideal of an economy but also—and in direct contradiction—because in reality different communities of Jewish immigrants entered Israel with little to share except their declared religion. 'Israeli' they were not; this social identity had to be constructed through state-based measures of integration: learning Hebrew, being trained in agricultural practices, becoming 'new Jews'. And, closely related, when immigrants settled in Israel only to find themselves in settlement camps, with little work or poor wages, the risk of social disturbance within the Jewish community became a threat to the state's central obsession with securing a strong and stable 'Israeliness'. Nevertheless, ethnic distinctions between Israelis of different social origin persisted throughout economic transformation.[77]

As a result, industrialization was based on the concentrated growth of state-backed mass-employment import-substituting industries. The industrial structure of Israel at this time was roughly 25 per cent state-owned, 25 per cent Histadrut-owned (and therefore in a complex fashion interlinked with the Labour Party government), and 50 per cent private.[78] If Israel's peculiar political circumstances led its import substitution industrialization to generate growing output and employment in basic sectors such as textiles and chemicals, it did not escape the limitations of this mode of accumulation. From the early 1960s, there were pressures on the current account and balance of payments, limits to the level of demand within the national consumer market, and narrowing technological development possibilities. The effective unity of state, organized labour, and capital bequeathed a static productivism

[75] Rivlin, *The Israeli Economy*: 7.

[76] For a time, Histadrut did provide contracts to Palestinians but in an ethnically differentiated fashion, reserving better-paid and full-time contracts to Israeli Jews.

[77] Deborah Bernstein and Shlomo Swirski, 'The Rapid Economic Development of Israel and the Emergence of the Ethnic Division of Labour' (1982).

[78] Rivlin, *The Israeli Economy*: 59.

that was strongly subjected to neither competition nor pressures from labour to increase productivity and seek new technologies of production. In our terms, Israel's industrialization generated a remarkable process of growth and industrialization in the absence of the kind of social relations that would drive it towards the innate dynamism that characterizes a fully fledged capitalist political economy.

From 1962, the government gradually liberalized the economy,[79] removing some restrictions on imports and seeking more proactively FDI. But it did so with no relinquishing of state remit. This was a partial and strategic statist liberalization within which government continued to control capital, support agriculture, and maintain the substantial social wage that assured it of civic peace among the Jewish Israeli population. Nevertheless, direct investment in housing and industry did start to decline.[80] Liberalization was also manifested in some loosening up of quota and tariff regimes that generated competition with imports and an increase in exports.

After the occupation of the Gaza Strip, Golan Heights, and West Bank, the Israeli state moved away from the ideal of an ethnically exclusive 'labourist' wage worker regime and towards something more hybrid. Palestinians in the Occupied Territories were employed as migrant and temporary labourers, managed carefully through a segmented labour recruitment structure.[81] By 1971, about half of all workers in the Occupied Territories were migrating to employment within Israel.[82] This generated a moderate recovery in the slumped growth rates of the mid-1960s as Israeli firms reorganized their labour forces around cheap Palestinian immigrant labour and better-paid permanent 'national' labour. Construction and agricultural labour expanded under this regime. A tendency emerged in which small firms—outside the state–Histadrut corporatism—relied on migrant Palestinian labour from the Occupied Territories and large firms remained within the established Histadrut model of relatively well-paid Jewish Israeli labour.

Nevertheless, from the 1960s, the Israeli political economy was defined by an innate crisis tendency. This was a result of its structural external current

[79] Paul Rivlin, *The Israeli Economy from the Foundation of the State through the Twenty-First Century* (2011): 40.

[80] Plessner, *The Political Economy of Israel*: 15.

[81] Zeev Rosenhek, 'The Political Dynamics of a Segmented Labour Market: Palestinian Citizens, Palestinians from the Occupied Territories and Migrant Workers in Israel' (2003). On the details of the political economy of reserve labour in the Occupied Territories see Shir Hever, *The Political Economy of Israel's Occupation* (2010).

[82] Gelvin, *The Israel–Palestine Conflict*: 185; Michael Shalev, 'Liberalisation and the Transformation of the Political Economy' (2000): 132.

account imbalance[83] in which it imported more than it exported. It maintained this imbalance through grants from German reparations and American aid, and experienced inflation[84] as a result of this and the rising consumerism of a near-fully employed (male) labour force. It went through piecemeal austerity measures. Increasing surplus of imports over exports, inefficiencies in production, expenditure on the military, consolidating 'cronyism' between state and capital, and the maintenance of near-full employment for Jewish Israelis subjected the economy to volatile and sometimes extremely high inflation. The industrialization that drives growth did not generate major structural change as much as expanded, consolidated, and exhausted a specific 'model'.[85] Nevertheless, the economy continued to grow—in the first half of the decade strongly, slumping mid-decade,[86] and recovering after 1967.[87]

1973 to the mid-1990s: Transformative Failure

From 1973, Israel moved into a major and protracted economic crisis. Between 1973 and 1984, GDP grew at just 1.6 per cent.[88] Between 1979 and 1985, inflation averaged 100 per cent per year.[89] Investment levels fell by an annual average of 4.7 per cent between 1974 and 1977.[90] Exports slumped until 1976.[91] Per capita income growth also significantly slowed.[92] This crisis was a result of the pressures on expenditure as a result of the 1967 and 1973 wars, occupation of south Lebanon, and—as with all non-oil-producing countries—oil price hikes in 1973.[93] Between 1967 and 1982 when the Israeli Defence Force invaded Lebanon, the country lost the vestiges of its image as a besieged nation or newly forged country seeking peaceful cohabitation in

[83] At its height, the external current account deficit was 17.5 per cent of GDP. Aharoni, *The Israeli Economy*: 76.

[84] Although most accounts focus on the hyperinflation of the mid-1980s, Israel's economy had always displayed high rates of inflation because of its near-full employment, rising demand, rounds of devaluation, and rising import dependence.

[85] Rivlin, *The Israeli Economy from the Foundation of the State through the Twenty-First Century*: 43. The extent to which the government had a 'plan' or responded to circumstance is debated in the literature.

[86] The mid-1960s slowdown was known as *mitun*, or 'recession'. In retrospect is seems fairly mild.

[87] A brief recovery that was supported by revived FDI and improved export performance. Rivlin, *The Israeli Economy*: 6, 59.

[88] Henri Barkey, 'When Politics Matter: Economic Stabilisation in Argentina and Israel' (1994): 47.

[89] Rivlin, *The Israeli Economy*: 1.

[90] Rivlin, *The Israeli Economy*: 13.

[91] Rivlin, *The Israeli Economy from the Foundation of the State through the Twenty-First Century*: 48.

[92] Plessner, *The Political Economy of Israel*: 13.

[93] Israel spent $600 million on oil imports in 1974 compared with $211 million in the preceding year. Plessner, *The Political Economy of Israel*: 30.

the region, and as a result immigration slowed and France (which had been Israel's main arms supplier) imposed an embargo on sales of military hardware.

But the slowdown was not only a result of Israel's regional aggressions and its repercussions. It was also a result of the increasing concentration of capital and its intensified interconnections with state patronage. The dominance of capital markets by the state generated an octopus-like network of state–capital integuments that favoured the rise of a small number of large firms that enjoyed strong political backing.[94] Holding companies and a convergence of production, technological change, and military build-up cemented this nexus. After 1967, this concentration was increasingly focused around the rise of military investments, to a degree that it was possible to speak of a military–industrial complex in Israel.[95] Between the mid-1960s and mid-1980s, Israel spent an average of 23 per cent of its GDP on the military.[96]

The economic slowdown eroded the 'labourist' regime in which Jewish labour organized within Histadrut received a kind of 'social wage' that connected to the Zionist ideology of Israel as a nation or workers forging a Jewish community. Most of the period from 1973 to the mid-1980s was spent executing unstable liberalization in the teeth of battles between political parties and Histadrut. In 1977, Likud gained leadership of the government within a coalition, seeking to weaken the corporatist labour regime constructed by the Labour Party and Histadrut. Nevertheless—as with the coming to power of many right-wing parties in the late 1970s and 1980s and the advent of economic liberalization—budgetary prudence was not achieved as much as a reallocation of spending towards capital or sections of capital.[97] Nevertheless, a slow liberalization of the economy took place. In 1974, Israel signed a free trade treaty with the European Economic Community, the purpose of which was to move trade towards a tariff-free regime.

In 1985, the Israeli government implemented the Emergency Economic Stabilization Plan. The Israeli currency was pegged to the dollar and incrementally devalued, international trade continued to be liberalized, incentives were re-oriented towards exports, subsidies on the prices of consumer goods were phased out, and the Bank of Israel was given more autonomy. This plan successfully reduced the budget deficit which was its main aim, although

[94] Nitzan and Bichler, *The Global Political Economy of Israel*: 108 *et seq*.
[95] Alex Mintz, 'The Military–Industrial Complex: The Israeli Case' (1983).
[96] Nitzan and Bichler, *The Global Political Economy of Israel*: 128.
[97] Nitzan and Bichler, *The Global Political Economy of Israel*: 134.

constraints on wage increases also ensured reduced inflation.[98] Labour became more differentiated between immigrant, low-skilled, and high-skilled workers. Unemployment among Jews from the Middle East increased and conditions of life in the peripheral 'development towns', where they were mainly located, declined.

Contrastingly, new centres of wealth and accumulation—connected to global circuits of investment and production—emerged around Tel Aviv and Haifa. Support for the kibbutzim was downscaled. As a result of all of these measures, the extreme levels of inflation—reaching 466 per cent in 1985—were dampened.[99] More generally, the economy grew at a low but steady pace and industry grew and moved into new technologies and sectors of production: machinery, chemicals, and electronics.[100] From the mid-1980s—and in keeping with the reorientation away from a national–labourist regime towards an export-oriented one—the government increased its support of research and development. The Histadrut gradually lost its power, although this involved a complex political battle in which changes within the Labour Party were at least as important as Likud's electoral victories.[101] Nevertheless, the government continued to exert considerable control over the economy, moving towards more direct and targeted support for capital and towards a more export-oriented strategy.[102] Concurrently, Israel endured the results of its own military actions. The *intifada* disrupted the managed flows of Palestinian labour from the Occupied Territories.[103] It also imposed heavy military expenditures on the economy and mobilized reservist military personnel in what is one of the most militarized societies in the world.[104] The invasion of Lebanon, continued settlement in the Occupied Territories, and the *intifada* also undermined Israel's attempts to present itself as a destination for investment and tourism.

The protracted slowdown and weak response to crisis that defined Israel's political economy throughout the 1970s and 1980s and the recovery from the 1990s are instructive. Israel's endeavours to generate capitalist development have most certainly been driven by the kind of existential politics that was

[98] Rivlin, *The Israeli Economy from the Foundation of the State through the Twenty-First Century*: 59.
[99] Shafir and Peled, 'The Socioeconomic Liberalisation of Israel': 6.
[100] Rivlin, *The Israeli Economy*: 63.
[101] Grinberg and Shafir, 'Economic Liberalisation and the Breakup of Histadrut's Domain'.
[102] Maman and Rosenhek, 'The Institutional Dynamics of a Developmental State': 352.
[103] On the economic effects of the first intifada on Israel's economic growth, see Shafir and Peled, 'The Socioeconomic Liberalisation of Israel'.
[104] Israel has, per capita, the second largest army in the world, losing out to North Korea (Gelvin, *The Israel–Palestine Conflict*: 211).

also very much present in our other case studies. But its articulation was in some ways distinctive. Growth, accumulation, and the reconfiguration of the social relations of work and property around capital were all front and centre of Israel's governance since independence, but they were profoundly interlinked with a politics of security and territory that imposed certain kinds of rigidity: 'Israel's strategic planning was based upon the concept of genuine danger to her national survival.'[105] The aspiration to full employment was a common 'developmental' aim—a way of legitimating accumulation through its social effects. It was also part of the 'social contract' of the Zionist state as a nation of Jewish labour. The building up of industry and agriculture was not only about the common developmental aim of generating a modernizing national economy, but also about 'creating facts on the ground': settlement, urban development, the construction of mass housing, water and energy supply, and road networks for Jewish communities throughout the territory Israel claimed after 1948. The insecurities that compelled Israel to seek rapid economic growth instituted rigidities in its governance that made it extremely difficult for the governing elite nimbly and adroitly to identify ways to restructure forms of accumulation and policy response during crisis.[106] Nevertheless, Israel remained ensconced in a politics of insecurity throughout its crisis years, and as its economy went into recession or inflationary bouts, its ability to control social unrest within its own borders or to maintain a vision of its future as a nation-state remained in question. The continued military and financial aid of America was pivotal to the continued sovereignty of Israel during this period. Without it, it seems reasonable to imagine that the country might have ceased to exist in the image generated by the Zionist project.

1990s Onwards: Transformation

Israel did eventually recover. Between 1985 and 1995, industrial production almost tripled; between 1991 and 1997, GDP increased at an average rate of 6 per cent and average incomes increased by 46 per cent.[107] Between 2003 and 2008, GDP increased by 27 per cent.[108] In the 1990s, immigration from the former Soviet Union brought new manufacturing skills and capital,

[105] Mintz, 'The Military–Industrial Complex': 104.
[106] Shalev, 'Liberalisation and the Transformation of the Political Economy'.
[107] Baruch Kipnis and Tamar Noam, 'Restructuring of a Metropolitan Suburban Industrial Park: Case Study in Metropolitan Tel Aviv, Israel' (1998): 217.
[108] Rivlin, *The Israeli Economy from the Foundation of the State through the Twenty-First Century*: 72.

followed by a less drastic wave of immigration of American Jews with high skill levels. Wage labour continued to become more differentiated as a result of the use of immigrant labour (less from the Occupied Territories and more from Africa) and increasing participation of women in wage labour (who were—as is common—more likely to be employed in lower-paid and less-secure jobs).

The state continued to advocate the ascendance of capital, albeit within a more liberalized regulatory regime. Incentives replaced subsidies.[109] This was also a period within which state strategy shifted towards the software and hardware of computer technology.[110] Support for research and development in computer technologies was strongly supported by the state,[111] and it was based on an already-existent high level of skill within the labour force,[112] a result of the rise of a large educated middle class (which was one side of the increasing differentiation from the late 1960s and a move away from 'labourism'). It was also a result of the continued integration of the Israeli with the American economy. This was expressed mainly in the sustained aid provided to the Israeli state, but also through networks of capital, often sustained through Jewish diaspora networks. Israeli firms increasingly raised capital in American markets.[113] As a result, the Israeli government constructed an infrastructure for technological development and succeeded in bringing in American tech companies not only to produce computer components but also to develop software and other new computer-related commodities. More generally, FDI increased substantially, as did the value of exports and imports. Israel had moved from an agrarian settler economy to an industrial one, transformed by technological upgrading and export success.[114] Industrial transformation progressed and the services sector grew absolutely and proportionately. As a result, the productivity of capital rose throughout this period.[115] Per capita GDP was $16,650 in 1997, 45 per cent higher than in 1991.[116] By the early 2000s, by some criteria, Israel's economy appeared

[109] Shalev, 'Liberalisation and the Transformation of the Political Economy': 134.

[110] Sean O'Riain, 'Dominance and Change in the Global Computer Industry: Military, Bureaucratic, and Network State Developmentalisms' (2006).

[111] Dan Breznitz, 'Industrial R&D as a National Policy: Horizontal Technology Policies and Industry–State Co-evolution in the Growth of the Israeli Software Industry' (2007). Since the mid-1980s, the Israeli government had one of the highest proportional spends on research and development. Rivlin, *The Israeli Economy*: 67.

[112] Aharoni, *The Israeli Economy*: 7.

[113] On the Israeli–American connection, see Amy Kaplan, *Our American Israel. The Story of an Entangled Alliance* (2018).

[114] By 1989, 4.7 per cent of the labour force worked in agriculture (Aharoni, *The Israeli Economy*: 3).

[115] Rivlin, *The Israeli Economy from the Foundation of the State through the Twenty-First Century*: 78.

[116] Kipnis and Noam, 'Restructuring of a Metropolitan Suburban Industrial Park': 217.

superior to Spain or Portugal's, and by 2010 Israel had joined the Organization for Economic Co-operation and Development (OECD).

Conclusion

We have argued that capitalist development is intrinsically crisis-driven and that developmentalism as a form of politics is defined by its ability to cope with crises during transition. All of our case studies this far have been distinguished by their success in enduring crisis and indeed emerging in some ways with stronger processes of growth and accumulation. Japan recovered from the destruction wrought by the American military remarkably well. Taiwan emerged from war and occupation facing hyperinflation but stabilized within a decade and then grew rapidly for a generation. Israel emerged from over a decade of economic crisis to become one of the fastest growing economies in the 1990s. Economic crisis is something of a stress test of capitalist transformation. Developmentalism is about not only surviving crisis but also recovering from it. In our three cases, this happened because crisis did not only cause plummeting rates of growth or increased unemployment (serious though these are). It also brought to the fore the basic legitimacy of the state itself.

The existential nature of crisis in the two cases treated in this chapter derived from the nature of the ruling elite itself. Taiwan and Israel were both created as conquest states: states in which the government immigrated into a territory, facing populations it was unfamiliar with. Consequently, governing elites promoted development as a way of establishing a basic legitimacy for their sovereignty. Economic crisis and state crisis were inextricably linked. Relatedly, both elites perceived their national territories in a distinct fashion. Rather than have a social base within the nation and a kind of 'embedded' familiarity with the public cultures of their territories, they saw their populations and territories as in good part external phenomena that needed to be controlled, socially engineered, and made in the state's image. Capitalist transformation seems both more possible and necessary if, in some degree, a state's citizenry appears as a tabua rasa.

Within a generation, these countries transformed from small low-growth economies in crisis to developed capitalist economies within which the masses achieved considerable improvements in their material well-being. The integrated and systemic nature of these transformations is palpable in the social and built environments of these countries. Japan, Taiwan, and Israel have gone through remarkable transitions. One could certainly add South Korea to this list, and arguably Singapore as well. This does not mean that these countries have solved problems of inequality and poverty; it simply means that the underpinning realities within which these phenomena exist and are expressed through political contention have transformed. The possibility of equality and an end to poverty is contained within the achievement of capitalist development. The proximity of that possibility is a political question realized within specific and fully capitalist processes of accumulation and labour. In Chapter 9, we shall consider two cases in which capitalist transformation is ongoing. Both of these have been described as exemplars of capitalist development but from very different perspectives. Our interest in presenting them together is to show in more realized form the politics of uncertainty that accompanies capitalist development.

9

Rwanda and China

Introduction

In this chapter, we examine the developmentalism of two 'in process' countries. One—Rwanda—is at best endeavouring to commence a developmentalist project. It is included mainly because it illustrates both the tenacity required in order to generate a capitalist transformation and how important uncertainty and adversity are. It is inescapable that an analysis of successful transitions tends to give the impression that some kind of plan worked and it worked for intelligible reasons. In real time, the politics of transition is a lot less certain. A secondary set of motivations for including Rwanda derive from the fact that it was Rwanda that started the research interest of this book. Rwanda's governance very starkly exemplified the analytical difficulties of developmentalism. It is difficult to find another country in Africa that has received such plaudits for those interested in economic growth and such condemnations from those interested in human rights. Conceptualizing these contrasts into a single analysis of Rwanda became a broader interest in how these same tensions are intrinsic to capitalist transformation. The second case study—China—is presented as something like a near-complete transition. It is also important for its own intrinsic reasons: China's economic size makes it globally important.

Rwanda

Historical Context

The beginnings of the modern state of Rwanda in the late nineteenth century derived from the expansion of the Rwandan monarchy, the consolidation of a system of rural authority over land and labour, and a class system based on

Developmentalism: The Normative and Transformative within Capitalism. Graham G.M. Harrison, Oxford University Press (2020). © Graham G.M. Harrison.
DOI: 10.1093/oso/9780198785798.001.0001

ownership of cattle, claims on labour, and clientship.[1] These processes were characterized by resistance, political manoeuvre, migrations, and conflict within a social landscape that was not primordially homogenous or integrated into the Rwandan state.[2] The Belgian colonial state introduced 'ossified'[3] and tribalized[4] versions of rural authority through chieftaincy that was increasingly associated with Tutsi social identity. This colonial/monarchical system imposed regimes of unpaid work and taxes throughout Rwanda's countryside. In rural areas and in manifold ways, peasants experienced colonialism as the loss of flexibility and accountability in the decentralized clientage that had previously defined land and livestock, and as a more concerted conquest of the state in what previously was a rather variegated set of alliances with the king. Throughout this period, there were constant migrations in order to escape monarchical power or colonial state exactions, or to modify political allegiances.[5]

Rwanda achieved independence in 1960 in extremely turbulent circumstances. It was only in the late 1970s, after a coup, that the government set out a programme of agricultural change based on four components: a conflation of the Rwandan peasantry with the virtuous hard-working Hutu,[6] the working up of good relations with donors and the profusion of projects,[7] an emphasis on the intensification of rural labour combined with an extension of land under cropping,[8] and a prioritization of food security based on sustained increases in food crop production. At the heart of this ethnic agrarian populism was 'the project': state-aligned and often donor-funded attempts to reorganize peasants' livelihoods.[9]

During the late 1980s, economic slowdown[10] and a damaging structural adjustment programme[11] were accompanied by President Habyarimana's

[1] Catherine Newbury, *The Cohesion of Oppression: Clientship and Ethnicity in Rwanda 1860–1960* (1988).

[2] David Newbury and Catherine Newbury, 'Bringing the Peasants Back in: Agrarian Themes in the Construction and Corrosion of Statist Historiography in Rwanda' (2000).

[3] Gerard Prunier, *The Rwanda Crisis: History of a Genocide* (1998).

[4] Mahmood Mamdani, *Citizen and Subject: Contemporary Africa and the Legacy of Late Colonialism* (1996).

[5] David Newbury, 'Returning Refugees: Four Historical Patterns of "Coming Home" to Rwanda' (2005).

[6] Philip Verwimp, *Peasants in Power. The Political Economy of Development and Genocide in Rwanda* (2013).

[7] Peter Uvin, 'Difficult Choices in the New Post-Conflict Agenda: The International Community in Rwanda after the Genocide' (2001).

[8] Catherine Andre and Jean-Philipe Platteau, 'Land Relations under Unbearable Stress: Rwanda Caught in the Malthusian Trap' (1988).

[9] Alice de Lame, *A Hill among a Thousand: Transformations and Ruptures in Rural Rwanda* (2005).

[10] Michel Chossudovsky, *Globalization of Poverty and the New World Order* (2003).

[11] Andy Storey, 'Structural Adjustment, State Power and Genocide: The World Bank and Rwanda' (2001).

refusal to address the question of return for over a hundred thousand Rwandan diaspora in neighbouring countries. Between 1985 and 1992, the international price of the two major peasant cash crops—coffee and tea—fell by 75 and 66 per cent respectively.[12] The government became increasingly authoritarian and explicit in deploying a discourse of ethnicity. During this period, attacks on Tutsi (re)commenced. In 1990, the Rwanda Patriotic Front (RPF) entered Rwanda over the Ugandan border, commencing a civil war that led to more mass migrations and livelihood disruption.

In 1994, over a period of 100 days, the remnants of the incumbent government and the militias that it had been training for 2 years rolled out a genocide against the Tutsi population after Habyarimana's plan was shot down. During the genocide and civil war, perhaps as many as 800,000 Tutsi and tens of thousands of Hutus were killed. Up to a million people fled the country. There were also large movements of people within the country—over one million people—leaving a profoundly uprooted and traumatized rural society by the time that the RPF had established full control.

During the genocide, militias also redistributed assets within agrarian society, justifying the killing of Tutsi in terms of their (supposed) material wealth and non-indigeneity. There was also the destruction of rural property and infrastructure, and what agribusiness remained and survived stopped production and became decrepit. The constant labour needed to maintain waterways and terraces on the hills also ceased. Perhaps the most striking example of this agrarian destructivism[13] was the mass import of machetes as weapons rather than tools.[14] The dynamics of the genocide also interacted with struggles over land and the emergence of large landowners in the context of increasing land scarcity.[15] The historical legacy that faced the post-genocide government was, then, one of a massively disrupted and traumatized agrarian society.

An Agrarian State

Agriculture matters a great deal for Rwanda. It is at the heart of the majority of the population's livelihood: 72 per cent of Rwandans have an agricultural

[12] Andy Storey, 'Economics and Ethnic Conflict: Structural Adjustment in Rwanda' (1999): 49.

[13] One manifestation of this was the fact that as men were mobilized to kill, leaders would often deploy agrarian metaphors about work and cutting. Although guns were distributed throughout the country, the main weapon of the genocide was the iconic farming tool the machete. The 'work' metaphor came out in the narratives for former *genocidaires* in Jean Hatzfeld, *Machete Season: The Killers in Rwanda Speak* (2006).

[14] Villia Jefremovas, *Brickyards to Graveyards. From Production to Genocide in Rwanda* (2002).

[15] Andre and Platteau, 'Land Relations under Unbearable Stress'.

base to their livelihood.[16] Geographically, outside Kigali, Rwanda's social landscape is one of homesteads and villages set in densely farmed hilly fields. Agriculture employs almost 90 per cent of Rwanda's active working population and represents about 45 per cent of its GDP.[17] It is also the case that rural society in Rwanda is perceived as the heart of 'traditional' social identities[18] and also the location for most of Rwanda's extreme and chronic poverty: it is estimated that over 70 per cent of the rural population are 'food poor'[19] and poverty rates in rural areas are twice as high as in urban areas.[20] Rwanda is a land-scarce country: there is very little unused land and average landholdings are very low: between 0.75 ha and 0.33 ha per household (World Bank, 2014: 3) depending on source.[21] There has always been an anxiety among Rwandan governments and development researchers that growing land scarcity will exacerbate contestations over land tenure and access; and there is some evidence that land scarcity and inequality were factors in provoking the genocide.[22] Rural population density is extremely high.[23] Climatic unpredictability leaves Rwandan smallholder agriculture (and agriculture in general) subjected to productivity declines and frequent 'hunger years'. Agricultural development is a major development concern.

We should start by recognizing the success Rwanda has achieved in relation to agriculture. Agricultural production doubled from 2000 to 2012.[24] 'The total production of maize, wheat and cassava tripled from 2007 to 2011, the production of beans doubled, and that of rice and Irish potato increased by 30 per cent.'[25] There has also been a fall in the prevalence of poverty in

[16] Pamela Abbott, Roger Sapsford, and John Rwirahira, 'Overcoming Poverty and Inequality: Rwanda's Progress Towards the MDGs' (2015): 927.

[17] An Ansoms, 'Striving for Growth, Bypassing the Poor? A Critical Review of Rwanda's Rural Sector Policies' (2008): 2. There is some variation in the estimates of people living primarily from agriculture, but they all demonstrate Rwanda's strong base in farming accompanied by a slow decline in its relative share of GDP.

[18] Verwimp, *Peasants in Power.*

[19] Patrick Vinck, *Rwanda: Comprehensive Food Security and Vulnerability Analysis (CFSVA)* (2006): 1.

[20] African Development Bank, *Africa Economic Outlook* (2013): 12.

[21] Xinshen Diao et al., *Agricultural Growth and Investment Opportunities for Poverty Reduction in Rwanda* (2010): 20; World Bank, (2014): 3.

[22] Andre and Platteau, 'Land Relations under Unbearable Stress'; Saskia van Hoywegen, 'The Urgency of Land and Agrarian Reform in Rwanda' (1999): 353–4; Alice des Forges, 'Land in Rwanda: Winnowing out the Chaff' (2006): 354.

[23] African Development Bank, *Rwanda 2015* (2015): 13.

[24] World Bank, *Managing Uncertainty for Growth and Poverty Reduction with a Special Focus on Agricultural Sector Risk Assessment* (2015): vi.

[25] International Fund for Agricultural Development (IFAD), *Climate Resilient Post-Harvest and Agribusiness Support Project (PASP) Including Blended Adaptation for Smallholder Agriculture Programme Grant* (2013): 2.

rural areas and in malnutrition,[26] although it is fair to say that these falls look moderate in comparison with increased outputs.[27] Inequality remains a major problem: the Gini coefficient has improved but not at a rate that reflects the high levels of economic growth.[28]

The current government of Rwanda—the RPF party-state—has explicitly and consistently declared an ambition to transform Rwanda's agriculture, to achieve and sustain high rates of economic growth, and to forge a more general capitalist transformation. Rwanda has grown at a remarkable pace, although there are important questions concerning the accuracy of the figures. It has sought out ways to generate investment capital, incentivized firms to expand and diversify, set out a strategy to develop services and technology, and encouraged foreign investment that might promote development. It has done all of this through an authoritarian state which has been both oppressive and effective. So there is a prima facie case to consider Rwanda as initiating a certain kind of developmentalism. As we have argued throughout, developmentalism's first and most pressing task is an agrarian one: the reorganization of rural areas into zones of capital in which productivity increases, wage labour expands, savings are generated, demand increases, and products serve the expansion of other sectors. First and foremost, Rwanda's developmentalism will be found in its agrarian strategy.

From Reconstruction to Agrarian Transformation

We will divide Rwanda's agrarian strategy into three phases. The period from 1994 to 1999 was one in which high-order issues of political order and sovereignty were paramount; the second period (2000–2006/7) was one of establishing the conditions for economic growth that involved increasing levels of donor development support and a conformity to donor orthodoxy; the third period commenced in 2007/8 and was characterized as one in which developmentalism emerged, coded into the meta-programme of Vision 2020 and the second Economic Development and Poverty Reduction Strategy.

[26] The percentage of those living in absolute poverty declined from 56.7 per cent to 44.9 per cent between 2006/7 and 2010/11 and there was a reduction in the Gini coefficient from 0.52 to 0.49 (UNDP, *Rwanda: Assessment of Development Results* (2008): 16). These are national figures, but bearing in mind that about 85 per cent of Rwanda's population live in rural areas, it seems reasonable to assume that national changes in inequality and poverty are reflected in rural areas. See Ansoms, 'Striving for Growth, Bypassing the Poor?'; IFAD, *Climate Resilient Post-Harvest and Agribusiness Support Project*.

[27] Vinck, *Rwanda Comprehensive Food Security*.

[28] IFAD, *Climate Resilient Post-Harvest and Agribusiness Support Project*: 1.

The first phase was characterized by two major and closely interrelated endeavours: ensuring order during resettlement, and consolidating state authority throughout Rwanda's territory. Between 800,000 and 1 million refugees from pre-1990s outmigrations aimed to return after the RPF came to power; additionally, 1.3–2 million refugees and internally displaced people from the civil war and genocide were moving back to their lands and residences,[29] and in all two-thirds of Rwanda's people were dislocated.[30] Resettlement was achieved through the creation of villages and a novel 'land sharing' arrangement that—although by no means perfect—was an effective means to deal with a period of considerable flux in rural areas. The major emphasis during this period was the basic assurance of nutrition for a population traumatized and uprooted. This involved heavy donor funding and little in the way of strategic development thinking. The measure of considerable success during this period was the avoidance of famine.

The second phase was characterized by the consolidation of a development strategy that was not transformative but was donor-friendly. In 2000, the war/counterinsurgency in the northwest formally ended, a Poverty Reduction Strategy Paper (PRSP) process commenced (leading to a PRSP in 2004), and the government's Vision 2020 was launched. Rwanda appeared to have recovered from the impact of the genocide and to have 'normalized' into a broadly PRSP framework. Supporting this, donors increased their lending and involvement in policymaking.[31] All of this was underpinned by a 'renaissance' and growth narrative in which international donors and politicians were highly impressed with Rwanda's recovery and growth.[32]

A donor-supported decentralization was introduced in 2001 that consolidated state power in the districts and a highly consultative land reform deliberation was commenced. By 2004/5 the national implementation of post-genocide *Gacaca* reconciliation courts[33] and further decentralization created a situation in which the government 'presence' in agrarian societies

[29] van Hoywegen, 'The Urgency of Land and Agrarian Reform in Rwanda': 354; Frederick Golooba-Mutebi, 'Political Economy of Agricultural Policy in Africa: Has CAADP Made a Difference? A Rwanda Case Study' (2013): 2.

[30] Jefremovas, *Brickyards to Graveyards*: 109.

[31] In the years after the genocide, aid to Rwanda was fairly limited and in fact more resource was probably going to the refugee camps in the DRC and therefore to some degree to the remains of the *genocidaire* militias.

[32] Uvin, 'Difficult Choices'; Stefaan Marysse, An Ansoms, and David Cassimon, 'The Aid Darlings and Orphans of the Great Lakes Region in Africa' (2007).

[33] In short: a neo-traditional open hearing process that aimed to process those suspected of participating in the genocide through confessionals, testament, and decisions by locally selected judges. The best overview of *Gacaca*'s fortunes is provided by Phil Clark, *The Gacaca Courts, Post-Genocide Justice and Reconciliation in Rwanda* (2010).

became authoritative and pervasive. At this juncture, the government rolled out its first comprehensive national agricultural strategy, the Programme for the Strategic Transformation of Agriculture 1 (PSTA1). Donor agricultural projects and the PSTA1 both aimed to support the poorest groups in rural areas and to promote increased production. As a policy text, PSTA1 focused on support for the intensified integration of smallholder agriculture into broader market relations, but there was little sense of agricultural development as a transformatory strategy.

The third phase commenced in 2007, a period distinguished by a considerable ratcheting up of institutional and political impetus behind a national agrarian strategy, based in a more focused strategic objective of chain integration and 'upgrading'. The reference to chain upgrading has become mainstreamed within Rwanda's agricultural policymaking circles. It refers to two processes that are seen as interrelated: first, the increasing connection of smallholder farming with upstream and downstream activities such as seed and fertilizer supply and the selling of crops to processors and traders; and second, efforts to improve the quantity and quality of agricultural production.

The third phase was first embodied in the Crop Intensification Programme (CIP 2007). CIP introduced the strategic decision to create macro-zones for cropping in an attempt to generate regional crop specialisms and to promote a scaling up in agriculture. The CIP's core objective was to promote increased agricultural productivity through the application of chemical fertilizers, the use of improved seeds, and the provision of extension services. CIP has been operationalized through the creation of government agencies: the Rwanda Cooperative Agency (RCA, 2008), Rwanda Agricultural Board (RAB, 2010), and National Agricultural Export Board (NAEB, 2011). The RCA, NAEB, and RAB all supply subsidized or free inputs: fertilizers, seeds, and seedlings for example. And CIP was integrated into the broader strategy of the PSTA2 in 2009, a programme that attained renewed donor support, met its declared targets early, and led to a PSTA3 in 2012, by which time, weighty commitments from some donors (particularly the World Bank, Department for International Development (DFID), European Union, Belgian Technical Cooperation (BTC), and the Dutch) and a broader refocusing on agriculture as the source of growth and development were integrated into the second Economic Development and Poverty Reduction Strategy (EDPRS) (2013).

In the second place, chain integration is connected to a process of upgrading. Chain upgrading involves implementing the production of new and improved crops, moving into processing. Most well known in this respect is the increasing number of coffee washing stations—from two in 2001 to over a hundred in 2007[34]—and in some cooperatives the establishing of marketing and branding activities (in tea and coffee). The government's programmatic focus here was the provision of improved and subsidized inputs, extension services, investment in post-harvest storage, and the selection of key crops for productivity increases.[35] Through CIP and a range of other projects and programmes,[36] cooperatives and smallholders are, it is expected, socialized into 'entrepreneurial' mindsets in which production is driven by the pursuit of new opportunities through deeper market-based networking. CIP has also pushed farmers to monocrop, fitting with the land consolidation, cooperativization, and villagization programmes.

Developmentalism

The concerted focus on agriculture from about 2007 has been underpinned by a steady increase in the proportion of the government's budget dedicated to agriculture,[37] rising by approximately 10 per cent per year.[38] It has been realized through considerable resource input and institutional innovation. It has also involved a substantial reorganization of rural settlement and agricultural production. There has been a push to gather smallholders into aggregated settlements—*imidugudu*. Production has been synchronized rather than collectivized and there has not been a large-scale movement of people into communal villages.

The RCA has registered over nearly 5,000 cooperatives,[39] each of which is based on a 'business plan' to increase productivity, value-added, and integrated agricultural activities. Indeed, the cooperative has been the basic unit for the bulk of agricultural strategic planning. The form of cooperative can vary from twenty or thirty households to thousands, and it might involve smallholders simply selling collectively, the creation of blocks of individual farming units that coordinate production, the creation of small agricultural enterprises (for example a coffee washing station or a mill), or the creation of cooperatives for workers on agricultural plantations.[40] Cooperatives are

[34] Abdul Murekezi, Jin Songqing, and Scott Loveridge, 'Do Organizational Forms of the Coffee Supply Chain Matter in Poverty Reduction?' (2012).

[35] Maize, wheat, cassava, beans, potatoes, and rice.

[36] These involve donors and the RCA.

[37] Ansoms, 'Striving for Growth, Bypassing the Poor?': 8.

[38] IFAD, *Climate Resilient Post-Harvest and Agribusiness Support Project*: 2.

[39] Ellen Verhofstadt and Miet Maertens, *Cooperative Membership and Agricultural Performance: Evidence from Rwanda* (2013): 8.

[40] An Ansoms et al., 'The Reorganization of Rural Space in Rwanda' (2014).

created by local initiative or through government fiat. Each of these kinds of cooperatives receives support from the government.

As noted in the section 'From Reconstruction to Agrarian Transformation', the government has developed a set of interconnected agencies that promote agricultural development. The National Agricultural Export Board promotes the development of higher-grade exports. This involves the provision of subsidized inputs, creating branding and quality assurance, and investing in larger and higher-specification crop processing. The Rwanda Agricultural Board intervenes in similar ways for a broader range of crops which are produced for food and domestic sale. The Ministry of Agriculture works with these agencies and with donors, upon which the government still heavily relies. The Ministry of Agriculture has various specific projects funded by donors in fertilizer provision, land management, and irrigation. Additionally, the Ministry of Agriculture has provided resources to support the introduction of new crops, irrigation techniques, terracing, and chemical fertilizers. Paralleling the 'core' agricultural support strategy, the government has supported the development of Savings and Credit Cooperatives (SACCOs) and other small-scale credit facilities. All of these initiatives are, characteristically for Rwandan governance generally, articulated within specific targets[41] and auditing procedures.

The point here is that agricultural development is underpinned by a substantial state effort to promote increased productivity within agriculture, largely through the agency of the agricultural cooperative. This support is, furthermore, oriented towards an ambitious transformation within Rwanda's agricultural areas. The transformation can be characterized as one in which peasant farmers move away from the diverse patterns of production and market integration based on the dispersed and small plots of land that pervade Rwanda's rural spaces towards an aggregated and intensified articulation to the rest of the economy. The ambition is that capital will move into agrarian social relations, work will intensify, and increased surpluses will be achieved. In this vision, the expectation is that smallholders will become entrepreneurs.

This transformative project is at most in an initial phase. Its commencement has required high levels of state presence in rural areas. The Rwandan government has projected its power into rural societies to a high degree and it has established through laws,[42] *imihigo*, and extension services a top-down

[41] A national political norm of target-based planning has been introduced under the neo-traditional rubric of *imihigo*. See An Ansoms, 'Re-engineering Rural Society' (2009): 305–8.

[42] Most importantly, decentralization of local government and the land laws that have been issued in after the cadastral survey and registration of land.

re-ordering of people's lives. The pervasive institutionalized imperative to at least meet growth targets and if possible exceed them produces not only a strong developmental ambition but also authoritarian state practice.[43] There is evidence of peasants being instructed to conform to a project with tacit rather than explicit consent and in these cases peasants might mistrust or fear that government while ostensibly participating. In some cases, crops have been dug up or destroyed if they do not conform to development plans, peasants have been fined for not growing the right crops, and peasants have even been beaten, incarcerated, and threatened with eviction after disobeying instructions.[44]

Developmentalism in Rwanda

There are three salient political motivations for Rwanda's determined agrarian developmentalism. In the first place, the core of the government is staffed by a group within the RPF who grew up in Uganda and returned through military action against the then-incumbent Rwandan government. Closely connected, there are many Rwandans who have returned from Europe and North America and moved into middle- and high-ranking positions within the ministries.[45] Both groups see in Rwanda a country that they return to, and which they desire to re-make in their own image. These two groups[46] have not grown up amid Rwanda's 'thousand hills' and they draw their political values from a more diffuse pool of ideas than those that prevail in Rwanda's villages and small towns.[47] Government programmes have been articulated through neo-traditional rural symbols,[48] but these are revealing not only for their attempts to render policy in culturally vernacular terms and in reference

[43] Ansoms, 'Re-engineering Rural Society'.

[44] Ansoms, 'Striving for Growth, Bypassing the Poor?' 17; Matthew Pritchard, 'Land, Power and Peace: Tenure Formalization, Agricultural Reform, and Livelihood Insecurity in Rural Rwanda' (2013).

[45] van Hoywegen, 'The Urgency of Land and Agrarian Reform in Rwanda': 365; David Booth and Frederick Golooba-Mutebi, 'Developmental Patrimonialism? The Case of Rwanda' (2012): 392.

[46] The 'Ugandan' and 'diasporic' groups might work in uneasy coexistence. My own and others' interviews with diaspora civil servants suggest both some admiration at Kagame's forcefulness of purpose and some fear.

[47] Ansoms, 'Re-engineering Rural Society': 294–5; des Forges, 'Land in Rwanda: Winnowing out the Chaff': 359.

[48] *Umuganda, ingando, gacaca, abunzi, ubudehe.* Phil Clark, 'Negotiating Reconciliation in Rwanda: Popular Challenges to the Official Discourse of Post-Genocide National Unity' (2014).

to a longer history of Rwandan nationhood,[49] but also in their purpose which is to fit within a strongly transformational and modernizing project.[50]

If there is a 'core' elite within the Rwandan state that shares experiences of return and a sense of alien-ness from Rwandan everyday life, this might give an insight into the desires to change Rwanda without strong attention to what already exists. But—and this is the second point—there is also something else in the 'mode of re-entry' into Rwanda that matters. The core of the ruling elite gained power in the throes of a genocide and civil war. It came to occupy power through force of arms. Although the post-1994 government was multi-ethnic and the RPF strongly eschewed ethnic politics, the core of government was largely made up of ethnic Tutsi, and they faced a country traumatized by violence and politically mobilized ethnic politics.[51] Few governments have come to power in such insecure circumstances.

It is difficult to imagine how these returning or immigrant groups at the heart of government would easily live in Rwanda without control of the state—it is the construction of statehood that defines this group and its place in Rwanda. The historical circumstances of Rwanda's post-genocide government are that it is staffed by a core elite that identifies extremely strongly with the party and state[52] and understands very well that its control of the state depends on its ability to assert and justify its rule to a rural population that is in some degree both alien and traumatized.[53]

These specific circumstances go a fair way to explaining why the Rwandan government has pursued a consistent and determined project of national development. The austere and unpropitious circumstances of Rwanda's political economy are both 'because' and 'in spite' of developmentalism: because of the fragility of the government in Rwanda the ruling party has embarked on a transformative project in spite of those adverse circumstances. One can see constantly in Rwandan media coverage of President Kagame's

[49] Rwanda's national history is—like many nationalisms—more recent and problematic than is often portrayed. See Catherine Newbury, *The Cohesion of Oppression: Clientship and Ethnicity in Rwanda 1860–1960* (1988); Alice des Forges, *Defeat is the Only Bad News: Rwanda under Musinga, 1897–1931* (2011). The notion of a long-standing national unity provides a vital resource for those who wish to move away from the erroneous notion that Rwanda has endured fixed antipathies between 'Tutsis' and 'Hutus'.

[50] Angélique Rwiyereka, 'Using Rwandan Traditions to Strengthen Programme and Policy Implementation' (2014). This is most clearly the case in respect to *imihigo* which has effectively become a universalized performance contracting system. Benjamin Chemouni, 'Explaining the Design of the Rwandan Decentralization: Elite Vulnerability and the Territorial Repartition of Power' (2014).

[51] van Hoywegen, 'The Urgency of Land and Agrarian Reform in Rwanda': 372.

[52] Esther Marijnen, and Jair van der Lijn, 'Rwanda 2025: Scenarios for the Future Political Stability of Rwanda' (2012): 17.

[53] Chemouni, 'Explaining the Design of the Rwandan Decentralization'.

visits throughout the country the same message: this government's legitimacy should be tested by its ability to deliver development. Development legitimacy is the key to the current core elite's security.[54] The corollary of this is that the pursuit of development is not based on rights and capabilities expansion but rather two other political values: first, a demonstration of the state's ability to act in an authoritative way—to get things done; and second, to generate results through resource inputs and modes of mobilization.

There is a third core component that reinforces the political motivations behind developmental governance in Rwanda. The reliance on developmental legitimacy is thoroughly intertwined with the government's nationalist discourse. This is not only another instantiation of the generic post-colonial phenomenon of national development as a tool to promote unity under state sovereignty. It is also the government's main way to address the legacy of genocide. The government has restricted all public expressions of ethnic political identity. Against ethnicized political discourses, the government propounds a strong discourse of Rwandan unity that poses a national identity above an ethnic one.[55] This is, like the claims to developmental legitimacy, a message repeated constantly by politicians. It is articulated through a historiography in which ethnic difference was constructed by colonial power and exacerbated by previous Rwandan governments, especially the Habyarimana regime. The counterpart to a public repression of political ethnicity is a positive proposing of a national identity based on 'Rwandan-ness' whose value derives from national economic growth and progress. A key purpose of development as social transformation is to create not only 'modern' Rwandans[56] but also social identities within which ethnicity is less prominent.[57] In short, development is a political project that aims to construct and enforce social identities that are less liable to generate political violence in the future: 'development for peace and stability'.[58] A great deal of this state project is oriented towards rural society.[59]

[54] Timothy Longman, 'Limitations to political reform. The undemocratic nature of transition in Rwanda' (2011): 41.

[55] Andrea Purdekova, 'Civic Education and Social Transformation in Post-Genocide Rwanda: Forging the Perfect Development Subjects' (2012).

[56] The quotation marks here simply signal that it is easy to produce stark oppositions between 'indigenous' and 'traditional' identities in ways that essentialize and reify what are heuristic terms that extract facets of social identities that often display more flexibility and hybridity than these terms allow.

[57] Frederick Golooba-Mutebi, 'Political Economy of Agricultural Policy in Africa': 5.

[58] van Hoywegen, 'The Urgency of Land and Agrarian Reform in Rwanda': 365.

[59] Andrea Purdekova, '"Even if I am not here, there Are so many Eyes": Surveillance and State Reach in Rwanda' (2011); Bert Ingelaere, 'What's on a Peasant's Mind? Experiencing RPF State Reach and Overreach in Post-Genocide Rwanda (2000–10)' (2014).

China

If there is one example of both the massive transformative potential and politically turbulent and troubled nature of capitalist development in the present day it is surely China. China's economic growth and transformation statistics amply illustrate a sustained, systemic, and profound transformation, one that, arguably, is the most rapid and radical in modern history.[60] It has been the fastest growing economy in the world for three decades.[61] From 1979 to 1995, GDP grew at an annual average rate of 9.5 per cent, with productivity improvements accounting for 40 per cent of that growth.[62] From 1980 to 2001, the proportion of Chinese villagers in poverty fell from 41 per cent to 5 per cent.[63] The number of people living in absolute poverty (by the World Bank's extremely austere definition) fell from 840 million to 84 million between 1981 and 2011.[64] China's growth and consequent poverty reduction has lifted one-tenth of the world's population out of extreme poverty.[65]

As a result of its peerless prominence in the discussion of global political economy and development, China has, unsurprisingly, become the point-of-reference for a range of claims about the nature of globalization. The most significant implication that we can take from China's capitalist transformation is that global poverty reduction has relied pivotally on the high economic growth rates in this most populous country. Put simply, for those who wish to present a picture of progressive global poverty reduction through crude headline aggregate figures, it is China that matters most. Between 1981 and 2010, 700 million were pulled out of poverty around the world, 627 million (89.6 per cent) of them in China.[66]

The Late Nineteenth to Mid-Twentieth Century: Conflict in the Absence of a State

We have encountered China before. We noted how the Opium Wars were a key moment in Britain's history of imperial capitalist expansion. In China, the

[60] Barry Naughton, *The Chinese Economy. Transitions and Growth* (2007): 143.
[61] Fred Bergsten et al., *China's Rise. Challenges and Opportunities* (2008): 106.
[62] Loren Brandt and Thomas Rawski, 'China's Great Economic Transformation' (2008): 1.
[63] Martin Ravallion and Shaohua Chen, 'China's (Uneven) Progress Against Poverty' (2007). There is much debate about the extent to which poverty and inequality have been reduced in China, but there are no arguments refuting that there has been a generalized process of poverty reduction.
[64] Arthur Kroeber, *China's Economy. What Everyone Needs to Know* (2016): 34.
[65] Linda Yueh, *China's Growth: The Making of an Economic Superpower* (2013): 1.
[66] World Bank, *Remarkable Declines in Global Poverty, but Major Challenges Remain* (2013).

Opium Wars are commonly called the 'humiliation',[67] an epitome of the failure of the late Qing dynasty to defend the country against increasingly invasive European and American influence. It was in the decades after the Opium Wars that China became aware of the 'Meiji' industrial development in Japan,[68] a transformation that led to Japanese occupation of Manchuria and subsequently a full-blooded invasion as part of Japan's regional–militarist regime of accumulation. Both western and Japanese projections of power showed how, throughout the late nineteenth and early twentieth century, China was subjected to the exigencies of other countries trying to sustain a capitalist transformation, and that was a major theme in its history during that period.

In the late 1800s, the Chinese dynastic system was in decline. The Qing dynasty faced an increasingly autonomous set of landlordly provincial powers, many with their own armies and revenue-raising systems. It also faced constant and intensifying pressures to open up its territories to foreign trade. Both Japan and Russia occupied territories on its frontiers and in other frontier areas (outside what has historically been the 'central' Chinese Han areas) and there were secessionist movements. Although the government did make some efforts to promote industry, the Chinese economy was not industrializing and what new industry there was was concentrated in the coastal towns and especially Shanghai. Within those towns, demands for an end to dynastic rule, or at least constitutional reform, grew through student movements and new literatures. In 1871, Russia occupied Ili and in 1895 the Qing government signed the Shimonoseki Treaty with the Japanese after the first Sino-Japanese War, a main outcome of which was the shifting of Korea's tributary status towards Japan. The emperor struggled to modernize Qing rule[69] or to establish a strong nationalist legitimacy. Discontent with foreign intervention—both 'Christian'[70] and Japanese—generated the Boxer Rebellion. Provincial governors contested political power through complex alliances. There were localized famines. The Qing government's efforts to create an effective national military were unsuccessful. By 1912, the Qing dynasty had failed and China became a republic.

[67] Julie Lovell, *Maoism. A Global History* (2019).

[68] Throughout the final years of the Qing dynasty, the example of a constitutional monarch in the Meiji imperial house, along with the remarkable industrialization over the same period, made Japan—as with other examples in this book—a point of reference for both hatred and emulation.

[69] Some piecemeal attempts to modernize were attempted but were too timid or failed. Part of the reason why Qing failed to adapt and maintain its power derived from its own familial dynamics and intrigues.

[70] The term used as a synonym for European.

The period from 1912 to 1949 might best be characterized as a relentlessly unstable, chaotic, and violent set of attempts to establish a Chinese nation-state under extreme external pressures.[71] The provincial powers that owned land, raised taxes, and maintained their own armies became autonomous powers. Japan occupied Manchuria and—as we have already noted—invested heavily in 'second wave' military zaibatsu.[72] In 1919 and 1921 respectively, the Guomindang[73] and Chinese Communist Party (CCP) were created, each cohabiting in a fitful and volatile nationalist alliance. From 1923 to 1927, the Revolutionary Alliance—which accepted members of the CCP individually[74]—undertook a Northern Expedition which aimed to subdue China's warlords and unify the country. From 1926 to 1928, a National Revolution, undertaken by a coalition of political movements under Guomindang dominance, made the only concerted attempt to unify the country, creating a national military, promoting a national-popular Chinese script, attempting to promote male literacy, and discussing constitutional reform. This period was truncated by rising Guomindang–CCP rivalries—largely held in place by pressures from Russia which saw China's politics as a 'national front' against Japanese imperialism. In 1934, after an attack of their military forces by the Guomindang, the CCP commenced its fabled[75] Long March, establishing a base in Yan'an. From 1934 to 1949, the CCP and Guomindang shifted from fighting a civil war to uniting to fight against the Japanese military. The entire first half of the twentieth century was an unremitting horror for the Chinese people in which millions perished, and at no point had a unified and stable national government emerged.[76]

1945–1958: Nation-Building and Modernization

After the defeat of Japan by the Allies, China was released from Japanese occupation. The final retreat of the Japanese was the trigger to re-ignite the

[71] That this was successful is historically remarkable: the only agrarian empire of the nineteenth century to have endured into the twenty-first. Wang Hui, *China's Twentieth Century* (2016): 14.

[72] Indeed, there was some industrialization during this period in Manchuria, Shanghai, and the Yangtze Delta, but it was disarticulated from anything that might be described as a national project. It was driven by imperialist occupation and entrepôt investments.

[73] Then the Revolutionary Alliance.

[74] The Guomindang held broadly socialist beliefs and has a Leninist democratic–centralist organization. Sun Yat-Sen's political thought was broadly egalitarian and suspicious of private business. The centralism and cynicism of business as a source of opposition were carried from the mainland into Taiwan, as we saw in Chapter 8.

[75] Recent histories offer good evidence that the Long March was not the arduous and heroic task that the CCP has claimed it was.

[76] John Keay, *China. A History* (2008): 480.

conflict between the Guomindang and CCP, one that had now taken on a broader Cold War dynamic. The Russian-supported People's Liberation Army (PLA) rapidly pushed south, and the Guomindang retreated to Taiwan, establishing a 'provisional' government there.[77]

In 1949, the PLA marched into Beijing. It took control of a putative nation-state. The CCP had established networks of dominance in its northern stronghold regions and supportive cadres in cities, but beyond these areas it faced diverse and partially governed territories, as well as its exiled rival across the South China Sea. After a half century of instability, two immediate major problems faced the CCP: flooding and rocketing inflation.[78] The nationalists had left a state that had never enjoyed a regularized and centralized fiscal infrastructure. Centralizing finance and taxation was the CCP government's first economic policy.[79] This enabled the government to reduce high and volatile rates of inflation. In 1950, the Agrarian Reform Law abolished landlordism throughout the country, redistributing 43 per cent land to peasants.[80] Executing this policy facilitated the projection of party-state authority throughout China's territories. All land was now owned by the state and the redistribution of land often involved military oversight. Party cadres drawn from the peasantry were established and the social class of landlords was liquidated either as a social identity or physically.

After a brief period of openness and inclusiveness, the CCP adopted a mode of governance that it cleaved to throughout the Mao years, and arguably in some form maintains to the present-day: the mass mobilization campaign. Using militarist rhetoric and authoritarian state action, China's population were in some form or another compelled to be good revolutionaries. Throughout all of the many campaigns that emitted from the state, this involved two core obligations: obedience to the state and hard work. The militarism in governance was reinforced by China's participation in the Korean War from 1950. It also maintained a militarized enmity with Taiwan and participated heavily in the Vietnam War from the early 1950s.[81]

Within this context, it is fair to say that the first 10 years of CCP governance were remarkably successful in constructing the beginnings of a national modernization project. An important reason for this was the experience that

[77] Keay, *China. A History*: 515. [78] Immanuel Hsu, *The Rise of Modern China* (2000): 652.

[79] Michael Dillon, *China: A Modern History* (2010): 284.

[80] Julia Lovell, *Maoism. A Global History* (2019): 99.

[81] Once the American military moved north of the 38th parallel, the Chinese government—with some justification—assumed that its own territory would come under military threat. Hui, *China's Twentieth Century*: 119.

the CCP accrued in its rural rear-guard in the north where the CCP 'fish' had to swim in a 'sea' of peasant farming communities. As noted, landlordism was abolished and substantial portions of land reallocated to peasant farmers. The efficacy of this was an outcome of the political practices through which it was realized. The CCP projected its party structures into rural areas through open meetings in which landlords were identified, vilified, and dispossessed. A normative discourse was constructed within which loyalty to the party became the foundation of authoritative political power. Land to the tiller was also power to the party. In 1952, villages under the administration of local party branches were encouraged to establish agricultural collectives. The model here was to co-ordinate large work tasks and eventually pool individual land. The reorganization of land and labour was driven by a desire to increase agricultural output, but it was also underpinned by a desire to extend state power. The Village Party Branch became the absolute power in China's villages.[82]

In 1953, the CCP passed the Unified Procurement and Marketing of Grain policy in which the state would monopolize the marketing of grain and set the prices of both crops and consumer goods. This policy shut down peasant agency and the possibilities for merchants to accumulate, and it established a means to extract resources from peasants for the purposes of bolstering the growing state-owned industry sector. In 1958, this projection of state power was consolidated through *hukuo* in which the party-state in all villages took a census of all families' property and social history in order to give them fixed citizenship identities.[83] It also connected them to a location and made it impossible for people to relocate without permission from the government. Modern Chinese citizenry was articulated through identities such as poor, middle, or rich peasant, ex-landlord, or ex-combatant, each of these categories conflating citizenship with the party-state. Thus, by the late 1950s, China's extensive and diverse agrarian space was integrated into the party-state. To stretch a metaphor, the fish reorganized and then swallowed the sea.

The First Five-Year Plan (1953–7) sought to extend and intensify state control over China's peasant societies through a commandist productivism, but the source of economic growth identified in the Plan was industry not agriculture. The core logic of the Plan was to industrialize and to engineer agriculture as the servant of this primary process. In line with the Stalinist

[82] An Chen, *The Transformation of Governance in Rural China. Market, Finance, and Political Authority* (2015): 30.

[83] Ying Chen, 'The Myth of Hukou: Re-examining Hukou's Implications for China's Development Model' (2019).

schema (and considerable state aid), heavy industrialization was seen as the route towards growth and transformation. Indeed, large-scale industrial plant was literally transported from Russia to Chinese cities, and the Plan set investment targets which exceeded the ability of other sectors to supply raw materials. The state took control of a massive amount of industrial property through either nationalization or 'partnerships' in which the state dominated. Ambitiously large-scale, the party-state failed to co-ordinate, incentivize, or adapt production in ways that would generate any sustained growth and transformation. What it did make some progress in was the spatial spread of industrial projects as a means to create a national industrial economy.[84] Nevertheless, the statistical record of this Five-Year Plan indicates that it enjoyed some success at least in comparison with other developing countries.[85]

In the countryside, agrarian strategies were accompanied by a broader social programme known as the National Campaign. Most pivotally, tax-raising was centralized so that all villages and towns were expected to generate tax revenues to be transferred to the central state. The CCP itself was establishing a 'democratic–centralist' set of institutions that involved a familiar Leninist core of localized representation in national policymaking through party elections and a central committee within which executive power was concentrated. In this period, Mao Zedong's personal power was not absolute.

By the end of the Five-Year Plan, the logic of centrally set targets and localized achievement (or excess) was intensified. Once the sinews of the state were in place, the expansion of state authority was realized through the Village Party Branch which exercised power through planning practices which imposed conformity and sanctioned disobedience. Targets for output and rates of collectivization were increased in order to subordinate social life to the Party. This dynamic also enabled the consolidation of power around Mao who used the discourse of failed targets to chastise pockets of the state that were not under his power. By the late 1950s, 'all the institutional arrangements the Chinese leadership then associated with a socialist state (collectives in the rural sector, effective state ownership of the means of production, and an articulated bureaucratic structure) were then in place'.[86]

[84] Roy Bin Wong, *China Transformed* (1997): 182.
[85] Jan Sevjnar, 'China in Light of the Performance of the Transition Economies' (2018).
[86] David Bachman, *Bureaucracy, Economy, and Leadership in China: The Institutional Origins of the Great Leap Forward* (1991): 13.

The Great Leap Forward, Cultural Revolution, and their Aftermath

By the end of the first Five-Year Plan, the auguries of a totalitarian 'commandist'[87] social engineering were evident. The 'socialist high tide' or 'small leap forward' of 1956 intensified collectivization in rural areas as the state imposed demands on peasant farmers, and a structure of governance in which localized obsessions with fulfilling targets became the primary purpose of the state. The Great Leap Forward completed a process in which the presence of the state throughout China became the near-absolute dominance of the state.[88]

The Great Leap Forward itself (1958–62) killed perhaps 50 million people.[89] Its declared overarching aim was to generate all-encompassing and rapid economic growth. The means through which this would be achieved was indicative planning: the planning organs of the state would set targets to be achieved based on information received from party cadres throughout the country, from villages to provinces, and throughout urban workplaces. It was in the very logic of this kind of planning that targets should be excessive and heroic, what Dikötter calls a 'frenzy of competitive bidding'.[90] The logic of planning shifted from the structuring of incentives to the imposition of quotas: from indirect planning to production planning.[91] It was also part of the politics of the Great Leap Forward that all social life—from production quotas to childcare—would be subordinated to the party. The ideological dominance of the CCP was so extreme as to be characterized as brainwashing.[92]

The process of collectivization was intensified and completed. What had been a more gradual move from individual tenure to co-operative work and a movement towards the commune became a systemic and imposed villagization accompanied by compulsory labour on larger government farms. The communal farm and the party cadres who exercised authority through it became the focus of absolute power in the newly formed villages. What product was produced by peasants outside of government farms on small private plots was requisitioned by the state, which had already monopolized marketing, using this to further extract value from farmers. The state became a coercive institution to work peasants to malnutrition or death while also

[87] A term first used in Nazi Germany, then Stalinist Russia.
[88] Chen, *The Transformation of Governance in Rural China*: 41.
[89] Frank Dikötter, *Mao's Great Famine* (2011): 128. [90] Dikötter, *Mao's Great Famine*.
[91] Nicholas Lardy, *Agriculture in China's Modern Economic Development* (1983).
[92] On Maoism and brainwashing, see Lovell, *Maoism. A Global History*.

commandeering their food at penurious prices. Work on the collective farms was rewarded through work points allocated by party cadres. These points could earn peasants the ability to buy food from the state. Furthermore, farmers (and relocated urbanites) were forced into massive public works labour to clear land, dig irrigation ditches, construct kilns for rural metallurgy, and so on. State-owned farms grew grains and some cotton for export or staple provisions for urban dwellers. Food availability and income levels for peasant farmers were stagnant. The famine caused by the Great Leap Forward (to which a period of drought contributed) killed up to 50 million people.[93]

The Chinese state nationalized almost all industry and also subjected it to commandist planning based on relentless output growth. For example, China's steel production was planned to increase from 30 million tonnes in 1959 to up to 90 million tonnes in 1962.[94] Target-setting was not primarily about estimating realistic achievements. It was rather about instituting a relentless push by the state—centrally and locally—to push factories and farms to higher levels of work through the exertions of party officials. This did produce growth and industrialization,[95] but through a regime in which industries were fixed into planning regimes that disallowed any dynamism, flexibility, or experimentation. Accounts of Great Leap Forward industrialization tend to show simply a relentless pressure to meet targets set from above through overwork. There was massive investment in large-scale industry—purchased from Russia through revenues earned from grain exports[96]—but this was extremely inefficient. The supply of materials for industries was insufficient and lacking quality. The management of factories was based on generating outputs even if the goods were faulty. Workers were often ill or injured. Although the Great Leap Forward is mainly known for its rural work brigades and famine, industry was the main priority of the CCP, driven in no small part by a desire to build up its military.[97]

The Great Leap Forward and Cultural Revolution constituted an extended period of severe social engineering in which the state relentlessly coerced people into intensified work through removal of almost all space for autonomous agency. There are two other facets of this period that are noteworthy because they feed directly into the nature of China's remarkable post-1978 transformation. In the first place, China's economy did grow for long periods

[93] Dillon, *China: A Modern History*: 317.
[94] Dillon, *China: A Modern History*: 305.
[95] Rawski, *Economic Growth and Employment in China*: 41.
[96] Dikötter, *Mao's Great Famine*: 140.
[97] Lardy, *Agriculture in China's Modern Economic Development*: 5.

between the early 1960s and late 1970s. Between 1952 and 1981, per capita output tripled and roughly over the same period the share of industry in GNP increased from 18 per cent to 50 per cent.[98] GNP increased at an annual average of 6 per cent from 1949 to 1978, which compared well with most post-colonial countries over the same period.[99] It built up a large industrial base within the state-owned enterprise sector. By 1979, China had 883,000 state-owned enterprises.[100] There was also investment in agricultural research, irrigation, and rural industry that increased rural production and absorbed a growing labour force.[101]

Second, this period did also witness the construction of a universal system of social provision. Primary education was massively expanded. The 'iron rice bowl' ensured that workers in urban areas had minimal access to nutrition. The growth, industrialization, and social infrastructure that emerged out of the totalitarian properties of Maoism did bequeath strategic possibilities for the reformist agendas that emerged after 1978. To put these into a nutshell, in the late 1970s, China had dominant and universal state power, a large (albeit undynamic) industrial sector, and a state ideology that conflated nationalism, mobilization to work, and order. It was within this context that the government sought ways to revitalize its authority as the commandism of the last 20 years faced a severe political and economic crisis.

Reorientation: 1978 to the mid-1990s

This is where the China development narratives usually start. Throughout this period, the Chinese government undertook what might be characterized as a changing combination of liberalization, regulatory reform, and state strengthening. Within this period there was a fair degree of experimentation[102] and some ambiguity as to how the state's structures of power might be changing. But the direction of travel seems clear: the securing of high rates of economic growth through expanded capitalist investment, accumulation, and transformation as a means to maintain the party-state and develop a legitimacy to

[98] Lardy, *Agriculture in China's Modern Economic Development*: 1.

[99] Naughton, *The Chinese Economy*: 140.

[100] Kroeber, *China's Economy*: 5.

[101] Thomas Rawski, *Economic Growth and Employment in China* (1979): 9; Jikun Huang, Keijiro Otsuka, and Scott Rozelle, 'Agriculture in China's Development Past: Disappointments, Recent Successes, and Future Challenges' (2018): 469, 471.

[102] Kelly Tsai and Barry Naughton, 'State Capitalism and the Chinese Miracle' (2015): 12. Yuen Ang's phrasing of 'directed improvisation' seems apt: *How China Escaped the Poverty Trap* (2016): 17.

its post-Maoist authority.[103] China has 'grown out of the plan'[104] in order to energize the process of economic growth through capitalist accumulation.

In 1978, Deng Xiaoping set out the Four Modernizations: agriculture, industry, defence, and science and technology. These hardly seem striking or unique. But in the post-Mao and Gang of Four politics of the late 1970s, this broad programmatic orientation served to open up the possibility of systemic change in the management of China's political economy. One concrete reform that was announced in the same year was the Open Door Policy which aimed to encourage FDI, initially in Special Economic Zones.[105] The response for transnational capital was strong: from a few billion dollars per year in the early 1990s to 100 billion in 2010.[106]

From 1979, the Household Budgetary Responsibility System (HBRS) was introduced. This was, at the time, a profound programmatic shift. Incrementally, peasant farmers were permitted to sell any surplus above that demanded by the village commune as they saw fit and to keep the revenues from those sales. Communes started to contract parcels of land to peasants for 'sideline production',[107] an arrangement that left an opaque hybrid tenure system in which land was still communally owned but worked by individual families with reduced obligations to the commune. This introduced incentives to agricultural production and allowed peasant farmers to grow what they wanted in their own fields. The introduction of the HBRS generated a strong production response, moving China from a net importer to a net exporter of foods, and generating an agricultural production growth rate of 8.2 per cent from 1978 to 1984[108] and a 78 per cent increase in productivity between 1979 and 1983.[109] Rural per capita incomes doubled between 1979 and 1984.[110] In 1988, the Land Management Law separated ownership rights and use rights in land, allowing landowners to lease the use of their land within an untransformed ownership structure. This generated markets in land and capital for

[103] In some accounts of China's growth in this period, a distinction is made between the period from 1978 to the mid-1980s and from the mid-1980s to the mid-1990s, the latter period only being one characterized by liberalization.

[104] Barry Naughton, *Growing out of the Plan. Chinese Economic Reform, 1978–1993* (1995).

[105] The first of these was in Shanghai in 1980.

[106] Carl Walter and Fraser Howie, *Red Capitalism. The Fragile Financial Foundation of China's Extraordinary Rise* (2012): 6. In an area of research so often characterized as about the relationship between China and America, it is worth noting that the major source of FDI in this period was the East Asian region, especially Japan.

[107] Hsu, *The Rise of Modern China*: 806.

[108] Huang et al., 'Agriculture in China's Development Past: 469, 478.

[109] Joshua Eisenman, 'Commune Kabuki: Development and Productivity Growth under Maoist China's Rural Collectives' (2018): 1554.

[110] Kroeber, *China's Economy*: 29.

leaseholders.[111] It also allowed increasingly decentralized local governments to generate revenue from land sales.[112] In essence, China's revived growth began in agriculture.[113]

This production response affirmed to the ruling elite that liberalizing reforms could generate economic growth. In this period between the late 1970s and the early 1980s, the Chinese party-state started to reorient its claims to authority and legitimacy away from Maoism and towards a growth-based legitimacy. In this period, the CCP redefined itself as the party that ensured economic growth. Economic growth could not be secured exclusively through the state. State-owned enterprises were largely bankrupt and inefficient. The party-state gradually saw liberalization as a means to bring capital into China and to generate accumulation within China's political economy. It prioritized the former over the latter because it was a way of generating new social dynamics that might undermine party power. As a result, the most drastic early change in China was the inflow of FDI. This has sometimes been seen as evidence of a radical shift towards 'neoliberalism' in China, but it is better understood strategically. FDI generated expanding processes of accumulation that did not threaten the party-state.[114] Indeed, the party-state has been apt to manage FDI in ways that fit with its plans to develop certain industries and technologies.[115] The government experimented with new forms of regulation and control and it gradually liberalized its domestic economy.[116]

It did all of this very clearly within a framework of socialism and nationalism, and, by doing so, it maintained an absolute dominance of the political sphere. The CCP endeavoured throughout to manage a considerable amount of internal debate and contestation about the direction of policy, and it also needed to ensure that the socio-economic changes ushered in through liberalizing reform did not generate significant centres of autonomous political power. As a result of these political imperatives, the CCP both maintained a complete conflation of party and state power and worked hard (and effectively) to marry liberalization with a reorganization of the practices of patronage and co-option.

[111] Meg Rithmire, *Land Bargains and Chinese Capitalism. The Politics of Property Rights under Reform* (2015).

[112] Minxin Pei, *China's Crony Capitalism* (2016): 54. [113] Yeuh, *China's Growth*: 23.

[114] Barry Naughton, 'A Political Economy of China's Economic Transition' (2008): 100, Roselyn Hsueh, *China's Regulatory State. A New Strategy for Globalisation* (2011): 3. Hsueh's notion of two-step liberalization catches the strategic and regulatory nature of the opening up of its economy well.

[115] Naughton, *The Chinese Economy*: 145.

[116] Sebastian Heilmann, 'Policy Experimentation in China's Economic Rise' (2008).

The 'responsibility' policy was extended to state-owned enterprises (SOE) in 1981, allowing firms to make their own profits once obligations to the state were fulfilled. In 1985, the Unified Procurement and Marketing of Grain was repealed, meaning that the state's monopoly on agricultural trading through village communes ended. In its wake, Township and Village Enterprises (TVE) emerged throughout China's rural societies.[117] TVEs transformed villages into highly varied institutional combinations of peasant farming and local cadre-run enterprises that used localized political support to make profits that would then be redistributed to those employed by the TVEs.[118] The property rights within TVEs were unclear, and some kind of localized blurring of political authority and economic sway underpinned the TVEs. TVEs were also the vehicles through which capitalists could invest semi-covertly in partnership with a recognized local CCP cadre—'wearing a red hat' or becoming a 'socialist landlord'. Throughout this period, although ownership and use have been separated, rural land remained officially under the purview of collectives run by party cadres.[119] The removal of the state's legal trade monopsony incentivized TVEs to seek new forms of production and organization of labour, and for the decade from the mid-1980s, it served to generate a massive increase in production. The annual rate of growth in grand output between 1957 and 1978 was 2.1 per cent; from 1979 to 1984 it was 4.9 per cent, and per capita farm incomes increased from Y134 in 1978 to Y463 in 1987.[120] The TVEs also significantly reduced the spatial concentration of growth, even if a rural–urban disparity intensified during this period. China's rural social landscapes came to be defined by agricultural production and wage labour. This represented an economically expanding and transformative agrarian dynamic, also manifested in the diversification of crops produced and a movement into more lucrative farm products.[121]

In 1986, following the consolidating logics of 'responsibility' and 'dual track' reforms, SOEs introduced labour contracts to their employees and commenced the retrenchment of labour. The profusion of small firms in urban areas absorbed much of the retrenched labour. Others took pensions which were often on attractive terms. It is important to bear in mind that throughout this period, one component of the Great Leap Forward remained

[117] Townships replaced communes in 1983.
[118] Yuen Ang, *How China Escaped the Poverty Trap* (2016): 80 *et seq.*
[119] Rithmire, *Land Bargains and Chinese Capitalism.*
[120] Hsu, *The Rise of Modern China*: 846.
[121] Huang et al., 'Agriculture in China's Development': 480. One example of this is Chinese farmers using genetically modified cotton crops, even if this is not yet regulated by the government.

in place. The *hukuo* system of migration control was not abolished and in 1982 a Custody and Repatriation System allowed the police forcibly to remove migrants to rural areas that did not have residence permits. As ever, the Chinese state identified political stability as a *sine qua non* of effective liberalized growth: urban residents had far greater job security, access to housing, and possibly pensions,[122] and immigration to urban areas was restricted and constantly policed.

Property rights were transformed. In 1984, individualized tenure of land for up to 15 years was legislated, and in 1986 it became possible for tenants of state-owned apartments to buy these outright. The Shanghai stock exchange was created in 1991, and in the same year grain markets were completely liberalized, removing state purchasing of grain altogether. By the end of the 1980s, China had recognizably transformed into an economically vibrant capitalist economy, defined by a competitive agrarian sector of TVEs and peasant farmers, increasingly competitive SOEs, and massive inflows of FDI. Inflation was stable and low, and the Chinese state had increased its fiscal take, introduced VAT, and unified its exchange rates, and became an international currency creditor in the early 1980s.

The government had maintained an absolute monopoly on political power, restructured SOEs, and maintained capital controls, and deployed the army to quell the student and worker rebellions in and around Tiananmen Square in 1989. It had established a form of decentralization within which township and provincial cadres maintained their political power not through reference to the Plan but through innovative and ambitious efforts to generate investment, employment, and growth, each and all of which did two things: generate revenue streams for personal income and patronage and produce statistical accounts of success within a state that was increasingly meritocratic and internally competitive. The CCP's governance was, then, characterized by substantial core stability—it faced no serious opposition—and an extremely dynamic capitalist ascendance. Throughout this period, there were real contestations about the speed and nature of liberalization, something that manifested itself in shifting balances of power, dismissals, and the exercise of the veto by major politicians.

By the mid-1990s, economic growth slowed slightly as a result of the Asian crash and the slowing growth of TVEs. The state struggled to raise revenues equal to its expenditure needs.[123] Also, growth in the Chinese economy was

[122] David Goodman, *Class in Contemporary China* (2014): 161; Chen, 'The Myth of Hukou': 294.

[123] Barry Naughton, 'A Political Economy of China's Economic Transition': 107.

accompanied by a laggardly growth in consumer demand. But the Chinese state had consolidated a central hierarchy of power, manifested in its centralization of revenues, reduction in rival centres of power within the party-state's apex institutions,[124] and increasingly stable ideological messaging. 'Development is the only iron law', declared Deng.[125] The government moved from an uncertain and experimental state socialism combined with a partial liberalization towards a state capitalism in which a legitimacy claim could be exercised by presenting the party as the representative of the dynamic growth of the 'advanced productive forces' of the country. The issue—as we have argued throughout the book—is not so much more or less liberalization or better liberalizing techniques but rather the recombinations of state power and accumulation and the possibilities that accumulation presents for generalized material improvements.

China's Transformative Development: The Early 2000s

Four discernible shifts took place at the start of the early 2000s.[126] In the first place, the government has made greater efforts to ensure that growth does not create drastic socio-economic processes of impoverishment. This shift in orientation was a result of increasing inequalities and also a shift in CCP leadership.[127] For most of the high-growth period from 1978, poverty reduction has coexisted with rising inequality.[128] In urban areas, the gradual lightening of migration regulation has generated a rising poor and precarious urban population. For the Chinese state, inequality and concentrations of increasing poverty present a threat to the continued authoritarian rule of the CCP.[129] In the early 2000s, there was a wave of peasant protest. There were up to 230,000 'public manifestations of discontent' in 2010.[130]

[124] One part of which was the subordination of the military, perhaps best exemplified when the party instructed the PLA to divest any companies it owned (1988).

[125] Kroeber, *China's Economy*: 8. This is sometimes translated as 'development is the only hard truth'.

[126] Bergsten et al., *China's Rise*: 109 *et seq.*

[127] Deng Xiaoping's 'some people become rich before others' was replaced by a stronger public discourse of shared wealth.

[128] Goodman, *Class in Contemporary China*: 13.

[129] I am not using the terms totalitarian and authoritarian arbitrarily in this discussion of China. During the Great Leap Forward and Cultural Revolution period, the government was totalitarian in that it aspired to dominate and regulate all aspects of social life. Gradually since 1978, the state has removed itself from the detailed control of people's lives while maintaining a centralized top-down governance that disallows opposition. This is broadly in keeping with how comparativists distinguish between the two terms.

[130] Goodman, *Class in Contemporary China*: 166, 172.

In 1999, the government introduced the minimum livelihood guarantee and in the mid-2000s this was rolled out from urban areas to the whole country. SOEs maintained social benefits to their employees and made payments to those retrenched. In 2007, a rural cooperative health insurance system aimed to provide basic healthcare to all. Local governments started to institute unemployment insurance. Eighty-nine million rural residents now have basic pensions.[131] Also in 2007, provincial development programmes of investment were rolled out. In 2000, the Campaign to Open up the West was introduced. In 2006, remarkably in comparison with other countries with large peasant populations, agricultural taxes were abolished. This was a measure to consolidate eroding state legitimacy in the countryside.[132] It left peasant farmers with no extractions imposed upon them by government. It is worth noting, of course, that China's capitalist transformation had—as with all other cases—led to a sectoral decline in agriculture and concomitantly a fall in the importance of peasant households to the state's fiscus. These measures represent a moderate strategic reorientation, under a changed leadership, to address the poverty effects of capital's ascendance. This is also a reflection of the fact that agriculture has become a residual in what is now an industrial and service political economy.

Second, the Chinese government reorganized the state-owned sector. This involved massive retrenchment, some privatization,[133] a refinancing of loss-making companies,[134] a listing of selected SOEs on the stock exchange, a new regulatory oversight structure, and the financial reorganization of SOEs.[135] As a result, China's state-owned companies are some of the largest companies in the world. Sinopec is the seventh largest company in the world with revenues in 2009 amounting to $187.5 million.[136]

Third, Chinese capital has grown and diversified. City governments generate capital from land sales, invest in infrastructure, and support firms. Privately owned Chinese companies employ the majority of the workforce. City and provincial governments compete and act innovatively to encourage investment and accumulation within their remits. Pearson categorizes China's capital into top tier large-scale enterprises dominated by restructured SOEs, middle tier companies largely state-owned but relatively autonomous and often provincially based, and bottom tier companies which are privately

131 Mark Frazier, 'The Evolution of a Welfare State under China's State Capitalism' (2015): 226.
132 On this see Chen, *The Transformation of Governance in Rural China.*
133 Kelly Tsai and Barry Naughton, 'State Capitalism and the Chinese Miracle' (2015): 9.
134 Shell companies were created to take non loss-making parts of enterprises.
135 Walter and Howie, *Red Capitalism.*
136 Walter and Howie, *Red Capitalism*: 12.

owned and constitute the vast majority.[137] In rural areas, TVEs have been transformed into private businesses run largely by 'entrepreneur cadres'.[138]

Fourth, from the mid-1990s and into the present-day, the Chinese state has invested very heavily in infrastructure. The most iconic early example of this was the completion of the Three Gorges Dam in 2006. This massive public work was undertaken after the World Bank withdrew its lending. It represents a keystone in China's endeavour to reduce dependence on oil imports—its own cheap coal is now nowhere near adequate to the energy demands of its economy.[139] Most importantly, the government has commenced the roll-out of the Belt and Road project which aims to pump prime the Chinese economy and integrate economies from China to Europe, Asia, and Africa.[140]

China has not only undergone protracted high economic growth. It has also become a capitalist political economy which has transformed its society. Industry and services have expanded. The average annual wage labourer income was $3,500 in 2008.[141] Agriculture has made considerable productivity gains.[142] Research and development and the deployment of technology in production has intensified. Millions of people have escaped poverty. There is a degree of social mobility that did not exist before.

However, income inequality is still extremely high. Compared to other northeast Asian developmentalisms, incomes have grown but at a far lower rate.[143] Millions of people are still extremely poor. The state has enhanced its authoritarian oversight rather than relinquished it, and it has done so by adopting the technologies of capitalism rather than refusing to change: big data, cyber monitoring, and CCTV and face recognition have endowed the Chinese government with a surveillance structure well in excess of any Stasi-like secret police or informer network (although these things also exist). China has the second highest number of people in prison—although as a ratio to the total population it is sixth. Especially from 2010, China's workers have struck against low pay[144] and hard work and also advocate for independent trade

[137] Margaret Pearson, 'State-Owned Business and Party-State Regulation in China's Modern Political Economy' (2015). Even by 1985 there were 17 million private businesses. Hsu, *The Rise of Modern China*: 852.

[138] Chen, *The Transformation of Governance in Rural China*: 13 *et seq.*

[139] This is why China's SOEs have invested heavily in Africa, although it would be a gross simplification simply to say that China is extracting oil from African oil exporters. See especially Deborah Brautigam, *The Dragon's Gift: The Real Story of China in Africa* (2011).

[140] Bruno Maçaes, *Belt and Road. A Chinese World Order* (2018).

[141] Kroeber, *China's Economy*: 174.

[142] Kroeber, *China's Economy*: 40–1.

[143] Ho-fung Hung, 'Rise of China and the Global Overaccumulation Crisis' (2008): 162.

[144] There is some evidence that unskilled wage rates are now growing at an accelerating rate. Xiaobing Wang et al., 'Wage Growth, Landholding, and Mechanization in Chinese Agriculture' (2016).

union organization.[145] China has more strikes than any country in the world.[146] The argument here is not of China's development success as much as its remarkable transformative progress.

Conclusion

It might seem odd to have reviewed Rwanda and China in one chapter. They are clearly very different countries. But, as suggested in the chapter's Introduction, they do offer contrasting examples of the singular challenge of developmentalism. They have both constructed a project of capitalist transformation: one early-stage example in a small economy with—let's be realistic—slender chances of success; and one in which the expanded accumulation of capital has been world-historic, but which still has a large peasant sector and mass poverty. In spite of repeated predictions of collapse, China's political economy continues to grow and transform and it seems likely that in the next twenty years or so, the problems China faces will be those of a developed capitalist political economy. The government of Rwanda, for its part, is well aware of the massive challenges it faces and which it identified in previously successful developmentalisms as points of reference for its own future, especially in relation to Singapore. We offer these cases, then, as diverse examples of capital ascendant precisely to illustrate how situated the developmentalist project is and how slender its chances. To have exclusively reviewed successes would be to give the false impression that there is a way and the chances are good if some kind of synthesis of existing successes can be forged. Rwanda shows us otherwise, but this is the project it is currently embarked upon, with no guarantees but with the future of the state itself pinned closely to its fortunes.

[145] Goodman, *Class in Contemporary China*: 163.

[146] Eli Friedman, 'Alienated Politics: Labour Insurgency and the Paternalistic State in China' (2014): 1002.

10
Conclusion

Recap

In Chapter 1, we identified a political project to generate capitalist accumulation in order to secure economic growth and possibly legitimacy. We have argued that this is a deeply political project and accordingly coined it developmentalism to signify its ideological features. Developmentalism consists of: a relationship between the state and capital which promotes transformative accumulation; a strong nationalism that endows the state with authoritative abilities to socially engineer society; a resilience of rule which means that regimes can both survive and adapt to crisis; and a socio-political dynamic of popular mobilization and contestation in pursuit of the commonwealth.

We have not offered developmentalism as an unequivocal model for successful development but have rather situated it within two broadly realist calibrations. In the first place, capitalist development might offer the most extensive means through which to provide significant improvements in mass material well-being, but it does not erase poverty or inequality. Nor does it address major social–structural injustices in relation to race, gender, or ethnicity. Capitalism—as a process of development or as a political economy more generally—is based on the exploitation of labour and dominance through the monopolization of property. This is, then, 'two cheers' for capitalist development, an acknowledgement of capitalism's dynamism in a historical period where there are no strong rivals which might promise better ways of generating growth and well-being. Second, capitalist development is itself realized through socio-political practices of dispossession, repression, authoritarian social engineering, intensified labour, and imperialism. These characteristics are not contingent or autonomous from development; they are part of it. This means that developmentalism is normatively agonistic: there is an incommensurability between the progress of growth and poverty reduction and the allocation of pain and suffering in its realization.

For developmentalism to have any possibility of succeeding, it must ensure some form of stability and authority in its modes of rule. We have drawn on contemporary political realism to understand how such an exacting and risky

Developmentalism: The Normative and Transformative within Capitalism. Graham G.M. Harrison,
Oxford University Press (2020). © Graham G.M. Harrison.
DOI: 10.1093/oso/9780198785798.001.0001

political project might succeed or even attain legitimacy. Realism understands politics as constituted through the exercise of authoritative political power by the state and its ability to create and enforce rules that enable or allow people to live in peaceful and orderly relations with each other. It is, then, a 'minimalist' understanding of politics and governance—not one based on detailed identifications of institutions or the fit between governance and an a priori value system which has been deduced as just. Developmentalism's strength derives from its ability to fulfil a modified version of Bernard William's basic legitimacy demand. Because Williams (and most others in his tradition) have focused on developed capitalist states, they have less insight into the ways in which the depth or extensity of poverty might generate mass deaths or major social upheavals, or profoundly destabilize prevailing property relations. Nor do they pay central attention to the fact that state sovereignty might be in construction and under siege in ways that pose existential threats to a national politics. We introduce a more materialist basic legitimacy demand for developmentalism that is based on a politics of constructing the ability of the state to manipulate the economy, to generate expanded accumulation and growth, to manage the major social instabilities generated by capitalist transformation, and to broadcast minimally convincing, or accepted, claims to be constructing a commonwealth based on a broadening of mass material well-being. Developmentalism is a legitimacy-seeking project in which the modern renditions of those things most political realists (and indeed most political theory generally) assume to be foundations for political analysis—the nation-state and the economy—are being constructed.

Political realism lends itself well to an analysis of the basis upon which politics can be practised. In relation to developmentalism this basis is more materially implicated than discussions of legitimacy in modern capitalist/liberal societies allow. There is another facet of the realist tradition that helps us understand developmentalism, and that is its non-idealism. Realism does not aim to stipulate the conditions of justice and then seek their realization through political relations and institutions. It sees justice as a contextual phenomenon that has no transhistorical or metaphysical identity. Although justice has proven to be the most commonly discussed norm in political theory, realism's mode of procedure denies any abstracted and deduced normative structure. Realism starts with an extremely parsimonious constitution of politics based on the necessity of an absence of arbitrary harm and fear, and it proceeds to recognize that the normative considerations that work through the heart of politics are not a meliorist seeking of a just system or of endeavouring to generate an institutional correspondence of politics with 'what justice requires'. Rather, it relies on the premise that all normative contestations and projects are unstable and agonistic. Normative improvement and political power do not synthesize as a result of the affinities of justice with order.

This matters for us because developmentalism is replete with normative agonism: social justice and capitalist development are not in comity with each other. The actual practices of developmentalism (as the case studies have amply shown) are defined by all manner of rights-denying actions, compromises, risks, and coercions. These are not simply violations of the requirements of justice. They are, instead, part of the political project of constructing a modern political order through capitalist transformation. As such, they create the conditions of possibility for both social justice (and other normative possibilities) and political mobilization that themselves realize the politics of rights, justice, and commonwealth. Realism has no need of a deduced notion of rights or justice. It understands rights and justice as historically and materially produced political practices that emerge within the teeth of capitalist transformation itself.

Realism is not an amoral theory of politics but rather a non-ideal one. It sets out a challenge that can only be engaged with through a consideration of the specific: how does the exercise of power generate normativity and what valuing and assessing judgements can we induce about that normativity and the politics from which it emerged? We will return to this in the section 'The World of Capitalist Development'.

Political realism has enjoyed a certain resurgence in the last decade or so and as it has grown it has moved beyond the often rather stereotyped renditions of realism offered by international relations theory textbooks which see realism as strictly a conservative doctrine. As realism has become a confident position within political theory, it seems possible to identify aspects of realism with a broadly Marxist tradition.[1] Indeed, reading the writing of Marx, Engels, or Lenin on the political struggles of their days, there is very little of the ideal or transcendental to be seen. What makes Marxism central to the construction of our theoretical framework can be condensed into two points. First, realism is in a sense not 'real' enough. It does not take political economy into its foundations and as a result does not give central attention in its considerations of power, authority, and legitimacy to the materiality of politics. This matters a great deal for our purposes. The concept of developmentalism is oriented towards the political exigencies of sustaining a process of expanded capital accumulation. And we have established a modified basic legitimacy

[1] On this, see Gregor McLennan, *Marxism and the Methodologies of History* (1981): Chapter 2.

demand in which poverty and inequality are not challenges to be met by established and legitimate government but are intrinsic to the establishing of government.

As a result, we offer a critical realist articulation to political realism in which we deploy the analytical categorizations of empirical actual and real. In this framework, the real is the process of expanded capital accumulation whose dynamics are intrinsic and generic to capitalism and which—for this author—are best set out by Marx in *Capital I*. This dynamic—which Marx often describes in metaphors—is not observable, which of course offers up a challenge for a realist ontology. Within critical realism, the real represents external phenomena that underdetermine the nature of the social dynamics. In our understanding, expanded accumulation of capital is the fundamental reality of a capitalism political economy. Without it, it is difficult to see how we can talk about capitalism in any kind of systemic way. Development is about the sustenance of this accumulation within conditions in which capitalist social relations are partially realized. Its 'actual' manifestations are the observable but massive and myriad forms of labour and investment that manifest expanded accumulation. These are rendered empirically through audit and research that might generate statistics, narratives, or models of how a political economy is growing, developing, declining, and so on.

The reality of capitalist development is expanded accumulation, a process that underpins economic growth and transformation but which can only be adumbrated theoretically as a concrete externality of capitalism. Its observable forms are constructed through empirical observations of actual socio-economic agency. At the heart of this process is capitalism's unequalled ability to generate wealth through increases in productivity. This property of capitalism creates the conditions of possibility for massive amounts of poverty reduction and improvements in mass material well-being. It is within these conditions of possibility that developmentalism might attain legitimacy, but in the throes of this transformative process, the ideologies of developmentalism often manifest themselves in tropes of national security, order, and necessity. These are hardly specific to successful developers, but it is most assuredly the case that successful developers have shifted from the authoritarianism of the latter to something more legitimate by achieving capitalist development. Within that transformation, government is characterized by a stable and legitimate state, widely accepted procedures through which policy is made, and perennial contestations of the modes through which inequality is minimized and the allocation of resources are justly managed. This is the 'two cheers' of a developed capitalist political economy.

To argue that development is nothing if not a social transformation driven by expanded accumulation under conditions of authoritarian governance is not commonplace within mainstream discourses of development. This is because development has been increasingly conceptualized through ideal rights theories within which poverty reduction and freedom not only coexist but also reinforce each other. We discuss this mainstream framing of development because it sets the greatest challenge both normatively and empirically to our approach, and we do so by focusing on the main point-of-reference in the rights/development canon which is capabilities. We argue that the capabilities approach struggles fully to understand the structural nature of development. It tends to manifest an ambition to make moderate and localized reductions in poverty, and it has generally failed to explain the major systemic improvements in material well-being that have taken place in the global history of capitalism. What it does do is identify a way of speaking about development in a normatively pleasing fashion. Development, in the liberal mainstream, involves the freeing up of agency, the allocation of rights, and the facilitation of socially harmonizing social processes. We respond to this approach by making a clearer distinction between a rights paradigm and a development one. We make a case that the synergy of rights discourse and development discourse might seem normatively attractive, but it comes at a considerable analytical cost. Furthermore, it tends to obfuscate or evade the very difficult—and in our view irreconcilable—normative issues that relate to capitalist transformation as a project that involves as much allocation of suffering as it does the allocation of benefit.

Section 2 sets out an historical account of how capitalist development has worked in concrete national instances. It treats Britain and America in some detail both because of their early and turbulent capitalist transitions and because these two capitalist nations construct the context within which development as a political project has taken place. Indeed, the term 'development' has no specific meaning in the absence of the world order constructed by these two. From the 1940s, development has been intrinsically a national project within and against a world made in the image of British and American capital. Britain and America reveal specific concrete histories of how capitalist development is a violent process. It involves states systemically dispossessing, reordering, engineering, colonizing, distributing patronage, and deceiving. Neither of these epitomes of capitalist transformation did any of its developing within a democratic frame of governance. Inasmuch as rights and democracy emerged as bones of normative contention, they did so as particular manifestations of the transformations themselves, not as the realizations of a clearly defined ideal. Nevertheless, we saw how remarkable the transformation was in each case: growth, improvements in mass well-being, and a dynamic set of innovations and investments in production. It is something of an inescapable teleology that capitalist transformation in these two countries and others from the nineteenth century—for all of the violence and exploitation—has created the most affluent and dynamic national economies in history.

The subsequent case studies—Japan, Taiwan, Israel, Rwanda, and China—exemplify the travails of developmentalism and illustrate the risk, effort, and potential of capitalist development. We identify analogous concrete manifestations of the same processes that we saw in Britain and America and which align broadly with our model of developmentalism: the coercion, the project to support expanded accumulation, the social engineering, the seeking of legitimacy in combinations of nationalism, security, and material progress. We end with Rwanda and China as examples of near-success and early endeavour. By many measures, China is the most remarkable capitalist transformation in world history, but it remains 'third world' in some ways. Rwanda has embarked on a developmentalist project under severely adverse circumstances and reveals very starkly the immense political pressures faced by states endeavouring to transform their societies.

The case studies do not serve to generate models. Each and all exemplify the political of capitalist transformation concretely and in historically and geographically distinct ways. What they all show us is how development requires the rise of a capitalist class that seeks to expand accumulation through new forms of production and through increased productivity and that this requires a political project. We now come to a position where we can explore the normativity in all of this—again not to seek institutional correspondence to an idealized rights position, but rather to assess and value the various actions of states within the midst of developmentalism.

The World of Capitalist Development: From the Miraculous to the Profane

Chapters 7–9 have set out five case studies of capitalist transformation during the era of modern development after the Second World War. Four of those cases—Japan, Taiwan, Israel, and China—offer us examples of exceptionally successful capitalist development. Each of these has been described as a 'miracle' in order to communicate the judgement that capitalist transformation has been against the odds, required exceptional levels of effort, and led to profound transformations in people's general material well-being. But although the miracle epithet offers a memorable stylization for each of these cases, there is nothing miraculous about any of them. We have seen how in each case capitalist transformation was a project. The project—developmentalism—required a consistent exercise of power to promote expanded accumulation, and the exacting nature of this project could only be met in each case through a conflation of development with the existential politics of security and sovereignty. Within this political context, major strategic decisions needed to be taken in relation to policy, adaptation, and risk. In each of these respects, strategic change was undertaken during periods of rapid social change: urbanization, the creation of large working classes, the emergence of increasingly powerful capitals, and the rise and fall of different threats and opportunities within regional and global systems. The concept of developmentalism re-inscribes miracles as hard-fought and prosaic successes, manifestations of both the unequalled promise of capitalist development and the adverse circumstances within which this might be achieved.

Sticking with the 'miracle' discourse a moment longer, we can note that there are other cases that have been given this accolade. South Korea and Singapore would be the most obvious. In the 1970s, Brazil's sustained growth was described as a miracle. Malaysia and Vietnam in the 1990s have also been characterized as miracles.[2] What we can see again, and more emphatically, is that extended periods of economic growth accompanied by transformative capitalist accumulation in our cases studies and these other 'miracle' countries show us how capitalism can generate mass material well-being. Each of these examples fixed a national–political project of socio-economic transformation and each experienced the emergence of a growing and dynamic capitalism that both pushed for increased productivity and technological change and brought into existence larger classes of wage labour. None of these countries fits into the notion of development associated with international aid, poverty reduction, capabilities, or any of the other signifiers of development that constitute the global development architecture.

We have understood capitalist development not as miraculous but rather as profane: a deeply material project, founded on the pursuit of growth, and

[2] One might add Ireland to the 1990s' list, but this would be misleading because Ireland did not go through a capitalist transformation as much as re-regulate its capitalist economy in the context of European integration.

immanently churning up all manner of social harms and repressions in the course of its business. But, as this book has argued throughout, it is within this milieu (and sometimes mêlée) that the vast majority of poverty reduction has taken place since the mid-nineteenth century. But what remains interesting about miracle discourse is its normative content. Everyone likes a miracle. The term is innately celebratory, in the same way that the literature on the resource curse is innately eschatological.[3] And there is something of the politics of the sublime in the notion of a miracle: that getting the policies right will generate positive effects that potentially will exceed predictions—amaze or even mystify. However much we might wish to add a dash of the mystical to a miracle, the normative positivity of the miracle is evident enough. One must, by definition, celebrate a miracle. This brings us back to a key theme throughout this book: the moral politics of development within a framework that denies the possibility of rights-affirming transformation.

Developmentalism's Normativity

Although our focus in the case studies has been on the transformative nature of capitalism and the politics of that transformation, we have taken care to note that many people have suffered and perished. We have argued that all of this harm is not amenable to analytical externalization. There is no transformation that does not involve dispossession, authoritarian state action, impoverishment, and death. But this does not mean that we should submit to some kind of ethical nihilism in which we focus on the growth statistics and leave the normativity to the human rights activists, or in which we throw our hands up at the tragic nature of progress and hope that in time the skyscrapers remain as the memories of sorrow dissipate. There are three ways in which a realist approach to ethical thinking allows us to assess the rights and wrongs of capitalist development.

Evaluating Practices of Development

In the first place, the practices of a developmentalist state are not simply covered by a kind of transformation performance carte blanche. We have

[3] In some more polemic literature, the quasi-antonym 'mirage' is used.

taken an approach to capitalist transformation in which specifics—and the particular ways in which states act—matter. Thinking normatively, we have to recognize that governments always exercise some choice in their actions and that those actions will have different relations to processes of growth, accumulation, and increased productivity. The inquiries that this position offers can only be pursued *in specifica*. Some actions—banning journalism or music, assassinating public speakers, and so on—either have nothing to do with development as we understand it, or their purported connections are so remote that they have no moral ambiguity. There are many states that carry out all manner of oppressive actions, accompanied by declarations of national progress or development, but in the midst of concrete empirical inquiry it appears that ideologies of development are largely smokescreens. In these contexts, the unpleasant acts of states require no developmental nuance.

A thought experiment might help illustrate where the nub of a normative judgement of developmentalism might lie. In some post-colonial states, people have been displaced in order for large civil engineering or commercial projects to be realized—say, a hydroelectric dam. In some cases, the project might be a conduit through which politicians and capitalists make money through patrimonially distributed contracts. The projects either fail, become highly costly and delayed, or are completed without due consideration to how they might be economically sustainable. In other cases, the project might generate cheaper energy for towns, cities, and industries. The companies completing the project might have been contracted to share technologies or training with local people and companies. In some cases, displacement might be through edict, handed down by a local official, backed up by force of arms, and with minimal planning for resettlement. In others, new settlements might be set up and some consultation—even if basically offering no choice—might have allowed some awareness and preparation. Small payments might be made to reduce resistance. Or the police might round people up and tell them to move. One might add other practical considerations to this hypothetical and each might make the evaluation of the execution of the project more involved. It is not *a priori* impossible that resettlement has benefits, such as proximity to health posts or schools, or new opportunities for wage labour. Perhaps for many women and people socially subordinate to dominant landowning lineages, resettlement opens up a certain release from former social constraints. It is within these concrete 'parcels' of developmental action that a great deal of normatively guided analysis can take place. Declaring that resettlement is a violation of the right to freedom of movement is ideally strong but for our purposes seems ethically impervious to the wide and significant ethical bandwidth of concrete developmental practice.

Considerations of economic policy contain much specificity for moral consideration. What kind of information is a government working with, how does it construct choices and make decisions, how does it identify expected harms in a policy measure and how—if at all—does it intend to ameliorate these? How, simply, do states make choices between a range of policies, all of which will be in part about the allocation of suffering as well as the allocation of benefits? Privatization, trade policy, social security, fiscal reform, land tenure changes... all of these involve some degree of choice and a range of ways in which the policy is actualized. And how do people respond to the execution of policies?—a question we will return to in the next section ('Rights, Social Mobilization, and Agency'.

We should recall that this is not an exercise in identifying the right form of policy or project, the one that corresponds to a perfected normative framework. None do, and none can. The realist approach we have taken is more akin to excavating the normative tensions and ethical specificities involved. That is as far as we can go without losing the central argument of the book. This is, to some degree, for an ideal normative theorist, unsatisfying.

Rights, Social Mobilization, and Agency

But we don't have to dwell on this dour historical note. The second normative consideration is a recognition that all aspects of a capitalist transformation contain within them the possibility of new forms of political agency and social identity. Developmentalism is necessarily about increased wage labour, greater possibilities for social well-being, urbanization, and mobility. In all of our case studies, whatever suppressions and oppressions were visited upon peoples were also generative of invigorated or novel forms of collective mobilization. In a realist framework, values do not exist *ex cathedra* but are realized through the exercise of political agency. And for those interested in politics, these agencies have to be collective, and their strength and tenacity have to be material. The point here is that the notion of human rights does not get at the historicity of political agency, at least in relation to capitalist transformation. Political agency is dynamic, not static. A rights violation is also a possibility of resistance, and the transformed conditions within which people might find themselves as they respond to the forces of expanded accumulation are also transformed conditions of possibility. To paraphrase inelegantly one of Marx's aphorisms: people make their own history but not in circumstances of their own choosing but in changing circumstances.

Towards Value Pluralism

If we take our focus of moral interest as the specific practices of developmentalism realized in concrete situations that we expect to generate their own normative contentions as a result of the agencies and resistances that they throw up, then we need also to recognize that rights are not the only value at play. As already mentioned, there is something of a monopoly of rights discourse over discussions of justice and a conflation of justice with what is normatively desirable. But, within our frame of reference, this seems rather narrow. We have just argued that values and norms are situated and political. Within the course of our theoretical and empirical explorations we have implied that questions of rights and justice cohabit with other values. We can set these out fairly directly here because they have been lurking throughout the body of the book. These values are: economic improvement;[4] political stability; a sense of valued national sovereignty, purpose, and progress; and the construction of a commonwealth. Taking values where one finds them, and aware of the antagonisms innate of capitalist development, we would be better placed to see individual rights as one value set that cohabits with these four others. There is no *a priori* move to establish rights as more important than economic improvement, being reasonably certain how life will be in a year, consolidating a social identity and shared destiny with many others in one's nation-state, or considering in some fashion that the transformation that is taking place is creating a shared sense of material improvement. We have five bundles of values that more comprehensively encompass the normativity of development and which one might expect to emerge in concrete settings where capitalist development is taking place. They might contest or complement one another and they most certainly will change as change takes place. The suggestion here is that a realist approach to development's normativity is not a degrading of values but a recognition of their plurality. Within capitalist development, it is within this plurality that legitimacy is constructed not only through the respect of human rights. How one might develop modes of

[4] Note the word 'improvement' here as a quick way to connect economic growth with an experience of improved incomes, opportunities, or quality of work. As ever, the connection between 'statistical' growth and these lived experiences is an empirical matter.

assessment or even more boldly predictions and recommendations might make for interesting research. This research would have the merit of being released from the Manichean incommensurability of the utilitarian and the idealist.

The Future

The historic promise of capital—and its ultimate claim to legitimacy—is that accumulation generates economic expansion that makes people's lives better. Clearly, globally, this is more promise than claim. Developmentalism is the ideology of a politics that aims to move a society from this promise to its reality, and it recognizes that this move is one that requires the distribution of suffering as well as benefits.

The trajectory from capital ascendant to capital dominant is in no sense a great historic resolution of poverty, overwork, or inequality. It is nothing more—or less—than a transformation of the realities upon which these material phenomena play out. To deny capitalism's progressiveness is as mistaken as denying its limits and contradictions. Development achieved is hardly the end of history. Indeed, as Marx insisted, within and against the historical engine of capitalism, anything is possible.

Bibliography

Abbott, P., Sapsford, R., and Rwirahira, J. (2015) Overcoming Poverty and Inequality: Rwanda's Progress Towards the MDGs. *Development in Practice* 25, 7.

Abernathy, D. (2000) *The Dynamics of Global Dominance. European Overseas Empires, 1415–1980*. New Haven: Yale University Press.

Abrams, P. (1988) Notes on the Difficulty of Studying the State. *Journal of Historical Sociology* 1(1), 58–89.

Ackroyd, S. and Karlsson, J. (2014) Critical Realism, Research Techniques and Research Designs. In: Edwards, P., O'Mahoney, J., and Vincent, S. (eds) *Studying Organizations Using Critical Realism*. Oxford: Oxford University Press, pp. 21–46.

African Development Bank (2013) *Africa Economic Outlook*. Abidjan: ADB.

African Development Bank (2015) *Rwanda 2015*. Abidjan: ADB.

Aharoni, Y. (1991) *The Israeli Economy. Dreams and Realities*. London: Routledge.

A'Hearn, B. (2014) The British Industrial Revolution in a European Mirror. In: Floud, R., Humphries, J., and Johnson, P. (eds) *The Cambridge Economic History of Modern Britain, Vol 1*. Cambridge: Cambridge University Press.

Alkire, S. (2002) *Valuing Freedoms: Sen's Capability Approach and Poverty Reduction*. Oxford: Oxford University Press.

Alkire, S. (2008) Using the Capability Approach: Prospective and Evaluative Analyses. In: Comim, F., Qizilbash, M., and Alkire, S. (eds) *The Capability Approach. Concepts, Measures and Applications*. Cambridge: Cambridge University Press, pp. 26–49.

Allen, C. (1972) *A Short Economic History of Modern Japan 1867–1937*. London: Allen and Unwin.

Allen, R. (2009) *The British Industrial Revolution in Global Perspective*. Cambridge: Cambridge University Press.

Allinson, G. (1993) The Structure and Transformation of Conservative Rule. In: Gordon, A. (ed.) *Postwar Japan as History*. Berkeley: University of California Press.

Alston, P. and Robinson, M. (eds) (2005) *Human Rights and Development—Towards Mutual Reinforcement*. New York: Oxford University Press.

Amsden, A. (1999) Taiwan's Industrialization Policies: Two Views, Two Types of Subsidy. In: Thorbecke, E. and Wan, H. (eds) *Taiwan's Development Experience: Lessons on Roles of Government and Market*. New York: Springer.

Anderson, B. (2008) *The Spectre of Comparisons*. London: Verso.

Anderson, K. (2010) *Marx at the Margins. On Nationalism, Ethnicity, and Non-Western Societies*. Chicago: Chicago University Press.

Anderson, R. and Gallman, R. (1977) Slaves as Fixed Capital. Slave Labor and Southern Economic Development. *Journal of American History* 64, 1.

Andre, C. and Platteau, J.-P. (1988) Land Relations under Unbearable Stress: Rwanda Caught in the Malthusian Trap. *Journal of Economic Behavior and Organization* 34, 1.

Ang, Y. (2016) *How China Escaped the Poverty Trap*. Ithaca: Cornell University Press.

Anievas, A. and Nicancioglu, K. (2015) *How the West Came to Rule. The Geopolitical Origins of Capitalism*. London: Pluto Press.

Ansoms, A. (2008) Striving for Growth, Bypassing the Poor? A Critical Review of Rwanda's Rural Sector Policies. *Journal of Modern African Studies* 46, 1.

Ansoms, A. (2009) Re-engineering Rural Society: The Visions and Ambitions of the Rwandan Elite. *African Affairs* 108, 289–309.

Ansoms, A., Cioffo, G., Huggins, C., and Murison, J. (2014) The Reorganization of Rural Space in Rwanda. In: Ansoms, A. and Hilhorst, T. (eds) *Losing Your Land. Dispossession in the Great Lakes*. Oxford: James Currey.

Arrighi, G. (1994) *The Long Twentieth Century*. Brooklyn: Verso Books.

Bachman, D. (1991) *Bureaucracy, Economy, and Leadership in China: The Institutional Origins of the Great Leap Forward*. Cambridge: Cambridge University Press.

Balogh, B. (2009) *A Government out of Sight: The Mystery of National Authority in Nineteenth-Century America*. Cambridge: Cambridge University Press.

Banajee, J. (2010) *Theory as History. Essays on Modes of Production and Exploitation*. Leiden: Brill.

Baran, P. and Sweezy, P. (1966) *Monopoly Capital: An Essay on the American Economic and Social Order*. New York: Monthly Review Press.

Barkan, J. D. (1994) *Beyond Capitalism Versus Socialism in Kenya and Tanzania*. Boulder: Lynne Rienner.

Barkey, H. (1994) When Politics Matter: Economic Stabilisation in Argentina and Israel. *Studies in Comparative International Development* 29, 4.

Batho, G. (1990) Landlords in England, 1500–1640. In: Thirsk, J. (ed.) *Chapters from the Agrarian History of England and Wales 1500–1750*. Cambridge: Cambridge University Press, pp. 21–71.

Bell, D. (2007) *The Idea of Greater Britain. Empire and the Future of the World Order 1860–1900*. Princeton: Princeton University Press.

Benjamin, W. (1969) Theses on the Philosophy of History. In: Zohn, H. (ed.) *Illluminations*. New York: Schocken Books.

Bensel, R. (2000) *The Political Economy of American Industrialisation 1877–1900*. Cambridge: Cambridge University Press.

Bensel, R. (2008) *Yankee Leviathan: The Origins of Central State Authority in America, 1859–1877*. Cambridge: Cambridge University Press.

Bergsten, C., Freeman, C., Lardy, N., and Mitchell, D. (2008) *China's Rise. Challenges and Opportunities*. Washington, DC: Peterson Institute for International Economics.

Berman, M. (2010) *All that Is Solid Melts into Air. The Experience of Modernity*. London: Verso.

Bernstein, D. and Swirski, S. (1982) The Rapid Economic Development of Israel and the Emergence of the Ethnic Division of Labour. *British Journal of Sociology* 33, 1.

Bernstein, H. (2010) *Class Dynamics of Agrarian Change*. Halifax: Fernwood Publishing.

Berry, S. (1993) *No Condition Is Permanent. The Social Dynamics of Agrarian Change in Sub-Saharan Africa*. Madison: University of Wisconsin Press.

Bhaskar, R. (1998) Philosophy and Scientific Realism. In: Archer, M., Bhaskar, R., Collier, A., Lawson, T., and Norrie, A. (eds) *Critical Realism*. London: Routledge, pp. 16–48.

Bigsten, A. and Danielson, A. (2001) *Tanzania: Is the Ugly Duckling Finally Growing up?* Uppsala: Nordiska Afrikainstitutet.

Bin Wong, R. (1997) *China Transformed*. Ithaca: Cornell University Press.

Blackburn, R. (1998) *The Making of New World Slavery: From the Baroque to the Modern, 1492–1800*. London: Verso.

Blaug, M. (2003) *Economic Theory in Retrospect*. Cambridge: Cambridge University Press.

Blecher, R. (2005) Citizens without Sovereignty: Transfer and Ethnic Cleansing in Israel. *Comparative Studies in Society and History* 47, 4.

Booth, D. and Golooba-Mutebi, F. (2012) Developmental Patrimonialism? The Case of Rwanda. *African Affairs* 111, 444.

Brandt, L. and Rawski, T. (2008) *China's Great Economic Transformation.* Cambridge: Cambridge University Press.

Brass, T. (1997) The Agrarian Myth, the 'New' Populism and the 'New' Right. *Journal of Peasant Studies* 24, 4.

Brass, T. (2011) *Labour Regime Change in the Twenty-First Century.* Leiden: Haymarket Books.

Brautigam, D. (2011) *The Dragon's Gift: The Real Story of China in Africa.* Oxford: Oxford University Press.

Bregman, A. (1987) Government Intervention in Industry. The Case of Israel. *Journal of Development Economics* 25, 4.

Brenner, R. (1976) Agrarian Class Structure and Economic Development in Pre-Industrial Europe. *Past & Present* 70, 1.

Brenner, R. (1977) The Origins of Capitalist Development: A Critique of Neo-Smithian Marxism. *New Left Review* Series I, 104.

Brenner, R. (1982) The Agrarian Roots of European Capitalism. *Past & Present* 97, 1.

Brenner, R. (1986) The Social Basis of Economic Development. In: Roemer, J. (ed.) *Analytical Marxism.* Cambridge: Cambridge University Press.

Brewer, J. (1989) *The Sinews of Power.* London: Routledge.

Breznitz, D. (2007) Industrial R&D as a National Policy: Horizontal Technology Policies and Industry–State Co-evolution in the Growth of the Israeli Software Industry. *Research Policy* 36, 6.

Brogan, H. (1999) *The Penguin History of the USA.* London: Penguin.

Brohman, J. (2005) *Popular Development.* Oxford: Blackwell.

Brown, A., Fleetwood, S., and Roberts, J. (eds) (2002) *Critical Realism and Marxism.* London: Routledge.

Bryant, C. (2017) *Entitled. A Critical History of the British Aristocracy.* London: Doubleday.

Bujra, J. (2000) *Serving Class: Masculinity and the Feminisation of Domestic Service in Tanzania.* Edinburgh: Edinburgh University Press.

Burnette, J. (2014) Agriculture, 1700–1870. In: Floud, R., Humphries, J., and Johnson, P. (eds) *The Cambridge Economic History of Modern Britain, Vol 1.* Cambridge: Cambridge University Press.

Burnham, P. (1994) Open Marxism and Vulgar International Political Economy. *Review of International Political Economy* 1(2), 221–31.

Byers, T. (1996) *Capitalism from Above and Capitalism from Below.* London: Macmillan.

Cain, A. G. and Hopkins, P. (2016) *British Imperialism.* London: Routledge.

Cain, P. J. (2001) Economics and Empire: The Metropolitan Context. In: Porter, A. (ed.) *The Oxford History of the British Empire. Volume III. The Nineteenth Century.* Oxford: Oxford University Press.

Callinicos, A. (2014) *Deciphering Capital. Marx's Capital and its Destiny.* London: Bookmarks.

Cardoso, F. and Faletto, E. (1979) *Dependency and Development in Latin America.* Berkeley: University of California Press.

Carlin, W. and Soskice, D. (2006) *Macroeconomics. Imperfections, Institutions, and Policies.* Oxford: Oxford University Press.

Carrier, J. G. (2018) Moral Economy: What's in a Name? *Anthropological Theory* 18(1), 18–35.

Chambers, R. (1983) *Putting the Last First.* London: Longman.

Chang, H.-J. (2002) *Kicking Away the Ladder. Development Strategy in Historical Perspective.* London: Anthem Press.

Chang, H.-J. and Grabel, I. (2004) *Reclaiming Development. An Alternative Economic Policy Manual.* London: Zed Books.

Chemouni, B. (2014) Explaining the Design of the Rwandan Decentralization: Elite Vulnerability and the Territorial Repartition of Power. *Journal of Eastern African Studies* 8, 2.

Chen, A. (2015) *The Transformation of Governance in Rural China. Market, Finance, and Political Authority.* Cambridge: Cambridge University Press.

Chen, Y. (2019) The Myth of Hukou: Re-examining Hukou's Implications for China's Development Model. *Review of Radical Political Economics* 51, 2.

Chibber, V. (2003) *Locked in Place. State-Building and Late Industrialization in India.* Princeton: Princeton University Press.

Chossudovsky, M. (2003) *Globalization of Poverty and the New World Order.* Montreal: Global Research Center.

Claassen, R. (2015) The Capability to Hold Property. *Journal of Human Development and Capabilities* 16(2), 220–36.

Clark, G. and Cummins, N. (2014) Inequality and Social Mobility in the Era of the Industrial Revolution. In: Floud, R., Humphries, J., and Johnson, P. (eds) *The Cambridge Economic History of Modern Britain, Vol 1.* Cambridge: Cambridge University Press.

Clark, P. (2010) *The Gacaca Courts, Post-Genocide Justice and Reconciliation in Rwanda.* Cambridge: Cambridge University Press.

Clark, P. (2014) Negotiating Reconciliation in Rwanda: Popular Challenges to the Official Discourse of Post-Genocide National Unity. *Journal of Intervention and Statebuilding* 8, 4.

Coates, D. (2000) *Models of Capitalism. Growth and Stagnation in the Modern Era.* Cambridge: Polity.

Cochran, T. and Miller, W. (1949) *The Age of Enterprise. A Social History of Industrial America.* New York: Macmillan.

Cohen, M. (2018) Reforming States, Agricultural Transformation, and Economic Development in Russia and Japan, 1853–1913. *Comparative Studies in Society and History* 60, 3.

Colley, L. (2005) *Britons. Forging the Nation 1707–1837.* New Haven: Yale University Press.

Conradie, I. and Robeyns, I. (2013) Aspirations and Human Development Interventions. *Journal of Human Development and Capabilities* 14(4), 559–80.

Cooke, B. and Kothari, U. (eds) (2001) *Participation: The New Tyranny?* London: Zed Books.

Cooper, F. (1987) *On the African Waterfront: Urban Disorder and the Transformation of Work in Colonial Mombasa.* London: Yale University Press.

Corbridge, S. (2002) Development as Freedom: The Spaces of Amartya Sen. *Progress in Development Studies* 2(3), 183–217.

Corbridge, S. and Shah, A. (2013) Introduction: The Underbelly of the Indian Boom. *Economy and Society* 42(3), 335–47.

Corrigan, P. and Sayer, D. (1985) *The Great Arch. English State Formation as Cultural Revolution.* Oxford: Blackwell.

Coulson, A. (2013) *Tanzania: A Political Economy.* Oxford: Oxford University Press.

Cowen, M. and Shenton, R. (1995) The Invention of Development. In: Crush, J. (ed.) *Power of Development.* London: Routledge.

Cowen, M. and Shenton, R. (1996) *Doctrines of Development.* Routledge: London.

Cox, G. (2016) *Marketing Sovereign Promises. Monopoly Brokerage and the Growth of the English State.* Cambridge: Cambridge University Press.

Crafts, N. (2004) Long Run Growth. In: Floud, R. and Johnson, P. (eds) *The Cambridge Economic History of Modern Britain, Vol 2.* Cambridge: Cambridge University Press.
Cumings, B. (1984) The Origins and Development of the Northeast Asian Political Economy: Industrial Sectors, Product Cycles, and Political Consequences. *International Organization* 38, 1.
Cumings, B. (1993) Japan's Position in the World System. In: Gordon A. (ed.) *Postwar Japan as History.* Berkeley: University of California Press.
Cunningham, H. (2001) *The Challenge of Democracy. Britain 1832–1918.* London: Pearson.
Currarino, J. (2006) The Politics of 'More': The Labor Question and the Idea of Economic Liberty in Industrial America. *Journal of American History* 93, 1.
Curtin, P. (1964). *The Image of Africa: British Ideas and Action, 1780–1850.* Madison: University of Wisconsin Press.
Cypher, J. and Dietz, J. (2004) *The Process of Economic Development.* London: Routledge.
Daunton, M. J. (2013) *Progress and Poverty. An Economic and Social History of Britain 1700–1850.* Oxford: Oxford University Press.
Davidoff, L. and Hall, C. (2002) *Family Fortunes. Men and Women of the English Middle Class 1780–1850.* London: Routledge.
Davidson, N. (2012) *How Revolutionary Were the Bourgeois Revolutions?* Chicago: Haymarket Press.
Davis, D. (1999) *The Problem of Slavery in the Age of Revolution.* Oxford: Oxford University Press.
de Angelis, M. (2004) Separating the Doing and the Deed: Capital and the Continuous Character of Enclosures. *Historical Materialism* 12(2), 57–87.
de la Rocha, M. (2007) The Construction of the Myth of Survival. *Development and Change* 38(1), 45–66.
de Lame, D. (2005) *A Hill among a Thousand: Transformations and Ruptures in Rural Rwanda.* Madison: University of Wisconsin Press.
De Soto, H. (2000) *The Mystery of Capital. Why Capitalism Triumphs in the West and Fails Everywhere Else.* London: Black Swan.
de Waal, A. (1997) *Famine Crimes. Politics and the Disaster Relief Industry in Africa.* Oxford: James Currey.
Deane, P. (1979) *The First Industrial Revolution.* Cambridge: Cambridge University Press.
Deaton, A. (2013) *The Great Escape. Health, Wealth and the Origins of Inequality.* Princeton: Princeton University Press.
Deneuilin, S. (2008) Beyond Individual Freedom and Agency: Structures of Living Together in the Capability Approach. In: Comim, F., Qizilbash, M., and Alkire, S. (eds) *The Capability Approach. Concepts, Measures and Applications.* Cambridge: Cambridge University Press, pp. 105–24.
des Forges, A. (2006) Land in Rwanda: Winnowing out the Chaff. In: Reyntjens, F. and Marysse, S. (eds) *L'Afrique des Grands Lacs: Dix Ans de Transitions Conflictuelles: Annuaire 2005–2006.* Paris: L'Harmattan, pp. 353–71.
des Forges, A. (2011) *Defeat Is the Only Bad News: Rwanda under Musinga, 1897–1931.* Madison: University of Wisconsin Press.
Diao, X., Shenggen, F., Kanyarukiga, S., and Bingxin, Y. (2010) *Agricultural Growth and Investment Opportunities for Poverty Reduction in Rwanda.* Washington, DC: IFPRI.
Dikötter, F. (2011) *Mao's Great Famine.* London: Bloomsbury.
Dillon, M. (2010) *China: A Modern History.* London: I. B. Taurus.
Dimmock, S. (2014) *The Origin of Capitalism in England 1400–1600.* Chicago: Haymarket Books.

Doner, R., Ritchie, B., and Slater, D. (2005) Systemic Vulnerability and the Origins of Developmental States: Northeast and Southeast Asia in Comparative Perspective. *International Organization* 59, 2.

Draper, N. (2010) *The Price of Emancipation. Slave Ownership and British Society at the End of Slavery.* Cambridge: Cambridge University Press.

Drescher, S. (1987) *Capitalism and Antislavery. British Mobilisation in Perspective.* Oxford: Oxford University Press.

Drescher, S. (2002) *The Mighty Experiment. Free Labour Versus Slavery in British Emancipation.* Oxford: Oxford University Press.

Dumenil, G. and Lévy, D. (2004) *Capital Resurgent: Roots of the Neoliberal Revolution.* Cambridge, MA: Harvard University Press.

Dunkerley, J. (2000) *Americana: The Americas in the World Around 1850.* London: Verso.

Eagleton, T. (2016) *Materialism.* New Haven: Yale University Press.

Edgerton, D. (2018) *The Rise and Fall of the British Nation.* London: Allen Lane.

Egan, T. (2006) *The Worst Hard Time.* New York: Mariner.

Eisenman, J. (2018) Commune Kabuki: Development and Productivity Growth under Maoist China's Rural Collectives. *Development and Change* 49, 6.

Ellis, F. (1982) Agricultural Price Policy in Tanzania. *World Development* 10(4), 263–83.

Ellis, F. (2000) *Rural Livelihoods and Diversity in Developing Countries.* Oxford: Oxford University Press.

Emmanuel, A. (1972) *Unequal Exchange: A Study of the Imperialism of Trade.* New York: Monthly Review Press.

Englander, D. (1998) *Poverty and Poor Law Reform in Nineteenth Century Britain, 1834–1914.* London: Longman.

Erikson, E. (2014) *Between Monopoly and Free Trade. The East India Company 1600–1757.* Princeton: Princeton University Press.

Escobar, A. (1995) *Encountering Development: The Making and Unmaking of the Third World.* Princeton: Princeton University Press.

Evans, E. (2001) *The Forging of the Modern State. Early Industrial Britain 1783–1870.* London: Longman.

Evans, E. (2011) *The Shaping of Modern Britain: Identity, Industry, and Empire 1780–1914.* London: Routledge.

Evans, P. (1995) *Embedded Autonomy: States and Industrial Transformation.* Princeton: Princeton University Press.

Evans, P., Rueschmeyer, D., and Skocpol, T. (1985) *Bringing the State Back in.* Cambridge: Cambridge University Press.

Evans, R. (2017) *The Pursuit of Power. Europe 1815–1914.* London: Penguin.

Ferguson, J. (1997) Anthropology and its Evil Twin: 'Development' in the Constitution of a Discipline. In: Cooper, F. and Packard, R. (eds) *International Development and the Social Sciences.* Berkeley: University of California Press.

Findlay, R. and O'Rourke, K. (2007) *Power and Plenty. Trade, War and the World Economy in the Second Millennium.* Princeton: Princeton University Press.

Fine, B. (2004) Economics and Ethics: Amartya Sen as Point of Departure. *New School Economic Review* 1(1), 151–62.

Fine, B. and Saad-Filho, A. (2004) *Marx's Capital.* London: Pluto Press.

Finkelstein, N. (1995) *Image and Reality of the Israel–Palestine Conflict.* London: Verso.

Flath, D. (2000) *The Japanese Economy.* Oxford: Oxford University Press.

Floud, R. (1994) Britain 1860–1914: A Survey. In: Floud, R. and McClockey, D. (eds) *The Economic History of Britain since 1700: Volume 2.* Cambridge: Cambridge University Press.

Foner, E. (1988) *Reconstruction. America's Unfinished Revolution 1863–1877.* New York: Harper.

Foner, E. (2012) *Give Me Liberty. An American History, Vol 2.* London: W. W Norton.

Foster, J. (1979) *Class Struggle and the Industrial Revolution.* London: Methuen.

Foster-Carter, A. (1978) The Modes of Production Controversy. *New Left Review* 107, 47–77.

Francks, P. (1979) The Development of New Techniques in Agriculture: The Case of the Mechanization of Irrigation in the Saga Plain Area of Japan. *World Development* 7, 4.

Francks, P. (1992) *Japanese Economic Development. Theory and Practice.* London: Routledge.

Francks, P. (1996) Mechanizing Small-Scale Rice Cultivation in an Industrializing Economy: The Development of the Power-Tiller in Prewar Japan. *World Development* 24, 4.

Francks, P. (2002) Rural Industry, Growth Linkages, and Economic Development in Nineteenth-Century Japan. *Journal of Asian Studies* 61, 1.

Francks, P., Boestel, J., and Kim, C. (1999) *Agriculture and Economic Development in East Asia.* London: Routledge.

Frank, A.-G. (1978) *Dependent Accumulation and Underdevelopment.* London: Macmillan.

Franklin, J. and Schweninger, L. (1999) *Runaway Slaves. Rebels on the Plantation.* Oxford: Oxford University Press.

Fransman, M. (1986) International Competitiveness, Technical Change and the State: The Machine Tool Industry in Taiwan and Japan. *World Development* 24, 12.

Fraser, D. (2009) *The Evolution of the British Welfare State.* Basingstoke: Macmillan.

Fraser, I. (2012) Distant Voices: Amartya Sen on Adam Smith's Impartial Spectator. *Culture and Dialogue* 2(2), 51–71.

Frazier, M. (2015) The Evolution of a Welfare State under China's State Capitalism. In: Naughton, B. and Tsai, K. (eds) *State Capitalism, Institutional Adaptation and the Chinese Miracle.* Cambridge: Cambridge University Press.

Frenkel, M., Shenhav, Y., and Herzog, H. (2000) The Ideological Wellspring of Zionist Capitalism: The Impact of Private Capital and Industry on the Shaping of the Dominant Zionist Ideology. In: Shafir, G. and Peled, Y. (eds) *The New Israel. Peacemaking and Liberalisation.* Boulder, CO: Westview Press.

Freund, B. (1985) The Modes of Production Debate in African Studies. *Canadian Journal of African Studies* 19(1), 23–9.

Friedman, D. (1988) *The Misunderstood Miracle. Industrial Development and Political Change in Japan.* Ithaca: Cornell University Press.

Friedman, E. (2014) Alienated Politics: Labour Insurgency and the Paternalistic State in China. *Development and Change* 45, 5.

Friedmann, H. (1987) International Regimes of Food and Agriculture since 1870. In: Shanin, T. (ed.) *Peasants and Peasant Societies.* Oxford: Basil Blackwell.

Fu, T. and Shei, S. (1999) Agriculture as the Foundation for Development: The Taiwanese Story. In: Thorbecke, E. and Wan, H. (eds) *Taiwan's Development Experience: Lessons on Roles of Government and Market.* New York: Springer.

Fukuda-Parr, S., Lawson-Remer, T., and Randolph, S. (2015a) Introduction. In: Fukudu-Parr, S., Lawson-Remer, T., and Randolph, S. (eds) *Fulfilling Social and Economic Rights.* Oxford: Oxford University Press, pp. 2–18.

Fukuda-Parr, S., Lawson-Remer, T., and Randolph, S. (2015b) Fulfilling Social and Economic Rights. In: Fukudu-Parr, S., Lawson-Remer, T., and Randolph, S. (eds) *Fulfilling Social and Economic Rights.* Oxford: Oxford University Press, pp. 101–27.

Gaido, D. (2000) A Materialist Analysis of Slavery and Sharecropping in the Southern United States. *Journal of Peasant Studies* 28, 1.

Gaido, D. (2002) The American Path of Bourgeois Development. *Journal of Peasant Studies* 29, 2.

Galtung, J. (1969) Violence, Peace, and Peace Research. *Journal of Peace Research* 6, 3.

Gao, B. (1997) *Economic Ideology and Japanese Industrial Policy. Developmentalism from 1931 to 1996*. Cambridge: Cambridge University Press.

Garon, S. and Mochizuki, M. (1993) Negotiating Social Contracts. In: Gordon A. (ed.) *Postwar Japan as History*. Berkeley: University of California Press.

Gelvin, J. (2007) *The Israel–Palestine Conflict. One Hundred Years of War*. Cambridge: Cambridge University Press.

Genovese, E. and Fox-Genovese, E. (1979) The Slave Economies in Political Perspective. *Journal of American History* 66, 1.

George, A. (2015) Explicating the Capability Approach through the Voices of the Poor: A Case Study of Waste-Picking Women in Kerala. *Journal of Human Development and Capabilities* 16(1), 33–46.

Geras, N. (1990) Seven Types of Obloquy. Travesties of Marxism. *Socialist Register* 26, 1–34.

Gilley, B. (2009) *The Right to Rule: How States Win and Lose Legitimacy*. New York: Columbia University Press.

Gold, T. (1986) *State and Society in the Taiwan Miracle*. New York: M. E. Sharpe.

Golooba-Mutebi, F. (2013) Political Economy of Agricultural Policy in Africa: Has CAADP Made a Difference? A Rwanda Case Study. *Future Agricultures Working Paper* No. 78. www.future-agricultures.org.

Goodman, D. (2014) *Class in Contemporary China*. Cambridge: Polity Press.

Goody, J. (2005) *Capitalism and Modernity. The Great Debate*. Cambridge: Polity Press.

Gordon, A. (2003) *A Modern History of Japan*. Oxford: Oxford University Press.

Gordon, D. (2016) *The Rise and Fall of American Growth*. Princeton: Princeton University Press.

Gough, I. and McGregor, A. (eds) (2007) *Wellbeing in Developing Countries*. Cambridge: Cambridge University Press.

Gray, H. (2018) *Turbulence and Order in Economic Development. Institutions and Economic Transformation in Tanzanian and Vietnam*. Oxford: Oxford University Press.

Griffin, E. (2010) *A Short History of the British Industrial Revolution*. London: Macmillan.

Griffin, E. (2013) *Liberty's Dawn. A People's History of the Industrial Revolution*. New Haven: Yale University Press.

Grinberg, L. (1991) *Split Corporatism in Israel*. New York: State University of New York Press.

Grinberg, L. (2014) *Mo(ve)ments of Resistance: Politics, Economy and Society in Israel/Palestine 1931–2013*. New York: Academic Studies Press.

Grinberg, L. and Shafir, G. (2000) Economic Liberalisation and the Breakup of Histadrut's Domain. In: Shafir, G. and Peled, Y. (eds) *The New Israel. Peacemaking and Liberalisation*. Boulder, CO: Westview Press.

Guess, R. (2001) *History and Illusion in Politics*. Cambridge: Cambridge University Press.

Guess, R. (2008) *Philosophy and Real Politics*. Princeton: Princeton University Press.

Hacker, J. and Pierson, P. (2002) Business Power and Social Policy: Employers and the Formation of the American Welfare State. *Politics & Society* 30, 2.

Haggard, S. and Pang, C. (2015) The Transition to Export-Led Growth in Taiwan. In: Abernach, J., Dollar, D., and Sokoloff, K. (eds) *The Role of the State in Taiwan's Development*. London: Routledge.

Hall, C. and Rose, S. (eds) (2006) *At Home with Empire. Metropolitan Culture and the Imperial World.* Cambridge: Cambridge University Press.

Harriss, J. (ed.) (1982) *Rural Development: Theories of Peasant Economy and Agrarian Change.* London: Hutchinson.

Harriss, J. (2002) *Depoliticizing Development: The World Bank and Social Capital.* London: Anthem Press.

Harriss-White, B. (2005) Poverty and Capitalism. *QEH Working Paper Series* QEHWPS134.

Harvey, D. (2009) The 'New' Imperialism: Accumulation by Dispossession. *Socialist Register* 40.

Harvey, D. (2010) *A Companion to Marx's Capital.* London: Verso.

Harvie, C. (1988) Revolution and the Rule of Law (1789–1851). In: Morgan, P. (ed.) *The Eighteenth Century and the Age of Industry.* Oxford: Oxford University Press.

Hatzfeld, J. (2006) *Machete Season: The Killers in Rwanda Speak.* London: Picador.

Havnevik, K. (1993) Tanzania: The Limits of Development from Above. Uppsala: Scandinavian Institute for African Studies.

Healey, J. (2014) *The First Century of Welfare. Poverty and Poor Relief in Lancashire.* Woodbridge: Boydell Press.

Heilmann, S, (2008) Policy Experimentation in China's Economic Rise. *Studies in Comparative International Development* 43, 1.

Hein, L. (1993) Growth Versus Success: Japan's Economic Policy in Historical Perspective. In: Gordon A. (ed.) *Postwar Japan as History.* Berkeley: University of California Press.

Hein, L. and Selden, M. (eds) (2000) *Censoring History. Citizenship and Memory in Japan, Germany, and the United States.* London: M. E. Sharpe.

Hever, S. (2010) *The Political Economy of Israel's Occupation.* London: Pluto Press.

Hewitt, V. and Duffield, M. (eds) (2013) *Empire, Development and Colonialism: The Past in the Present.* London: James Currey.

Heyer, J., Roberts, P., and Williams, G. (eds) (1981) *Rural Development in Tropical Africa.* London: Macmillan.

Hickel, J. (2017) *The Divide. A Brief Guide to Global Inequality and its Solutions.* London: William Heinemann.

Hilton, B. (2006) *A Mad, Bad, and Dangerous People? England 1783–1846.* Oxford: Oxford University Press.

Himmelfarb, G. (1991) *Poverty and Compassion. The Moral Imagination of the Late Victorians.* New York: Vintage Books.

Hirschman, A. O. (2002) *Development Projects Observed.* Washington, DC: Brookings Institution Press.

Hobbes, T. (1996) *Leviathan.* Cambridge: Cambridge University Press.

Hobsbawm, E. (1999) *Industry and Empire.* London: Penguin Books.

Hobsbawm, E. and Ranger, T. (eds) (1982) *The Invention of Tradition.* London: Canto.

Hodgson, G. (2004) Some Claims Made for Critical Realism in Economics: Two Case Studies. *Journal of Economic Methodology* 11(1), 53–73.

Hopgood, S. (2013) *The Endtimes of Human Rights.* Ithaca: Cornell University Press.

Hoppit, J. (2017) *Britain's Political Economies. Parliament and Economic Life 1660–1800.* Cambridge: Cambridge University Press.

Howe, A. (2002) Restoring Free Trade: The British Experience, 1776–1873. In: Winch, D. and O'Brien, P. (eds) *The Political Economy of the British Historical Experience, 1688–1914.* Oxford: Oxford University Press.

Hsu, C. (2000) *The Rise of Modern China.* Oxford: Oxford University Press.

Hsueh, R. (2011) *China's Regulatory State. A New Strategy for Globalisation.* Ithaca: Cornell University Press.

Huang, J., Otsuka, K., and Rozelle, S. (2018) Agriculture in China's Development: Past Disappointments, Recent Successes, and Future Challenges. In: Brandt, L. and Rawski, T. (eds) *China's Great Economic Transformation.* Cambridge: Cambridge University Press.

Hui, W. (2016) *China's Twentieth Century.* London: Verso.

Hung, H.-f. (2008) Rise of China and the Global Overaccumulation Crisis. *Review of International Political Economy* 15, 2.

Hunt, E. and Lautzenheiser, M. (2011) *History of Economic Thought.* A Critical Perspective. New York: E. M. Sharpe.

Hyden, G. (1980) *Beyond* Ujamaa *in Tanzania: Underdevelopment and an Uncaptured Peasantry.* London: Heinemann.

Ingelaere, B. (2014) What's on a Peasant's Mind? Experiencing RPF State Reach and Overreach in Post-Genocide Rwanda (2000–10). *Journal of Eastern African Studies* 8, 2.

Inikori, J. (2002) *Africans and the Industrial Revolution in England.* Cambridge: Cambridge University Press.

International Fund for Agricultural Development (IFAD) (2013) *Climate Resilient Post-Harvest and Agribusiness Support Project (PASP) Including Blended Adaptation for Smallholder Agriculture Programme Grant.* Project No. 1497. East and Southern Africa Division Programme Management Department. Rome: IFAD.

Jefremovas, V. (2002) *Brickyards to Graveyards. From Production to Genocide in Rwanda.* New York: SUNY Press.

Jennings, M. (2002) 'Almost an Oxfam in itself': Oxfam, *Ujamaa* and Development in Tanzania. *African Affairs* 101(405), 509–31.

Jessop, B. (2002) Capitalism, the Regulation Approach, and Critical Realism. In: Brown, A., Fleetwood, S., and Roberts, J. (eds) *Critical Realism and Marxism.* London: Routledge, pp. 88–116.

Johnson, C. (1982) *MITI and the Japanese Miracle. The Growth of Industrial Policy 1925–1975.* Stanford: Stanford University Press.

Johnson, C. (1995) *Japan: Who Governs? The Rise of the Developmental State.* London: W. W. Norton.

Joseph, J. (2002) Five Ways in which Critical Realism Can Help Marxism. In: Brown, A., Fleetwood, S., and Roberts, J. (eds) *Critical Realism and Marxism.* London: Routledge, pp. 23–43.

Joseph, J. (2012) *The Social in the Global.* Cambridge: Cambridge University Press.

Josephson, M. (1962) *The Robber Barons: The Great American Capitalists, 1861–1901.* New York: Harcourt Brace Press.

Kadri, A. and Macmillen, M. (1998) The Political Economy of Israel's Demand for Palestinian Labour. *Third World Quarterly* 19, 2.

Kang, D. (2010) *China Rising. Peace, Power, and Order in East Asia.* New York: Columbia University Press.

Kant, I. (2017) *The Metaphysics of Morals.* Cambridge: Cambridge University Press.

Kaplan, A. (2018) *Our American Israel. The Story of an Entangled Alliance.* Cambridge, MA: Harvard University Press.

Kaplinsky, R. (2005) *Globalization, Poverty and Inequality.* Cambridge: Cambridge University Press.

Kay, G. (1975) *Underdeveloped and Development. A Marxist Analysis.* London: Macmillan.

Keay, J. (2008) *China. A History.* London: Harper Press.

Kellman, M. and Landau, D. (1984) The Nature of Japan's Comparative Advantage. *World Development* 12, 4.

Kennedy, D. (1999) *The American People in the Great Depression: Freedom from Fear.* Oxford: Oxford University Press.

Khenin, D. (2000) From *Eretz Israel* to *Yisrael Hashnia*: The Social Discourse and Social Policy of Mapai in the 1950s. In: Shafir, G. and Peled, Y. (eds) *The New Israel. Peacemaking and Liberalisation.* Boulder, CO: Westview Press.

Kipnis, B. and Noam, T. (1998) Restructuring of a Metropolitan Suburban Industrial Park: Case Study in Metropolitan Tel Aviv, Israel. *Geografiska Annaler* 80, B.

Kislef, Y. and Hoffman, M. (1978) Research and Productivity in Wheat in Israel. *Journal of Development Studies* 14, 2.

Kitching, G. (2001) *Seeking Social Justice through Globalization.* Philadelphia: University of Pennsylvania Press.

Kleiman, E. (1967) The Place of Manufacturing in the Growth of the Israeli Economy. *Journal of Development Studies* 3, 3.

Kohli, A. (2004) *State-Directed Development. Political Power and Industrialisation in the Global Periphery.* Cambridge: Cambridge University Press.

Kroeber, A. (2016) *China's Economy. What Everyone Needs to Know.* Oxford: Oxford University Press.

Kukathas, C. (2018) Justicitis. In: Knoll, M., Snyder, S., and Şimsek, N. (eds) *New Perspectives on Distributive Justice: Deep Disagreements, Pluralism, and the Problem of Consensus.* Berlin: De Gruyter.

Kuo, S. (1999) Government Policy in the Taiwanese Development Process: The Past 50 Years. In: Thorbecke, E. and Wan, H. (eds) *Taiwan's Development Experience: Lessons on Roles of Government and Market.* New York: Springer.

Kuo, T.-C. and Myers, R. (2012) *Taiwan's Economic Transformation. Leadership, Property Rights, and Institutional Change 1949–1965.* London: Routledge.

Kydd, J., Dorward, A., Morrison, J., and Cadisch, G. (2004) Agricultural Development and Pro-Poor Economic Growth in Sub-Saharan Africa. *Potential and Policy Oxford Development Studies* 32(1).

Laderchi, C. (2008) Do Concepts Matter? An Empirical Investigation of the Differences between a Capability and a Monetary Assessment of Poverty. In: Comim, F., Qizilbash, M., and Alkire, S. (eds) *The Capability Approach. Concepts, Measures and Applications.* Cambridge: Cambridge University Press, pp. 203–41.

Lardy, N. (1983) *Agriculture in China's Modern Economic Development.* Cambridge: Cambridge University Press.

Lefebvre, H. (1984) *The Production of Space.* Oxford: Blackwell.

Leftwich, A. (2000) *States of Development: On the Primacy of Politics in Development.* Cambridge: Polity Press.

Levi-Faur, D. (1998) The Developmental State: Israel, South Korea, and Taiwan Compared. *Studies in Comparative International Development* 33(1).

Levine, B., Brier, S., Brundage, D., et al. (1989) *Who Built America? Working People and the Nation's Economy, Politics, Culture, and Society, Volume 1.* New York: Pantheon Books.

Lin, C.-y. (1973) *Industrialisation in Taiwan, 1946–74. Trade and Import Substitution Policies for Developing Countries.* New York: Praeger.

Lin, J. (2012) *The Quest for Prosperity.* Princeton: Princeton University Press.

Lindert, P. and Williamson, J. (2016) *Unequal Gains. American Growth and Inequality since 1700.* Princeton: Princeton University Press.

Linebaugh, P. (2003) *The London Hanged.* London: Verso.

Lofchie, M. (2014) *The Political Economy of Tanzania: Decline and Recovery.* Philadelphia: University of Pennsylvania Press.

Longman, T. (2011) Limitations to Political Reform. The Undemocratic Nature of Transition in Rwanda. In: Straus, S. and Waldorf, L. (eds) *Remaking Rwanda. State Building and Human Rights after Mass Violence.* Madison: University of Wisconsin Press.

Lovell, J. (2011) *The Opium War.* London: Picador.

Lovell, J. (2019) *Maoism. A Global History.* London: Bodley Head.

Maçaes, B. (2018) *Belt and Road. A Chinese World Order.* London: Hurst and Company.

Magee, G. (2004) Manufacturing and Technological Change. In: Floud, R. and Johnson, P. (eds) *The Cambridge Economic History of Modern Britain, Vol 2.* Cambridge: Cambridge University Press.

Maman, D. and Rosenhek, Z. (2012) The Institutional Dynamics of a Developmental State: Change and Continuity in State–Economy Relations in Israel. *Studies in Comparative International Development* 47, 4.

Mamdani, M. (1996) *Citizen and Subject: Contemporary Africa and the Legacy of Late Colonialism.* Princeton: Princeton University Press.

Marijnen, E. and van der Lijn, J. (2012) Rwanda 2025: Scenarios for the Future Political Stability of Rwanda. In: Campioni, M. and Noack, P. (eds) *Rwanda Fast Forward. Social, Economic, Military and Reconciliation Prospects.* Basingstoke: Macmillan.

Marley, B. (2016) The Coal Crisis in Appalachia: Agrarian Transformation, Commodity Frontiers and the Geographies of Capital. *Journal of Agrarian Change* 16(2).

Marshall, P. J. (2001) The British in Asia: Trade to Domination, 1700–1765. In: Marshall, P. J. (ed.) *The Oxford History of the British Empire. The Eighteenth Century.* Oxford: Oxford University Press.

Marx, K. (1964) *Pre-Capitalist Economic Formations.* London: Lawrence and Wishart.

Marx, K. (1973) *Grundrisse [Outlines of the Critique of Political Economy].* London: Penguin.

Marx, K. (1987) *A Contribution to the Critique of Political Economy.* London: Lawrence and Wishart.

Marx, K. (1992) *Capital III.* London: Penguin.

Marx, K. (1995) *Capital I. A New Abridgement.* Oxford: Oxford University Press.

Marysse, S., Ansoms, A., and Cassimon, D. (2007) The Aid Darlings and Orphans of the Great Lakes Region in Africa. *European Journal of Development Research* 19(3).

Mathias, P. (1969) *The First Industrial Nation. An Economic History of Britain 1700–1914.* London: Methuen.

McLennan, G. (1981) *Marxism and the Methodologies of History.* London: Verso.

McMichael, P. (2013) *Food Regimes and Agrarian Questions.* Halifax: Fernwood Publishing.

McMillan, M. and Rodrik, D. (2011) Globalization, Structural Change and Productivity Growth. *NBER Working Paper* No. 17143.

McPherson, C. B. (2010) *The Political Theory of Possessive Individualism: Hobbes to Locke.* Oxford: Oxford University Press.

McPherson, J. (1988) *Battle Cry of Freedom. The Civil War Era.* Oxford: Oxford University Press.

Meaney, C. (2015) State Policy and the Development of Taiwan's Semiconductor Industry. In: Abernach, J., Dollar, D., and Sokoloff, K. (eds) *The Role of the State in Taiwan's Development.* London: Routledge.

Meiksins-Wood, E. (1981) The Separation of the Economic and the Political in Capitalism. *New Left Review* Series I, 127.

Meiksins-Wood, E. (2016) *Democracy Against Capitalism: Renewing Historical Materialism*. Cambridge: Cambridge University Press.
Meillasoux, C. (1981) *Maidens, Meal and Money: Capitalism and the Domestic Community*. Cambridge: Cambridge University Press.
Merritt, K. (2017) *Masterless Men: Poor Whites and Slavery in the Antebellum South*. Cambridge: Cambridge University Press.
Milanovic, B. (2005) *Worlds Apart. Measuring International and Global Inequality*. Princeton: Princeton University Press.
Mills, C. (1997) *The Racial Contract*. Ithaca: Cornell University Press.
Milly, D. (1999) *Poverty Equality and Growth. The Politics of Economic Needs in Postwar Japan*. Cambridge, MA: Harvard University Press.
Milonakis, D. and Fine, B. (2009) *From Political Economy to Economics. Method, the Social, and the Historical in the Evolution of Economic Theory*. Abingdon: Routledge.
Mintz, A. (1983) The Military–Industrial Complex: The Israeli Case. *Journal of Strategic Studies* 6, 3.
Mitchell, W. F., Wray, L. R., and Watts, M. (2016) *Modern Monetary Theory and Practice*. CreateSpace.
Mokyr, J. (2011) *The Enlightened Economy: Britain and the Industrial Revolution, 1700–1850*. London: Penguin.
Mooers, C. (1991) *The Making of Bourgeois Europe*. London: Verso.
Morgan, C. (2001) *Women Workers and Gender Identities, 1835–1913*. London: Routledge.
Morgan, K. (2000) *Slavery, Atlantic Trade and the British Economy 1660–1800*. Cambridge: Cambridge University Press.
Morgan, K. (2002) Mercantilism and the British Empire, 1688–1815. In: Winch, D. and O'Brien, P. (eds) *The Political Economy of the British Historical Experience, 1688–1914*. Oxford: Oxford University Press.
Morris-Suzuki, T. (1994) *The Technological Transformation of Japan. From the Seventeenth to the Twenty-First Century*. Cambridge: Cambridge University Press.
Moseley, W, Schnurr, M., and Bezner Kerr, R. (2015) Interrogating the Technocratic (Neoliberal) Agenda for Agricultural Development and Hunger Alleviation in Africa. *African Geographical Review* 34(1), 4.
Mosk, C. (2008) *Japanese Economic Development. Markets, Norms, Structures*. London: Routledge.
Mosse, D. (2005) *Cultivating Development*. London: Pluto Press.
Mouffe, C. (2005) *The Return of the Political*. London: Verso.
Moyn, S. (2010) *The Last Utopia. Human Rights in History*. Cambridge, MA: Harvard University Press.
Murekezi, A., Songqing J., and Loveridge, S. (2012) Do Organizational Forms of the Coffee Supply Chain Matter in Poverty Reduction? *Development in Practice* 22(7).
Murtazashvili, I. (2013) *The Political Economy of the American Frontier*. Cambridge: Cambridge University Press.
Myers, R. and Ching, A. (1964) Agricultural Development in Taiwan under Japanese Colonial Rule. *Journal of Asian Studies* 23(4).
Naughton, B. (1995) *Growing out of the Plan. Chinese Economic Reform, 1978–1993*. Cambridge: Cambridge University Press.
Naughton, B. (2007) *The Chinese Economy. Transitions and Growth*. London: The MIT Press.
Naughton, B. (2008) A Political Economy of China's Economic Transition. In: Brandt, L. and Rawski, T. (eds) *China's Great Economic Transformation*. Cambridge: Cambridge University Press.

Naughton, B. (2015) The Transformation of the State Sector: SASAC, the Market Economy, and the New National Champions. In: Naughton, B. and Tsai, K. (eds) *State Capitalism, Institutional Adaptation and the Chinese Miracle*. Cambridge: Cambridge University Press.

Nayar, D. (2013) *Catch Up. Developing Countries in the World Economy*. Oxford: Oxford University Press.

Neeson, J. (1993) *Commoners: Common Right, Enclosure, and Social Change in England, 1700–1820*. Cambridge: Cambridge University Press.

Newbury, C. (1988) *The Cohesion of Oppression: Clientship and Ethnicity in Rwanda 1860–1960*. New York: Columbia University Press.

Newbury, D. (2005) Returning Refugees: Four Historical Patterns of 'Coming Home' to Rwanda. *Comparative Studies of Society and History* 47(2).

Newbury, D. and Newbury, C. (2000) Bringing the Peasants Back in: Agrarian Themes in the Construction and Corrosion of Statist Historiography in Rwanda. *American Historical Review* 105(3).

Nitzan, J. and Bichler, S. (2002) *The Global Political Economy of Israel*. London: Pluto Press.

North, D. (1966) *The Economic Growth of the United States 1790–1860*. New York: W. W. Norton.

North, D. C., Wallis, J. J., and Weingast, B. R. (eds) (2013) *In the Shadow of Violence. Politics, Economics, and the Problems of Development*. Cambridge: Cambridge University Press.

Nussbaum, M. (2011) *Creating Capabilities: The Human Development Approach*. Cambridge, MA: Harvard University Press.

Nussbaum, M. (2015) Philosophy and Economics in the Capabilities Approach: An Essential Dialogue. *Journal of Human Development and Capabilities*, 16(1), 1–14.

Nussbaum, M. (2016) Introduction: Aspiration and the Capabilities List. *Journal of Human Development and Capabilities* 17(3), 301–8.

O'Brien, P. (1993a) Modern Conceptions of the Industrial Revolution. In: O'Brien, P. and Quinault, R. (eds) *The Industrial Revolution and British Society*. Cambridge: Cambridge University Press.

O'Brien, P. (1993b) Political Preconditions for the Industrial Revolution. In: O'Brien, P. and Quinault, R. (eds) *The Industrial Revolution and British Society*. Cambridge: Cambridge University Press.

O'Brien, P. (2001) Inseparable Connections; Trade, Economy, Fiscal State, and the Expansion of Empire 1688–1815. In: Marshall, P. J. (ed.) *The Oxford History of the British Empire. The Eighteenth Century*. Oxford: Oxford University Press.

Ohkawa, K. and Rosovsky, H. (1998) Postwar Japanese Growth in Historical Perspective: A Second Look. In: Smitka, M. (ed.) *Japanese Prewar Growth. Lessons for Development Theory?* New York: Garland Publishing.

O'Mahoney, J. (2014) Critical Realism as an Empirical Project. In: Edwards, P., O'Mahoney, J., and Vincent, S. (eds) *Studying Organisations Using Critical Realism*. Oxford: Oxford University Press, pp. 1–21.

O'Riain, S. (2006) Dominance and Change in the Global Computer Industry: Military, Bureaucratic, and Network State Developmentalisms. *Studies in Comparative International Development* 41(1).

Palan, R. and Abbott, J. (1999) *State Strategies in the Global Political Economy*. London: Bloomsbury.

Parisot, J. (2019) *How America Became Capitalist*. London: Verso.

Parker, M. (2012) *The Sugar Barons. Family, Corruption, Empire, and War*. London: Windmill.

Pearson, M. (2015) State-Owned Business and Party-State Regulation in China's Modern Political Economy. In: Naughton, B. and Tsai, K. (eds) *State Capitalism, Institutional Adaptation and the Chinese Miracle*. Cambridge: Cambridge University Press.
Peet, R. (2003) *Unholy Trinity: The IMF, World Bank and the WTO*. London: Zed Books.
Peet, R. and Watts, M. (1996) *Liberation Ecologies: Environment, Development and Social Movements*. New York: Routledge.
Pei, M. (2016) *China's Crony Capitalism*. Cambridge, MA: Harvard University Press.
Penn, T. (2012) *Winter King: The Dawn of Tudor England*. London: Penguin.
Phillips, A. (2015) *The Politics of the Human*. Cambridge: Cambridge University Press.
Plessner, Y. (1994) *The Political Economy of Israel. From Ideology to Stagnation*. New York: State University of New York Press.
Polanyi, K. (2001) *The Great Transformation*. Boston: Beacon Press.
Pomeranz, K. (2000) *The Great Divergence. China, Europe and the Making of the Modern World Economy*. Princeton: Princeton University Press.
Porpora, D. (1998) Four Concepts of Social Structure. In: Archer, M., Bhaskar, R., Collier, A., Lawson, T., and Norrie, A. (eds) *Critical Realism*. London: Routledge, pp. 339–56.
Post, C. (2003) Plantation Slavery and Economic Development in the Antebellum Southern United States. *Journal of Agrarian Change* 3(3).
Post, C. (2012) *The American Road to Capitalism. Studies in Class Structure, Economic Development and Political Conflict 1620–1877*. Chicago: Haymarket Books.
Pritchard, M. (2013) Land, Power and Peace: Tenure Formalization, Agricultural Reform, and Livelihood Insecurity in Rural Rwanda. *Land Use Policy* 30(1).
Prunier, G. (1998) *The Rwanda Crisis: History of a Genocide*. London: Hurst.
Purdekova, A. (2011) 'Even if I Am not here, there Are so many Eyes': Surveillance and State Reach in Rwanda. *Journal of Modern African Studies* 49(3).
Purdekova, A. (2012) Civic Education and Social Transformation in Post-Genocide Rwanda: Forging the Perfect Development Subjects. In: Campioni, M. and Noack, P. (eds) *Rwanda Fast Forward: Social, Economic, Military and Reconciliation Prospects*. London: Palgrave Macmillan.
Rahnema, M. and Bawtree, V. (eds) (1997) *The Post-Development Reader*. London: Zed Press.
Ravallion, M. (2016) *The Economics of Poverty: History, Measurement, and Policy*. Oxford: Oxford University Press.
Ravallion, M. and Chen, S. (2007) China's (Uneven) Progress against Poverty. *Journal of Development Economics* 82(1).
Rawls, J. (1971) *A Theory of Justice*. Cambridge, MA: Harvard University Press.
Rawls, J. (1999) *The Law of Peoples*. Cambridge, MA: Harvard University Press.
Rawski, T. (1979) *Economic Growth and Employment in China*. Oxford: Oxford University Press.
Reddy, S. (2012) Economics and Human Rights: A Non-Conversation. In: Elson, D., Fukuda-Parr, S., and Vizard, P. (eds) *Human Rights and the Capabilities Approach. An Interdisciplinary Dialogue*. London: Routledge, pp. 63–73.
Reinert, E. (2007) *How Rich Countries Got Rich and Why Poor Countries Stay Poor*. London: Constable.
Reynolds, D. (2010) *America. Empire of Liberty*. London: Penguin.
Richardson, D. (2000) The British Empire and the Atlantic Slave Trade. In: Marshall, P. J. (ed.) *The Oxford History of the British Empire. The Eighteenth Century*. Oxford: Oxford University Press.

Rithmire, M. (2015) *Land Bargains and Chinese Capitalism. The Politics of Property Rights under Reform*. Cambridge: Cambridge university Press.

Rivlin, P. (1992) *The Israeli Economy*. Bolder, CO: Westview Press.

Rivlin, P. (2011) *The Israeli Economy from the Foundation of the State through the Twenty-First Century*. Cambridge: Cambridge University Press.

Robeyns, I. (2005) The Capability Approach: A Theoretical Survey. *Journal of Human Development* 6(1), 93–117.

Robeyns, I. (2016) Capabilitarianism. *Journal of Human Development and Capabilities* 17(3), 397–414.

Robins, N. (2012) *The Corporation that Changed the World: How the East India Company Shaped the Modern Multinational*. London: Pluto Press.

Rodrik, D. (ed.) (2003) *In Search of Prosperity. Analytical Narratives on Economic Growth*. Princeton: Princeton University Press.

Rodrik, D. (2007) *One Economics, Many Recipes: Globalization, Institutions, and Economic Growth*. Princeton: Princeton University Press.

Rodrik, D. (2011) *The Globalisation Paradox. Why Global Markets, States, and Democracy Can't Coexist*. Oxford: Oxford University Press.

Rodrik, D. (2015) *Economics Rules. Why Economic Works, When it Fails, and How to Tell the Difference*. Oxford: Oxford University Press.

Rorty, R. (1989) *Contingency, Irony and Solidarity*. Cambridge: Cambridge University Press.

Rosenfeld, H. (1978) The Class Situation of the Arab National Minority in Israel. Comparative Studies in Society and History 20(3).

Rosenhek, Z. (2003) The Political Dynamics of a Segmented Labour Market: Palestinian Citizens, Palestinians from the Occupied Territories and Migrant Workers in Israel. *Acta* Sociologica 46(3).

Rosenzweig, R., Lichtenstein, N., Brown, J., and Jaffee, D. (2008) *Who Built America? Working People and the Nation's History, Volume 2*. New York: St Martin's.

Rostow, W. (1971) *The Stages of Economic Growth*. Cambridge: Cambridge University Press.

Royle, E. (2012) *Modern Britain. A Social History 1750–2011*. London: Bloomsbury.

Rubenstein, M. (1994) The Taiwan Miracle. In: Rubenstein, M. (ed.) *The Other Taiwan 1945 to the Present*. London: Routledge.

Rubenstein, M. (2007) Taiwan's Socio-Economic Modernisation 1971–1996. In: Rubenstein, M. (ed.) *Taiwan: A New History*. London: Routledge.

Rueschmeyer, D., Stephens, E., and Stephens, J. (1992) *Capitalist Development and Democracy*. Cambridge: Polity Press.

Rwiyereka, A. (2014) Using Rwandan Traditions to Strengthen Programme and Policy Implementation. *Development in Practice* 24, 1.

Sachs, J. (2005) *The End of Poverty. How we Can Make it Happen in our Lifetime*. London: Penguin.

Sassen, S. (2014) *Expulsions: Brutality and Complexity in the Global Economy*. Cambridge, MA: Harvard University Press.

Satia, P. (2018) *Empire of Guns. The Violent Making of the Industrial Revolution*. London: Penguin.

Sayer, A. (2000) *Realism and Social Science*. London: Sage.

Schatzberg, M. (2001) *Political Legitimacy in Middle Africa*. Bloomington: Indiana University Press.

Schneider, L. (2014) *Government of Development. Peasants and Politicians in Tanzania.* Bloomington: Indiana University Press.

Scott, J. (2000) *England's Troubles. Seventeenth-Century English Political Instability in European Context.* Cambridge: Cambridge University Press.

Scott, J. C. (1977) *The Moral Economy of the Peasant: Rebellion and Subsistence in Southeast Asia.* New Haven: Yale University Press.

Scott, J. C. (1999) *Seeing Like a State. How Certain Schemes to Improve the Human Condition Have Failed.* New Haven: Yale University Press.

Sen, A. (1981) *Poverty and Famines. An Essay on Entitlement and Deprivation.* Oxford: Oxford University Press.

Sen, A. (1997) Development Thinking at the Beginning of the 21st Century. DEDPS, 2. London: Suntory and Toyota International Centres for Economics and Related Disciplines, London School of Economics and Political Science.

Sen, A. (1999) *Development as Freedom.* Oxford: Oxford University Press.

Sen, A. (2009) *The Idea of Justice.* London: Penguin.

Shafir, G. and Peled, Y. (2000) The Socioeconomic Liberalisation of Israel. In: Shafir, G. and Peled, Y. (eds) *The New Israel. Peacemaking and Liberalisation.* Boulder, CO: Westview Press.

Shalev, M. (2000) Liberalisation and the Transformation of the Political Economy. In: Shafir, G. and Peled, Y. (eds) *The New Israel. Peacemaking and Liberalisation.* Boulder, CO: Westview Press.

Shilliam, R. (2018) *Race and the Undeserving Poor.* London: Agenda Publishing.

Shivji, I. G. (1986) *The State and the Working People in Tanzania.* Dakar: Codesria.

Shklar, J. (1989) The Liberalism of Fear. In: Rosenblum, N. (ed.) *Liberalism and the Moral Life.* Cambridge, MA: Harvard University Press.

Skocpol, T. (1995) *Protecting Soldiers and Mothers: Political Origins of Social Policy in the United States.* Cambridge, MA: Harvard University Press.

Slack, P. (2015) *The Invention of Improvement.* Oxford: Oxford University Press.

Sleat, M. (2013) *Liberal Realism. A Realist Theory of Liberal Politics.* Manchester: Manchester University Press.

Smith, J. (2016) *Imperialism in the Twenty-First Century.* New York: Monthly Review Press.

Smith, S. D. (2006) *Slavery, Family, and Gentry Capitalism in the British Atlantic.* Cambridge: Cambridge University Press.

Smith, T. (1959) *The Agrarian Origins of Modern Japan.* New York: Atheneum Press.

Smith, T. (1965) *Political Change and Industrial Development in Japan: Government Enterprise 1868–1880.* Stanford: Stanford University Press.

Smitka, M. (ed.) (1988) *Japanese Prewar Growth. Lessons for Development Theory?* New York: Garland Publishing.

Specht, J. (2019) *Red Meat Republic. A Hoof-to-Table History of how Beef Changed America.* Princeton: Princeton University Press.

Stedman Jones, G. (1971) *Outcast London. A Study in the Relationship between Classes in Victorian Society.* Oxford: Oxford University Press.

Stedman Jones, G. (2004) *An End to Poverty? A Historical Debate.* Exmouth: Profile Books.

Steinmo, S. (2010) *The Evolution of Modern States. Sweden, Japan, and the United States.* Cambridge: Cambridge University Press.

Stevenson, J. (1993) Social Aspects of the Industrial Revolution. In: O'Brien, P. and Quinault, R. (eds) *The Industrial Revolution and British Society.* Cambridge: Cambridge University Press.

Storey, A. (1999) Economics and Ethnic Conflict: Structural Adjustment in Rwanda. *Development Policy Review* 17(1).

Storey, A. (2001) Structural Adjustment, State Power and Genocide: The World Bank and Rwanda. *Review of African Political Economy* 28(89).

Sumner, A. (2014) Global Poverty and the New Bottom Billion: What if Three-quarters of the World's Poor Live in Middle-Income Countries? *IDS Working Paper* 349.

Sumner, A. (2015) Global Poverty and the New Bottom Billion Revisited: Exploring the Paradox that most of the World's Extreme Poor no Longer Live in the World's Poorest Countries. *IDS Working Paper* 14 May.

Sumner, A. (2016) *Global Poverty. Deprivation, Distribution, and Development since the Cold War*. Oxford: Oxford University Press.

Svejnar, J. (2018) China in Light of the Performance of the Transition Economies. In: Brandt, L. and Rawski, T. (eds) *China's Great Economic Transformation*. Cambridge: Cambridge University Press.

Teschke, B. (2009) *The Myth of 1648: Class, Geopolitics, and the Making of Modern International Relations*. London: Verso.

Therborn, G. (2001) Into the Twenty-First Century. *New Left Review* Series 2, 10.

Thirlwall, A. P. (2002) *The Nature of Economic Growth. An Alternative Framework for Understanding the Performance of Nations*. Cheltenham: Edward Elgar Publishing.

Thompson, E. P. (1980) *The Making of the English Working Class*. London: Penguin.

Thorbecke, E. and Wan, H. (1999) The Lessons from Taiwan: Relevance, Limitations and Transferability. In: Thorbecke, E. and Wan, H. (eds) *Taiwan's Development Experience: Lessons on Roles of Government and Market*. New York: Springer.

Todaro, M. and Smith, S. (2015) *Economic Development*. London: Pearson.

Tombs, R. (2015) *The English and their History*. London: Penguin.

Totman, C. (2005) *A History of Japan*. London: Blackwell.

Trafzer, C. and Hyer, J. (1999) *Exterminate them: Written Accounts of the Murder, Rape, and Enslavement of Native Americans during the California Goldrush*. East Lansing: Michigan State University Press.

Trattner, W. (1989) *From Poor Law to Welfare State. A History of Social Welfare in the United States*. New York: Free Press.

Trentmann, F. (2008) *Free Trade Nation. Commerce, Consumption, and Civil Society in Modern Britain*. Oxford: Oxford University Press.

Tribe, M., Nixson, F., and Sumner, A. (2010) *Economics and Development Studies*. London: Routledge.

Tsai, K. and Naughton, B. (2015) State Capitalism and the Chinese Miracle. In: Naughton, B. and Tsai, K. (eds) *State Capitalism, Institutional Adaptation and the Chinese Miracle*. Cambridge: Cambridge University Press.

Turner, M. (2004) Agriculture 1860–1914. In: Floud, R. and Johnson, P. (eds) *The Cambridge Economic History of Modern Britain, Vol 2*. Cambridge: Cambridge University Press.

UNDP (2008) *Rwanda: Assessment of Development Results*. www.oecd.org/countries/rwanda/41105593.pdf. New York: UNDP.

Uvin, P. (2001) Difficult Choices in the New Post-Conflict Agenda: The International Community in Rwanda after the Genocide. *Third World Quarterly* 22(2).

Uvin, P. (2004) *Human Rights and Development*. Bloomfield, CT: Kumarian Press.

Uyan-Semerci, P. (2007) A Relational Account of Nussbaum's List of Capabilities. *Journal of Human Development* 8(2), 203–21.

Van der Pijl, K. (1998) *Transnational Classes and International Relations.* London: Routledge.
van Hoyweghen, S. (1999) The Urgency of Land and Agrarian Reform in Rwanda. *African Affairs* 98(392).
Verhofstadt, E. and Maertens, M. (2013) Cooperative Membership and Agricultural Performance: Evidence from Rwanda. *Bioeconomics Working Paper Series Working Paper* 2013/6.
Vernon, J. (2007) *Hunger. A Modern History.* Cambridge, MA: Harvard University Press.
Verwimp, P. (2013) *Peasants in Power. The Political Economy of Development and Genocide in Rwanda.* Dordrecht: Springer.
Vestal, J. (1993) *Planning for Change. Industrial Policy and Japanese Economic Development 1945–1990.* Oxford: Clarendon Press.
Vinck, P. (2006) *Rwanda: Comprehensive Food Security and Vulnerability Analysis (CFSVA).* Kigali: World Food Programme.
Vogel, J. (2006) The Tragedy of History. *New Left Review* I(220), 36–61.
von Tunzelmann, G. N. (1994) Technological and Organisational Change in Industry during the Early Industrial Revolution. In: O'Brien, P. and Quinault, R. (eds) *The Industrial Revolution in British Society.* Cambridge: Cambridge University Press.
Wade, R. (1990) *Governing the Market. Economic Theory and the Role of Government in East Asian Industrialisation.* Princeton: Princeton University Press.
Waldron, J. (1999) *Law and Disagreement.* Oxford: Oxford University Press.
Waldron, J. (2009) Judges as Moral Reasoners. *International Journal of Constitutional Law* 7(1), 2–24.
Walter, C. and Howie, F. (2012) *Red Capitalism. The Fragile Financial Foundation of China's Extraordinary Rise.* Singapore: John Wiley and Sons.
Walton, G. and Rockoff, H. (2014) *History of the American Economy.* London: Cengage Learning.
Wang, X., Yamauchi, F., Otsuka, K., and Huang, J. (2016) Wage Growth, Landholding, and Mechanization in Chinese Agriculture. *World Development* 86(1).
Warren, B. (1980) *Imperialism: Pioneer of Capitalism.* London: Verso.
Watts, M. (2013) *Silent Violence: Food, Famine, and Peasantry in Northern Nigeria.* Athens: University of Georgia Press.
Weber, M. (2010) *Political Writings.* Cambridge: Cambridge University Press.
Weeks, J. (2010) *Capital, Exploitation, and Economic Crisis.* London: Routledge.
Weil, F. (1998) Capitalism and Industrialization in New England, 1815–1845. *Journal of American History* 84, 4.
Weiss, J. (1986) Japan's Post-War Protection Policy: Some Implications for Less Developed Countries. *Journal of Development Studies* 22, 2.
Weiss, L. (1998) The Myth of the Powerless State. Governing the Economy in a Global Era. Cambridge: Polity Press.
Westra, R. (2019) Roy Bhaskar's Critical Realism and the Social Science of Marxian Economics. *Review of Radical Political Economics* 51(3), 365–82.
White, R. (2003) Information, Markets, and Corruption: Transcontinental Railroads in the Gilded Age. *Journal of American History* 90, 1.
Whiteside, M. (1998) *Living Farms.* London: Earthscan.
Wickberg, E. (1969) Japanese Land Policies in Taiwan, 1895–1945. *Agricultural History* 43, 3.
Williams, B. (2002) *Truth and Truthfulness.* Princeton: Princeton University Press.
Williams, B. (2003) *In the Beginning Was the Deed.* Princeton: Princeton University Press.

Williams, G. (1976) Taking the Part of Peasants: Rural Development in Nigeria and Tanzania. In: Gutkind, P. C. W. and Wallerstein, I. (eds) *The Political Economy of Contemporary Africa*. London: Sage.

Wolpe, H. (ed.) (1980) *The Articulation of Modes of Production: Essays from Economy and Society*. London: Routledge.

Woo-Cumings, M. (1999) *The Developmental State*. Ithaca: Cornell University Press.

World Bank (2001) *World Development Report 2000/2001: Attacking Poverty*. Washington, DC: World Bank.

World Bank (2013) *Remarkable Declines in Global Poverty, but Major Challenges Remain*. Washington, DC: World Bank.

World Bank (2014) *Rwanda Agriculture Policy Note. Promoting Agricultural Growth in Rwanda: Recent Performance, Challenges and Opportunities. Report No. ACS9719*. Washington, DC: World Bank.

World Bank (2015) Managing Uncertainty for Growth and Poverty Reduction with a Special Focus on Agricultural Sector Risk Assessment. *Rwanda Economic Update*, Issue 7.

Wrigley, E. A. (2010) *Energy and the English Industrial Revolution*. Cambridge: Cambridge University Press.

Wu, Y. (2007) Taiwan's Developmental State: After the Economic and Political Turmoil. *Asian Survey* 47(6).

Yang, M. (1970) *Socio-Economic Results of Land Reform in Taiwan*. Honolulu: East-West Center Press.

Yueh, L. (2013) *China's Growth. The Making of an Economic Superpower*. Oxford: Oxford University Press.

Zahavi, G. (1983) Negotiated Loyalty: Welfare Capitalism and the Shoeworkers of Endicott Johnson, 1920–1940. *Journal of American History* 71(3).

Zinn, H. (2015) *A People's History of the United States*. New York: Harper Collins.

Zmolek, M. (2013) *Rethinking the Industrial Revolution. Five Centuries of Transition from Agrarian to Industrial Capitalist in England*. Chicago: Haymarket Books.

Zysman, J. (1994) *Governments, Markets and Growth. Financial Systems and the Politics of Industrial Change*. Ithaca: Cornell University Press.

Index

For the benefit of digital users, indexed terms that span two pages (e.g., 52–53) may, on occasion, appear on only one of those pages.

Basic Legitimacy Demand 77–82
Basic needs 17
Belt and Road 246
Bhaskar, Roy 23
BRICS 4–5

Charitable Organization Society 124–5, 160
Chinese Communist Party 233–8, 241–2, 244
Christian 105, 125–6, 159–60, 232
Civil War 109–10, 140–1, 146–55, 162, 220–1, 229, 233
Clearances 41, 138
Colonialism 27, 38, 122, 133, 138–9, 168–9, 175–6, 219–20
Corn Law 104–5, 122–3, 129
Corruption 33, 155

Daimyo 177–8, 181
Dar es Salaam 3–4
Democracy 52, 70–1, 74, 128, 191, 252–3
Dependency 36–8, 41–2, 132–3, 160
Dialectic 11, 14, 16–17, 37–8

East India Company 111, 115–16, 121–2
Eretz Israel 203
Eurocentric 6–8

Famine 78–9, 91–2, 145, 224, 237–8
Foreign Direct Investment 199, 211, 240–1, 243

Gender 9, 14, 75–6, 248
Gini 16–17, 222–3
Gold Standard 154
Great Depression 156–7, 161–2
Great Leap Forward 237–9, 242–3

Histadrut 204, 208–11, 213–14
Hobbes, Thomas 78–9
Hutu 220

Individualism 55–6, 58–60, 73–4
International Monetary Fund 171–2

Joint Commission on Rural Reconstruction 197

Keiretsu 187–8, 200
Keynes, J. M. 8
  Keynesianism 147–8, 185
Kibbutz 205–6, 209
Korean War 185, 201–2, 234
Kuomintang 198, 201–2

Landlordism 91–3, 98, 108, 114, 117, 132, 135–6, 177–8, 185–7, 195, 234–5
Liberalism 126

Marxism 128, 250–1
Meiji 178–84
Ministry of International Trade and Investment 189–91
Moral economy 16–17

Navigation Acts 111, 116, 138–9
Neoliberal 29, 58
Neoliberalism 28–9, 43, 58, 170, 241
NGO 7, 48–9, 52, 85

Ontology 22–4, 29, 49–50, 56, 58, 251
Opium Wars 179–80, 231–2
Organization for Economic Cooperation and Development 216–17

Peasantry 27–9, 80–1, 191, 220, 234
People's Liberation Army 233–4
Poor Law 124–6
Privatization 41, 43, 245, 257
Proletarianization 9, 162–3, 168–9, 181–2
Proletariat 95, 98–100, 124–5

Qing 231–2

Rawls, John 66–9
Realpolitik 74
Rwandan Patriotic Front 220–1, 223–4, 228–9

Sen, Amartya 20, 50, 56, 66
Smith, Adam 13
State-Owned Enterprise 242–3, 245–6
Supreme Commander for the Allied Powers 184–6

Teleology 58, 252–3
Tokugawa 177–80
Town and Village Enterprise 242–6
Tudor 92–3
Tutsi 219–21, 229

Ujamaa 11–13
UNDP 52
Urbanization 97–101, 165–6, 253–4, 257–8
Utilitarianism 8–9, 50, 53, 68, 73, 82, 126, 129, 159–60, 258–9

Williams, Bernard 15–16, 67–8, 77–8, 80–1, 248–9
World Bank 52, 171–2, 221–2, 225, 246

Zaibatsu 177, 185, 187–8, 195–6, 200, 233
Zionism 209–10